THE BIRTH OF OPERA

DATE DUE

NO 5'98			
~~SET 10~~			

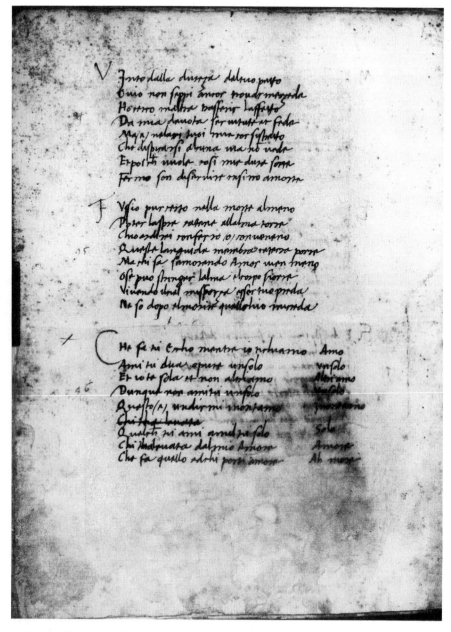

The earliest MS of Poliziano's echo poem 'Che fa' tu Echo', late fifteenth century, Florence, Biblioteca Riccardiana, MS 2723, fo. 49ᵛ.

The Birth of Opera

F. W. STERNFELD

CLARENDON PRESS · OXFORD

Walton Street, Oxford OX2 6DP
d New York
nd Bangkok Bombay
Calcutta Cape Town Dar es Salaam Delhi
Florence Hong Kong Istanbul Karachi
Kuala Lumpur Madras Madrid Melbourne
Mexico City Nairobi Paris Singapore
Taipei Tokyo Toronto
and associated companies in
Berlin Ibadan

Oxford is a trade mark of Oxford University Press

Published in the United States by
Oxford University Press Inc., New York

First published 1993
Paperback edition 1995

British Library Cataloguing in Publication Data
Data available

Library of Congress Cataloging in Publication Data
Sternfeld, Frederick William, 1914–   .
The birth of opera / F. W. Sternfeld.—Pbk. ed.
p.   cm.
Includes bibliographical references (p.   ) and indexes.
1. Opera—Italy.   2. Libretto.
ML1733.2.S73   1995   782.1'0945'09031—dc20   95–13375
ISBN 0–19–816573–0

1 3 5 7 9 10 8 6 4 2

Printed in Great Britain
on acid-free paper by
Bookcraft Ltd., Midsomer Norton, Avon

*To my colleagues
at Oxford and Florence*

Preface

It was in the Shakespeare year of 1964 that I first realized to what extent my work on English stage music lacked foundation and depth without a better knowledge of the practices of stage music in Italy. I then immersed myself in a particular study of comedies, pastorals, and tragedies, in addition to intermedi and the lesser-known early operas, and was much influenced by D. P. Walker's edition of the Florentine intermedi of 1589 and his ' publications on Italian humanism, and also by Konrat Ziegler's work on the Orpheus myth. Both Walker and Ziegler were generous enough to let me have the benefit of their criticism and counsel, and, thus encouraged, I proceeded to lecture on 'The Birth of Opera: Ovid, Poliziano, and the *lieto fine*' at a number of universities, including Göttingen in 1974, when I had the opportunity of discussing with Ziegler, shortly before his death, the importance of Ovid and Hyginus for Monteverdi. Portions of this lecture were published in my article of the same title in 1979; others were presented at an unpublished Round Table on Monteverdi's *Orfeo* held by the Royal Musical Association at Birmingham in 1984. The present volume constitutes an attempt to sketch in context the *disiecta membra* of my investigations.

It was the provocative title of Nietzsche's *The Birth of Tragedy out of the Spirit of Music*, first purchased and devoured in Vienna in the 1920s, that suggested to me 'The Birth of Opera out of the Spirit of Humanism'. In my youth I was passionately involved with opera, frequently attending performances three or four times a week. At the age of twelve, armed with the vocal score of *Don Giovanni* at a performance at the Vienna State Opera, I was struck by the fact that the *lieto fine*, the happy ending, was omitted. When discussing this with the habitués of the opera-house, I found that most of them defended this cut, which went back to the hallowed practice of Gustav Mahler in the 1900s and was considered in tune with the serious, demonic aspects of *Don Giovanni* and late Mozart in general. The problem of the *lieto fine*, also posed by Monteverdi's and Gluck's *Orfeo*, took hold of me, and I made bold to discuss it with composers and conductors. A few persons agreed that faithfulness to the original score and a perception of the aesthetics of opera before the nineteenth century demanded a restoration of the buffo finale. Among them were composers such as Richard Strauss (who had conducted an uncut *Don Giovanni* in 1895), Egon Wellesz, and Karl Weigl (who had served as a solo coach under Mahler in Vienna); poets such as Hofmannsthal (whose libretti amply document his attitude towards the *lieto fine*); and conductors such as Bruno Walter (who argued for the restoration of the finale in the twenties, and carried his plans out at the Salzburg Festival in 1934, to the surprise of conservative Viennese opinion); I also talked with scholars such as Guido Adler and Egon Wellesz (in his capacity as music historian). I might add that, in Vienna, discussions pertaining to opera were by no means restricted to professional musicians: the general public argued about revivals of Mozart or Gluck, or the director-ship of the state opera, with a fanatic seriousness reserved in the English-speaking world for debates on the budget or national elections.

Discussions of the *lieto fine* within the dramatic and tonal structure of opera have continued throughout my career, but I must acknowledge here, as particularly relevant to this book, two persons, Edward Dent and Stravinsky. Dent, who through his various publications has so profoundly influenced the history of opera, assisted both my research on Shakespeare and on Italian opera, and I particularly remember the prolonged sessions we had on the finales of Cavalieri's *Rappresentazione di anima e di corpo* and Peri's *Euridice*. It was a great privilege to submit my views on Stravinsky's *Orpheus* and *Rake* to the composer, after performances he conducted in New York and Boston. I came to know Stravinsky through Nikolai Nabokov, who greatly assisted my article on *Petrouchka*. Discussing *Orpheus* with the composer and Balanchine, and the *Rake* with him and Auden, revealed Stravinsky's fascinating grasp of the aesthetics behind Monteverdi's *Orfeo* and Mozart's *Don Giovanni*, and of his indebtedness to his models.

The spirit of opera was born out of Renaissance humanism, the study of which I pursued for many decades in the libraries of the Old and the New Worlds. In order to deal with humanist drama and its meaning one has to investigate history, literature, visual arts, and philosophy in addition to music, and in the 1940s, teaching at Wesleyan University and cut off from European libraries, I decided that the groves of academe were sorely in need of an interdisciplinary journal. In 1945, therefore, as chairman of the New England Conference on Renaissance Studies, I consulted with scholars in music (Einstein, Schrade), history (Gilbert, Gilmore), visual arts (Panofsky, Stechow), literature (Seznec, Bennett), and philosophy (Kristeller), and librarians and bibliographers about starting such a periodical. As a result I became, *nolens volens*, the editor of *Renaissance News* (now *Renaissance Quarterly*), which first appeared in Armen Carapetyan's *Journal of Renaissance and Baroque Music* (now *Musica disciplina*). In 1954–5 I spent a year at the Institute for Advanced Study at Princeton, working closely with Erwin Panofsky, who put me in touch with Frances Yates and D. P. Walker; they in turn involved me in the team of Renaissance scholars who participated so congenially in the French colloquia organized by Jean Jacquot and Geneviève Thibault. It was at these conferences that performances of the intermedi of 1589 were first heard, paving the way for the BBC revival under Andrew Parrott in 1979.

Guided by Panofsky, I had come to appreciate the iconographic, allegorical, and symbolic aspects of Renaissance humanism. But delving more deeply into the vicissitudes of the Orpheus myth, it became necessary to study Italian literature more closely, and to consult editions of Poliziano, Correggio, and other humanists. In this I was greatly aided by scholars such as Antonia Tissoni Benvenuti. Once more my investigations had to be widened, for Poliziano and his successors in the sixteenth and seventeenth centuries showed not only an intensive interest in the themes and myths of the Greco-Roman world, but also exhibited the desire of humanists to vie with antiquity for new laurels, and in doing so they created a new genre—opera.

The first chapter of the present book attempts to sketch the main themes: the classical heritage, particularly Ovid's *Metamorphoses* and *Heroides*, and the humanistic interpretations of a few archetypal myths, last but not least that of Orpheus. It deals also with important building-stones of opera: the pangs of love that generate the 'laments', and the shaping of the plot that leads to the *lieto fine*. In fact, a detailed consideration of two primary elements in early opera, namely the solo lament and the ensemble finale, are the main preoccupations of this volume. The growth and articulation of the finale is traced in Chapters 3 to 5; the sixth chapter shows the development of the doleful lament, which acts as a foil for the *lieto fine*; and the seventh and final chapter chronicles the employment of repetition and echo, which so powerfully enhance and intensify the emotions of the lament, and which are among the main tools of humanist rhetoric used by the early librettists.

The gestation of this book was long and difficult. For decades I had been gathering material on Orpheus, the finale, the lament, and the echo device, planning to finish the actual writing fairly rapidly. But major surgery and failing eyesight intervened, and the health of my wife, who had edited and typed all my previous publications, also deteriorated. Still, after extensive eye surgery, I started writing the book, aided by graduate students who acted both as typists and research assistants. They were Ewan West, Laura Davey, Sally Roper, and Malgosia Czepiel; their devotion and encouragement have been a great help. But at the conclusion of the sixth chapter, medical circumstances severely restricted the number of hours I had for reading and writing. I decided to forgo the planned seventh chapter on echo and repetition and submitted a first draft of my typescript to Wolfgang Osthoff and to Tim Carter. They both encouraged me to publish my material and gave me the benefit of their advice and criticism, for which I am most grateful. Then the publishers sent the typescript to Bonnie Blackburn, who made further valuable observations, and also volunteered to revise some of my earlier articles dealing with repetition and echo and mould them into a seventh chapter. She also copy-edited the entire book, in the course of which we agreed on many additional minor revisions. The improvements due to the observations of these three scholars are considerable, but I must stress that any remaining imperfections are my sole responsibility.

No doubt, other monographs will be written in due course upon other building-blocks of opera, such as the recitative, the aria, the overture, or the inserted ballet. (As for myself, I hope to publish articles on 'Aria' and on 'Ovidian myths other than that of Orpheus'). But for the present it seemed worth while to supplement the admirable studies of my main predecessors, Nino Pirrotta and Wolfgang Osthoff, with observations of my own, particularly on the problems of the dramatic structure of opera plots with more extensive consideration of the role played by Poliziano, and contribute towards a lively discussion of a genre that, in spite of rumours to the contrary, resolutely refuses to die or fade away. And whereas my main efforts have been focused on the period from Poliziano to Monteverdi, frequent comparisons are made with works from other centuries, whether by Gluck or Stravinsky, in an effort to view 'The Birth of Opera' as a necessary first step towards an understanding of the genre as a constant challenge to poets and composers of four centuries.

In addition to the acknowledgements already made, I wish to single out the fellowship and camaraderie that I have enjoyed at Oxford and Florence for over a quarter of a century. In Oxford I belonged to three clubs, as it were. One was the Faculty of Music, where tutorials, lectures, and graduate seminars were punctuated by chats with colleagues and pupils (and I learned a good deal from my pupils). Another was the Bodleian Library, where study of printed sources, manuscripts, and microfilms was equally punctuated by coffee-breaks with fellow scholars and chats with an unusually well-informed, helpful library staff (who often put readers in touch with the authors of the books they were reading). A third gathering-place was Exeter College, where I partook of meals and interdisciplinary enlightenment. I must also record the encouragement and helpful advice I received from my patient publishers, the Clarendon Press. For several decades I spent part of each year in Florence, working in the libraries there, and when these were closed, in the excellent library of the Villa I Tatti. I also cannot think of a better place to meet historians of humanism, of literature, the visual arts, palaeographers, bibliographers, and other helpful students of the subject. In these libraries (and at the Vatican Library in Rome) coffee punctuations also framed intense working sessions, and functioned like intermedi in Renaissance comedies and pastorals, providing invaluable information and stimulation.

Finally, it is a pleasant duty to acknowledge grants-in-aid and residential grants received from the following institutions, in addition to sabbaticals and leaves of absence from my own university: The British Academy, The British School at Rome, The Harvard Center of Renaissance Studies (Villa I Tatti), The Hinrichsen Foundation, The Leverhulme Trust, Music and Letters Awards, and The Musicians Benevolent Fund.

F.W.S.

Oxford, 1992

Contents

List of Tables   xii
List of Music Examples   xiii
List of Abbreviations   xiv

1. Orpheus, Ovid, and Opera   1

2. Definitions and Non-Definitions   31

3. The Problem of the Finale and Poliziano's Solution   48

4. The Finale in the Sixteenth Century   65

5. The Operatic Finale   99

6. The Lament   140

7. Repetition and Echo in Poetry and Music   197

Bibliography   227
Index of Subjects   255
Index of Names, Titles, and First Lines   259

List of Tables

1.1.	Settings of the Orpheus myth, 1599–1698	2
1.2.	Orpheus and related tales in Ovid's *Metamorphoses*	10
1.3.	Poliziano's *Orfeo* and some *rifacimenti*	22
2.1.	'Recitar cantando' and 'stile recitativo', 1600–1638	39
3.1.	Proportions of choral section of finale, 1480–1608	57
3.2.	Sixteen poems by Poliziano in ottonari	62
4.1.	Intermedi in Machiavelli's comedies	69
4.2.	Pastorals, 1341–1637	78
4.3.	Sixth intermedio, 1589	88
4.4.	Design of the sixth intermedio, 1589	95
5.1.	Early operas with extant score or libretto	99
5.2.	Concluding choruses of *Dafne*	103
5.3.	Concluding choruses of *Euridice*	109
5.4.	Concluding choruses of *Orfeo*	112
5.5.	Division into three and five acts	127
5.6.	The Orpheus myth after Rinuccini and Monteverdi, 1619–1986	128
6.1.	Five laments	144
6.2.	Four laments in Poliziano's *Orfeo*	146
7.1.	Selective list of echo passages in Italian stage music	225

List of Music Examples

Ex. 4.1.	Examples of melodies for ottonari	73
Ex. 4.2a.	Cavalieri, concertino section of 'O che nuovo miracolo'	93
Ex. 4.2b.	Peri, concertino section of finale of *Euridice*	94
Ex. 5.1.	Corsi, final chorus of *Dafne*	105
Ex. 5.2.	Gagliano, final chorus of *Dafne*	106
Ex. 5.3a.	Monteverdi, final chorus of *Orfeo*	115
Ex. 5.3b.	Landi, final chorus of *Morte d'Orfeo*	115
Ex. 6.1.	Monteverdi, Ottavia's lament from *Poppea*, Act III	142
Ex. 6.2.	Monteverdi, Orfeo's lament from *Orfeo*, Act II	142
Ex. 6.3.	Settings of Orfeo's lament from Poliziano, *Orfeo*	148
Ex. 6.4.	Festa, 'Qual sarà mai'	150
Ex. 6.5.	Stravinsky, harp accompaniment to Orfeo's lament in *Orpheus*	152
Ex. 6.6.	Peri, 'Dunque fra torbid'onde'	154
Ex. 6.7.	Peri, Orpheus' lament from *Euridice*	162
Ex. 6.8.	Schematic outline of bass of 'Possente spirto'	169
Ex. 6.9.	Comparison of bass of 'Possente spirto' with ostinato basses	169
Ex. 6.10.	Cavalli, Erisbe's lament from *Ormindo*	176
Ex. 6.11.	Monteverdi, *Lamento d'Arianna*, opening section	180
Ex. 6.12.	Variant versions of melody to 'lasciatemi'	182
Ex. 6.13.	Descending tetrachords in Cavalli, *Ormindo*	188
Ex. 6.14a.	Cavalli, Hecuba's lament from *Didone*	190
Ex. 6.14b.	Cavalli, Climene's lament from *Egisto*	190
Ex. 6.14c.	Purcell, Dido's lament from *Dido and Aeneas*	190
Ex. 6.15.	Cavalli, Cassandra's lament from *Didone*	191
Ex. 7.1.	Anon., 'La pastorella'	202
Ex. 7.2.	Anon., 'Soffrir i' son disposto'	204
Ex. 7.3.	Anon., 'Gridan vostri occhi'	206
Ex. 7.4.	Isaac, 'Quis dabit capiti meo'	207
Ex. 7.5.	Isaac, 'Quis dabit capiti meo'	210
Ex. 7.6.	Claude Le Jeune, 'Quae celebrat Thermas Echo'	214
Ex. 7.7.	Tromboncino, 'S'i 'l dissi mai'	217
Ex. 7.8.	Antonio Cifra, 'Sa quest'altier'	219
Ex. 7.9.	Striggio, 'Fuggi speme mia'	220

List of Abbreviations

AcM	*Acta musicologica*
AMw	*Archiv für Musikwissenschaft*
AnMc	*Analecta musicologica*
BHR	*Bibliothèque d'Humanisme et Renaissance*
CHM	*Collectanea historiae musicae*
CMM	Corpus mensurabilis musicae
EMH	*Early Music History*
GSLI	*Giornale storico della letteratura italiana*
HJMw	*Hamburger Jahrbuch für Musikwissenschaft*
JAMS	*Journal of the American Musicological Society*
JRMA	*Journal of the Royal Musical Association*
JWCI	*Journal of the Warburg and Courtauld Institutes*
Mf	*Die Musikforschung*
MGG	*Die Musik in Geschichte und Gegenwart*
ML	*Music and Letters*
MQ	*The Musical Quarterly*
MR	*The Music Review*
MSD	Musicological Studies and Documents
New Grove	The New Grove Dictionary of Music and Musicians, ed. Stanley Sadie, 20 vols. (London, 1980)
NRMI	*Nuova rivista musicale italiana*
Nuovo Vogel	F. Lesure and C. Sartori, *Bibliografia della musica italiana vocale profana pubblicata dal 1500 al 1700*, 3 vols. (Pomezia and Geneva, 1977)
PRMA	*Proceedings of the Royal Musical Association*
RIM	*Rivista italiana di musicologia*
RMI	*Rivista musicale italiana*
RRMBE	Recent Researches in the Music of the Baroque Era
SCMA	Smith College Music Archives
SM	*Studi musicali*
SMw	*Studien zur Musikwissenschaft*
THR	Travaux d'Humanisme et Renaissance

I

Orpheus, Ovid, and Opera

ORPHEUS

In the beginning was the myth, and the myth was that of Orpheus. It provided the key plot for intermedi and the first operas, and looms impressively, both in quantity and in quality, at the inception of the genre. Indeed it is a plot that continues to act as a springboard for the imagination of composers of operas and ballets, even after the seventeenth century, as witnessed by the works of Gluck, Offenbach, and Stravinsky. Two excerpts are particularly fascinating for the historian, namely the echo laments of Orpheus from the last act of Monteverdi's opera and from Gluck's opening act, and their connection with the history of the echo lament from Euripides (Andromeda) to Verdi (Desdemona) in general, and with Peri's echo lament (Arion) from the Florentine intermedi of 1589 in particular.

In tracing the literary antecedents of the stories of Orpheus and of Echo, one arrives inevitably at the most widely read manual of classical mythology in the last two millennia, Ovid's *Metamorphoses*. But the elusive figure of Orpheus is also reflected in many other writings, notably those of Virgil and Hyginus. Here we are fortunate to possess two thought-provoking articles: K. Ziegler's article on 'Orpheus in Renaissance und Neuzeit' of 1951 and D. P. Walker's essay on 'Orpheus the Theologian and Renaissance Platonists' of 1953.

In discussing the reflections of the story of Orpheus in the arts, we deal with a great mass of material, heterogeneous in its artistic formulations, and chronologically extending from the sixth century BC to our own age. Greek vases, early Christian frescoes, and Renaissance painting and sculpture are relevant; in literature the thread leads from the poetry of Ibycus (second half of the sixth century BC) through the playwrights of the fifth century (a trilogy of Aeschylus, the *Lycurgeia*, and the *Alcestis* and *Hippolytus* of Euripides) to Rilke's sonnets of 1923 and Cocteau's play and film (1926 and 1950 respectively); and in Western music relevant items stretch from the fourteenth century (for example Landini's madrigal 'Si dolce non sono') to the operas of Krenek and Milhaud (1926), Stravinsky's ballet (1947), and Birtwistle's opera (first performed 1986). There can be no doubt, however, that it was in early and the earliest opera that the ancient myth found its greatest resonance, as the accompanying calendar of twenty items from 1599 to

1698 will show at a glance (see Table 1.1). This calendar, which is restricted to the more obvious items, culled from standard works of reference, also shows the crucial role of the years surrounding the inception of opera: eight out of the twenty works stem from the period 1599 to 1619, and all are Italian (for we may be fairly certain that the *Orfeo* performed at Salzburg in 1614 was an Italian composition).

TABLE 1.1. *Settings of the Orpheus myth, 1599–1698*

Date	Place	Title	Composer	Author of text, scenario, etc.
1599	Milan	*Orfeo* (intermedio)	?	Schiaffinati
1600	Florence	*Euridice*	Peri	Rinuccini
1602	Florence	*Euridice*	Caccini	Rinuccini
1606	Rome	*Eumelio*	Agazzari	De Cupis and Tirletti
1607	Mantua	*Orfeo*	Monteverdi	Striggio
1614	Salzburg	*Orfeo*	?	?
1616	Florence	*Orfeo* (intermedio)	Belli	Chiabrera
1619	Rome	*La morte d'Orfeo*	Landi	?Landi
1634, 1663	?Madrid	*El divino Orfeo*	Hidalgo	Calderón
1638	Dresden	*Orpheus* (ballet)	Schütz	Buchner
1640	Paris	*La descente d'Orphée*	?	Chapoton
1647	Paris	*Orfeo*	Rossi	Buti
1659	Wolfenbüttel	*Orpheus*	Loewe	U. v. Braunschweig
1672/3	Venice	*Orfeo*	Sartorio	Aureli
1673	London	*Orpheus* (masque)	Locke	Settle
1683	Vienna	*La lira d'Orfeo*	Draghi	Minato
1685	Paris	*La descente d'Orphée*	Charpentier	?
1690	Paris	*Orphée*	L. Lully	Duboullay
1697	(near) Oxford	*Orpheus* (masque)	Goodson, Weldon	?
1698	Brunswick	*Orpheus*	Keiser	Bressand

The role of Rinuccini, who provided librettos for Peri and Caccini, but who also collaborated with Cavalieri and Monteverdi on projects not restricted to the Orpheus myth, cannot be overestimated. If any single person can be said to have made possible the new *stile rappresentativo* and the birth of opera, the Florentine poet and humanist was that man. His *Dafne* pointed the way to the chosen land, and with his *Euridice* he arrived there: the works of Agazzari, Monteverdi, Belli, and Landi are all indebted to him. And so, indeed, is Gluck's court opera of the eighteenth century. As a matter of fact, it is difficult to imagine any historical perspective in opera (let alone articles on the Orpheus plot) without the success of Gluck's *Orfeo* in the eighteenth and nineteenth centuries (for example, the revivals under Liszt and Berlioz). A word should perhaps be said about the opera *Eumelio* (1606), which does not name Orpheus in the title, or include the Thracian singer in the cast of characters. Here we must remember that presentation in a Jesuit seminary in Rome forced the Sienese composer to purify his cast by making it all-male, referring to the age-old device of allegory in the preface: Apollo (not Orpheus) rescues Eumelio (not Eurydice) from the underworld, and even this rescue by the Sun-god symbolizes a deeper and more spiritual meaning. (The role of allegory in adapting the pagan tales of Ovid's *Metamorphoses* to the Christian era will be dealt with in greater detail later.) Suffice it to say that spiritual stage works, whether dealing with the Orpheus theme overtly or covertly (Agazzari, Calderón), or dealing with different topics (Cavalieri's *Rappresentazione di anima e di corpo*, Landi's *Sant' Alessio*), has remained a comparatively minor branch of the main operatic stream, and cannot be considered in the present context.

After 1619 the new genre of opera and the distribution of the Orpheus theme spreads rapidly to France, Spain, Germany, Austria, and England. At the same time the frequency with which the ancient myth provides the main action of the plot, either in Italy or abroad, decreases steadily through the later seventeenth and entire eighteenth century. Gluck's *Orfeo* of 1762, although a 'reform' opera in terms of Calzabigi's programme, is still a courtly entertainment written for the emperor's name-day, and thus connected with the centuries-old tradition of royal, ducal, and aristocratic pastimes. But with the demise of the *ancien régime* at the end of the eighteenth century, the previously ubiquitous plot becomes even rarer, and when it reappears it frequently quotes or refers to Gluck (who, after all, provided one of the few pre-Mozartian operas in the repertoire): Liszt's symphonic poem *Orpheus* preceded a performance of Gluck's opera under Liszt's direction at Weimar in 1854; Offenbach's clever satire of 1858 has Orpheus play Gluck's tunes on the fiddle; and in Cocteau's film *Orphée* of 1950 (with a score by Auric) Gluck's music comes out of the loudspeaker of a wireless set.

As to the treatments of the Orpheus theme before 1599, they must of necessity be chronicled in a summary manner in an essay devoted to the genre of opera. Most belong to the category of princely entertainments, banquets, or intermedi, offered as a rule by secular patrons but occasionally by princes of the Church, such as popes or cardinals. Orpheus appears in festivities at Rome in 1473, at Pesaro in 1475, at Milan in 1489, at Ferrara in 1529, and so on. I have endeavoured to indicate this connection with the tradition of the Italian Renaissance intermedi by including the Milan intermedi of 1599 in my calendar. What all these interludes or tableaux have in common is that the Orpheus plot, as a rule, provides only one of several mythological topics for the diversion of the guests. The occasion for the 1599 intermedi was the ceremonious entry of members of the Habsburg family into the city of Milan. A pastoral play, Visconti's *Armenia*, was punctuated by intermedi devised by Schiaffinati, and the intermedio after the first act told the ancient woeful tale, complete with Orpheus' echo lament, a device already prominent in Ovid. Obviously our calendar of treatments of the myth of Orpheus in the seventeenth century would be increased substantially if we included occasional and passing references to the topic in stage works whose main theme was not concerned with Orpheus, such as Campion's *Lord's Masque* (London, 1613) or Cavalli's *Egisto* (Venice, 1643). On the other hand, it is probably unfair not to mention Poliziano's *Orfeo* as a predecessor of Peri's and Rinuccini's *Euridice* simply because it is not an opera. True, it is listed in most histories of Italian literature as a play, and indeed as Italy's first secular drama in the vernacular. Also, it does contain a sizeable portion of spoken lines, which Peri's, Monteverdi's, and Cavalli's operas do not. But by my reckoning the number of sung lines of this remarkable harbinger of opera exceeds the number of lines spoken. By any account, Poliziano's *Orfeo*, performed at a Gonzaga banquet at Mantua in 1480, is the most important work in the prehistory of opera. But since this play with music has been discussed at some length by Osthoff, Pirrotta, and myself, I must forgo extensive consideration of this fascinating fifteenth-century author in the present context. Suffice it to say that the title of Pirrotta's book of 1969, *Li due Orfei*, referring to Poliziano's and Monteverdi's *Orfeo*, has given the significance of Poliziano a rhetorical emphasis that no later scholar can hope to rival. Reference to Poliziano's precedent, however, will be made at appropriate moments in our discussion of the changes the Ovidian tale has undergone in the operas of Peri, Monteverdi, and others. In any event, future research on Poliziano's Orfeo has, at long last in 1986, received its indispensable foundation in A. Tissoni Benvenuti's edition of the work, which with its textual apparatus, explanatory notes, and introductory essays greatly enhances our understanding of Italian humanism.

OVID

It has often been asked from which sources the allusions to classical mythology in Shakespeare's plays are derived, and there is agreement that the influence of Ovid is four times as great as that of Virgil. One would not hesitate to say the same of the history of opera, in spite of the Virgilian roots of Cavalli's *Didone*, Purcell's *Dido and Aeneas*, and Berlioz's *Troyens*. The significance of Ovid for opera, particularly early opera, has been discussed in several articles, among others by H. C. Wolff in 1971, and by myself in 1979 when I presented a calendar of fifty-five pieces based on the *Metamorphoses*, extending from 1475 to 1654. Had I included more operas from the seventeenth century (notably those of Lully) and moved chronologically forward to the twentieth century (to cover Strauss, Milhaud, and others) one could easily arrive at a list of well over a hundred pieces by composers of some stature. Such a selective chart could be extended further by automatic inclusion of all titles, no matter how insignificant. But our concern here is not with an encyclopaedic roll-call, for the material already gathered is of sufficient number and weight for our argument, but rather with the reasons behind the importance of Ovid. Some would merely refer to Ovid's stature as a great poet, but that will not do, for who would claim that Homer or Virgil are not great? Obviously, problems of such aesthetic sophistication cannot be exhaustively answered in a book, let alone a paragraph. But at the danger of being simplistic, one might single out three qualities of the *Metamorphoses*: narrative skill, sensuous eroticism, and prominence of the miraculous element.

The concatenation of some 250 plots within Ovid's narrative framework, extending in time from primeval chaos to Augustan Rome, has always and justly been admired. Ovid is a master of suspense: he spins a good yarn full of surprises, and he tells stories aplenty. (Such goodly numbers are always characteristic of best-sellers: one hundred in the *Decameron*, 1001 in the *Arabian Nights*. It is the astute awareness of the public's curiosity that makes the success of a *Rahmenerzählung*.) As to eroticism, such matters are hard to assess. One would not accuse Ovid of catering to a cheap desire for titillation of the senses, but one can readily see why the Christians accepted the manly restraint of Virgil without question, but felt that they had to expurgate and 'moralize' Ovid to make him acceptable. (They never expelled his works from their libraries, however: they were too good a read.) As to the miraculous, it is almost self-explanatory that this element would appeal to the dramatists and stage designers of the seventeenth century.

The staple diet of opera, from its inception, has been one of love stories, and it is the tales of passionate *amours* that the librettists have culled from Ovid, who provides them so abundantly if not exclusively. It is the pangs of love, disappointed, frustrated, and thwarted, that have led to the famous laments that established the emotional climate in which the genre has thrived from the seventeenth to the twentieth centuries. The main attraction of the myths from the *Metamorphoses* for the librettists, whether they be Rinuccini or Hofmannsthal, has been these laments so effectively positioned within the plot: Orpheus bewails the loss of Eurydice, Ariadne of Theseus, Venus of Adonis, Phaedra of Hippolytus, and so on *ad infinitum*. It will be noticed that the last three examples are taken from tales where passionate women bewail their woe; and indeed it is the feminine lament, in which heroines rather than heroes mourn their fate, that has featured so prominently in stage plays and operas throughout the centuries. And here one collection of stories by Ovid is supplemented by another, the *Heroides*, a gathering of verse epistles by women in straits of love. A striking example is the myth of Ariadne. What would Monteverdi's opera be without its famous lament, praised by contemporaries more copiously than any other excerpt from the composer's stage works, and repeatedly appearing in print during his lifetime? Clearly this is a case where the poignancy of Ariadne's fate, as expressed in the verse epistle from the heroine to Theseus, augments the scenario in the *Metamorphoses*. (The *Heroides*, well known to Hofmannsthal, were equally a contributing influence on the laments of Strauss's Ariadne in our own century.) In similar fashion, the searing, sensuous love-letter that Phaedra writes to Hippolytus in the *Heroides* amplifies and intensifies the operas based on the account given in the *Metamorphoses* (from Vannarelli at Spoleto in 1661 to Rameau at Paris in 1733 and to Gluck at Milan in 1745).

Much more could be said about the role of Ovid's *Heroides* in the history of operatic topics, not only as a fillip to the ubiquitous *Metamorphoses*. Among several examples, the verse epistles of Penelope and of Dido come to mind as sources for Monteverdi's *Ulisse* and Cavalli's *Didone*, intensifying the tales told by Homer and Virgil. Still, when all is said, the overall influence of a collection of the stories of eighteen unhappy heroines cannot rival the storehouse of hundreds of plots contained in the *Metamorphoses*. From this latter and ampler collection come such operatic favourites as the myths of Orpheus, Daphne, Echo, Andromeda, Medea, Ariadne, and Venus (and Adonis). Of these and some fifteen others only two (Ariadne and Medea) are complemented by the *Heroides*.

Of the others, the most popular in the seventeenth century, apart from the Orpheus plot, seem to have been the myths of Andromeda, Daphne, and Echo. Here the laments of Andromeda, chained to a rock, and of Apollo bewailing the loss of Daphne and Echo that of Narcissus without question loom large. In connection with these laments it must be stressed that Ovid received from his Greek predecessors and passed on to his Renaissance imitators not only the *topoi*, that is various subject-matters, but also the modes of expression with which these topics are treated. Repetition and echo were among the standard rhetorical devices thus employed. One of the best-known examples in classical literature of what the French have called 'rimes en écho' is the story of the nymph Echo and her unhappy love for Narcissus. But Echo's lament harks back to that in Euripides' *Andromeda*, where the heroine laments her fate, softly answered by echo. Aristophanes parodies this passage in his *Thesmophoriazusae* by having one of the protagonists, bound to a plank, tell his tale of woe, punctuated by echo repetitions. What these passages in Greek plays, in Ovid's verse (both *Metamorphoses* and *Heroides*), and in Renaissance poetry have in common is subject-matter and technique. Topically, the repeated words are characteristic of a plaint ('bewail', 'woe', 'alas', 'death'); technically, the terms of the lament receive emphasis by being echoed. One of the finest poetic examples from the late sixteenth century is Shakespeare's *Venus and Adonis*, where the Ovidian tale is treated in a most Ovidian manner:

> And now she beats her heart, whereat it groans,
> That all the neighbour caves, as seeming troubled,
> Make verbal repetitions of her moans;
> Passion on passion deeply is redoubled:
> 'Ay me!' she cries, and twenty times, 'Woe, woe!'
> And twenty echoes twenty times cry so . . .
>
> (ll. 829 34)

But to proceed from narrative poetry by Shakespeare to opera, and ignoring for the moment Manelli's *Adone* written for Venice in the 1630s and Blow's *Venus and Adonis* written for London in the 1680s, there survives in an example from the eighteenth century the *topos* of Andromeda's lament in a strange and unexpected context. The plaint in question is rather confusingly sung by a character called Ariadne and occurs in an opera by Vivaldi performed at Rome in 1724. In his *Giustino*, whose plot is largely concerned with Byzantine history, Ariadne, the empress, is chained to a rock, lamenting her fate, and her cries for help are answered by a double echo (rather similar to Arion's lament from the Florentine intermedi of 1589, set to music by Peri as an 'ecco con due risposte').

Enough has probably been said to suggest the importance of the Ovidian matrix for the history of opera both in regard to the stories provided and the rhetorical techniques therein employed. Concerning the traditions of poetry behind the works of Poliziano and Shakespeare there exist numerous studies of the topic by classical and literary historians. Without consideration of these literary models, the verse of the operatic librettos, which permits the composers to allow their protagonists to lament and to 'make verbal repetition of their moans', cannot be understood.

ALLEGORY

So far we have dealt with various plots provided by Ovid largely in a manner comparable to that of a surveyor. We have noted the frequency with which certain myths occur at the birth of opera and persist throughout the seventeenth century (and even beyond that) when different subject-matters supplant, by and large, the plots of classical mythology. But we must now proceed to ask ourselves what the meaning of the Orpheus figure was: what it meant to Poliziano, Rinuccini, and Striggio; to the academies and coteries with which these poets and humanists were associated; and to the audiences for which they wrote. The tale of Orpheus as told by Ovid is a long and circumstantial one. It is far more detailed than the account given by Virgil, even if we subtract from it the several other stories intercalated by Ovid between the stations of the main myth. (One of these inserted plots is that of Venus and Adonis.) Some of the aspects of the tale of Orpheus seem, on the surface, ideal for an operatic subject, such as the hero's mastery of music and his ardent love for Eurydice. The nature of the latter has been disputed by many observers from Boethius to our own century. Ziegler considers unproven the hypothesis that the erotic and uxorial elements were added to the original myth at a later stage. More about that later. But what of the aspect of the musical powers of our protagonist? Certainly, the capacity to perform remarkable feats is not restricted to this myth: Amphion builds the walls of Thebes to the sound of his lyre, Arion's song causes the dolphin to rescue him, and the strains of Timotheus assuage the fury of Alexander. And these musical tales have found resonance in compositions by Peri, Handel, and others, but not—be it noted—in opera, and not nearly as often as the Orpheus plot. Are there other aspects and associations attached to this tale that have fascinated poets, librettists, and composers through the ages?

When one examines the voluminous literature dealing with Orpheus, extending from passing references (such as those in Euripides or Plato) to continuous and artistically shaped stories (such as those in Virgil or Ovid, Poliziano or Monteverdi, Stravinsky or Birtwistle), one cannot help feeling that the figure of Orpheus stands for more than the well-known plot suggests superficially. The multitude might be touched and diverted by the traditional tale, but those who know, who have been initiated, perceive a deeper meaning. For them Orpheus becomes a sage, a courageous seeker after divine wisdom, a conqueror of death, a religious prophet (if not the founder of a religious cult, Orphism), an *allegory* for Apollo, Dionysus, Osiris, or Christ. This last suggestion may seem surprising, if not shocking, to some modern minds; but to classical, medieval, or biblical historians this view is not unfamiliar.

The etymology of the word 'allegory' contains the root *allos* (other), and it is this otherness that matters, this difference between the ostensible content of discourse and its real meaning. As early as the sixth century BC the stories told in Homer, particularly the accounts of the gods and their sometimes unseemly squabbles, were treated in this fashion. Similarly, the Church Fathers subjected the Bible to an analogous process of interpretation: the Song of Songs, for instance, with its love poetry was in especial need of spiritualization. What was true of sections of Holy Writ was inevitably more urgently required of the world of classical mythology. In these medieval spiritualizations of Orpheus one of his several qualities, mentioned earlier, is prominent: his success in conquering Hades. He is the superhuman figure who 'discovers', who penetrates the realm of the dead, who 'harrows Hell'. He miraculously returns from that 'undiscovered country from whose bourn no traveller returns'. In various Christian accounts Orpheus is depicted either as Christ the good shepherd, or as Christ who harrowed Hell and rose again.

An example of Christ as shepherd is found in the catacombs of San Callisto at Rome (third century AD). This is a surprisingly early survival, but to find Orpheus serving as a *figura* for the rapidly spreading new religion is far from astonishing. Early Christian art, after all, is always allegorical, a fact partially explained by the prohibition against graven images in the Ten Commandments. The first Christian artists (that is, in the third and fourth centuries) had to resort to Old Testament figures (Adam, David) or to Graeco-Roman figures (Orpheus, Apollo) to evolve their pictorial vocabulary. As Stravinsky said: 'I think of Noah as an Old Testament Christ figura ([in] Auerbach's sense).'[1] Here Stravinsky's reference to Auerbach's term *figura* (rather than allegory, or metaphor, or symbol) reminds us of the brilliant contributions made to our understanding of the survival of pagan elements in Christian art by historians of the visual arts and of literature, such as Schlosser (1894), Auerbach (1938), Seznec (1940), and Kitzinger (1980).

Of the narrative accounts of Orpheus as a Christian *figura* the most influential ones stem from the fourteenth century, the age of Dante, Petrarch, Boccaccio, and Chaucer. It is this period that gave rise to the French allegorical treatment of Ovid, the *Ovide moralisé* and its Latin derivative, the *Ovidius moralizatus*. (Of the latter, four printed editions survive from the sixteenth century, that is between Poliziano and Striggio.) In these moralizations Orpheus' descent equals Christ's harrowing of Hell. To a humanist the analogy of such a descent, such a *katabasis*, with that of Ulysses in Homer's *Odyssey*, with Aeneas in Virgil's *Aeneid*, and, last but not least, with Dante under the guidance of Virgil in the *Divine Comedy*, would be obvious. It is the symbolism of the *figura* of Orpheus that distinguishes him from other musical figures of antiquity (such as Arion or Amphion). Moreover, the allegorical interpretation would make it acceptable to use a pagan plot, though the nature of the occasion had connections with organized religion, such as a commission from a Gonzaga cardinal for a play with music by Poliziano, or a performance at the Seminario Romano of an opera by Agazzari. In fact, in his preface Agazzari states that he had chosen the plot of his work because of its allegorical meaning: 'per la bella et utile allegoria'.

It would seem appropriate at this point to consider several witnesses for the interpretation of Orpheus as a *figura*: Ovid, Dante on Ovid, the *Ovide moralisé*, and Terrasson's description of the trials of Orpheus. Ovid himself,

---

[1] Igor Stravinsky and Robert Craft, *Dialogues and a Diary* (2nd edn., London, 1968), 90.

it would seem, suggests that the tale of Orpheus, as told by him, is out of
the ordinary by its sheer size: it sprawls over two books of the *Metamorphoses*,
from book x, line 1, to book xi, line 84, occupying a total of 823 lines. In a
way this count is deceptive, for Ovid, with his consummate narrative skill,
uses two devices to maintain both continuity and suspense, namely
propagation and interruption. The story of Orpheus begets other stories,
which interrupt and prolong it. The interspersed tales are sometimes told
by the narrator, though mostly by Orpheus, making the intercalations even
more organic. And to top it all, Ovid inserts a portion of the narrative
framework between two intervening stories: a marvellous example of
Rahmenerzählung, a genre to whose popularity Ovid and later Apuleius
contributed so much, and thus led the way to Boccaccio and other
vernacular poets. Consequently, a patchwork of eight tales enlarges the
myth of Orpheus from 201 to 823 lines, as shown in Table 1.2. What
concerns us here is not the way in which all the insertions reflect on love
profane, if not love sacred, but how clearly they are connected with the
main plot or with each other: Orpheus' power moves rocks and trees,
among them the cypress, which leads to the story of Cyparissus; an
analogue to that is the myth of Hyacinthus; the incestuous tale of Myrrha,
mother of Adonis, leads to the story of Adonis, bisected by the
metamorphosis of Atalanta. The quilt is so complex that it is hard to
separate its component parts. At the same time, these parts differ greatly in
size: 7 lines for Ganymede, 73 for Adonis, 221 for Myrrha. Yet the resulting
total—over 800 lines—is exceptional. Ariadne in book viii is given 14 lines,
Daphne in book i takes 116, and Echo's 153 lines in book iii are longer than
average. By sheer length Ovid makes the myth of Orpheus stand out from
the hundreds of tales told in his fifteen books.

TABLE 1.2. *Orpheus and related tales in Ovid's* Metamorphoses

1.	Orpheus, part I	x. 1–105
2.	Cyparissus (told by Ovid)	106–42
3.	Orpheus, part II	143–54
	(further tales told by Orpheus himself:)	
4.	Ganymede	155–61
5.	Hyacinthus	162–219
6.	Propoetides	220–42
7.	Pygmalion	243–97
8.	Myrrha	298–518
9.	Adonis, part I	519–59
10.	Atalanta	560–707
11.	Adonis, part II	708–39
12.	Orpheus, part III (resumed from x. 143–54)	xi. 1–84

It is, therefore, not surprising that in his discussion of literal and allegorical poetry Dante offers as a single example of the latter the story of Orpheus in the *Metamorphoses*. In his *Convivio* (ii. 1. 3) he discusses the allegorical understanding of poetic tales. These tales constitute a hidden truth (*veritade ascosa*) under the mantle of a beautiful lie (*bella menzogna*). The instance given is

when Ovid says that Orpheus with his lyre made wild beasts tame and trees and rocks move . . .

The power of Orpheus is viewed by Dante as an allegory for the faculties of man who, in his wisdom and rationality, can tame and move, according to his will, those creatures who do not partake of arts and letters.[2]

Dante's illustration of the *senso allegorico* is complemented by another work of the early fourteenth century, the *Ovide moralisé*. This widely read compilation added to Ovid's stories suitable allegories, moralizations, and sometimes even alternative allegories for the same story. The stories themselves had become increasingly useful during the millennium that separates the wall-paintings in the Roman catacombs from the age of Dante and Petrarch. As the knowledge of Latin spread across Europe the number of readers increased, but, conversely, the protagonists of the Ovidian tales became more remote. Hence an ancient household book acquired a new usefulness. As Curtius has succinctly put it:

. . . the *Metamorphoses* were also a repertory of mythology as exciting as a romance. Who was Phaethon? Lycaon? Procne? Arachne? Ovid was the *Who's Who* for a thousand such questions.[3]

At the same time, the string of allegories and interpretations attached to the *Metamorphoses* seemed to merit compilation. The stories were too attractive and useful to be ignored, but their content was too pagan and erotic (if not lascivious) to be left unexplained. As these apologetic moralizations increased in number a catalogue of catalogues seemed to be in order. The anonymous *Ovide moralisé* (*c*.1310) was one of the most widely distributed *Who's Who* type of collections, which informed its readers not only as to who was who, but also who stood symbolically for whom. The passage that compares the *katabasis* of Orpheus with Christ's descent into hell and his deliverance of the soul begins significantly with the noun *alegorie*:[4]

---

[2] An analogous passage on the civilizing powers of Orpheus occurs in Daniello's *Poetica* (Venice, 1536), 11; ed. Bernard Weinberg, *Trattati di poetica e retorica del Cinquecento*, 4 vols. (Bari, 1970–4), i. 234.

[3] Ernst R. Curtius, European Literature and the Latin Middle Ages, trans. W. R. Trask (London, 1953), 18.

[4] The quotation is based on Cornelius de Boer's edition, *Ovide moralisé, poème du commencement du quatorzième siècle*, 5 vols. (Verhandelingen der K. Akademie van Wetenschappen te Amsterdam, Afdeeling Letterkunde, NS, 15, 21, 30, 37, 43; Amsterdam, 1915–38). The French verse has been compared with manuscripts now at Paris and London, notably the beautiful manuscript formerly in the possession of the Duc de Berry, now Paris, Bibl. Nat., MS fr. 373, fo. 220ᵛ.

Par alegorie puis metre
Autre sentence en ceste letre.
Puis que Dieu fu en crois pendus
Et vis en enfer descendus,
Pour l'ame querre et delivrer,
Pour qui se vault à mort livrer
Et souffrir mainte grief dolour,
Mes li mauves por lor folour
Demorerent à dapnement
En enfer pardurablement,
Et là sont pris et retenus;
Puis que Dieu fu d'enfer venus,
Il monte en la haute plaine
De verdour pardurable plaine,
Mes n'i avoit encor plenté
Des sains, qui or i sont planté.
Cil prophetes, cil bon harperres,
Cil delitables preechierres
Asseia son procureour,
Son apostre, son prescheour,
Saint Pere, et les autres ensamble
L'un pour tous, et tous, ce me samble,
Sor le hault mont de sainte yglise,
Si lor comanda la joustise
De lier et de deslier,
D'absoudre et d'escommenier.

By way of allegory we may put
another meaning to this story.
After God was hung on the cross
and descended alive to hell
to seek out and deliver the soul
(for whose sake he was willing to undergo death
and to suffer many a grievous pain;
but the evil ones, for their folly,
remained damned
in hell eternally,
and are held and retained there)
after God came back from hell
he climbed up to the high plain,
full of everlasting greenness.
(But there was not the host of saints
who are now situated there.)
That prophet, that good harper,
that delightful preacher
set up his deputy,
his apostle, his preacher,

St Peter, and the others along with him,
one for all, and all, it seems to me,
on the high hill of Holy Church,
giving over to them the legal power
to bind and to release,
to absolve and to excommunicate.

In the *Ovide moralisé*, then, Dante's hidden truth consists in the fact that Orpheus-Christ rescues and delivers the human soul, and in the *Ovidius moralizatus* of *c.*1340 (an even more popular derivative, since it was written in Latin, not in French verse) he liberates human nature:

Dic allegorice quod . . . Orpheus Christus in infernum personaliter voluit descendere et sic uxorem suam i.e. humanam naturam rehabuit; ipsamque de regno tenebrarum ereptam . . .

Let us say allegorically that . . . Orpheus Christ wanted to descend to Hades himself and thus regain his wife, that is to say, human nature, liberating her from the rule of Hades . . .

This victory over Hades—death, hell—could of course be interpreted in a variety of ways, both by medieval commentators and Renaissance humanists; by and large both religious and philosophical annotators tended to view it as reason gaining the upper hand over passion. Thus, when Orpheus breaks the proscription and looks back, he turns to passion, to hell, and loses first Eurydice and consequently his own life. As Boethius points out the moral of the Orpheus myth in the sixth century:

This tale refers to you . . . for whosoever seeks to lead his mind to the upper regions [i.e. the light], should he, defeated, turn his eyes back to Hades [i.e. the darkness] loses whatever excellence he has gained . . .[5]

This excellence is Dante's 'wisdom and rationality' in the fourteenth century. And the tales, the fables, the myths always conceal this deeper, Neoplatonic truth. The element of concealment, allegorization, is quite common in literary accounts from the sixth century (Boethius, Cassiodorus) to the sixteenth century. Dante's mantle (*manto*) reappears as Ronsard's 'manteau' when he recounts how he became the disciple of the humanist Jean Dorat (1508 – 88) who

> Taught me poetry, and showed me how
> One must feign and conceal fables properly,
> And how to disguise the truth of things
> With a mantle of fables wrapped around them
> (*D'un fabuleux manteau, dont elles sont encloses*)[6]

[5] *De Consolatione Philosophiae*, iii. 12. 52–8.

[6] From 'Hynne de l'automne à Claude de l'Aubespine', *Œuvres complètes*, ed. Gustave Cohen, 2 vols. (Paris, 1950), ii. 241.

The distinction drawn by the Neoplatonists between the overt, literal meaning of the Orpheus myth and its covert, symbolic significance throws some light on Poliziano's preface to his *Orfeo*. There he apologizes for this secular trifle, dashed off in a mere two days and written, moreover, not in Latin but in the vernacular, for the better understanding of the spectators. What Poliziano seems to say in so many words is that he (the poet, humanist, and scholar) has deliberately written a play to please the million (to use Hamlet's hyperbole), not offering caviare to the general. Nevertheless, the concealed meaning of the plot would have been obvious to the circle around Ficino of which Poliziano was a member. This circle regarded the philosopher as a new Orpheus who had brought back from Hades the true Eurydice, that is wisdom and control in terms of Plato's philosophy.

Perhaps we can show the persistence of the allegorical interpretation of the Orpheus plot when we turn our attention briefly to the eighteenth century, where we find not only the operas of Fux (1715), Wagenseil (1750), and Gluck (1762), but also Dittersdorf's *Orpheus der Zweite* (Hamburg, 1788), which antedates the clever irony of Offenbach (1858). But it is Mozart's *Zauberflöte* of 1791 that needs to be brought in here for a moment. The connection between the quest of Tamino and that of Orpheus is allegory. In some way the twentieth century has rediscovered the greatness of the *Zauberflöte*. Its popularity was never in doubt, but particularly in the English-speaking world it seemed more farce than high art. Dent, in his masterly study of Mozart's operas, quotes from a review of 1942:

Suffice it that *The Magic Flute* contains some of the most beautiful music ever written to a nonsensical libretto.[7]

But modern critics, heirs of Frazer, Jung, and Lévi-Strauss (let alone Stith Thompson's invaluable *Motif-Index of Folk-Literature*), are aware of the archetypal and mythical aspects of Schikaneder's libretto. The concealed truth behind the jumble of action and the babble of Papageno's speech becomes clear when we read Abbé Jean Terrasson's book of 1731, to which Dent has introduced historians of opera.

Terrasson, who taught Greek and Latin philosophy at the Collège de France, published his *Sethos, histoire ou vie tirée des monumens anecdotes de l'ancienne Egypte* in 1731, with three further French editions appearing by 1813; two German translations were in print by 1778; an Italian translation came out in Venice in 1734.[8] There is no need to rehearse here the importance of *Sethos* for Mozart: certain of his numbers, such as 'O Isis und Osiris' and 'Wer da wandelt diese Straße voll Beschwerden', are clearly paraphrases of Terrasson's text, but these and other related Mozartian matters have been

---

[7] *Mozart's Operas* (2nd edn., London, 1947), 229.

[8] The present brief account is based on a copy of the English translation (London, 1732) in the Bodleian Library, Oxford.

investigated by Dent and others. On the other hand, three aspects of the curious romance, or *histoire*, concern us here: the Egyptian connection, the reference to *katabasis*, and the attainment of knowledge through trials involving self-control. As to Egypt, D. P. Walker, whose knowledge of Orpheus in Neoplatonism was unrivalled, wrote:

Usually it was supposed, not without some historical evidence, that Plato and his main predecessors, *Orpheus* [my emphasis] and Pythagoras, had visited Egypt . . .[9]

The other connection with Egypt is the mythological element of dismemberment, of being torn to pieces, which is common to the tales of Orpheus, Dionysus (Bacchus), and Osiris. Such stories of decay and rebirth are, of course, not restricted to a single myth. It was Plutarch (*De Iside et Osiride*, 364F – 365A) who first pointed out the analogies between Dionysus and Osiris, and these matters have been discussed in various classical and religious glosses, as well as in modern monographs.

The element of *katabasis* is found in Terrasson's accounts both of the Egyptian prince Sethos and the Thracian poet Orpheus. Both of them 'descend' through a well to the subterranean portion of a pyramid that allows them access to the realm of the dead. The non-Egyptian Orpheus wished to visit Egypt and be initiated, like Sethos, into its ancient rites since he was

persuaded that his poetry would become more sublime, when he had gain'd a thorow knowledge of theology, morality, and nature, of which he had been inform'd the Egyptians were the true and only masters.[10]

It is this search for wisdom through trial that makes Sethos and Orpheus (and Tamino in the *Zauberflöte*) undergo the examinations demanded of them. Having attained such wisdom, they would be endowed with two powers important in the Orpheus myth: to parley with the gods of death in order to rescue the dead, and to converse with the dead to divine the future (and thus to counsel the followers of the cult).

Obviously these remarks constitute the merest sketch of the archetypal connections between Osiris, Sethos, Orpheus, and Tamino. In addition to Dent and Walker, already mentioned, the publications of Raymond Clark, Mircea Eliade, and Walter Strauss would be found helpful, as well as encyclopaedias of ancient and Christian religions such as that of James Hastings. Sometimes the very titles of these monographs suggest avenues of further reading, such as Clark's *Catabasis, Vergil and the Wisdom-Tradition*, Eliade's *Rites and Symbols: The Mysteries of Birth and Rebirth*, Strauss's *Descent and Return: The Orphic Theme in Modern Literature*.

| Alles Vergängliche | All things transitory |
| Ist nur ein Gleichnis | Are but a symbol . . . |

[9] 'The *Prisca Theologia* in France', *JWCI* 17 (1954), 212.
[10] Terrason, *Sethos*, trans. [Thomas] Lediard, 2 vols. (London, 1732), i. 168.

It is with these lines that Goethe concludes his *Faust*, and it is in this spirit that we should endeavour to perceive the figure of Orpheus as symbol, as metaphor. With reference to Yeats ('High Talk'), and through Yeats to Goethe, Tippett opens his *Mask of Time* with the words

> All metaphor, Malachi, stilts and all.
> Malachi, Malachi, all metaphor.

(In the same work Tippett quotes Rilke's *Sonette an Orpheus* and refers to Strauss's *Descent and Return*.) There can be little doubt that in the wake of Nietzsche and Existentialism we are more likely to view again works of art and myths in a metaphorical way, and that the theme of Descent and Return in the tale of Orpheus clearly stands for more than the surface of the story would suggest. We are thus in a better position to grasp the allegorical associations that the Orpheus plot evoked in the humanistically trained portions of the audiences who attended a performance of the works of Poliziano or Monteverdi. I would say that in the days of Poliziano these associations were both Christian and Neoplatonic. By the time of the seventeenth century (Peri, Monteverdi, Belli) the accent had probably shifted more to the Platonic and Neoplatonic traditions. And with increasing secularization, the quests of Orpheus and Tamino, in the eighteenth century of Gluck and Mozart, represent a striving for wisdom and control of the passions more in line with the Age of Enlightenment. By that time the figura of Orpheus had been subjected to an intellectual and symbolic treatment that far transcended the confines of a 'Jack and Jill' plot. Goethe's remarks about the *Zauberflöte* could readily be applied to the tradition of allegory in general. When speaking to Eckermann about the second and final part of his own *Faust* he said:

I am content if the general public enjoys what it sees; at the same time the higher meaning will not escape the initiated, just as is the case with *Die Zauberflöte* and other things.[11]

THE 'ACADEME'

In *Love's Labour's Lost* (I. i. 13) the King of Navarre's edict is

> Our court shall be a little academe

and the young men, bent on a régime of self-improvement and austerity, are asked

> . . . to live and study here three years.
> But there are other strict observances:
> As not to see a woman in that term . . .

11 Quoted in Dent, *Mozart's Operas*, 255.

At the end of the comedy Berowne comments (v. ii. 863)

> Our wooing doth not end like an old play;
> Jack hath not Jill . . .

I have therefore subtitled this section 'Academe' to focus on the main operatic crux of the Orpheus plot: Orpheus hath not Eurydice, and elements of misogyny and related attitudes are readily observed in Ovid, Poliziano, and Monteverdi.

The old 'country proverb' about Jack and Jill also surfaces in the *Midsummer Night's Dream* (III. ii. 462) when Puck uses his magic juice to reunite the former lovers in the Athenian pastoral:

> Jack shall have Jill;
> Naught shall go ill.

And indeed, few are the operas where this precept is not observed, at least during the first two centuries of the genre: naught goes ill, and *lieto fine* rules.

The term 'academe' or academy could not but remind Italian humanists and Elizabethan authors of Plato's school in ancient Athens; and it goes without saying that Ficino's academy in the Florence of the Medici, and the *Académie française*, described in Primaudaye's book of 1577, are all-male institutions. Shakespeare's contemporary Greene says that

Plato admitted no Auditour in his *Academie*, but such as while they were his schollers woulde abstaine from women . . .[12]

And apropos of Greene and the Elizabethans I cannot forgo quoting some misogynistic lines where Orpheus rather perversely blames Eurydice, attributing her loss to the fickleness with which she prefers Pluto to him. He says of her:

> In Thesaly, so bright none euer was,
> But faire and constant hardly may agree.
>> False harted wife to him that loued thee well:
>> To leaue thy loue and choose the Prince of hell.[13]

In fact, references to woman's inconstancy and lack of emotional control abound in the time-span from Plato's account of the death of Socrates to the *Zauberflöte*, where the Queen of the Night is dismissed as 'Sie ist ein Weib, hat Weibersinn', a comment not surprising in a patriarchal society, a fact of which present-day readers are more aware since Bachofen's classic study of matriarchy. In the nineteenth century, which initiated the general admission of women to church choirs, singing societies, and universities, Verdi's duke still sings 'Donna è mobile'.

   [12] *The Royal Exchange, contayning sundry aphorismes of phylosophie* (1590); *The Life and Complete Works in Prose and Verse of Robert Greene*, ed. Alexander B. Grosart, vii (London, 1881–3), 314.
   [13] Greene, '*Orpheus* Song', *Orpharion* (1599); *Complete Works*, xii. 22.

If anti-feminism, the other pole of the adoration of a madonna beyond reach, is prominent in 'academe', an institution devoted to the improvement of the philosopher-king and his fellow rulers (or magistrates), another attitude crops up in the description of such establishments that has some bearing on Poliziano and Monteverdi, namely, homoeroticism. The first account attributing such an inclination to Orpheus dates from the third century BC. It is a fragment by Phanocles, a rather shadowy Hellenistic figure, that survives in an anthology by Stobaeus of the fifth century of our era.[14] The fragment, short as it is, was known to Poliziano and rightly commended by Schlegel, who translated and published it in 1798, for its poetic polish. Its plot contains the fundamental outlines used by Virgil in his brief account in the *Georgics* (77 lines) and the slightly later and certainly more extensive tale as told in Ovid. In Phanocles Orpheus loves a boy, but the Thracian women resent his introduction of pederasty into their country, kill him, and throw his head and lyre into the water, which carries both to the Isle of Lesbos, where song and poetry have ruled ever since. But the cruel women were punished for their misdeed.

The different kind of artistry characteristic of Virgil and Ovid is telling in how divergently they used the outline of the myth they inherited, whether from Phanocles or some similar source, no longer extant. There is, of course, both gain and loss in Virgil's brevity. But a poet of his rank could not fail to achieve the greatest eloquence even within a short space. There are also some notable omissions. The love for young boys is gone and therewith one motive for the dismemberment by the Thracian women. We are merely told that no thought of love [for woman] or [another] wedding would soften Orpheus' heart—'Nulla Venus, non ulli animum flexere hymenaei'—and the women tear their 'contemptor' (as Ovid called him: ix. 7) limb from limb simply because they are spurned. Economy of narration here, but also, perhaps, circumspection and restraint, which may partially explain why Virgil died as the emperor's favourite, while Ovid finished his life in exile. But no critic could cavil at Virgil's conclusion; these three lines with their threefold articulation of the word 'Eurydice' by the severed head floating down the river (once as lament, then as repetition, and finally as echo) are as poignant and as finely chiselled as poetry can be:

> . . . Eurydicen vox ipsa et frigida lingua,
> a miseram Eurydicen! anima fugiente vocabat;
> Eurydicen toto referebant flumine ripae.

Ovid copied the passage by a threefold 'flebile' ('woeful': *Metamorphoses*, xi. 52–3), but most judges of poetry, particularly of echo poetry, would concede that Virgil retains the palm.

¹⁴ J. U. Powell, *Collectanea Alexandrina* (Oxford, 1925), 106 7.

Otherwise little needs to be said about Ovid's treatment of love, passionate and illicit or controlled and approved, in the myth of Orpheus. Of the eight subsidiary stories interrupting the main tale (see Table 1.2), only the first three involve pederasty, amplifying and exemplifying the *topos* of love for young boys (x. 83):

> ille etiam Thracum populis fuit auctor amorem
> in teneros transferre mares . . .

But it goes without saying that a poet of Ovid's rank has moulded these stories with a perfection reminiscent of the handiwork of Pygmalion. Moreover, the manner in which these sub-plots throw light on the main plot, and enliven it by suspense, has always been assessed as one of the finest examples of story-telling. Some critics have felt it incumbent upon them to praise Virgil at the expense of Ovid, which confuses preference with merit. To talk about lack of moral stamina in the character of Orpheus or on the part of Ovid, or to view either of them as 'flawed poets', shows a strange insensitivity to poetry. Rarely has the symbolic contrast between the lyre of Apollo and the wind instruments and drums of Dionysus been more poignantly described than when the Thracian women start their attack on Orpheus. At first their spears and stones cannot touch him who is protected by the magic of his lyre. Only when the clangour of winds (*tibia, cornu*) and percussion (*tympana*) drowns the lyre (*cithara*) does cruelty prevail (xi. 8 – 18). Surely, to censure the poet who has served as a model for Shakespeare's poetry, Monteverdi's libretto, and Stravinsky's scenario is to misconstrue the critic's function, which is not to moralize but to explicate.

To proceed to Hyginus, whose *Astronomica* date from the second century of the Christian era. Hyginus, like other writers on astronomy (such as Manilius) in describing the constellations of the stars, deals also with the Lyre and consequently with the myth of Orpheus. This touches inevitably on the problem of rebirth, for a tale involving dismemberment and resurrection poses the question as to what happens to Orpheus after the Thracian women have killed him. In Phanocles his head and lyre float on the water to Lesbos, where both are interred and function as symbols, nay as tokens, of the flourishing of poetry and music. In Virgil, the afterlife of Orpheus is less extravagantly described: the head (not accompanied by the lyre) floats down the river (we do not know where to) and laments poignantly, as we have seen. Still, the fact that the severed head is capable of speech betokens some kind of immortality, or, at least, of an indestructible afterlife. In Ovid, the lyre is reinstated; both head and lyre lament, not only the head as in Virgil. As in Phanocles, they float to Lesbos, but nothing is said about the flourishing of poetry and music on that island. Instead, we have a coda that curiously anticipates the *lieto fine* of Peri and Gluck: Jack hath Jill. The shade of the dead Orpheus leaves earth for the lower regions ('umbra subit terras'), seeks for Eurydice in the blessed fields, and the two shades are at last happily united.

The conclusion of Hyginus is not concerned with the uxorial bliss of Orpheus and Eurydice, but introduces a new and important event in regard to the lyre. As in previous accounts, the head floats to Lesbos (nothing is said about the lyre at this point), is interred there, and as a result music flourishes at Lesbos. But the lyre (as a symbol of Orpheus) is translated to heaven: Orpheus is truly and gloriously reborn. This was obviously the conclusion that appealed to Monteverdi and Stravinsky. It also had the advantage that for the Renaissance humanists it made the Orpheus plot compatible with two Platonic themes, namely, anti-feminism and an interpretation of *eros* suggested by the *Symposium*. As to the former, Orpheus' spurning of Venus (to quote Virgil) and the consequent cruel reaction of the Thracian women are duly rehearsed by Hyginus, who also adds that it is rumoured ('nonnulli aiunt') that Orpheus originated love for boys. Hyginus strikes one as a mere compiler rather than a profound judge of the relative importance of the various motifs he has collected. Nevertheless, the *Astronomica* were widely read, and with Orpheus' lyre gloriously translated from Lesbos to heaven by the Muses, and Eurydice conveniently forgotten, any Neoplatonic humanist was free to interpret the ubiquitous myth as an allegory for the progress of the quest of Eros for beauty, proceeding from the love for a beautiful human to the love of heavenly beauty (and the renunciation of human love).

Poliziano seemed particularly endowed to do justice to the Orpheus myth. As a brilliant classical scholar, both in Greek and in Latin literature, he had the raw materials ready to hand; and as a poet who had proved his mettle both in Latin and Italian, he possessed the imaginative strength to mould the bits and pieces into a new shape. Reading Phanocles, Virgil, and Ovid for him meant not only to add new glosses to old ones, but also to vie for new laurels. The success of his endeavour may be gauged from the number of times his *Fabula di Orpheo* was reprinted between the *editio princeps* of 1494 and the publication of the score of Monteverdi's *Orfeo* in 1609. If we add to these printings various *rifacimenti* (reworkings, rearrangements) of Poliziano's original, the number of publications over these 110-odd years easily amounts to thirty items or more, and that leaves out of consideration the circulation of manuscript copies. But in order to assess the influence of Poliziano, we must also give due regard to a number of other plays, largely from the closing decades of the fifteenth century, that are not *rifacimenti* of his *Orfeo*, but nevertheless modelled upon it. Obviously this short play of 342 lines exercised a seminal influence. The plays indebted to Poliziano are now conveniently reprinted in Antonia Tissoni Benvenuti's *Teatro del Quattrocento*, whose comments there, and also in her more recent *L'Orfeo del Poliziano*, make further discussion unnecessary here.

The conclusion of Poliziano's play (ll. 261 – 342) is of particular relevance to our discussion. It consists primarily of two large musical 'numbers', Orpheus' lament after the second loss of Eurydice (ll. 261 – 92) and the chorus of the women after they have killed Orpheus (ll. 309 – 42). The lament consists of four stanzas of eight lines each. In the first stanza Orpheus bemoans his loss in Petrarchan terms and concludes that 'never again does he wish to love any woman (*donna alcuna*)'. In the second stanza he expresses the wish 'to pluck new flowers, the springtime of the better sex' (*del sexo migliore*, meaning the masculine sex). The third stanza is frankly misogynistic:

> Quant'è misero l'huom che cangia voglia
> per donna . . .
>
> How wretched is the man who changes his intentions
> for [the sake of pleasing] woman . . .

and expands on the fickleness of woman. We have already discussed this common cliché of a patriarchal society, and Tissoni Benvenuti cites an impressive array of literary parallels, among them examples from Virgil, Ovid, Petrarch, and Boccaccio. She also rightly refers to other plays of the fifteenth century clearly inspired by Poliziano's stanza, for example an answer poem recited by the heroine in Visconti's *Pasitea*, in the same metre of ottava rima:

> Quant'è meschina donna che se fida
> in omo . . .
>
> How wretched is the woman who trusts
> in man . . .

The fourth and final stanza repeats the Ovidian examples of pederasty (Jove and Ganymede, Apollo and Hyacinthus) and adds a further instance (Hercules and Hylas; perhaps influenced by Theocritus xiii). There is no *lieto fine* in Poliziano, Orpheus hath not Eurydice either in this world or in the nether-world: the angry women kill the man who spurns them, sever his head, tear his body limb from limb, and the play concludes with a Bacchanalian song in octosyllabic verse (ottonari), also in four stanzas, with a choral refrain, thus pointing the way to the type of operatic finale devised by such librettists as Rinuccini, Chiabrera, and Striggio. It was a brilliant dramatic stroke to transpose the noisy Dionysian revels of the women and have them succeed the death of Orpheus rather than cause it, as in Ovid. Thus the play concluded on a festive note and with a maximum of sonority, which the tale of Orpheus and his last song could not provide.

This last lyric of the protagonist, though, was clearly objectionable to some, even if acceptable to an élitist 'academe'. And here a brief glance at the various *rifacimenti* of Poliziano's play shows that quite a few of them attenuate or omit Orpheus' lament. And when they refer to the practice of pederasty, they castigate it as 'sodomia' or 'contra natura' or 'fuor di

TABLE 1.3. *Poliziano's* Orfeo *and some* rifacimenti

Title	Date	Number of ottave rime		Number of lines	Lament
		total	from Poliziano		
Poliziano:					
Fabula di Orpheo	c.1480 (first printed 1494)	—	—	342	4 stanzas
Rifacimenti:					
Orphei tragoedia 4 MSS: Florence, Modena, Paris, Parma	c.1485	—	—	450	stanzas 1–3 modified, 4 omitted
Historia de Orpheo[a]	printed c.1495	88	17	704	omitted ('sodomia')
Historia de Orpheo (dalla dolce lira)[b]	printed c.1525, c.1550, etc.	80	15	640	omitted ('contra natura' or 'fuor di natura')
Tractato de Orpheo (fiol del sole)[c] (variant of the above)	printed c.1510, c.1532, etc.	80	15	640	omitted ('contra natura')
Historia et fabula de Orpheo[d] (variant closest to Poliziano)	printed c.1530, c.1567, etc.	96	24	768	4 stanzas

[a] Ugolini, *I cantari*, 'C' (only one copy extant).
[b] Ugolini 'E'.
[c] Ugolini, p. 139.
[d] Ugolini 'M'.

misura'. In Table 1.3 a summary of these *rifacimenti* is given. All are anonymous, and with the exception of *Orphei tragoedia* (which is another play, and survives in various manuscripts rather than in print) they are narrative poetry: what the Italians call *cantari*, meaning literally 'songs' (as in 'Song of Roland'), though 'mini-epics' might be a more suitable term for today's English-speaking readers. These *cantari*, usually comprising less than a thousand lines, do not, as a rule, indicate date or place of publication on title-page or colophon, and must be dated by typography and illustrations.

The metre is the hendecasyllabic line, organized into that favourite secular stanza of the fifteenth century, the ottava rima, and in Table 1.3 the number of ottave lifted from Poliziano into these *cantari* is indicated. As will be seen, the original 342 lines are gradually extended to over 700 lines. Much spadework has been done on these *cantari* by Francesco Ugolini (1933), Erhard Lommatzsch (1950 – 63), and Antonia Tissoni Benvenuti (1986). Much further work and more exact cataloguing is still required. For the present book some ten different versions of the *cantari* have been examined, scattered through various libraries at Oxford, London, Florence, Venice, and Rome (including a recently discovered version in private possession at Oxford); for copies in German libraries (Wolfenbüttel, Zwickau) I have relied on Ugolini and Lommatzsch.

Before turning to operatic matters, notably Monteverdi, we must look briefly at another source of misogyny in allegorical plots, namely Terrasson's book, mentioned earlier as a source for the *Zauberflöte*. Mozart's Queen of the Night was modelled on the character of Daluca, stepmother of Sethos, who is described in Terrasson's *Sethos* as a rather disreputable lady,

desirous of becoming omnipotent at court, [she] did her best to get rid of the wise philosophers who had frequented it in the days of the late queen.

'The method she pitched on . . . was to give the sole empire of conversation to such ladies of the court as she had observed the most vain, and who had the faculty of talking loud and long upon nothing. These ladies . . . were always ready to interrupt any discourse that might savour of learning or ingenuity; but they were not often put to the trouble: for their own perpetual talk was so vain, and so little approved, that no man of sense could find room, or thought it worth while, to put in a word.'[15]

MONTEVERDI

The librettists of the Orpheus myth, then, inherited from their classical and Italian sources a fascinating and inspiring protagonist, but a difficult plot. Operatic audiences from Peri's *Euridice* to the twentieth century have ever wished for a tale with powerful passionate and erotic accents. The public also has always wanted star singers to project the leading roles: in Peri's *Euridice* of 1600 this was the tenor–composer Peri himself, in Monteverdi's *Orfeo* of 1607 probably the tenor–composer Francesco Rasi, in Gluck's *Orfeo* of 1762 the castrato Gaetano Guadagni (one of the finest performers of the century), and in Berlioz's revival of Gluck in 1859 Pauline Viardot Garcia (a striking member of a family of vocal virtuosi). At the end of an opera, audiences are not interested in Thracian women, or in the stars, or in

---

[15] Dent, *Mozart's Operas*, 225 6; Dent quotes the second paragraph from the English translation of *Sethos*, 1732.

Apollo, let alone in religious or philosophical tenets. What people want to see and hear in the finale is a resolution that has a bearing on the main pre-occupation and fate of the protagonist-star. Leaving aside for the moment the *lieto fine* that held such sway in the seventeenth and eighteenth centuries, it is readily seen that even in an opera with a tragic ending, Radames, for example, would deeply disappoint his audience were he to declare at the end that he was no longer interested in 'fickle woman'. But in the Orpheus plot it is impossible for hero and heroine to be together on the stage at the conclusion of the drama, whether they are to live or to die. The poet who realized that *impasse* between mythological tradition and operatic necessity was Rinuccini, the librettist of Peri's *Euridice* (and Monteverdi's *Arianna*). His insight is surprising because he stands at the beginning of the genre, and rarely does a pioneer foresee the laws to be deduced from the evolution of a new art-form. The two acts of surgery that the Florentine poet performed were to delete the Thracian women entirely and thus the tension between them and the hero. But Rinuccini went further: his Pluto returns Eurydice without any stipulation, Jack and Jill live happily thereafter, and the chorus, in festive and sonorous strains, congratulates the couple—and implicitly mankind—on this felicitous conclusion. In the preface to the libretto, the poet, knowing full well that any schoolboy could fault his plot, apologizes for his departure from the classical tradition:

> ma così mi è parso convenevole in tempo di tanta allegrezza . . .
>
> but thus it seemed to me suitable at a time of such rejoicing . . .

The *allegrezza* referred to was, of course, occasioned by the Medici wedding in October 1600, though this did not preclude a general satisfaction with the dramatic advantages of a *lieto fine*. In any event, Rinuccini's decision had several consequences. In the first place, he was able to provide Peri with a 'scaffolding' for music of an amplitude, a sonority, and a variety that made for a suitable finale. The libretto's eight stanzas were transformed by Peri into a sizeable concertato structure providing contrasts between ripieno and concertino, duple and triple time, vocal sections and instrumental ritornellos. (In Howard Mayer Brown's edition the finale occupies about 200 bars.)

This joyful conclusion not only contributed to the continued popularity of the work itself, it also proved a model for the next decade. The libretto that Striggio provided for Monteverdi at Mantua in 1607 has a choral finale, employing like Poliziano and Rinuccini the metre of ottonari, and providing concertino episodes. Nor was the finale formula of *Euridice* restricted to operas based on the Orpheus plot. When Peri's younger colleague and friend Gagliano was asked to contribute to the Mantuan festivities of 1608 he reset Rinuccini's Ovidian libretto of *Dafne* to music: again ripieno vs. concertino, duple vs. triple time, vocal stanzas vs. instrumental ritornellos. But taking a longer view of the history of opera, which today spans close to

four centuries, the most important consequence of Rinuccini's radical alter-
ation of the Orpheus myth was its influence on Calzabigi, the librettist of
Gluck. Calzabigi had the best of two worlds: at the end of the drama Amor
intervenes, reunites the lovers, and a concertato choral finale celebrates the
lieto fine. On the other hand, Gluck's librettist reinstated an element of the
traditional plot: Orpheus loses Eurydice a second time, which gives him a
chance for another lament and Gluck the opportunity to compose 'Che
farò senza Euridice'. Thus the two main requirements for a successful opera
were fulfilled: expression of the affections in memorable music, and a finale
that satisfied the expectations and emotional requirements of the audience.
It was Calzabigi's and Gluck's critical intelligence, and their astute assessment
of their predecessors, that caused them to create the one opera based on
the Orpheus myth that has enjoyed continuous success for over two centuries
on the boards of opera-houses, institutions no less fickle than the 'donne
mobili'. It may be surprising to have scholars citing the influence of a
libretto, dating from 1600, on a work more than a century and a half later.
But Rinuccini was far from forgotten in the second half of the eighteenth
century. The two most articulate historians of opera of that age, Algarotti
and Arteaga, refer to him with particular praise, and Algarotti's *Saggio*
(second, augmented edition, 1762) was published in the same year in which
Gluck's *Orfeo* was first performed.

Back to Monteverdi, there is first of all the knotty problem of the two
finales, one in Striggio's libretto published in 1607, the other in Monteverdi's
score printed in 1609, and reprinted in 1615. It is usually thought that
Striggio's finale was prepared for the two performances under the auspices
of the Accademia degli Invaghiti at Mantua on 24 February and 2 March
1607. (No further performances are known in the seventeenth century, nor
is there any record of a reprinting of the libretto before the present century.)
The 1607 finale is sixty-two lines long, and its mainstay is a choral song of
five stanzas comprising thirty-five lines, the remainder being taken up by
concertino episodes. (Throughout the present discussion such terms as
'chorus' and 'choral' refer either to an ensemble of solo voices, such as all
the singers employed in an opera, or a chamber choir with about two
voices to a part—any thought of an opera chorus or choral society of the
size customary in the nineteenth century would suggest an inappropriate
fullness of sound.) As far as the action goes, the finale has little to do with
either Orpheus or Eurydice. After the hero has lamented his second loss of
the heroine, and voiced his misogynistic thoughts, he is interrupted by a
troop of women indulging in their Dionysian revels, who resent his anti-
feminist attitude; he draws apart (that is, he presumably leaves the scene),
and the women sing their concertato finale, which has little connection
with the main plot. On the surface, it is not clear why Orpheus thinks all
women vile simply because he has lost Eurydice, nor is it clear whether

the women are going to kill the protagonist once they have found him (presumably after the end of the opera).

It is usually assumed that Monteverdi disliked a conclusion that left Orpheus lamenting his loss and fearfully cowering in the wings to avoid confrontation with a troop of hostile, inebriate, and noisy women; and sometime between the printing of the libretto in the carnival of 1607 and the publication of the score in 1609 he obtained the text of the so-called Apollo-finale, the only final scene of his opera for which the music survives. Just why he agreed to the publication of a score that was never, as far as we know, performed between 1609 and his death in 1643 we can only surmise; he did revive *Arianna* in his Venetian years, but not *Orfeo*.[16] Perhaps one reason for the publication was a kind of competition that went on between 1600 and 1609, in which various composers had their scores printed to establish their contribution to the new genre of opera, the *stile rappresentativo*.

Whatever the motives for publication, the fifth and final act of Monteverdi's score deserves close scrutiny. It consists of three sections:

1. Orpheus' echo lament, ll. 563–612 (50 lines). These are, for all practical purposes, identical with the corresponding section of the Striggio finale, including references to 'vile womanhood' (*vil femina*).
2. The Apollo section, ll. 613'–44' (32 lines).[17] Apollo descends from heaven and admonishes Orpheus to lift his mind from personal and self-indulgent grief to a higher approach and follow him to heaven. When Orpheus asks whether he will see his beloved Eurydice (*amata Euridice*) again, Apollo counsels him that he will behold her lovely likeness (*le sue sembianze belle*) in the sun and the stars. Orpheus states that he would not be the son of great Apollo, were he not to follow his counsel. They both sing a short duet, and the same cloud-machine that brought Apollo down to the stage takes them both up to heaven—surely a *deus ex machina* ending if ever there was one.
3. Choral finale, ll. 645'–56' (12 lines). A chorus (or ensemble of soloists) articulates the moral conclusion of the play in two stanzas of six lines each. The judgement sounds more biblical (Ps. 126: 5) than pagan: 'from the seeds of sorrow grace shall be reaped':

> E chi semina fra doglie
> D'ogni gràzia il frutto coglie.

---

[16] The best way to compare the 1607 and the 1609 finale is to consult Barbara Russano Hanning, *Of Poetry and Music's Power: Humanism and the Creation of Opera* (Studies in Musicology, 13; Ann Arbor, Mich., 1980), where both finales are printed, or John Whenham, *Claudio Monteverdi: Orfeo* (Cambridge Opera Handbooks; Cambridge, 1986), where the Striggio finale is reprinted and translated; the 1609 finale, with translation, is readily available in sleeve-notes.

[17] Line-numbers with primes refer to the alternative text of the finale in the 1609 score, and are thus numbered in Hanning's monograph.

One offers so detailed a synopsis with apologies to any student of Monteverdi. But the main lines of thought, discussed above under the headings of 'Allegory' and 'Academe', require citing of chapter and verse concerning this opera, which lay dormant for almost three centuries until Eitner published excerpts from the score in 1881, and the revivals at Paris in 1904 and Oxford in 1925.[18] Clearly, anyone reading the Bible or Homer allegorically would find no difficulty in interpreting the protagonist of Rinuccini, Striggio, or Monteverdi as a *figura*. Even the eventual happiness of Gluck's Orpheus could be and was interpreted by some court officials as a happy omen for the Emperor's well-being. One could perhaps add that of the four finales between 1600 and 1762 here compared, Monteverdi's is Neoplatonic in a manner more pronounced than the others. As to misogyny, it is common to the versions of 1607 and 1609, and was avoided by Peri and Gluck only by deliberate omission. The librettists of these two latter composers also deleted any trace of homoeroticism; nor is there any mention of it in Striggio, but in Monteverdi anyone familiar with classical mythology in general and Ovid or Poliziano in particular would notice that the manner in which Apollo takes Orpheus to heaven could easily be construed as an analogue to the stories about Jove and Apollo that Orpheus sings in Ovid. (In passing we may note that Apollo similarly rescues Eumelio in Agazzari's opera of 1606, and in Landi's *Morte d'Orfeo* the hero is brought by Mercury before the throne of Jove and joins the gods in a finale, detached from the main plot.) On the other hand, if secular or sacred authorities objected to such overtones, these could always conveniently be explained away as allegories.

There are, however, two aspects of Monteverdi's apotheosis we have not yet discussed: the spatial and dramatic consequences that follow from the differences from Striggio's plot. In Striggio, ripieno and concertino are intertwined; we have a total of 62 lines, 35 of them choral. By contrast, the 1609 finale neatly separates concertino and ripieno: after 32 lines for Apollo and Orpheus (a texture of one or two vocal parts) there are 12 lines for the chorus (a texture of five vocal parts). These two choral stanzas, of 6 lines each, seem a rather puny conclusion of the drama, to act as a dismissal of the audience, a *licenza*, after the prolonged diet of solo singing that precedes it. One wonders whether this was one of the reasons why neither Monteverdi nor his many admirers in the first half of the seventeenth century ever revived the work after 1607. Certainly contemporary critics, when they praise Monteverdi as an operatic composer, single out that other Ovidian opera of his, *Arianna*. Speaking in the first person, I must admit that I have always felt let down by the conclusion of the opera, in spite of the glorious passages preceding the finale. After discussing this problem with Dent, who was consulted before the Oxford revival of 1925, with

---

[18] For a calendar of modern edns. and revivals see Nigel Fortune's article in Whenham's monograph.

Westrup, who edited the score for that occasion, and with Stravinsky, who wrestled with the *licenza* problem both in his *Orpheus* and *The Rake's Progress*, I find myself in a minority, but not entirely isolated. In any event, a composer of the stature of Monteverdi, whose laurels are not restricted to stage music, does not require uncritical adulation. To proceed from value-judgements to statistics, the final chorus of the 1609 score seems the shortest in the history of early opera. Peri's *Euridice* concludes with 48 lines (of which 36 are choral), Agazzari's *Eumelio* with 30 lines (18 choral, interlaced with 12 lines concertino), Gagliano's *Dafne* has 48 lines (of which presumably 36 are choral), the libretto for Monteverdi's *Arianna* ends with 47 lines (of which 18 are choral), and Landi's *Morte d'Orfeo* has 70 lines (of which at least 29 must be reckoned as choral).

The other aspect of the 1609 finale concerns the question of *fine tragico* vs. *lieto fine*. In the libretto finale of 1607 the main plot can hardly be said to be terminated; rather it is superseded by the Dionysian revels of the spurned women. There is no doubt that Monteverdi preferred a happy ending for his protagonists; he said so in a much-quoted letter to Striggio about the libretto of *Narciso* (7 May 1627), and the librettos of *Arianna*, *Ulisse*, and *Poppea* bear out this approach. In the 1609 finale Orpheus is at least not left lamenting (or hiding from inimical women), but his earthly afflictions are succeeded by his apotheosis. His final ascent to heaven is the glorious complement and reward for his fearless descent. This archetypal success of death and transfiguration, of dismemberment and rebirth, is in accord with some of the classical sources, as we have seen, and is also aesthetically satisfying. It may well have influenced Landi's fifth act, tacked on to the main plot, and it certainly affected Stravinsky's ballet, written in collaboration with Balanchine. In fact, this twentieth-century score, created by two men with a good knowledge of classical mythology, is perhaps the most successful descendant of Monteverdi's apotheosis. The orchestra is a better medium than the singing voice to symbolize deification, and it is no discourtesy to Stravinsky's choreographers to state that his ballet scores have always done well in the concert hall, where—in fact—for social and economic reasons they have been more often performed than as stage music. The contrast between the harp (and other softly played instruments) and the ripieno is the perfect concertato between the protagonist and the Bacchic women who attack him and tear him to pieces.[19] The quiet fading-away of action and music is an apt accompaniment to this version of the myth:

Apollo appears. He wrests the lyre from Orpheus and raises his song heavenwards.

Throughout the history of drama and opera, Apollo plays an important role in the Orpheus myth. In the *Lycurgeia* of Aeschylus (fifth century BC)

---

[19] In the score, rehearsal numbers 125 and 137 for the ripieno of the women; 143 for the concertino of Orpheus' apotheosis.

Orpheus, after his *katabasis*, neglected the worship of Dionysus and instead honoured the sun, whom he identified with Apollo. In Peri's *Euridice* the final chorus opens with a grateful praise to the 'biondo arcier' (blond archer) Apollo, and the god's role looms even more prominently in Agazzari's *Eumelio* of 1606. There is ample precedent, then, for Monteverdi's and Stravinsky's apotheosis, both in mythological terms and in the history of the stage.

Monteverdi's *Orfeo* has often been called 'the first great opera', begging a definition of each of the three terms employed in that phrase. 'First composed' or 'first extant'? If the latter, *Dafne* of 1598 is out, and Cavalieri's *Rappresentazione di anima e di corpo* (February 1600) and Peri's *Euridice* (October 1600) vie for the chronological pride of place. But is a spiritual opera, such as Cavalieri's, a serious and significant contender in the history of a genre overwhelmingly and essentially secular? By dictionary definition Cavalieri wins, and about his (or Caccini's) pioneering contributions there can be little doubt, yet most historians would, I think, agree that Peri's was the work that exercised the first significant influence in opera's development. This leaves the extremely difficult definition of greatness unresolved. In terms of what the Germans call *Rezeptionsgeschichte*, success during a composer's lifetime can be measured, and perhaps the 'resonance' a work creates in its own age, and through the ages, is the only quality that can be assessed objectively. But timeless greatness may lie for ever in the eye of the beholder. In a thought-provoking article of 1984 Osthoff has dealt with the questions raised in this essay, though in greater depth and more detail.[20] Happily, we have come independently to similar conclusions on several problems. Of Monteverdi's work Osthoff states that it may be regarded as the 'first opera', a statement that applies perhaps in a 'higher sense', since we know that several years before Monteverdi Florentine literati and musicians had erected 'the fantastic structure of opera' ('das abenteuerliche Gebäude der Oper', a suggestive phrase of Goethe's that rivals Dr Johnson's 'exotic and irrational entertainment').

In musicological literature Peri has tended to be treated as a poor relation of Monteverdi, somewhat in the manner in which 'Papa Haydn' was considered in the nineteenth century as a symphonic predecessor of Beethoven. There is a vast literature on Monteverdi, but no book on Peri (though the publications of Brown, Carter, and Hanning add much to our knowledge). By two criteria of 'resonance' in the early seventeenth century, the operas based on librettos by Rinuccini were more successful than the *Orfeo* of Striggio and Monteverdi, namely, the frequency with which the librettos were reprinted, and the praise bestowed upon them by contemporary commentators (such as Doni). But then, Rossini found more resonance in Vienna than Beethoven or Schubert. (And who would deny that he had

---

[20] Wolfgang Osthoff, 'Contro le legge de' fati: Poliziano und Monteverdis *Orfeo* als Sinnbild künstlerischen Wettkampfs mit der Natur', *AnMc* 22 (1984), 11–68.

at his disposal librettists more knowledgeable about the requirements of the genre than either of the Viennese masters?) Could it be that the taste of the operatic public is as fickle and eager for novelty as the women whom Orpheus (and other tenors) despise? And are Monteverdi's *Orfeo* and Beethoven's *Fidelio* 'great' not in the sense of the box-office or *Rezeptions-geschichte*, but because they were written by stubborn men of genius whose major compositions we cannot ignore, even if they exhibit occasional flaws according to the canons of the genre within which their creators chose to work? One would have to be a veritable Beckmesser to deny immortality to 'Possente spirto' or to the canonic quartet in *Fidelio*. And yet most historians of opera would understand why Monteverdi and Beethoven so radically revised their respective operas. Can a work be great and yet flawed? Unless care is exercised the critic is drawn into a discussion of flaw, and even Aristotelian *hamartia*. Perhaps one should exhibit some of the moderation and control, for the absence of which Apollo chides Orpheus. Suffice it to say that even a flawed masterpiece can exert considerable influence and fascination, though the impact might be delayed by as much as centuries. But the soft strains of Orpheus' *kithara* or lute are powerful indeed:

> Orpheus with his lute made trees,
> And the mountain tops that freeze,
> Bow themselves when he did sing.

2

Definitions and Non-Definitions

OPERA, INTERMEDIO, MONODY

Before proceeding to a discussion of the main ingredients of early opera, such as lament and finale, a word must be said about the definitions of such terms as 'opera' and 'intermedio', or—rather—the non-definitions of these labels. For this study approaches the question pragmatically rather than aiming at comprehensive and strict statements of meaning. Brief working descriptions of opera are, of course, readily found in standard dictionaries, for example:

1. 'A drama in which music is the essential factor, comprising songs . . . orchestral preludes and interludes' (*Webster's Dictionary*, quoted in *Harvard Dictionary of Music*).
2. ' . . . musical dramatic works in which the actors sing some or all of their parts' (*New Grove Dictionary of Music*).

But there are always borderline cases that create controversy, and what would historical monographs be without controversy? Two such debates are easily derived from the above-quoted definitions by students of opera: one concerns style, the other content.

If music is the *essential*, not the exclusive factor in the drama, and if the actors sing *some*, but not necessarily all their parts, then, clearly, there exists a choice between spoken dialogue (occasionally encountered outside Italy, for example in Beethoven's *Fidelio* or Bizet's *Carmen*) and speech-song or recitative (as almost invariably met in Italian operas of the standard repertoire). Fortunately, we are not concerned with what happened in Vienna or Paris in the nineteenth century, but with events in Florence, Mantua, and Rome in the early seventeenth century; and Italian librettists and composers accepted the humanistic theory that ancient Greek drama was sung from beginning to end, and that therefore the new genre of opera was bound to proceed likewise. This involved the need to connect the full-blooded lyrical passages with the rapid declamation of the recitatives, which ever since opera's inception has been a subject of controversy. Speech-song, particularly in its more expository and narrative sections, has frequently engendered boredom (*tedio*) while audiences waited for more exciting musical fare. As early as 1626 Mazzocchi, in a printed score, complained about the 'tedio del recitativo', which must be interrupted and relieved by more full-blooded arias (*arie*). However that may be, most historians would agree that over the centuries the success of operas has not depended on whether the composer dared to switch from song to speech and back to song again, but on the quality of the songs. It is the magic by which the words of the libretto are translated into another realm that counts, by which we leave the genre of spoken drama and move into the sphere of opera (but more about that in the next section of this chapter).

The second controversy concerns content. The definitions quoted do not concern themselves with subject-matter. But it does not require much astuteness to observe that most operas deal with the pangs of love. Need they? The original version of *Boris Godunov* does not. Does opera have to be secular? Is there a clear dividing-line between opera and oratorio? As an instance of such debates, an authoritative and comprehensive survey of the oratorio, recently published, called Cavalieri's *Rappresentazione di anima e di corpo*[1] an opera, not an oratorio, since its production required full stage action, although its subject matter was spiritual (and allegorical at that) rather than secular. An equally authoritative student of oratorio detected a flaw here and considered the presence or absence of stage action a narrow and impractical criterion by which to distinguish between opera and oratorio. Most authors dealing with the earlier seventeenth century would agree that a stage performance involving actors who sing constitutes an opera, at least in that period. Accordingly, Cavalieri's *Anima e corpo*, Agazzari's *Eumelio* (an allegorical pastoral), and Landi's *Sant'Alessio* are relevant to this study. Moreover, Cavalieri's priority as one of the architects of the nascent genre of opera makes his exclusion from the history of early opera undesirable. It would remove the first complete opera (performed February 1600) from a slim corpus of extant scores, although its methods of construction and its pastoralism could be exemplified from other available sources. On the assumption that a student who consults a book on early opera has a working knowledge of a work so labelled, no slavish adherence to either of the two definitions quoted is to be expected.

It is equally difficult to construct a concise, yet comprehensive definition of intermedio. The intermedi of the fifteenth and sixteenth centuries, one of the main roots out of which opera grew, were as varied as opera itself. Most were secular, a few spiritual. Some early specimens were short madrigals lasting a minute or so; others involved intricate concertato structures and lasted ten or twenty minutes. In several instances complex stage action and machinery were required; in others the intermedio provided musical variety in a non-musical activity (such as spoken drama) but without stage action. Equally, whereas the most influential predecessors of opera punctuated spoken drama, notably the five acts of a comedy, such musical interludes could also diversify a variety of activities, such as banquets and tournaments.

---

[1] The original spelling is *Rappresentatione di anima, et di corpo*; all future references to this work will be abbreviated as *Anima e corpo*.

In fact, any series of episodes involving music, whatever the occasion, form a welcome addition to our source material, for whereas the descriptions of these interludes are numerous, the extant scores are few indeed. The main difference between opera and intermedio (though not the only one) is one of time-scale: hence opera enjoys the prominence associated with being the principal business of an afternoon's or evening's entertainment. When such prominence is given to an opera, comedy, or banquet, these events constitute the main entertainment, whereas the intermedi (or interludes) punctuate the main event but do not constitute it. When, for instance, their lavish and conspicuous character seems to obscure the principal entertainment, authors have complained that the tail appears to wag the dog (Il Lasca, alias Anton Francesco Grazzini, in his description of the intermedi of 1565.)

A good example of the difference in time-scale and in relative prominence is provided by the Ovidian myth of Orpheus, which forms the basis of both intermedi and full-length operas. At Florence in 1616 another of the many performances throughout Italy of Tasso's *Aminta* took place. The five acts of this pastoral play provided the main show, which was, however, punctuated by intermedi. These intermedi of 1616 (text by Chiabrera, music by Belli) adumbrated the topic, the sufferings of Orpheus, but were merely a sideshow. In Peri's *Euridice* and Monteverdi's *Orfeo*, however, the same Ovidian myth constitutes the main business. The length of these works gives them an exclusive and appropriate prominence. To use the five acts of Monteverdi's *Orfeo* as giant intermedi in some unusually protracted entertainment would be artistically offensive, if not impractical, because of the time-scale required. To introduce considerations of time into a discussion of the 'time' arts of drama and music is germane and proper. After all, the dimension of time is the main distinguishing characteristic between such miniature gems of expression as certain madrigals and 'monodies' and opera proper. Monteverdi's *Lamento della ninfa* is thoroughly dramatic, has interplay between soloist and an ensemble that observes and comments, but the work is too short to function as an opera. There are, of course, a few exceptions to any rule, and those that are to be found here and there usually have their origin outside Italy. As an instance, Lully's ballet interludes for Cavalli's operas performed in Paris were too long for the success of the operas they punctuated, or, indeed, for Cavalli's liking. But examples of this kind hardly exist in the annals of musical drama in Italy.

Reference has just been made to fully-fledged operas and brief monodies. Indeed so many of the latter are preserved as to make monody an ideal genre for studying the evolution of the operatic style. It is a sad fact that the extant operatic scores, from Peri's *Dafne* (1598; only fragments survive) to Landi's *Morte d'Orfeo* (1619) may be counted on the fingers of two hands, while monodies survive in hundreds—indeed, in thousands of specimens. Nor is the importance of monody dependent only on quantity; in quality some monodies rival the finest pages of the surviving operatic scores, including the greatest monody of them all, Monteverdi's *Lamento d'Arianna*. By a curious quirk (infuriating to the bedevilled music historian) Monteverdi never published a score of his opera *Arianna*, although it received more praise from his contemporaries than any other of his operas and although this work, based on a master libretto by Rinuccini, was mounted under Monteverdi's musical direction at Mantua in 1608 and at Venice in 1640. Fortunately, however, the traditions and economies of printing music as well as Monteverdi's desire to experiment and revise induced publication of the lament of the heroine three times: in 1614 there appeared an arrangement of the opening four sections as a madrigal, in 1623 a monody for solo voice and accompaniment, and in 1640/1 a contrafactum with its own sacred text.[2] A brief working definition of the term monody may be appropriate here. The term appears in antiquity, for instance in discussions of Greek drama (in which it is sometimes associated with lament), as well as in textbooks on music of the twentieth century. In the seventeenth century Milton called his *Lycidas*, a lament on the death of a friend, a monody. In ancient Greece, a single actor, not a chorus, was involved in the performance of a monody, which literally means 'solo-song'.

And obviously Monteverdi felt that the poignancy of the 'affetti' of Ariadne was enhanced by solo singing, for which reason he published the lament as a monody; otherwise melody, harmony, and text of the madrigal arrangement would have sufficed. It is equally clear that in the dramas of Sophocles and Euripides, as well as in the many published collections of monodies, and in the operas of Monteverdi (or, for that matter, of Verdi in the nineteenth century), the glories of monodic expression are reserved for laments. (We have already alluded to the lament as a constituent element of early opera, indeed of opera altogether.) It is therefore not surprising that such diverse works of reference as the *Oxford English Dictionary* and *Die Musik in Geschichte und Gegenwart* mention lament as an aspect of monody. At the same time this tragic element highlights the difference between a working definition and an all-embracing definition that brooks no exception to the rule. Technically speaking, all the songs and duets published in volumes of 'musiche' and 'arie' in the early seventeenth century display both in their vocal melodies and in their basses what we now call the operatic or monodic style, and are—*ipso facto*—monodies, whether they are plaintive or jubilant. Statistics may tell us that a more sizeable proportion of them is plaintive than otherwise. The discerning judgement of the contemporaries of Caccini, Peri, Gagliano, Sigismondo d'India, and Monteverdi bears out the statistics. Yet we must face the fact that the all-embracing term 'monody' is a modern,

---

[2] A more detailed consideration of words and music in the *Lamento d'Arianna* and a discussion of extant printed and manuscript sources will be found in Ch. 6. The sources for our knowledge of the 1640 revival of the opera are few: the libretto (1640) and a comment by Ivanovitch (1681).

musicological usage, designed to hold the mirror up to the new style of music in the early seventeenth century. Systematic musical history usually embodies its insight in newly invented terms: for instance, Ludwig felt impelled to coin the adjective 'isorhythmic' to catch an important aspect of fourteenth-century polyphony. Similarly, Ambros and Riemann, Solerti and Ghisi knew more precisely what they meant by monody than did Caccini and Peri when the latter published their 'musiche'. These men helped to create opera and monody, but how adept and interested they were in framing accurate definitions is hard to say. In any event, modern scholars in establishing such terms as monody endeavoured to take into account testimony from the seventeenth century, notably that of G. B. Doni, however sparse and inconsistent that testimony was likely to be. Another lexicographic difficulty is that in some musical textbooks of our century 'monodic' is employed as a synonym of 'monophonic', which refers to a single unaccompanied line. But the very essence of the operatic or monodic style lies in the tension between the vocal line and its bass. Nothing is more crucial to an appreciation of the monodies of Peri or Monteverdi than the composer's refusal to have the melodies 'ballare al moto del basso', dance to the motion of the bass. We may adumbrate this much-quoted phrase of Peri's as the crucial difference in the rate of harmonic change between melody and bass, and the deliberate anticipations and delays in the melody that prevent strict conformity at those points where the bass changes.

'RECITAR CANTANDO' AND 'PARLAR CANTANDO'

A useful aid to our understanding of such terms as 'monodic style', 'stile recitativo', and 'recitar cantando' is provided by an important and unusually explicit letter of Monteverdi's. The letter concerns a piece of dramatic music that the composer never completed and the sketches of which are not extant. In 1616 the Mantuan court approached Monteverdi to provide music for a maritime tale by Agnelli, entitled *Le nozze di Tetide*. The details of this abandoned commission need not detain us here; they are chronicled in Monteverdi's correspondence between 9 December 1616 and 14 January 1617.[3] Suffice it to say that the plot of *Tetide* concerned the wedding of the sea-nymph Thetis to Jupiter's grandson Peleus; other characters involved in the story are Venus, the sirens, and (most objectionally to Monteverdi) personifications of winds (*venti*), who cannot be expected to sing (the composer claims). In the course of formulating his objections to the plot, which Monteverdi believed to be the outline for an opera (it actually turned out to be a set of intermedi), he makes revealing remarks about the suitability of a

---

[3] *Lettere, dediche, prefazioni*, ed. Domenico de' Paoli (Rome, 1973), 85–99; *Letters of Claudio Monteverdi*, tr. Denis Stevens (London, 1980), 113–29.

text for an opera, about his own *Orfeo* and *Arianna*, and—last but not least—about 'parlar cantando'. This phrase we may interpret as a synonym for 'recitar cantando' used by Cavalieri in 1600 (*Anima e corpo*) and by Gagliano (*Dafne*, 1608), for Peri's 'imitar col canto chi parla' (*Euridice*, 1601), and for Caccini's 'in armonia favellare' (*Nuove musiche*, 1602).[4]

We can be certain that the composers quoted, as well as the theorists, such as Doni, were unanimous that the verbal text constituted the inevitable starting-point for a musical setting: it delineated the story, the characters, and the emotions. It is therefore the words that a composer closely examines before he decides that the text is suitable for a musical setting. Whether he refers to these words as 'parlare' or 'recitare' or 'favellare' is immaterial for our purposes. What matters is that these words, in opera, must be transmuted into something else; the text remains no longer verbal

> But doth suffer a sea change
> Into something rich and strange.

The libretto is merely the scaffolding on which the composer erects his score, or—to change metaphors—'the wire-frame on which to hang music' (Hofmannsthal to Strauss). This realization that in opera 'music must always be the vehicle of expression' (again Hofmannsthal to Strauss) and must be given a chance to function in such manner, runs strongly and plaintively through Monteverdi's letter. He finds the proposed plot of *Tetide* devoid of the strong and direct story-line, of the powerful emotions that he was able to invoke at the lyrical climaxes of *Orfeo* and *Arianna*. In the following quotation I have consulted the Italian original, and the glosses of Paoli's edition and Stevens's translation. But the English version offered here is my own and aims more at conveying the meaning across the centuries than at a literal translation.[5]

Monteverdi to Striggio, 9 December 1616

I received your letter . . . also the sketch of the libretto containing the maritime tale, the wedding of Thetis . . . I am asked to peruse it carefully and then to give my judgement as it is my duty to set it to music to serve at the celebration of the forthcoming wedding . . . If you add that I may speak freely, I am ready to obey with due respect and promptness . . . I shall say, first of all, generally that music wishes to be mistress of the air and not only of water; I want to say in my own language that the ensembles described in this tale are all placed low on the stage (*tutti bassi*) and near the ground, a great hindrance to beautiful [vocal] ensembles

---

⁴ A more detailed discussion of these and other terms, with a chronological list extending from 1600 to 1638, will be found later in this chapter.

⁵ Cf. *Lettere*, ed. de' Paoli, 85 9; *Letters*, tr. Stevens, 113 18; Heinz Becker *et al.*, *Quellentexte zur Konzeption der europäischen Oper im 17. Jahrhundert* (Musikwissenschaftliche Arbeiten, 27; Kassel, 1981), 30 3; Denis Arnold and Nigel Fortune, *The New Monteverdi Companion* (London, 1985), 33 5; Silke Leopold, *Monteverdi: Music in Transition*, trans. Anne Smith (Oxford, 1991), 191. I am much indebted to Osthoff's interpretation of this difficult letter.

(*belle armonie*) . . .[6] I see that among the actors of the plot are winds . . . and furthermore that these winds have to sing, namely Zephyrs and Boreals. How, dear Sir, can I imitate the speech of the winds if they do not speak? And how can I by such means move the emotions (*affetti*)? Ariadne moved [the audience] by being a woman, and similarly Orpheus moved [the listeners] by being a man and not a wind. Music can imitate their emotions, if not their speech, and even the roaring of winds, the bleating of sheep, the neighing of horses, and what not; but it does not imitate the speech of the winds because that does not exist . . . I feel that the entire tale, as far as in my humble ignorance I can judge it, does not move me, and I also have difficulty understanding it, nor do I feel that it carries me in a natural progression to a climax which moves me. Ariadne carried me to a proper lament (*giusto lamento*), Orpheus to a true prayer [*giusta preghiera*: a reference to 'Possente spirto' from Act III of *Orfeo*], but this [story]—I do not know to what climax [it leads] . . . If this [plot] were to lead to a single climax (*sol fine*), like in *Arianna* or *Orfeo*, it would require a single hand [i.e. not a team of composers], it would lead to words, though transformed into song, retaining primary importance (*parlar cantando*) and not, as in this tale, to song with underlaid words of secondary importance (*cantar parlando*) . . .

It will be seen that Monteverdi, in this letter, as in other documents, is vitally concerned with 'imitation', or with 're-creation' (as those unfamiliar with the term 'mimesis' from Plato and Aristotle may prefer to call it). But what is re-created is not a set of words ('oratione'), but rather the universal emotions ('affetti') of human beings. As an opera composer, Monteverdi starts from the words of the libretto, where the characters express themselves in words ('parlare', 'favellare', etc.). But only some words (some stories, some emotions) are capable of being transformed into music ('cantare', 'armonie'). When this is the case, communication through music (notably, but not exclusively vocal music) as the vehicle of expression is possible. In this case, the words give rise to the music, but are ultimately left behind, because inspired song ('canto') supersedes them, we are 'translated' (to use a biblical term) into another realm, and when this wondrous process takes place, Italians, influenced by humanism, speak of 'parlar cantando' or 'recitar cantando'.

There exist, however, also other, more recalcitrant, texts, not amenable to such transmutations. Music here performs an agreeable function, but does not serve as a vehicle of expression for the emotions of the text. This second kind of setting words, this 'incidental' music, Monteverdi calls 'cantar parlando'.

These pregnant phrases, employing only two terms (an infinitive and a gerund), are clear to readers conversant with the Italian prefaces and letters

---

[6] In the preceding sentence Monteverdi makes a distinction between plots where singers are placed low on the stage and those where they occupy a high position. A capacious stage and high positioning of the actors, so that their voices carry well through the air, are required for a euphonious ensemble ('belle armonie'), which might be accompanied by instruments, played backstage.

of the period. They probably require some gloss or paraphrase for many non-Italian students. The above remarks are offered with diffidence. Further discussion will be found in earlier publications dealing with the concepts and terminology of the birth of opera.[7]

'STILE RECITATIVO' AND MONODIC STYLE

Discussions of the new operatic style frequently involve the term 'stile recitativo' as synonymous with monodic style. This raises the question as to when the Italians first used that term. To students of English literature, the question acquires additional interest since it is frequently stated that as early as 1617 an *entire* masque by Ben Jonson 'was sung (after the Italian manner) Style Recitativo'. This phrase, first printed in the Jonson folio of 1640, is relevant to the date of the introduction into England of the monodic style, as well as the possibility of accompanying an *entire* masque with music, analogous to an Italian opera, sung from beginning to end, not merely punctuated by music here or there.[8]

It would seem that the first Italian scores to employ the new dramatic style do not use the term 'stile recitativo' either on the title-page or in the preface, though they usually display a phrase that implies that a story is told, not in words, but in music. A few of the phrases employed have just been mentioned in connection with Monteverdi's letter on 'parlar cantando'. In addition to *parlare* the following terms are used for story-telling: *recitare, recitando, rappresentare, rappresentativo, favellare, favola,* etc. The musical terms, in addition to 'cantare' and its derivatives, include: *armonia* (plural: *armonie*), *posta in musica, in musica,* etc. A glance at some prominent title-pages, prefaces, and other relevant passages from 1600 to 1638 will clarify matters (see Table 2.1).

From this short survey of printed scores dating from Cavalieri and Caccini (born in the 1540s or early 1550s) to Peri, Monteverdi, and Giacobbi (born in the 1560s), and to Gagliano (born in the 1580s) it would appear that the adjective 'rappresentativo' was the term most widely employed to announce the new Italian style. This makes sense: the verb *rappresentare* appears on most title-pages of operas and intermedi, conveying representation on the stage. Of course, *recitare* in the sense of stage recitation is, in this context, a synonym for *rappresentare*. Therefore, the phrase *recitar cantando* employed by Cavalieri in 1600 and Gagliano in 1608 was another formula for the same style. And one suspects that the terms 'stile monodico' or 'stile recitativo'

---

[7] See the section on 'recitar cantando' vs. 'cantar recitando' in Nino Pirrotta, *Music and Theatre from Poliziano to Monteverdi*, trans. Karen Eales (Cambridge, 1982), 241–5; also Leopold, *Monteverdi* (1982), 237–9 (1991 edn., pp. 188–9).

[8] See Peter Walls, 'The Origins of English Recitative', *PRMA* 110 (1983–4), 25–40; see also Doni's remark that it is still possible 'to recall the time when one began to sing all the drama in its entirety', quoted in the Annexe to this chapter.

TABLE 2.1. *'Recitar cantando' and 'stile recitativo', 1600–1638*

Date	Composer and opera	Title-page	Other places
Sept. 1600	Cavalieri, *Rappresentatione di anima e di corpo*	posta in musica . . . per recitar cantando	
Dec. 1600	Caccini, *Euridice*	composta in musica in stile rappresentativo	
Feb. 1601	Peri, *Euridice*	Le musiche . . . rappresentate	preface: imitar col canto chi parla
1602	Caccini, *Nuove musiche*		preface: in armonia favellare . . . rappresentate cantando
1606	Agazzari, *Eumelio*	Dramma . . . recitata . . . con le musiche	
1608	Gagliano, *Dafne*	rappresentata	preface: recitare cantando
1609	Monteverdi, *Orfeo* (first performed 1607)	favola in musica . . . rappresentata	
1608	Giacobbi, *Aurora ingannata*	canti rappresentativi	
1609	D'India, *Musiche*		p. 25: Madrigale in stile recitativo (*Ferma, Dorinda mia*)
1613	Bonini, *Lamento d'Arianna*	in istile recitativo	
1615	Bonini, *Affetti spirituali*	in istile di Firenze o recitativo	
1619	Monteverdi, *Settimo libro de madrigali*		p. 33: Lettera amorosa in genere rappresentativo
1620	Saracini, *Seconde Musiche*		p. 25: in stile recitativo. *Lamento della Madonna*
1620	Saracini, *Terze Musiche*	Pianto della Beata V.M. in stile recitativo	
1623	Monteverdi, *Lamento d'Arianna*	Lettere amorose in genere rappresentativo	
1626	Mazzocchi, *Catena d'Adone*		last page of score: rompono il tedio del recitativo
1632	Monteverdi, *Scherzi musicali*	in stil recitativo	
1638	Monteverdi, *Madrigali guerrieri et amorosi*	con alcuni opuscoli in genere rappresentativo	preface: rappresentativa; pp. 18, 55, 63: rappresentativo

would have been readily accepted as synonymous with 'stile rappresentativo' by the Italian musicians in the period tabulated above, that is, 1600–38. This assumption is based on a survey of extant treatises.

Three authors provide us with glosses on the term 'recitativo' in treatises written between 1607 and 1647. The earliest and briefest of these is Agazzari's *Del sonar sopra 'l basso*, published in 1607. Agazzari, born in 1578, that is, a generation or so after Cavalieri and Caccini, undoubtedly knew *Euridice*, since his own opera *Eumelio* (Rome, 1606) derives from it in ways more than one. His brief treatise of 1607, a mere twelve pages, mentions 'recitativo' in a passing remark at the bottom of p. 10. The basso continuo is useful for the modern style (*stile moderno*) of singing and composing in the 'recitativo' way (*di cantar recitativo e comporre*). The composer Bonini (born 1582) never published his treatise on *Discorsi e regole sopra la musica*, but on internal evidence it may be dated *c.*1620–45. Bonini was a pupil of Caccini, whom he praises highly and whom he also credits with being the inventor of the new and modern style. As with Agazzari, he calls this style 'recitativo'. Bonini is also interesting as a composer who, like Monteverdi, set Rinuccini's 'Lamento d'Arianna' to music. By far the most consequential author of treatises on the subject was Giovanni Battista Doni, born 1595, that is, too late to serve as an ear- or eyewitness to the developments that happened at Florence around 1600. But he was passionately interested in the subject, conducted a good deal of research, and his writings (between 1633 and the year of his death in 1647) form the main basis of modern musical scholarship. Doni's writings include four treatises, in all of which the 'stile recitativo' is discussed.[9]

Doni, a Florentine whose career kept him largely at Rome between 1623 and 1640, returned to Florence in 1640, where he died in 1647. His taste was conservative and Florentine, and he seems to have preferred Peri's *Euridice*, Caccini's *Nuove musiche*, and Monteverdi's *Arianna* to the Roman and Venetian operas of the 1630s and 1640s. Thoroughly aware of the new operatic style created around 1600, he asked Pietro Bardi, son of Giovanni Bardi (patron of Caccini), to provide him with historical information. Pietro Bardi's letter of 1634 to Doni is extant in manuscript and now usually studied in Solerti's reprint.[10] Bardi calls the modern manner 'stile rappresentativo', as did Caccini and Monteverdi (the latter speaks of 'genere rappresentativo'). Most of Bardi's information reappears in Doni's *Trattato*, largely in ch. IX. There he speaks of the modern style, which he sometimes

[9] 1. *Trattato della musica scenica*, largely written in 1633 5, revised c.1635 40, not published in the 17th c. but included in the *Lyra Barberina*, ed. A. F. Gori, 2 vols. (Florence, 1763; repr. Bologna, 1975).

    2. *Compendio . . . della musica* (1635).

    3. *Annotazioni sopra il compendio . . . della musica* (1640).

    4. *De praestantia musicae veteris . . .* (1647).

[10] Angelo Solerti, *Le origini del melodramma* (Turin, 1903; repr. 1969), 143 7. Solerti also includes excerpts from Bonini and Doni.

calls 'melodie odierne' (music of today) or 'vera musica teatrale' (true stage music).[11] But more often than not he speaks of 'stile recitativo', possibly influenced by such Roman composers as Mazzocchi and Della Valle: 'in stile communemente detto recitativo', 'suddetto stile recitativo', etc. On the other hand, in ch. XI of the same *Trattato* Doni splits the 'new style' (*nuovo stile*) into three subdivisions: 'recitativo', 'rappresentativo', and 'espressivo'. In the *Compendio* of 1635 he refers to the unpublished *Trattato* as a matter of course, and it is likely that those who received complimentary copies of the *Compendio*, for example Monteverdi, also received manuscript copies of the *Trattato*. In any case, in the *Compendio* (p. 101) Doni refers to the modern style, which with its single vocal line differs from madrigals as the 'stile detto recitativo'. But on second thought the passage did not seem detailed enough, and in the *Annotazioni* of 1640 he glosses the term 'stile detto recitativo', dividing it this time into three subsections, slightly different from his own Trattato, namely, 'narrativo', 'speciale recitativo' (in the narrower sense), and 'espressivo'.[12]

The umbrella term that Doni applies (*Annotazioni*, p. 60) for these three subdivisions is 'stile monodico'. Finally, in his *De praestantia* of 1647, the terms 'recitativo' and 'monodico' are treated as synonymous, as the following Latin passage shows: 'stylus recitativus, ac monodicus potius vocandus' (recitativo style or, better, monodic style).[13]

Obviously one could go into much greater detail, and Doni's attitude towards music, whether of ancient Greece or of Caccini and Monteverdi, deserves a separate study. But enough has been said to show that the term 'stile recitativo' was not forged by the five composers who established the new style at Rome, Florence, and Mantua: Cavalieri, Caccini, Peri, Monteverdi, and Gagliano. If any term predominates in the scores before 1610, it is 'stile rappresentativo'. Things remained fluid and unsettled, however; and as late as the 1630s and 1640s the terms 'rappresentativo', 'recitativo', and 'monodico' were used interchangeably. In a lecture given in 1624 Doni spoke of 'the style called "recitativo", that is to say "rappresentativo"'.[14] Largely as the result of Doni's influence, 'recitativo' has become the generally

[11] Substantial excerpts from the *Trattato* are quoted, translated, and discussed in the Annexe to this chapter.

[12] As an example of 'narrativo' Doni gives the messenger's report of Euridice's death from Peri's *Euridice*, 'Per quel vago boschetto', which entails, in addition to the more expressive turns, a certain amount of speech-like reiterations of the same note over long-held notes in the bass. (Today this would be called recitative.) As an instance of 'recitativo in the narrower (or special) sense' Doni gives the Prologue sung by Tragedy in Peri's *Euridice*, 'Io che d'altri sospiri', which in terms of fully-fledged, expressive music is half-way between 'narrativo' and 'espressivo'. (This would be called strophic variations, which frequently occur over an ostinato bass.) As an example of 'espressivo' Doni gives Ariadne's lament from Monteverdi's *Arianna*, 'Lasciatemi morire', obviously referring to the most intense and pathetic species of expression within the monodic style. (This would be called arioso.)

[13] *De praestantia*, 57; reprinted *Lyra Barberina*, i. 116 17.

[14] 'cioè rappresentativo'; *Lyra Barberina*, ii. 148.

accepted term, both in eighteenth-century opera and in modern scholarship. When foreigners such as Ben Jonson (*Lovers made Men*, 1617) or Schütz (*Psalmen Davids*, 1619) use the term, it testifies to the international influence of the new Italian style.[15] But it tells us little about the terminology used by composers from Cavalieri to Monteverdi. An English masque, with its aristocratic amateur performers and its revels, was miles away from Florentine or Mantuan opera, and Schütz's polychoral motets are similarly removed from Caccini's 'stile rappresentativo'.

This new style accommodated a whole gamut of musical expressiveness, ranging from speech-song to fully-fledged lyrics. When Doni attacks Cavalieri for his use of old-fashioned 'ariette', this does not imply that closed forms, such as strophic (or sectional) songs, did not occur in the scores of the first operas, but that a preponderance of them was inimical to the dramatic and emotional impact upon the audience. It also raises the question of the term 'aria', which has meant many things to many writers at various periods. To define it is well-nigh impossible, since the modern historian cannot easily discard his knowledge of 'aria' and 'recitative' in Metastasian and later opera. Certainly, such terms as 'aer', 'aere', 'aria', and other derivations from the same root are encountered in Italian music from the fourteenth century on.[16] Sometimes it refers to the skeleton of a bass or of a melody or both, suitable for the recitation of a stanza, or several stanzas of a text, for example ottave rime from Ariosto's *Orlando furioso*. At other times it seems to function as a synonym for music, but usually solo music, and quite frequently in strophic form. Such strophic solo songs, framed by instrumental ritornellos, and striking the listener as 'closed' forms, do occur in early opera, for instance Tirsi's 'Nel pur ardor' in Peri's *Euridice*, scene 2, or Orpheus' 'Vi ricorda o boschi ombrosi' in Monteverdi's *Orfeo*, Act II. But these function as pleasant pastoral interludes rather than as pillars of the dramatic structure. The famous, memorable solo pieces are either irregular (as Ariadne's lament in Monteverdi's *Arianna*) or the strophic structure is not clear to a lay audience.

[15] Another work that bears witness to this influence is the first extant German opera, *Seelewig* (1644, music by Staden, libretto by Harsdörffer). The opera boasts a score that sets the libretto to music in its entirety. The librettist refers to this Italian practice as 'set to music entirely in the form of recitation' ('durch und durch erzählungsweis in die Musik gesetzt'), and adds parenthetically in the margin the Italian phrase 'in genere recitativo'. Cf. Steven R. Huff, 'The Early German Libretto: Some Considerations Based on Harsdörffer's "Seelewig" ', *ML* 69 (1988), 345 55 at 348.

[16] Cf. standard musical dictionaries; also James Haar, *Essays on Italian Poetry and Music in the Renaissance, 1350–1600* (Berkeley, Calif., 1986), s.v. 'aer', 'aere', 'aria'; Pirrotta, 'Early Opera and Aria' in *Music and Theatre*, 237 80; Carolyn Gianturco, 'Nuove considerazioni su il tedio del recitativo delle prime opere romane', *RIM* 18 (1982), 212 39; Silke Leopold, ' "Quelle bazzicature poetiche . . .": Dichtungsformen in der . . . italienischen Oper (1600 1640)', *HJMw* 3 (1978), 101 41; Stuart Reiner, 'Vi sono molt'altre mezz'arie', in Powers (ed.), *Studies in Music History*, 241 58; James Haar, '*The Madrigale Arioso*: A Mid-Century Development in the Cinquecento Madrigal'; *SM* 12 (1983), 203 19; Howard M. Brown, 'Towards a Definition of Antonio Barré's *Madrigali ariosi*', *RIM* 25 (1990), 18 60. I hope to contribute an article on 'Aspects of Aria' to a volume of *Essays on Italian Baroque Opera and Song*, to be edited by T. Carter and I. Fenlon.

For instance, in 'Possente spirto' in Monteverdi's *Orfeo*, Act III, the text is strophic, and at least five of the six stanzas employ a skeleton of melody as well as of bass. But the melodic profile lies below the surface: the ordinary listener is not likely to notice it, let alone remember it. In order to establish a piece as an aria in the mind and memory of an audience, the old-fashioned devices of repetition and echo, for which Doni chides Cavalieri, must be employed. Certainly the great laments of Monteverdi and Cavalli are detachable from their context and could function as separate 'numbers' in recitals, but they do not strike us as 'closed' because the very fluidity with which they shift from recitative to arioso, from long-held bass notes to a moving bass, marks them as being composed in the new fashion of 'stile recitativo'.[17]

To discover the criteria of such terms as 'monodic style' or 'aria' one must examine the poetic and musical vocabulary of extant Italian sources from the seventeenth century, rather than impose rigid definitions on a fluid development.

ANNEXE

Doni on Cavalieri and the New Style

The various remarks that Doni makes about Cavalieri are scattered in several of his writings, but occur mostly in the *Trattato della musica scenica*, of which two versions were reprinted in the *Lyra Barberina*, ii, one at the beginning of the volume, the other (a second edition) in the Appendix, separately paged. One passage (ii. 22–3 and Appendix, pp. 12–13) deals with the rival claims of Cavalieri, Caccini, and Peri to be the originators of the new operatic style. The other passage (ii. 95 and Appendix, p. 60) deals with the needs of dramatic poetry for a chorus, to accommodate dancing as well as singing.

In the first passage, influenced no doubt by the letter of Pietro Bardi, but also by the more poignant vocal and harmonious expressiveness of Peri (and other rivals of Cavalieri), Doni criticizes Cavalieri's music as old-fashioned, containing too many 'ariette', that is, (strophic) closed musical forms, and not a sufficient number of samples of the new style to which he attaches such adjectives as 'recitativo', 'rappresentativo', or 'monodico'. These criticisms are largely levelled at the prefatory remarks printed at the beginning of the score of Cavalieri's *Anima e corpo*, which remarks were undoubtedly intended to advance the claims of Cavalieri against Caccini and Peri.

The second passage does not deal with Cavalieri's Roman sacred opera of 1600, but with the choral finale he composed for the Florentine intermedi of 1589. Here his dual competence as a choreographer as well as

---

[17] Monteverdi's 'Possente spirto' and *Lamento d'Arianna*, and Cassandra's lament from Cavalli's *Didone* are discussed in some detail in Ch. 6, which contains also a section on 'Lament as Number'.

musician is accorded high praise indeed: superlatives are applied to him as a composer ('most experienced') and to his finale ('most beautiful'). Why such high praise for the intermedi of 1589 and such low marks for *Anima e corpo* of 1600? Three reasons seem probable. First, *Anima e corpo* was rushed into print at Rome in September 1600 in order to claim priority over the efforts of Caccini and Peri, which were to be staged at Florence in October of that year. About Cavalieri's priority and Peri's acknowledgement of that claim there can be no doubt.[1] But priority and merit and the influence on subsequent composers are dissimilar matters. The strength of Cavalieri's opera (and of so much later Roman opera) lies in the sheer length of some of his musical structures and the greater utilization of choral and orchestral sonorities. There is to be found solo singing in the new monodic style, and some of it is harmonically quite striking. But the amount of solo singing and the proportion of what we would call 'in stile recitativo' is smaller than in the *Euridice* of either Peri or Caccini.

Therefore, Doni, writing a generation after the event, that is to say, in the 1630s, awards the palm to Caccini, Peri, and Monteverdi. Secondly, the so-called 'stile recitativo' does not occur in the intermedi of 1589, to which Cavalieri, Caccini, and Peri all contributed without controversial claims, at least without staking such claims in print. There is no reason why Cavalieri's enormously popular finale should not have been recognized for what it was worth. Thirdly, one detects perhaps some of that intense Florentine pride, so characteristic of the natives of that city, in Doni's remarks, when he ignores the claims of Roman opera against those of Florence. Florentine operas and north Italian operas by Florentine librettists (such as Monteverdi's *Arianna*) dominated the first decade of the century. Against them the Roman operas by Cavalieri and Agazzari of 1600 and 1606, and particularly allegorical sacred operas, constituted no major challenge to the Florentine claim to have established the 'new' style in Tuscany, a region whose eminence in poetry and music was no less pronounced than that in the visual arts.

Trattato della musica scenica

Capitolo IX. Dell'origine che ebbe a' tempi nostri il cantare in Scena[2]

In ogni tempo si è costumato di frammettere alle Azioni dramatiche qualche sorte di cantilena, o in forma d'Intermedi tra un Atto, e l'altro, o pure dentro l'istesso Atto, per qualche occorrenza del soggetto rappresentato. Ma quando si cominciassero a cantare tutte le Azioni intere, fresca ne è ancora la memoria; perciocchè avanti a quelle, che fece il Sig. Emilio del Cavaliere Gentiluomo Romano, e intendentissimo della Musica, non credo si sia praticato cosa, che meriti di essere mentovata. Di costui và attorno una Rappresentazione intitolata *Dell'Anima, e del*

---

[1] Cf. Sternfeld, 'The First Printed Opera Libretto', *ML* 59 (1978), 121–38 (esp. p. 121).

[2] *Lyra Barberina*, ii. 22–3.

Corpo, stampata quì in Roma nel 1600, e in essa si fa menzione di una Commedia grande rappresentata in Firenze nel 1588, per le Nozze della Serenissima Granduchessa, nella quale erano molti frammessi di Musica, da lui medesimo composti: dove anco due anni appresso si rappresentò il Satiro con le Musiche dell'istesso. Conviene però sapere, che quelle melodìe sono molto differenti dalle odierne, che si fanno in stile, comunemente detto *Recitativo*; non essendo quelle altro, che ariette con molti artifizi, di repetizioni, echi, e simili, che non hanno che fare niente con la buona, e vera Musica Teatrale, della quale il Sig. Emilio non potè aver lume per mancamento di quelle notizie, che si cavano dagli antichi Scrittori. E ciò si conosce chiaramente da certe massime, che egli mette avanti, le quali sono al tutto contrarie a quello, che richiede il Teatro. Tra l'altre cose ei vuole, che i versi siano piccoli, come di sette, e di cinque sillabe, e anco di otto con sdruccioli, e con le rime vicine, che è giustamente un volere ridurre la Musica scenica a barzellette, e villanelle, che come accennai di sopra, servono propriamente per framessi, e ripieni delle Commedie, massimamente giocose. Vuole anco, che bastino tre atti, e che il Poema non passi settecento versetti, e altre sue chimere, cavate dall'odierna pratica corrotta. Non vorrebbe anco, che la Sala fosse capace, che di mille persone al più; perchè i Cantori non avessero a sforzare troppo la voce: cose tutte, che si potrebbono dare per legge ad una Commedia da Monache, o da Giovani studenti, e non per Azioni rappresentate con reale apparato, che tra le altre condizioni, richiedono un sito di competente grandezza, e Cantori eletti: potendosi anco trovare rimedi per ingagliardire la voce degli Attori, come più abbasso si dirà. Questa dunque si può dire, che sia stata la prima ett [*recte* 'età'] della Musica Teatrale, dopo tanti secoli rinata in Firenze, come tante altre nobili professioni, nella maniera, che si è visto, benchè con principi molto deboli, e bassi. Ma notabile accrescimento fece poi con l'introduzione del suddetto stile recitativo; il quale è stato universalmente ricevuto, e praticato oggi da molti, accortisi che universalmente diletta più, che la maniera madrigalesca, per la gran perdita, che vi si fa del senso delle parole. Questo stile cominciò parimente in Firenze, intorno i medesimi tempi; sebbene più tardi fu introdotto nelle Scene, cioè là intorno al 1600, principio di questo secolo, e della seconda età di questa Musica scenica.

At all times it has been the custom to intersperse dramatic presentations with some kind of music, be it in the form of an intermedio between one act and another, or within the act, in accordance with the subject-matter dramatically presented. But it is still within the reach of memory to recall the time when one began to sing all the drama in its entirety. Because I do not think that anything was practised that merits mentioning before those works that were written by Signor Emilio de' Cavalieri, a Roman nobleman and excellent connoisseur of music. From him we have a stage work entitled *Body and Soul* [*Dell'Anima e del Corpo*], printed here at Rome in 1600, and in it [i.e. the Preface to the Reader, 'A' Lettori'] there is mention of a great comedy presented at Florence in 1588 [*recte* 1589] for the wedding festivities of the most Serene Grand Duchess, in which comedy there were interspersed many interludes of music composed by him; where also [i.e. in Florence] two years further on [i.e. 1590/1] there was presented *The Satyr* [*il Satiro*], with music by the same. It is, however, as well to know that these melodies [i.e. this music] are very different from those of today, written in a style commonly called 'recitativo'—the former being nothing else but *ariette* [strophic, old-fashioned, 'closed' musical forms] with many artful devices such as repetitions, echo effects, and similar devices, which have nothing to do with good and true theatrical music. Of such [dramatic] matters Signor Emilio could not have possessed insight for lack of knowledge of what the ancient writers say. And this one knows clearly from certain maxims that he puts in front [of the score], which are altogether contrary to that which the theatre requires. Among other matters he wishes that the lines be short, such as comprising seven or five syllables, and also nine with the accent on the antepenultimate syllable, and with paired rhymes, which is really a wish to reduce dramatic music to popular vocal forms (*a barzellette, e villanelle*) which, as I have indicated above, serve properly for intermedi and interludes (*per framessi e ripieni*) for comedies of a largely joyful nature.[3] He [Cavalieri] also wishes to have only three acts, and that the libretto not be longer than 700 lines, and pursues other hobby-horses of his, taken from the corrupt practices of today.[4]

Nor does he wish that the hall be too capacious: it should contain 1,000 spectators at most, so that the singers would not have to force their voices too much. All these are considerations out of which one could make rules for a comedy of nuns or of juvenile students, but not for stage presentations with stage machinery appropriate for grand occasions, which among other conditions require a site of sufficient amplitude and select singers; one could also find remedies for strengthening the voice of the actors, as will be stated later. But this one can say: that theatrical music in its first stage was reborn after so many centuries in Florence, like so many other notable achievements, in a manner which has been seen, in spite of weak and humble beginnings. But the notable step forward was made with the introduction of the so-called 'stile recitativo', which has universally been accepted and is practised today by many; it is recognized that it universally delights more than the madrigalian style because of the great loss suffered in the sense of the words. This style began likewise in Florence about the same time; though later it was introduced in the theatre around 1600, that is, the beginning of this century and of the second age of this theatrical music. [Doni then proceeds to discuss Giovanni Bardi, Vincenzo Galilei, Caccini, Peri, and Monteverdi.]

Capitolo XIX. Della Musica Corica[5]

. . . onde poteva agevolmente il Poeta nel comporre i suoi Cori (che di varie sorti di versi sogliono essere) usare metro, e ritmo tale, che fosse capace di una bell'aria di Canto, e di Ballo: nel che consiste la maggior parte dell'eccellenza dell'antica Musica, come vedremo appresso. Il che averebbe potuto molto bene imitare il Sig. Emilio del Cavaliere in quelle Rappresentazioni, che egli modulò in Firenze, se di queste cose avesse avuto notizia; poichè egli era non solo peritissimo Compositore, ma leggiadrissimo danzatore, e da lui fu inventato quel bellissimo ballo, detto del Granduca, o l'Aria di Firenze, con quell'aria tanto stimata per certa gravità, e magnificenza, che ha . . .

---

[3] Modern readers must remember the concern of Florentine humanists with tragedy and the 'high', pathetic tone of tragedy.

[4] Ancient plays were divided into five, not three acts; early operatic librettos, if divided into acts at all, follow this ancient practice, e.g. Caccini's *Cefalo* of 1600 or Monteverdi's *Orfeo* of 1607.

[5] *Lyra Barberina*, ii, Appendix, p. 60.

... wherefore the poet could readily compose his choruses (which are usually in various kinds of verse) using metre and rhythm in such a way as to be capable [of accommodating] a beautiful melody suitable for singing as well as dancing: this is what the major part of the excellence of ancient music consisted of, as we shall shortly see. He [i.e. such a poet] could have done very well to imitate Signor Emilio de' Cavalieri in regard to those stage works which he [Cavalieri] composed in Florence, if he had had knowledge of them. Because Cavalieri was not only a most expert (*peritissimo*) composer but also a very graceful dancer [i.e. an excellent choreographer]; and by him was devised that most beautiful 'Ballo' called 'Ballo of the Grand Duke' or 'Aria of Florence'.[6] The music for this 'Ballo' is highly esteemed for a certain solemnity and magnificence that it possesses . . .

[6] These are alternative titles for the music of the Finale of the intermedi performed at Florence in 1589 for the wedding festivities of the Grand Duke of Tuscany. It involved choreography as well as singing.

3

The Problem of the Finale and Poliziano's Solution

THE DIMENSION OF TIME AND THE SHAPING OF THE PLOT

In a spoken drama the playwright says his last word in the concluding scene, and so does the operatic composer in his finale. In such time-arts as poetry and music the placing of the component parts within the time-dimension of the whole is crucial.[1] Therein lies the importance of the finale, whether 'tragico' or 'lieto', whether logical or arbitrary. The prologue sets the tone and guides the expectation; near the centre there is often an impassioned plea; before the end a poignant lament (frequently one of several laments within the opera) is favoured; and after that the finale relaxes tension and attention, tells the listener the outcome of the plot, and at the same time the audience that the show is over:

> Our revels now are ended. These our actors
> . . . .
> Are melted into air . . .
> . . . .
> . . . We are such stuff
> As dreams are made on . . .

Any component part of the whole that strikes the ear and mind and imagination of the listener at the end of the total time-span, at the moment when he realizes that the theatrical illusion has run its course, is bound to be memorable, and destined to be fashioned with great care by librettist and composer alike. Here was usually found the climax of scenic splendour, of music's sonority and texture. Whether the theatrical machinery transported a god, or demigod, or the spirit of harmony, or the three Graces (or what not when not) on to and off the stage, the *lieto fine* seemed to provide a fitting culmination for the aristocratic spectacles that operas in the seventeenth and eighteenth centuries largely were. When, on the other hand, in subsequent periods other effects were desired, then the final portion of the music induced by appropriate means hushed calm, or clangorous din, or

---

[1] In these pages such authors as Shakespeare, Tasso, Rinuccini, Metastasio, and Hofmannsthal are considered poets.

deep compassion, or an epilogue or summation. One might vary the biblical maxim that 'the last shall be the first' to 'the last shall be the foremost'. In the hybrid genre of opera, where the time-arts of drama and music intermingle, the final unit tends to confirm the reaction of audiences and critics, in establishing a work as a *magnum opus*, or a flawed masterpiece, or another humdrum specimen of irrational entertainment.

To achieve the *lieto fine* we are often wrenched from expected catastrophe to an unforeseen solution. This is not a procedure restricted to the seventeenth century: the apotheosis of Orpheus in Monteverdi is comparable to that of the musician's lyre in Stravinsky, and the sudden peripeteia of the arrival of Bacchus after Ariadne's lament in Rinuccini and Monteverdi is no less sudden than in Hofmannsthal and Strauss. The whole procedure of having a god appear to untie the knot (the 'denouement'), and appear at that by virtue of some theatrical contraption, has been epitomized in the term *deus ex machina*. In ancient Greek tragedy the intervening deity was often lowered from above by some device such as a crane or pulley (Greek *mechane*, Latin *machina*). And historians of drama use the term *deus ex machina* not infrequently for any arbitrary resolution of the plot. (It was Paul Valéry who said that all endings are arbitrary.) It has usually been assumed that these gods who are hoisted on to the stage intervened in order to please the aristocratic patron. It is true that *Euridice* was performed to celebrate a Medici wedding, that Lully's *tragédies lyriques* had to gratify the 'Roi-Soleil', and that Gluck's *Orfeo* was performed for the name-day ('giorno onomastico') of an emperor. (And indeed few interventions are more jolting than that of Amor in Gluck's opera.) But patronage and social considerations do not offer satisfactory solutions for the entire corpus of early opera. Not all the operas of the first half of the seventeenth century were written for name-days, birthdays, betrothals, or weddings. Monteverdi's *Orfeo* was written for no particular occasion, just the pleasure of a Mantuan academy. True, it has been argued that the descent of Apollo, certainly a *deus ex machina* ending, represents a revision of the original finale with a view to a forthcoming Gonzaga wedding. But I remain unconvinced that this offers a total explanation: an artist of Monteverdi's stature (and temperament) never writes exclusively for the satisfaction of his patron's whims and commands, and in view of his letter already referred to[2] we may safely assume that the composer preferred a *lieto fine* to a *fine tragico*, as satisfying the emotional expectations of the audience and his own aesthetic views. Similarly, the love duets that so happily conclude the Venetian operas of Monteverdi and his pupil Cavalli cannot be said to satisfy anything but the tastes of the Venetian public. To be sure, a significant portion of that public was aristocratic, but a fondness of pleasure and of endings that appeal to an escapist desire for happiness

---

[2] Concerning Monteverdi's dislike of a *fine tragico*, expressed in his letter of 7 May 1627, cf. Ch. 1.

are not restricted to an audience of high rank. Nor can social considerations entirely account for the plots of Strauss and Stravinsky.

This is not to say that the social setting is wholly unrelated to the development of the libretto over the centuries. Certainly, the manner in which the *fine tragico* supersedes the *lieto fine* in the last three-quarters of the nineteenth century is striking and symptomatic of the demise of the genre of opera buffa. After the Congress of Vienna (1814–15), which probably provides a more convenient dividing-line than the French Revolution, opera ceases increasingly to be merely court opera and tends more to be an impresario's opera. It therefore becomes also the vehicle for the star, the diva (Grisi, Lind, Viardot-Garcia). The diva appealed to a wider public and its sentimentality (a taste also catered to by the novelists of the period). When we speak of the broader stratification of the audience and the sentiments it relishes, we acknowledge, of course, as we must, social factors. In the majority of nineteenth-century novels and operas women are weak and fallible, but their pathos is moving. Listeners go to the opera not only to admire the vocal gymnastics, but also to have a good 'sob'. There is no reason why Desdemona (Rossini, 1816), Norma, Lucia, Leonora (in *Forza*), Aida, Carmen, Mimì, Tosca, and Mélisande should not die at the end of the opera; there is no court party, no state banquet to follow. That is why in so many nineteenth-century productions of *Don Giovanni* the curtain comes down on the death of the Don.[3]

The Romantic imagination relished the tragic ending, and this attitude extended to the close of the century and beyond (verismo, symbolism, expressionism, and what not); nevertheless, there are qualifications and exceptions to that rule too. At the beginning of the period Rossini still experimented with *lieto fine* in *opera seria*. He tampered with the ending of *Otello*, providing variant finales; and in his *Semiramide* the death of the heroine is succeeded by a happy conclusion. At the end of the period, too, a haze of transfiguration at times succeeds the death of the heroine or hero (or both). For instance, in Verdi's *Otello*, the protagonist who has killed Desdemona commits suicide, as he does in Shakespeare. But in the orchestral postlude he is consoled by recollections of tranquillity and bliss. Still, one must admit that the exceptions in Italian opera are few. However, such concepts as 'transfiguration' or 'redemption' loom large in German opera of the period. In all Wagner's operas from *Der fliegende Holländer* to *Parsifal* the key concept is 'redemption', and all endings are ambivalent: 'Verklärung' (transfiguration) makes it difficult to discern whether the fate of the protagonists is despondency or felicity (albeit in another and better world). Does Senta in *Holländer* commit

---

[3] Curiously, it was left to two ardent Wagnerians, Hermann Levy and his young assistant Richard Strauss (Munich, 1895), to reinstate the final, happy sextet in the major mode. Concerning other details about tragic and happy variants of this Mozart finale, see below the discussion of the versions conducted by Gustav Mahler and Bruno Walter.

suicide, or does she 'redeem' the Dutchman who appears miraculously with her, 'verklärt', on the horizon? Is Elsa despondent on being deserted by Lohengrin, or is she redeemed? But the fate of Isolde in *Tristan* and of Brünnhilde in *Götterdämmerung* is more crucial for students of opera. There can be no doubt that both couples, Tristan and Isolde, Siegfried and Brünnhilde, meet their death. But the conclusion is again ambivalent: Verdi's Traviata and Desdemona die unwillingly, but Isolde finds fulfilment in death: in the very process of dying she joins Tristan in that mysterious realm where night, love, and death are united. It is significant that Wagner's own title for the 'Love-death' was 'Verklärung'.[4] Indeed, the whole concept of 'Verklärung', namely that in spite of fate an ultimate happiness or delight prevails, is important for Wagner's successors: see, for instance, Strauss's *Tod und Verklärung* and Schönberg's *Verklärte Nacht*. Perhaps this is a pertinent point at which to remember Aristotle's remarks on the function of 'catharsis' in tragedy, a term for which 'purgation' seems more of a literal translation than an idiomatic English expression. Milton, when paraphrasing Aristotle in the preface to *Samson Agonistes*, says of tragedy that it has the power to raise pity, fear, or terror 'to purge the mind of such like passions, that is to temper and reduce them to just measure with a kind of *delight* . . .' (my emphasis). It is this 'delight' in tragedy that in the wake of Schopenhauer's philosophy begins to affect the tragic endings of some operas of the later nineteenth century.

The remarkable German musician Furtwängler, who was far from being merely a conductor, addressed himself to the problem of mingling tears with laughter, sorrow with joy. Armed with references to Aristotle and Goethe, he referred primarily to instrumental works of the nineteenth century, stressing how appropriate it was to give *music* the role of sounding a joyful note at the conclusion of a work. Here is the excerpt:[5]

Beethoven . . . succeeds in attaining within . . . a sonata the kind of effect which Aristotle ascribed to tragedy . . . In a tragedy, the catastrophe . . . tears apart and refashions those who participate in it, establishing thereby a harmony on a higher plane, that 'tragic catharsis' of which Aristotle speaks. If we apply this to the realm of music we find, curiously enough, that music itself is incapable of achieving tragic effects of this kind, and that a real musical tragedy has therefore never been written. In a work with a tragic ending . . . like *Tristan* . . . it is the subject, the drama, which is tragic, not the music as such. Attempts have of course been made in this direction from time to time, even in the field of pure music—the most recent of these

---

[4] It was only the publisher who coined the title 'Liebestod'. See John Deathridge, Martin Geck, and Egon Voss, *Wagner Werk-Verzeichnis* (Mainz, 1986), 445. See also p. 412 of the same work on the final scene of *Götterdämmerung*. Wagner seems to have hesitated over the ultimate shape of this scene a good deal. See also John Deathridge and Carl Dahlhaus, *New Grove Wagner* (London, 1984), 84, on the ambivalence of all Wagner's finales. I am indebted to John Deathridge, who is preparing an article on the conclusion of the *Ring*, for several stimulating ideas concerning 'Verklärung' in Wagner.

[5] Wilhelm Furtwängler, *Concerning Music*, trans. L. J. Lawrence (London, 1953), 32–3.

was made by Tchaikovsky in the *Pathétique* ... but their effect is nevertheless very different from that of the great spoken tragedy. Not 'tragic catharsis' but gloom, despair, and resignation have the last word. One cannot help feeling that a climate of sorrow and struggle and conflict can only be transitory, because in music the tragic element does not possess the same liberating power as in poetic tragedy ... It is by no means accidental that the funeral march is only the second movement of the *Eroica*. The *ultimate* effect of tragedy (a subject on which Goethe and Schiller conducted an extensive correspondence), its liberating effect, its power to save, is released by music—and this shows the profound difference between the two arts— by the opposite of the 'tragic element', that is, by *joy*. It is at this point that the essentially Dionysian character of music stands revealed. And no one has shown this more clearly than Beethoven. No matter what the prevailing mood of individual movements may be, every sonata, every string quartet is in its way a drama, not infrequently a real tragedy, whose concentrated ecstasy is altogether beyond the reach of poetry ... This is fundamentally the explanation of Beethoven's great finales in a major key, a monumental example being the finale of the ninth symphony.

These remarks about Beethoven's last movements in general, and the D major finale of the D minor symphony in particular, may well be extended to earlier centuries. The finale to *Don Giovanni*, already referred to, provides a good instance of the different emotional stance between the age of Goethe and Mozart, and that of Chopin and Tchaikovsky. The attempts of Hermann Levy and Richard Strauss to remove the nineteenth-century cuts and restore the music and spirit of the original buffo ending were unsuccessful. The cuts persisted even under so sensitive an interpreter and conductor as Gustav Mahler at the Vienna opera. It was not until the 1930s, under Walter at Salzburg and Busch at Glyndebourne, that the reinstatement of the sextet in D major took place to general applause and approbation.

These considerations of Beethoven and Mozart may seem far removed from the operas of Peri and Monteverdi, but they tend to emphasize the universality of the problem of the finale, of optimistic versus pessimistic endings. In the Italian Renaissance, from Poliziano to Striggio, humanists and librettists struggled with Aristotle's *Poetics*, Horace's *Art of Poetry*, and other ancient texts to sort out various kinds of drama, and their appropriate setting and emotional climate. In order to assess the different genres of the theatre ('generi teatrali') Poliziano drew on many sources in addition to Aristotle and Horace. Among these were the writings of the Byzantine polymath Tzetzes of the twelfth century, and the views of Vitruvius on the construction of ancient theatres, transmitted to the Italian Renaissance largely through a treatise of the humanist Leon Battista Alberti (1404 72), *De re aedificatoria*.[6]

---

[6] Poliziano's translations of the relevant passages from Tzetzes, with appropriate bibliographical references, are quoted by Antonia Tissoni Benvenuti, *L'Orfeo del Poliziano, con il testo critico dell'originale e delle successive forme teatrali* (Padua, 1986), 94 5. She also quotes (pp. 98 9) the relevant paragraph from Alberti's Latin treatise, drawing attention to the fact that Poliziano himself edited the first printed text of Alberti (published after Alberti's death in Florence in 1485). Alberti's influential treatise was translated

Tzetzes writes about a genre that—unlike tragedy or comedy—combines the tragic and comic, calls it *fabula satyrica* (the term, used by Italian writers, is their translation of Tzetzes' *drama satyricon*, which they imagined was a mingling (Latin 'satura') of laughter and tears), and says that 'the satyrical genre mingled laughter with tears, and concluded sorrow with joy' (as translated by Poliziano: 'satyrica hilaritatem lacrymis admiscebat, atque ab eiulatu in laetitiam desinebat'). (It will be seen that the concluding lines of Monteverdi's *Orfeo*, that sorrow shall be followed by grace, have not only biblical, but also classical models.)[7]

When Alberti speaks of the three genres he calls them 'tragicum', 'comicum', and 'satyricum', but in Leoni's English translation 'pastoral' is substituted for 'satyricum':

And as there are three sorts of poets concerned in theatrical performances, the tragic, who describe the misfortunes and distresses of princes (*tyrannorum miserias*); the comick, who represent the lives and manners (*curas et sollicitudines*) of private persons; and the pastoral, who sing (*cantarent*) the delights of the country and the loves of shepherds (*pastorumque amores*): there was a contrivance upon the stage of a machine (*machina*) which turning upon a pin changed the scene to a palace for tragedy, an ordinary house for comedy, or a grove for the pastoral, as the nature of the fable required.[8]

One could easily write a book on the nature of the pastoral or tragicomedy or *fabula satyrica*.[9] For our purposes it will be enough to remember that the *fabula satyrica* or pastoral occupies a middle ground between the pomp and circumstance of tragedy with its formal setting and the intrigues of comedy placed in a domestic milieu. The background of the pastoral is bucolic, even idyllic, with its charming groves and meadows, hills and grottos (never

into Italian by Cosimo Bartoli (published Florence, 1550; Venice, 1565), and this Italian translation was put into English by the Venetian architect Giacomo Leoni in the 18th c. (published London, 1726; reprinted 1739 and 1755). The 1755 text of Leoni forms the basis of the widely used modern English edition of Alberti, that of J. Rykwert (London, 1965).

⁷ Concerning the choral finale of Monteverdi's *Orfeo* and its allusion to the Psalms, cf. Ch. 1.

⁸ *Ten Books of Architecture, translated into Italian by Cosimo Bartoli and into English by James Leoni*, ed. J. Rykwert (London, 1965), 177. The same oft-quoted paragraph is also discussed by Wolfgang Osthoff (with many perceptive remarks on the genres of tragedy, comedy, and pastoral) in his 'Die Opera buffa', in W. Arlt *et al.* (eds.), *Gattungen der Musik in Einzeldarstellungen: Gedenkschrift Leo Schrade* (Berne, 1973), 678–743 at 681. Osthoff also refers to the remarks of Licisco Magagnato, *Teatri italiani del Cinquecento* (Venice, 1954), 39–40.

⁹ Cf., for instance, the *Compendio della poesia tragicomica* (Venice, 1601), by Guarini, probably the most popular pastoral dramatist of the period, whose *Pastor fido* provided a veritable anthology of excerpts set to music by Monteverdi and his contemporaries. Cf. also Hermann Jung, *Die Pastorale: Studien zur Geschichte eines musikalischen Topos* (Neue Heidelberger Studien zur Musikwissenschaft, 9; Berne, 1980). Further discussion will be found in Osthoff's article 'Opera buffa' and in Tissoni Benvenuti's edn. Pirrotta, in the section 'The pastoral aura' (*Music and Theatre*, 263–70), examines both Guarini's views and the musical prowess and social status of the mythological shepherds of Arcadia, which represented a more elevated order than ordinary, uneducated farmers. See also the chapters on the 'Power of Music' and 'Pathos, Homeopathy', in Hanning, *Music's Power*, 1–19 and 21–41. Pirrotta and Hanning disagree about the significance of the term 'Tragedia', employed in the prologue of *Euridice* and the title-page of *Arianna*, but agree about the mingling of tears and laughter in the librettos of the early operas.

underestimate the usefulness of caves and grottos for echo effects). This Arcadian habitat is almost more important than its inhabitants, but something can be said about those who dwell in this idyllic setting. Their natural speech is poetry and music; socially they occupy a half-way stage between the heroes of tragedy and the servants (or slaves) of comedy. Its mythological representatives include satyrs, sileni, and other followers of Dionysus, whose inebriation may afford comic relief or be reminiscent of a ritual sacrifice, but they are not menial slaves or avid for financial gain. Poliziano himself, when discussing the middle way of the *fabula satyrica* between tragedy and comedy, instances the one complete satyr-play that has come down to us from ancient Greek drama, namely the *Cyclops* of Euripides. At the end of this play the drunkenness of Polyphemus and the presence of satyrs and Silenus remind us of the ribald choruses at the conclusion of Poliziano's and Striggio's plays, and of the 'Dionysian character of music' that Furtwängler discerns in the art of tones when it exercises its liberating effect at the conclusion of tragedy, or in succession to tragic or pathetic or poignant incidents.[10]

There has been considerable controversy as to whether the many references to the tragedies of the ancients, both in the deliberations of north Italian humanists and in the extant librettos, represent a mere lip-service to the learned discussions of the academies or are of real dramatic significance. The prologue to Peri's and Rinuccini's *Euridice* is sung by Tragedia, the personification of tragedy, and on the title-page of Rinuccini's libretto for Monteverdi's *Arianna* the work is called *Tragedia . . . Rappresentata in Musica*, whereas the title-pages of *Euridice* ('Rappresentata') and *Orfeo* ('Favola . . . Rappresentata in Musica') make either no reference to dramatic genre or use the neutral term 'favola' (here signifying either 'tale' or 'play'). If, however, one examines the extant scores, or librettos where no scores survive, the mingling of tears and laughter, of sorrow and joy, sometimes in rather sudden succession, is unmistakable, whether the plot concerns Orpheus and Eurydice, Theseus and Ariadne, or Narcissus and Echo. In the case of the Orpheus plot, both Peri and Monteverdi provide happy and idyllic (not comic) strains until the hero is apprised of the death of Eurydice. The pathos and poignancy then ensuing is pronounced. (Some critics praise Monteverdi exclusively, and feel that Peri can never be great. In this writer's humble opinion Orpheus' lament 'Non piango, e non sospiro', sung at Florence by Peri himself, is one of the most moving passages in the history of early opera, and one does not hesitate to call it 'great'. But more

---

[10] Cf. Tissoni Benvenuti, *Poliziano*, 96 7 and 165 7 for the passage in Poliziano's *Miscellaneorum centuria secunda*, with its reference to Euripides' *Cyclops*, and for verbal and dramatic echoes of the *Cyclops* in Poliziano's own finale. Tissoni Benvenuti also provides bibliographical references for Poliziano, and generally for the revival of Euripides in the Italian Renaissance. Furtwängler's reference to music's 'Dionysian character' is obviously derived from Nietzsche.

about that in Ch. 6.) Comedy seems absent from the Florentine and Mantuan operas up to 1608. True, Monteverdi's Charon appears to be a rather ineffectual guardian of the confines of the underworld, but he is not a truly ribald figure as encountered in Roman opera, later in the century. Nor is comedy, in the traditional sense, present in the jubilation of the finale. Dionysian revelry may include an element of the grotesque, but the triumph of Bacchus in Poliziano and Striggio and the apotheosis of Orpheus in Monteverdi lack the elements of disguise and revelation, of intrigue and resolution, associated with comedy.

To call, then, the succession of idyllic happiness, followed by sorrow and misery, and ultimately succeeded by triumph, either pastoral, or *fabula satyrica*, or tragicomedy seems appropriate. As is so often the case, the terminology is less important than an aesthetic awareness of the synthesis of diverse elements.

POLIZIANO: THE DIMENSION OF TIME

Poliziano's finale is the only choral piece in the drama, a work that otherwise relies exclusively on solo speech or solo song. Three major families of versions of the play are extant, representing three successive stages in the evolution of the drama, and are edited by Tissoni Benvenuti as Texts I, II, and III. The first of these represents what most scholars consider the original version: it is also the shortest, whereas Texts II and III expand this original by several insertions. In the following discussion the three stages of Poliziano's play, and the proportion allotted to the finale within the total length, correspond to Tissoni Benvenuti's three texts.[11]

I. The earliest extant text is primarily derived from a manuscript in the Biblioteca Riccardiana at Florence, and is 342 lines long. The choral finale occupies 34 lines, namely four stanzas of six lines each, punctuated by five two-line 'riprese' or refrains. If we assume that the refrain was first intoned by the leader of the chorus (choragus), then repeated by the chorus monophonically (i.e. not polyphonically), and that thereafter the chorus concluded each of the stanzas by repeating the choral refrain, we arrive at a total of 36 lines, a concertato of which 10 lines are choral. It seems reasonable to assume that the refrain was accompanied by percussion instruments (e.g. cymbals, tambourines) and possibly also by other concealed instruments.[12] Poliziano's finale, then, represents in length as well as in sonority a not inconsiderable portion of this version of 342 lines.

---

[11] Cf. Tissoni Benvenuti, *Poliziano*, 41 52, for the manner in which three insertions, totalling 64 lines, expand Text I from 342 lines to form Text II. Text I is given ibid. 133 67, of which the finale occupies pp. 165 7. Concerning this finale, cf. also Pirrotta, *Music and Theatre*, 19, 21.

[12] Concerning a tambourine ('cembalino') with bells ('sonagli'), used in the finale of the intermedi of 1589, cf. Ch. 4.

II. A longer variant of the play, totalling 406 lines, is mainly derived from the first printed edition of 1494. Here the drama has been expanded by three insertions, namely a long passage of Latin verse (comprising 52 lines), a much shorter interpolation of Latin verse (4 lines) and 8 lines of Italian verse. The total of these added 64 lines makes for the longer Text II of 406 lines. By my reckoning, the majority of these (namely 241) were sung and only 165 spoken:[13] these proportions establish this play with music as a true ancestor of opera, if not an 'opera' in the sense of the Florentine monodists. In this enlarged version, then, the choral finale remains unchanged in length; it obviously constituted a major and indispensable pillar of the poet's structure.

III. Another version of Poliziano's text, comprising 450 lines, is represented by an anonymous *rifacimento* (rearrangement), entitled *Orphei tragoedia*. It is largely derived from north Italian manuscripts and dates probably from the middle 1480s, whereas Text II must date from before 1483 (when Cardinal Gonzaga died).[14] The anonymous *rifacimento* contains two pieces of choral music, namely a chorus of Dryads (Chorus Dryadum) and, at the conclusion of the play, the chorus of Bacchic women or Maenads (Chorus Maenadum). The latter is again 34 lines long, composed of four six-line stanzas and five two-line refrains. In other words, structurally, metrically, and verbally the *rifacimento* is very close to the model, and could be sung to the same music. Verbally, though, there are several variations, notably in the first stanza, and in character the entire lyric resembles more a sacrifice to Dionysus than the mere drinking-song (*brindisi*) of Texts I and II, though the element of inebriation is not absent from the revels either.

It has seemed desirable to deal in such detail with Poliziano's finale because many observers (Pirrotta, Osthoff, Tissoni Benvenuti, the present writer, and others) consider this early, vernacular, secular drama as the fountain-head of so much poetry-cum-music to come. Three aspects of the finale are of historical importance: sonority, length, and its creation of a festive conclusion to the drama (the shaping of the plot). Of these, assessments of length, that is to say of the time-dimension, loom large in the history and prehistory of opera. A fairly rudimentary procedure for judging proportions of time lies in a consideration of the number of pertinent lines. (In any

---

[13] Cf. Tissoni Benvenuti, 183 4 for the finale in this longer version. That the finale was sung, not spoken, is accepted by all commentators. As to the other lyrics in the play, they are judged to be sung either in accordance with stage directions or the dramatic context. My hypothesis of 241 lines sung agrees, on the whole, with that of Pirrotta, except that both C. M. Pyle and I believe that the ottave rime preceding Orpheus' death (ll. 261 92) were also sung, which Pirrotta, p. 25, doubts. For further discussion of this point, irrelevant to the problem of the finale, see Ch. 6, on 'The Lament'.

[14] Concerning *Orphei tragoedia* cf. Ch. 1. On the vexed question of the precise date of the first performance of Text II (at Mantua before 1483) cf. Tissoni Benvenuti, *Poliziano*, 58 70, where no particular year is postulated. Pirrotta and Mirella Vitalini favour the widely accepted date of 1480; cf. Pirrotta, *Music and Theatre*, 3 12 *et passim*, and Vitalini, 'A proposito della datazione dell'*Orfeo* del Poliziano', *GSLI* 146 (1969), 245 51. As to the two choral pieces in *Orphei tragoedia*, cf. Tissoni Benvenuti, 194 6 and 207 9.

event, in the case of Poliziano's *Orfeo*, Peri's *Dafne*, or Monteverdi's *Arianna* there is no extant score that makes it possible to count bars of music rather than lines of text.)

In the earliest version, which Poliziano dismisses as having been dashed off in two days ('in tempo di dua giorni'), the finale occupies 34 lines out of a total of 342 lines. In the expanded version, frequently reprinted between 1494 and 1608, the finale occupies 34 out of 406 lines. If we keep in mind that at least 165 of these 406 were spoken, not sung, that is moved faster rather than slower, 34 out of 406 is a sizeable proportion. In Peri's and Rinuccini's *Dafne* of 1598 the finale occupies 48 out of 445 lines, a slight increase in comparative size. In Peri's and Rinuccini's *Euridice* of 1600 the figures are 48 out of 790; in Striggio's *Orfeo* libretto of 1607: 62 out of 678; in Monteverdi's *Orfeo* score: 12 out of 602. Finally, in Monteverdi's and Rinuccini's *Arianna* of 1608 the finale takes 47 out of 1,115 lines.

From this rapid and cursory survey three deductions may be drawn:

1. Poliziano's finale, in the version printed in 1494, represents a sizeable proportion of the total time-span, a good 8 per cent (probably more, since the spoken sections of the play move more quickly than recitative). On the other hand, the choral portion of the final concertato is small (10 out of 34 lines).
2. The statement made earlier, in Chapter 1, that the final chorus in Monteverdi's *Orfeo* score of 1609 'seems the shortest in the history of early opera', is borne out by these statistics: 2 per cent is quite pithy compared with 4 per cent for *Arianna* and 6 per cent for *Euridice*.
3. On the other hand, the choral element of the final concertato tended to increase after Poliziano, that is, after stage music shifted from oral and improvisatory practices to printed scores with five-part textures for the chorus. Even *Arianna* (38%), which has the lowest choral proportion after Poliziano (29%), gives the chorus more of a chance, as Table 3.1 shows.

TABLE 3.1. *Proportions of choral section of finale, 1480–1608*

Date	Author	Title	Lines	
			for chorus	total
1480	Poliziano	*Orfeo*	10	34
1598	Peri	*Dafne*	?36	48
1600	Peri	*Euridice*	36	48
1607	Striggio	*Orfeo*	35	62
1609	Monteverdi	*Orfeo*	12	12
1608	Monteverdi	*Arianna*	18	47

POLIZIANO: THE SHAPING OF THE PLOT

From what has been said both in this chapter and in our earlier discussion of the Orpheus plot it will be seen that the need for a festive, affirmative conclusion was recognized from the age of Poliziano to that of Monteverdi and beyond. The question was how to achieve such an ending when the myth in Ovid ended tragically. Two good examples are afforded by the tales of 'Cephalus and Procris' and 'Narcissus and Echo': about the tragic death of Procris in the former and that of Narcissus in the latter there can be no doubt. But in Niccolò da Correggio's *Cefalo* (Ferrara, 1487) and Gluck's *Echo et Narcisse* (Paris, 1779) the festive note is achieved by radically altering the plot. In Correggio it is the goddess Diana who intervenes and brings Procris back to life, and in Gluck it is the god Amor who restores the happy union of Narcissus and Echo. And, as we have observed, the same medicine of *lieto fine* was administered to the Orpheus plot by Peri and Rinuccini in 1600, and by Gluck and Calzabigi in 1762. That such divine and somewhat arbitrary intervention owes much to the *deus ex machina* convention of ancient drama has often been recognized. Poliziano utilized another method, but before examining it, a word must be said about the role of the chorus.

Renaissance humanists were aware of the great importance of the chorus in ancient Greek drama, and their own plays tended to place a chorus at the end of each of the five acts. (This is still true of Monteverdi's *Orfeo*.) Of course, Poliziano's drama had no act-division and only a single chorus, as we have seen. But *Orphei tragoedia* already increased the number of choral pieces and, at least superficially, carved up the brief action into five acts (the third act comprises only 44 lines). Influenced, no doubt, by *Orphei tragoedia*, Correggio's *Cefalo* has five real acts, and each of them concludes with a chorus, accompanied by instruments and dancing. The opportunity such choruses (or ensembles) afforded for the participation of music in the dramatic whole is obvious. In this connection it is well to remember the choruses Andrea Gabrieli composed for the presentation of *Edipo tiranno* at the inauguration of the Teatro Olimpico at Vicenza in 1585, and the roles presented to the chorus in Rinuccini's first two librettos, the *Dafne* of 1598 and the *Euridice* of 1600.

But to return from the descendants of Poliziano's *Orfeo* in the 1480s (namely *Orphei tragoedia* and Correggio's *Cefalo*) to the model itself. Here the author, aware of the dramatic and social drawbacks of concluding the play with Orpheus' lament and his subsequent death at the hands of the Bacchae, decides to bring the action to an end with a chorus of the Bacchae. This chorus is connected with the plot—it is not an intermedio (a 'divertissement') that offers musical and choreographic variety, but the connection with the fate of the protagonist is slight, although no doubt it acts as a foil to his downfall. (The choruses in Correggio's *Cefalo* also formed part of the action, and were not of the intermedio type). The Bacchic women in

Poliziano justifiably celebrate the destruction and punishment of the man who spurned them. It is a tragicomic scene, absorbing—as it were—models from Greek tragedy and the Greek satyr-play. That a chorus should follow the scene where the protagonist is torn to pieces is reminiscent of Euripides' *Bacchae*.[15] On the other hand, comic relief is achieved by the drunken, 'tipsy' note of Poliziano's chorus, rather reminiscent of the only ancient satyr-play known to Italian humanists, the *Cyclops* of Euripides. (Poliziano was not only a brilliant poet, capable of combining and transforming a great variety of models, he was also a fiercely and profoundly learned connoisseur of ancient literature.)

To conclude a play with a scene that is not directly concerned with the suffering or happiness of the protagonists, but reflects upon them in some oblique way, such as triumph, or eulogy, or drawing a moral, or sketching a contrast, is not unknown in the history of drama or opera. Shakespeare does not finish the last act of *Hamlet* with the hero's death, but with the eulogies pronounced upon him by Horatio and Fortinbras. In Mozart, the death of Don Giovanni is followed by the sextet of the survivors who point out the moral to the audience. (This method of addressing the spectators, talking *to* them rather than performing *for* them, has left its mark upon two later finales, those of Verdi's *Falstaff* and Stravinsky's *Rake*.) And in twentieth-century opera we may instance both comic and tragic foils. In *Rosenkavalier*, after the poignant trio (really, the lament of the Marschallin) and the duet of the lovers, we are treated to what? The little page-boy who retrieves the handkerchief of the Marschallin. Hofmannsthal is a master of such 'distancing', of relaxing the dramatic tension and telling the audience that the entertainment has finished, and that the time for curtain-calls and applause has come. (The comments that Zerbinetta, a woman of the world, makes on the moanings and consolations of the tragic Ariadne perform a similarly choric and distancing function in another Strauss–Hofmannsthal work.) Finally, we may turn a brief look at the operas of Alban Berg, where in *Wozzeck* the murder of Marie is followed by the orphaned child riding its hobby-horse, and in *Lulu* the death of the heroine by the eulogy pronounced by the countess.

POLIZIANO: THE PROSODY

So far we have considered Poliziano's finale as the progenitor of those of Rinuccini and Striggio in two respects: the dimension of time and the shaping of the plot. But nothing has been said about the metrical mould that served

---

[15] Cf. the triumphal chorus addressed to Bacchus after the account of the terrifying death of Pentheus (ll. 1152 ff.). Cf. also the traditional Bacchanalian shout of joy 'Evoe' in the long chorus at the beginning of the play (ll. 64 ff., particularly l. 142).

as a model for the librettists of the late sixteenth and early seventeenth centuries. However, Italian metrics are usually treated as a stepchild in the musicological literature on opera. It is quite possible to read articles and monographs on Peri and Monteverdi, on Mozart and Verdi, without a single reference to versification. Yet to an Italian-speaking audience, that is, the people for whom intermedi and early operas were written, the prosody helped to establish the tone: whether the plot concerned 'high' or 'low' matters. In order to classify a play as a tragedy, a comedy, or a tragicomedy (or pastoral or *fabula satyrica*), a sensitivity to the number of syllables contained in a line, and the rhythmical and rhyming schemes employed, was important. Fortunately, several modern studies assist the English-speaking student to define terms and to assess the musical consequences of the librettist's choice between high, courtly verse, and low, popular metres.[16]

The dialogue of an Italian play or libretto usually proceeds in lines of eleven syllables (endecasillabi) or seven syllables (settenari), and quite frequently in a free mixture of the two, called versi toscani. But a shorter line of eight syllables and a half-line of four syllables (ottonari and quaternari) are frequently associated with a rustic or pastoral atmosphere. Also involved in the distinction between the 'high' tone of tragedy and the 'lower' tone of the pastoral was the type of rhythm employed.

Italian verse is classified in two ways: first by the count of syllables per line as we have just seen, and secondly by the conclusion of the line. Most Italian words are accented on the penultimate syllable, and this accentuation is called 'piano'; the majority of words are 'parole piane', and hence the normal line of verse concludes with a 'parola piana' and is called a 'verso piano'. This classification of verse by the conclusion of the line is natural for several reasons: we do pause normally at the end of a verse, and in the Middle Ages the conclusion of the line received additional importance by the rhyme that acted as a signpost. Since the Renaissance, however, we speak of 'endecasillabi piani' or 'ottonari piani' whether we deal with blank verse or rhymed verse. (In fact, the 'closed' musical numbers discussed here, laments and final chorus, are almost invariably rhymed.) It happens more rarely that the final word of a line bears the accent on the last syllable, and in that case we speak of a 'verso tronco'. For instance, an 'ottonario tronco' consists only of seven syllables, since the last unaccented syllable of the metrical scheme is omitted. The least frequent occurrence is provided by a line of verse concluding with a word accented on the antepenultimate syllable: here a 'parola sdrucciola' produces a 'verso sdrucciolo'. An 'ottonario sdrucciolo', then,

---

[16] W. Theodor Elwert, *Versificazione italiana* (2nd edn., Florence, 1976); Silke Leopold, 'Madrigali sulle egloghe sdrucciole di Iacopo Sannazaro: Struttura poetica e forma musicale', *RIM* 14 (1979), 75–127; ead., 'Iacopo Sannazaro et le madrigal italien', in Vaccaro (ed.), *Chanson à la Renaissance*, 255–74; Friedrich Lippmann, 'Der italienische Vers und der musikalische Rhythmus', *AnMc* 12 (1973), 253–369; 14 (1974), 323–410; 15 (1975), 298–333; Wolfgang Osthoff, 'Musica e versificazione', in Bianconi (ed.), *Drammaturgia musicale*, 125–41.

would consist of nine syllables, comprising an extra unaccented syllable at the end of the line, for instance, lines 3 and 5 of Poliziano's final chorus (see below).

When we look at the first stanza of Poliziano's finale, we can readily see that it consists of ottonari that are exclusively 'tronchi' or 'sdruccioli'. In other words, the wild, orgiastic tone is indicated not only by the absence of versi toscani but also by the lack of feminine endings ('versi piani'):

Og-	nun	se-	gua,	Bac-	co,	te!
Bac-	co,	Bac-	co,	eu-	o-	è!
Chi	vuol	be-	ver,	chi	vuol	be-ve-re,
veng'	a	be-	ver,	ven-	ga	qui.
V'im-	bot-	ta-	te	co-	me	pe-ve-re:
I'	vo'	be-	ver	an-	cor	mi!
Gl'è	del	vin'	an-	cor	per	ti,
la-	scia	be-	ver	prim'	a	me.

Refrain:
Each one join thee, Bacchus,
Bacchus, Bacchus, hail!

Stanza:
Whoever wants to drink, wants to drink,
let him come to drink, let him come here.
You guzzle like a funnel:
I want to drink some more!
There is also wine for you,
but let me drink first.

Refrain:
Each one . . .

The next three stanzas are composed of ottonari 'piani' and ottonari 'tronchi', that is, of lines of eight and seven syllables. The first stanza made a considerable impact on later poets. It is referred to, among the examples of metrical variety suitable for musical composition, in the preface to Chiabrera's *Le maniere de' versi toscani* (1599),[17] which also mentions another poem in ottonari, ascribed to Lorenzo de' Medici, but at other times ascribed to Poliziano. Just which of the many lyrics of the late fifteenth century that adopted the popular tone ('tono popolaresco') of the ottonari instead of the courtly stance ('poesia aulica') of the versi toscani are by Poliziano and which by Lorenzo is a moot question. Between the 1490s and the 1560s there were in circulation six anthologies that reprinted quite a few poems by Lorenzo, Poliziano, and others. They bore such titles as *Canzone* [the modern plural would be 'canzoni'] *a ballo dal Magnifico Lorenzo de Medici et da Messer Agnolo Poliziano*, or *Ballatette del . . . Lorenzo . . . et di . . .*

---

[17] Cf. Gabriello Chiabrera, *Canzonette*, ed. Luigi Negri (Turin, 1964), 194. The other poem in 'ottonari' is 'Io non l'ho perchè non l'ho'; cf. Ferdinando Neri, *Il Chiabrera e la pleiade francese* (Turin, 1920), 94; Poliziano, *Le Stanze, L'Orfeo e le rime*, ed. G. Carducci (2nd edn., Bologna, 1912), 338; the poem is nowadays thought to be of uncertain authorship.

Politiani . . . et di molti altri.[18] Among the lyrics circulating in these six printed collections (in addition to countless manuscript anthologies between the 1490s and Chiabrera's *Maniere* of 1599) there were ten canzoni a ballo (or ballate or ballatette) by Poliziano in the metre of ottonari. This deliberate espousal of a popular, non-courtly tone was undoubtedly one of the reasons why Poliziano's reputation was still high at Florence in 1600, when the Medici court celebrated a wedding with performances of *Euridice* and *Cefalo*. In the same month, on 8 October 1600, in a garden entertainment given at the Riccardi Palace in Florence, some of the occasional verses addressed to Maria de' Medici were delivered by a speaker dressed up as Poliziano.[19]

At this point it will be useful to demonstrate the popularity of the ottonario by tabulating sixteen of Poliziano's lyrical poems couched in that metre (see Table 3.2). The first column gives the incipit, the second the page-number in Sapegno's modern edition,[20] the third indicates the ten poems invariably reprinted in the six anthologies up to the 1560s, and the last column lists another six poems in the same metre readily found in modern editions of Poliziano's ballate or canzoni a ballo.

TABLE 3.2. *Sixteen poems by Poliziano in ottonari*

Incipit	Page in Sapegno	Number in anthologies[a]	Ballate in other sources
Cant'ognun ch'io canterò	156	1	—
Deh udit'un poc'amanti	169	—	11
Doloros'e meschinella	143	2	—
Donne mie io potre' dire	178	—	12
Donne mie voi non sapete	149	3	—
E' non c'è niun più bel giuoco	185	—	13
Egl'è ver ch'i port'amore	150	4	—
Già non siàn perch'a te paia	153	5	—
I' conosc'el gran disio	170	—	14
I' ho rott'el fuscellino	161	6	—
I' son dam'el porcellino	158	7	—
Io vi vo' donn'insegnare	172	8	—
Io vi vo' pur raccontare	165	9	—
Io vi voglio confortare	183	—	15
Non potrà mai dir'Amore	133	—	16
Una vecchia mi vagheggia	162	10	—

[a] Six, published between the 1490s and 1560s.

[18] Cf. Daniela Delcorno Branca, *Sulla tradizione delle rime del Poliziano* (Florence, 1979), 160 ff.

[19] 'stanze in persona del Poliziano'; cf. Angelo Solerti, *Musica, ballo e drammatica alla corte medicea* (Florence, 1905; repr. Bologna, 1969), 248.

[20] Poliziano, *Rime*, ed. Natalino Sapegno (2nd edn., Rome, 1967), section 'Ballate', pp. 131–87; cf. also Poliziano, *Poesie italiane*, ed. Saverio Orlando (Milan, 1976), section 'Canzoni a ballo', pp. 129–70.

Among the poets who contributed notable lyrics couched in ottonari to the anthologies of the sixteenth century one must also mention Serafino (born 1466), one of the imitators of Lorenzo (born 1449) and Poliziano (born 1454). His barzelette are usually cast in octosyllabic verse, whereas his strambotti are as a rule hendecasyllabic. Both genres were generously represented in the ever-popular volumes of frottole, so well known to music students from the publications of Petrucci. It is as well to remember that perhaps more than half the lyrics in Petrucci's anthologies were octosyllabic.[21]

To return from the canzoni a ballo or barzelette of Lorenzo, Poliziano, and Serafino to Poliziano's finale for his *Orfeo*: among the prosodic features that establish its popular tone are not only the ottonario, but also the verso sdrucciolo. A good idea of the general esteem in which the sdrucciolo was held in the Italian Renaissance may be gleaned from the various treatises on poetics, literary criticism, and rhetoric written in the sixteenth century. One of these was the *Poetica* of Trissino (1478–1550), to which he added at the end of his career (*c.*1549) some afterthoughts:[22]

First let us say something about the pastoral, which belongs to the same genre as comedy, that is to say the more lowly and humble (*dei più bassi e dei peggiori*). Also, the characters introduced in these [pastorals] are even more lowly and humble (*più umile e più basse*) than in those [comedies], because whereas comedies deal with citizens of middling importance, the pastoral is about peasants, that is ploughmen, shepherds, goatherds, and other rustic personages, removed from civilized life . . . and sdruccioli are not much praised by the more fastidious critics of our age, because they are not much used by Petrarch or Dante.

Certainly, in Poliziano's *Orfeo* the versi sdruccioli are not associated with the hero, but with lowly characters: the shepherd Mopso has an entire ottava rima (lines 88–95) with three-syllable rhymes that include the very term 'sdrucciolo' in the concluding pair of rhymes, 'cucciola–sdrucciola'.[23]

[21]   Concerning the importance of ottonari for the genre of the barzeletta (for our purposes another term for canzone a ballo or ballata) in Serafino, and in the corpus of frottole in general, cf. Barbara Bauer-Formiconi, *Die Strambotti des Serafino dall'Aquila* (Munich, 1967), 10, 102, 342 ff.; also *MGG*, article 'Frottola' by Walter Rubsamen, particularly col. 1021.

[22]   Trissino's testimony as to the regard in which the 'sdrucciolo' was held is valuable and corroborated by other sources from the second half of the 16th c. (The relevant passage will be found in Weinberg, *Trattati di poetica*, ii. 87.) His judgement about the hierarchy of literary genres is more idiosyncratic. Certainly his placing the pastoral (or tragicomedy) at the bottom of the scale, i.e. below comedy, represents an aesthetic attitude not shared by such poets as Guarini and Rinuccini, or such composers as Peri and Monteverdi. It must be balanced by the influential views held by Guarini and the statements by other Italian writers, referred to above.

[23]   On the significance of this pseudo-rustic rhyme in *Orfeo*, and its similarity to the 'sdrucciola–lucciola' rhyme in one of Poliziano's canzoni a ballo (namely 'Cant'ognun ch'io canterò', no. 1 in Table 3 of this chapter), see Ch. 7. Tissoni Benvenuti, *Poliziano*, 146, rightly observes that the dialogue between the shepherds Mopso and Tirsi hits the most humble tone in *Orfeo*: 'il registro umile . . . tocca la sua punta più bassa'; these are the very epithets with which Trissino characterizes the pastoral milieu ('più umile e più basse'). Finally, it is worth remembering that the names of such characters as Mopsus (Virgil's *Eclogues*), Mopsa (Shakespeare's *Winter's Tale*), or Mopso (Poliziano) are of course in themselves pointers to the pastoral atmosphere.

Another occurrence of the lowly verse-endings is to be found in the lines allotted to the Bacchic women before they sing their choral finale (lines 307–8); here again the emotional stance is distinctly anti-heroic and un-heroic. The women who boast to Dionysus that they have torn Orpheus to pieces, and who taunt the dismembered corpse about having spurned legitimate and natural love, are anything but sympathetically depicted. They are inimical to poetry and to what Trissino would call 'civilized society'. Lastly, there is the drinking-song itself, the finale proper. The two 'parole sdrucciole', namely *bevere* (to drink) and *pevere* (funnel) are far removed from a 'high' tone, and the whole lyric is, as has been said, more characteristic of inebriation than of a ritual sacrifice. In this regard the scene is not dissimilar to the denouement of the *Cyclops*, the satyr-play of Euripides, where Polyphemus and Silenus 'guzzle' rather than drink (as do Osmin and Pedrillo in Mozart's *Entführung*: after all, such scenes are archetypal in the history of drama).

The mention of a satyr-play introduces another aspect of Poliziano's *Orfeo* in which it has served as a model for posterity. To some sensitive souls of the nineteenth and twentieth centuries it has seemed strange that the Greeks should conclude a trilogy of tragedies with an unceremonious satyr-play. Similarly, some students of Shakespeare are surprised to learn that at the conclusion of an Elizabethan tragedy, such as *Julius Caesar*, it was customary to perform a jig. In fact, the jig is a close parallel to the Italian moresca, which so often comes at the end of Italian stage entertainments of the sixteenth century. (It still appears, as an instrumental postlude, in Monteverdi's *Orfeo.*) What such terms as canzone a ballo, jig, and moresca have in common are connotations of gaiety and of dancing, also to be found in several of the finales still to be discussed. In particular, the element of deliberate merriment, the progression from tears to laughter, which Furtwängler so admired in Beethoven, is one of historic importance for Poliziano's mythological drama. To its conclusion the poet gave prominence by the proportions of time he allotted to the component parts of the play, by his shaping of the plot, and by his prosodic experiments.

4

The Finale in the Sixteenth Century

INTRODUCTION

A survey of the constituent elements of opera, including the finale, as they evolve in the century or so before *Dafne* of 1598, is largely concerned with intermedi. True, a few plays with incidental music cannot be ignored, amongst them Poliziano's *Orfeo* from the late quattrocento, or Giustiniani's *Edipo* (a translation of Sophocles' *Oedipus Tyrannus*, Vicenza, 1585). But by and large, it is the intermedi that rely heavily on the support of music, not the events they punctuate and articulate. The event itself is usually a spoken comedy or pastoral, but all kinds of pomp and circumstance may serve to celebrate an occasion, extending from banquets and tableaux vivants to naval battles (whether on the river Arno or an artificial lake). In most cases the music has not survived (the intermedi of 1539 and 1589 are notable and fortunate exceptions), but the ceremonious nature of the occasion usually has left printed traces behind. Among the chief sources for our purposes are the elaborate and encomiastic descriptions that were published to commemorate state visits, weddings, or similar events. From these accounts we are able to gather a fair picture of the subject-matter, and of the manner in which it was treated. It is no surprise that the mythological, pastoral, and Ovidian world of the operas can be traced in the intermedi antedating *Dafne* and *Euridice* by more than a century.

Among the topics deriving wholly or partially from Ovid's *Metamorphoses* we may single out, apart from the ubiquitous Orpheus, such protagonists as Andromeda (Rome, 1473; Pesaro, 1475), Apollo (Lyons, 1548; Florence, 1589), Ariadne (Rome, 1473), Jason (Rome, 1473; Tortona, 1489; Florence, 1608), Narcissus (Florence, 1525), and Silenus (Pesaro, 1475; Tortona, 1489; Florence, 1539). Orpheus, with all the significance and allegorical meaning attached to that myth, occurs much more frequently: Rome, 1473; Pesaro, 1475; Tortona, 1489; Ferrara, 1529; Milan, 1599; Florence, 1608; and Florence, 1616. These examples are all associated with Italian festivals and comedies. (Even the Lyons intermedi of 1548 celebrated the entry of Henri II and his bride Caterina de' Medici into the city; the comedy was Bibbiena's *Calandria*; the (lost) music for the intermedi was by the Italian composer Piero Mannucci. Lyons, which boasted a sizeable Italian colony, was altogether the main gateway into France for Italian letters, art, and music.) If an attempt were made here to chronicle the evolution of the French ballet de cour and the English court masque as well, other topics, such as Circe and Ulysses (adumbrated in Ovid, Homer, and other poets), would have to be investigated.

In addition to protagonists (gods, demigods, humans) there were also certain subject-matters that were favourite topics of intermedi and early opera. Reference has already been made to Silenus, the elderly and jolly follower of Bacchus. But clearly he stands for the pleasure of imbibing, associated with Dionysus (Bacchus) and his train of satyrs; perhaps 'Bacchanalian' would be the proper adjective to associate with this important aspect of the dramatic content. Another characteristic of these intermedi is a hankering after a lost golden age, a fairyland so eloquently and prominently described in the first book of Ovid's *Metamorphoses*, where the ages of gold, silver, brass, and iron are contrasted. In the age of gold, spring is eternal, and so is peace, since there are no weapons.[1] No wonder the golden age is celebrated in several important sets of intermedi (Florence, 1539; Lyons, 1548; Florence, 1589).[2]

THE EARLIER SIXTEENTH CENTURY

From the 1520s we have two plays with intermedi where the music is either extant or may be gleaned from the stage directions. One of these is *Santa Uliva* (Saint Olive), a sacra rappresentazione, dated by Becherini and others as from about 1525. The Florentine sacre rappresentazioni were religious and spiritual but, as in the case of the Roman *Anima e corpo*, far removed from either liturgy or the modern notions of oratorio. These plays were enacted in costume and with stage representation, and with their mingling of comedy and tragedy and their colourful interpolations, they were genuine theatre. The story of Uliva and her tribulations tells of a saint maligned and persecuted. But such heroines are not restricted to hagiography: under various names (Griselda or Grissell, Geneviève or Genoveva, Constance, Florimonda) they appear in the pages of Boccaccio and Chaucer, in operas from Scarlatti and Vivaldi to Schumann, and in countless other

---

[1] A useful monograph on the Golden Age ('Età dell'oro') is Gustavo Costa, *La leggenda dei secoli d'oro* (Cultura moderna, no. 731; Bari, 1972).

[2] For a discussion of 15th-c. intermedi (Rome, 1473; Pesaro, 1475; Tortona, 1489) and their bearing on the stage history of Poliziano's *Orfeo*, with up-to-date bibliographical references, cf. Tissoni Benvenuti, *Poliziano*, 89 91. Three comprehensive studies of the role of music in intermedi are Wolfgang Osthoff, *Theatergesang und darstellende Musik in der italienischen Renaissance*, 2 vols. (Münchner Veröffentlichungen zur Musikgeschichte, 14; Tutzing, 1969); Howard Mayer Brown, *Sixteenth-Century Instrumentation: The Music for the Florentine Intermedii* (MSD 30; Rome, 1973); and Pirrotta, *Music and Theatre*. Pirrotta's volume has the advantage of ample and generous bibliographical references to the research of Osthoff, Brown, Slim, and others. Concerning the intermedi at Rome in 1473 (and an analogous entertainment at Urbino in 1474, with a vocal finale in ottonari) cf. Pirrotta, pp. 9 and 286; Osthoff, i. 33 8. Regarding the intermedi at Ferrara in 1529, cf. Brown, 'A Cook's Tour of Ferrara in 1529', *RIM* 10 (1975), 216 41.

plots, easily investigated with the help of Stith Thompson's *Motif-Index* and other reference works. Obviously the story itself was of considerable interest, but for good measure it was enlarged by no fewer than fourteen interludes, which made it possible to extend the stage presentation over two consecutive days. As that great historian of the Italian theatre, D'Ancona, remarked, he who expects merely the pious story of a saint will be disappointed, for this is a legend of knights errant and ladies maligned ('cavalieri erranti e dame perseguitate'), much in the manner of the tales of Genoveva or Griselda. What is distinctive about the intermedi of *Santa Uliva* is their profusion, the importance that music plays in them, and the clarity with which the stage remarks refer to particular extant lyrics (a hunting-song in the first intermedio) or to the manner in which the music is to be performed (an echo song of Narcissus in the second intermedio). No specific music for the finale is known, but the dramatic context and the description of the action make it clear that the shaping of the plot leads to the expected *lieto fine*. In actual fact, there are two finales, both concluding festively. One intermedio acts as a postlude to the entire action—that is, the conclusion of the second day of the presentation—and includes several dances ('balli') as well as a collation, of which, if possible, the audience should also partake ('una universal colazione'). To this the extant text also adds an optional intermedio to function as a finale at the end of the first day, which likewise ends with general rejoicing.[3]

Since the intermedi framing the scenes or acts of spoken plays are as a rule not extant, it is therefore particularly fortunate that in the case of the two comedies by Machiavelli some of Verdelot's music for the intermedi has been preserved, providing at least the conclusion for acts, if not the entire play. Traditionally, Italian humanists felt that choruses constituted the proper postludes for acts of a tragedy, and intermedi for acts of a comedy, but in practice the dividing-line between the two genres was not sharply drawn. Either choruses or intermedi (and sometimes both) functioned as postludes to acts of plays.[4]

---

[3] Concerning the general theme of the maligned and persecuted heroine, cf. Wilhelm Kosch, *Deutsches Literatur-Lexikon* (3rd edn., ed. B. Berger *et al.*; Berne, 1968   ); Dominic P. Rotunda, *Motif-Index of the Italian Novella* (Indiana University Publications, Folklore series, no. 2; Bloomington, Ind., 1942); Stith Thompson (ed.), *Motif-Index of Folk-Literature, Folktales, Ballads, Myths, Fables, Medieval Romances* (rev. and enl. edn., 6 vols., Copenhagen, 1955 8). For specific monographs dealing with the Constance–Geneviève–Griselda–Uliva topic cf. K. Laserstein, *Griseldis-Stoff in der Weltliteratur* (Weimar, 1926); M. Schlauch, *Chaucer's Constance and the Accused Queens* (New York, 1927); H. Schneider, 'Motif der Geneviève' (Diss. Paris, 1952); O. Siefken, *Konstanze-Griseldistypus* (Rathenau, 1904). Concerning *Santa Uliva* and its music, cf. Luigi Banfi (ed.), *Sacre rappresentazioni del Quattrocento* (Turin, 1963), 752 841; Bianca Becherini, 'La musica nelle "Sacre rappresentazioni" fiorentine', *RMI* 53 (1951), 193 241 at 215 17; Alessandro D'Ancona, *La rappresentazione di Santa Uliva* (Pisa, 1863); id., *Sacre rappresentazioni dei secoli XIV–XVI*, 3 vols. (Florence, 1872), iii. 235 315; Knud Jeppesen, *La frottola*, 3 vols. (Copenhagen, 1968 70), iii. 75; Francesco Luisi, *Del cantar a libro – a sulla viola: La musica vocale nel Rinascimento* (Turin, 1977), 47; Osthoff, *Theatergesang*, i. 42 n. 19, ii. 45 54; Pirrotta, *Music and Theatre*, 59 64; and below, Ch. 7.

[4] Concerning the role of the chorus and end-of-act choruses, cf. Ch. 3, and also the discussion of practice and theory of these choruses later in the present chapter.

For the presentation of his *Clizia* at Florence in 1525 and of his *Mandragola* at Faenza in 1526 Machiavelli had in mind intermedi performed by a vocal ensemble of four soloists, namely the soprano Barbara Salutati and three male voices. (Whereas women were not, as a rule, permitted to sing in church, they did occasionally sing in secular performances.) These intermedi, or canzoni, as Machiavelli called them, were in effect a prelude to the first act and postludes to the other acts. In the case of the *Clizia* six intermedi were required, of which three survive in music. In the case of the *Mandragola* again only three canzoni are extant in Verdelot's composition, although Machiavelli prescribed five intermedi (the last act not requiring a postlude).

The canzone after Act IV of the *Mandragola*, 'O dolce notte', is of particular importance in the history of stage music. Here, as in all the Machiavelli–Verdelot intermedi, music conjures up a poetic aura that is absent from the play itself. Machiavelli's prose, with its sardonic wit and anti-clericalism, unfolds a tale of human foibles in a contemporary and almost urban setting. Verdelot's music, on the other hand, sung by a nymph and shepherds, evokes the pastoral atmosphere of a lost golden age. 'O dolce notte' apostrophizes 'notte' (night) where 'desiosi amanti' (ardent lovers) find 'sante ore notturne e quete' (sacred hours, nocturnal and quiet), and it is worth remembering that the plots of most of the extant intermedi and early operas deal with love in a pastoral setting, and neither with affairs of state nor the pomp and circumstance of war. 'O dolce notte' does not introduce another action in another stage setting, as many of the later intermedi do; rather, it complements and extends the play, by supplying the dimension of poetry-cum-music in a manner that seems to anticipate the famous Belmont scene in *The Merchant of Venice* (V. i. 1 ff.), where the phrase 'In such a night' is repeated seven times before Jessica protests to Lorenzo 'I would out-night you' and Lorenzo refers to the music of the orbs of the spheres and quotes 'the poet' (that is Ovid) on Orpheus (ll. 60 and 80).

As a 'finale' to Act IV, 'O dolce notte' fulfils several functions. Dramatically it suggests the nocturnal pleasure of the lovers (Callimaco and Lucrezia). Modern audiences must of course realize that the kind of amorous affairs Machiavelli portrays are of a rather earthier kind than those encountered in the operas of the late nineteenth century. Callimaco's infatuation with Lucrezia (who is another and an older man's wife) is very different from the attitudes of Tristan and Pelléas, but not so dissimilar to Machiavelli's own fondness for Barbara Salutati (described in one source as 'a very beautiful courtesan') or—for that matter—to Lorenzo's love of Jessica and Bassanio's of Portia. The intermedio establishes continuity of action between Acts IV and V and makes certain that the entertainment, offered in the interval, is artistically and emotionally controlled by the playwright and not by some theatrical hack. The mention of intervals brings up another point: the intermedio assures that the audience knows that Act IV has come to its close, in lieu of the curtain of the modern proscenium theatre. As an interlude then, 'O dolce notte' acts both as a prelude to Act V and as a postlude to Act IV. But obviously it is the latter function that is of primary importance. It conspicuously concludes the preceding act by way of contrasts: verse (versi toscani) is substituted for prose, singing for speaking, the suggestion of the pleasures of 'sweet night' for the intrigues of the day.

The transmission of the three extant intermedi for the *Mandragola* is quite complicated: it is summarized in Table 4.1. From the *Clizia*, performed at Florence in 1525, we have the prelude to Act I, printed in Verdelot's *Primo libro de' madrigali*. For the *Mandragola* the extant material for the performance planned for Faenza in 1526 preserves the postlude to Act IV printed in Verdelot's *Terzo libro de' madrigali*. But the remaining intermedi were deemed lost, until manuscript part-books containing Verdelot madrigals were discovered in the Newberry Library at Chicago. Actually, the altus part was missing in the Newberry parts, but eventually located at Oscott College in Sutton Coldfield. (The abbreviation 'Newberry' stands not only for Newberry Library, but also for the remaining part from Sutton Coldfield.) But before acknowledging the valiant sleuthing of Nino Pirrotta and Colin Slim in an appropriate bibliographical note, it will be useful to proceed to Table 4.1 from which can be seen that two of the intermedi from the *Clizia* were reused in the *Mandragola*. The table also lists reprints of Verdelot's music in the monographs of Osthoff and Pirrotta. 'O dolce notte' is a fairly short piece of music, lasting perhaps a minute or two: eleven lines of verse occupy twenty-seven bars of music in Pirrotta's transcription, and forty-two in that of Osthoff. (Pirrotta halves the note-values, and there are also other minor differences of transcription.) In the history of the finale, then, this music must be judged as occupying a very small space of time in spite of

TABLE 4.1. *Intermedi in Machiavelli's comedies*

Incipit	Clizia (1525)	Mandragola	Source	Reprint
Quanto sia lieto	prel. I	—	*Primo libro*, 1537	Osthoff, ii. 68 Pirrotta, p. 161
Chi non fa prova	postl. I	postl. I	Newberry	Pirrotta, p. 135
Si suave è l'inganno	postl. IV	postl. III	Newberry	Pirrotta, p. 138
O dolce notte	—	postl. IV	*Terzo libro*, 1537	Osthoff, ii. 65 Pirrotta, p. 142

the fact that the last line of verse is repeated twice in the lower parts and once in the superius part (Pirrotta, bars 21–7).[5]

Whereas from 1473 to 1526 there is a paucity of sources, musical and otherwise, the intermedi that were performed at Florence in 1539 are well documented. The arrangements for the wedding of Cosimo de' Medici with Eleonora di Toledo were of the utmost dynastic and geopolitical importance, allying the Duke of Tuscany with the Spanish viceregal court of Naples, and thereby with the all-powerful Emperor Charles V. Accordingly, the festivities were on a sumptuous scale, and several printed sources survive to commemorate them, including the comedy *Il commodo*, which constituted the climax of the proceedings. Also extant is the music that framed the comedy as well as enhancing other ceremonious moments (such as the entry of the bride into Florence). Briefly, the main printed sources are:

1. Giambullari's description of the festivities, which includes *Il commodo*, a comedy in five acts by Landi, and the text of the intermedi by Strozzi, 1539;
2. the publication of the music in part-books, containing nine pieces of music for the preliminary festivities from 29 June to 6 July (by Corteccia, Festa, and others), and seven intermedi for the comedy on 9 July (with all the music by Corteccia), 1539;
3. the republication of eight out of nine pieces of Corteccia's music in madrigal and motet collections of 1547 and 1564;
4. a reprint of Landi's comedy with the intermedi, 1566.[6]

The quantity of the extant music is impressive: the comedy is framed by seven, not by six intermedi, since the fifth and the final act receives two postludes, extending the time-dimension of the finale. One also notes the number of parts in the musical pieces: the lyrics for *Clizia* and *Mandragola* were set to music in four parts, a standard scoring for frottolas and madrigals of the period. But three out of seven of the 1539 intermedi are scored for five and six parts (nos. 2, 3, and 6), and of the preliminary nine pieces, two are written for eight and nine parts, namely an eight-part Latin motet and a nine-part Italian wedding lyric, addressed to the god Hymen. (The opening line 'Sacro e santo Hymeneo' anticipates the choral finale of the

[5] For a more extended discussion of the complicated stage history of the *Mandragola* between 1518 and 1526, and the various musical sources for Verdelot, cf. Pirrotta, *Music and Theatre*, 123–4 and 130–46, where further references to Osthoff, *Theatergesang*, i. 213–49 and to various publications of Colin Slim will be found. Among Slim's contributions the following are particularly relevant: *A Gift of Madrigals and Motets*, 2 vols. (Chicago, 1972), ii. 344–9; 'A Motet for Machiavelli's Mistress', in S. Bertelli and G. Ramakus (eds.), *Essays Presented to Myron P. Gilmore*, 2 vols. (Florence, 1978), ii. 457–72; 'A Royal Treasure at Sutton Coldfield', *Early Music*, 6 (1978), 57–74; 'Un coro della "Tullia" di Lodovico Martelli messo in musica e attribuito a Philippe Verdelot', in Garfagnani (ed.), *Firenze e la Toscana dei Medici*, ii. 487–511.

[6] For a more detailed discussion of the 1539 intermedi, with ample bibliographical references, cf. Andrew C. Minor and Bonner Mitchell (eds.), *A Renaissance Entertainment: Festivities for the Marriage of Cosimo I, Duke of Florence, in 1539* (Columbia, Mo., 1968); Osthoff, *Theatergesang*, i. 334–42; *Nuovo Vogel*, nos. 628–9; Pirrotta, *Music and Theatre*, 154–69.

Pastor fido, 'Vieni, santo Imeneo'; both lyrics are couched in *versi toscani*.) Obviously no expense or rehearsal time was spared, and every effort was made to achieve ornate and elaborate textures. The nine-part canzone addressed to Hymen, performed by the nine Muses, is preceded by extensive solo singing. Apollo, accompanying himself, sings encomiastic ottave rime, the last of which exhorts the Muses to proceed with their canzone. The music for Apollo's ottave is not extant, but if one adds this to the sixteen lyrics that have been preserved, the total amount of music is quite large. (We note again how frequently the figure of Apollo appears in these mythological entertainments. Apollo was, after all, not only the protector of Orpheus, but also the leader of the Muses [again Stravinsky!], and—last but not least—the source of light and truth.) Nor was solo singing restricted to Apollo. In the fourth intermedio of the comedy, the postlude to Act III, Silenus sings the praises of the Golden Age, accompanying himself.

But our main interest is inevitably centred on the finale, that is, on intermedi 6 and 7. This is the first known instance where an Italian play in five acts receives a conclusion consisting of two distinct numbers. The first of these, intermedio 6, is scored for a solo singer: 'Notte' (night), accompanied by four trombones.[7] Dramatically, Night, which, by its return, brings 'blessed repose and banishes day', expresses sentiments not so different from those encountered in Verdelot's 'O dolce notte' at the end of Act IV of the *Mandragola*. But musically, there are differences of sonority and texture. In Verdelot's lyric the superius was accompanied by a vocal male trio; in Corteccia it is supported by an instrumental quartet. (In some ways, the original publication in part-books, and the modern transcriptions of Minor and Mitchell and Osthoff are deceptive, for the lower four parts are not on a par with the superius, and have the unmistakable character of an accompaniment. Although it is possible to fit words to them and perform them vocally if need be, it is preferable to have them played by an ensemble of trombones, as Giambullari's description of 1539 indicates. Pirrotta's transcription of these lower parts, in short score and without words, is therefore more helpful in suggesting the original performance style.)

But this solo postlude, in *versi toscani*, was judged too soft and gentle a conclusion to the play, or, to quote Giambullari,

the singing was so sweet that in order not to let the audience fall asleep there appeared suddenly on the stage twenty followers of Bacchus, ten of whom were females and the others satyrs. Among all these, eight played, eight sang and danced in the middle of the stage, and two on each side of the stage acted as if they were drunk . . . Those who danced and sang were four satyrs and four Bacchic women, all with various things in the left hand, some with drinking vessels . . . and all of them had in their right hand small burning torches. The words they sang over and

7   Minor and Mitchell, 343; Osthoff, ii. 101; Pirrotta, 164.

over were 'Bacchus, Bacchus, euoe'. They engaged in very loud laughter and performed various actions and pranks, full of joy and drunkenness . . .[8]

In other words, from the lyrical nocturne of the sixth intermedio the listeners were roused (or awakened?) by a raucous and boisterous intermedio. Here solo singing was contrasted with a chorus of eight singers (two for each of the four parts, supported and doubled by an ensemble of eight instrumentalists), slow with fast tempo, piano with forte dynamics. Dramatically, this last intermedio is strikingly similar to the Bacchanalian scenes encountered in Poliziano's earlier finale, and that of Striggio's libretto to come. All three scenes employ the Bacchic shout 'Euoe', they all evoke gladness and laughter rather than sorrow and tears, and they suggest choral singing accompanied by choreographic action on the stage. Clearly we deal here with what the Italians term moresca and the Elizabethans jig.[9]

There is also a metrical contrast between the Song of the Night and the Song of Bacchus. The sixth intermedio consists of eight rhymed lines in versi toscani—the traditional courtly metre of drama and intermedio. (Versi toscani or endecasillabi are also employed in Corteccia's other pieces composed for the 1539 festivities.) But the seventh intermedio consists of a single line, sung, as Giambullari informs us, 'over and over': 'Bac-co, Bac-co, e-u-o-e'.[10] It will be seen that these three words consist of eight syllables, and indeed the octosyllabic verse produces eight-note tunes on Corteccia's part. In order to show the kind of melody engendered by eight syllables, examples are given in Ex. 4.1: the opening bars of the finale of the 1539 intermedi (Ex. 1a); the beginning of the finale of the 1589 intermedi in the scoring for five vocal parts, as originally published (Ex. 1b); a hypothetical simplified version of the 1589 music, suitable for a chordal instrument such as harpsichord or lute (Ex. 1c); and another version of the 1589 music, with the same bass and fairly similar melody, preserved in a dance manual published in 1600, Caroso's *Nobiltà di dame*, where it is entitled 'Laura suave' (Ex. 1d).[11] The first line of the 1589 intermedi finale, a settenario sdrucciolo, has the eight syllables: 'O che nuo-vo mi-ra-co-lo' (O what new miracle).

Considering specially composed, extant intermedi for five-act plays, the 'Bacco, Bacco' finale of 1539 offers, in terms of sonority, the fullest sound described up to that date: a chamber choir of eight voices, doubled by an ensemble of eight instrumentalists, including a tamburo (drum), a cornetto (zink), a storta (crumhorn), and a tromba (trumpet). It is difficult accurately

---

[8] Minor and Mitchell, 349 50.

[9] Cf. above, Ch. 3; cf. also Osthoff, index s.v. moresca. Concerning any possible connection between the English morris tune and the music for the moresca (including the instrumental postlude to Monteverdi's *Orfeo*) cf. John Ward, 'The Morris Tune', *JAMS* 39 (1986), 294 331, esp. 331 n. 49.

[10] The Bacchanalian shout 'Euoe' (or 'Evoè') could prosodically be trisyllabic, as in Poliziano's finale, discussed in Ch. 3, or quadrisyllabic, as here.

[11] Cf. Fabritio Caroso, *Nobiltà di dame*, ed. and tr. J. Sutton and M. F. Walker (Oxford, 1986), 165; cf. also below, n. 43.

Ex. 4.1. Examples of melodies for ottonari

(*a*) Corteccia, 'Bacco, Bacco' from 1539 intermedi

Bac - co, Bac - co   e - u - o - e,   Bac - co, Bac - co,   e - u - o - e,

Bac - co, Bac - co,   e - u - o - e,   Bac - co, Bac - co,   e - u - o - e

(*b*) Cavalieri, 'O che nuovo miracolo' from 1589 intermedi

(*c*) simplified version of Ex. 4.1*b*

(*d*) Anon., 'Laura suave', transposed from F to G

to gauge the total length of the finale, that is, the sixth plus the seventh intermedio: at a fair estimate it would take twice the time of the Verdelot canzoni. In Minor and Mitchell's transcription, 'Notte' occupies sixty-three bars and 'Bacco' thirty-two bars. But one would guess that the 'Bacco' piece was repeated *ad libitum* until the festive choreography had run its course. Such jolly pieces, in triple or compound duple time, sometimes bear the rubric 'questo ritornello va replicato più volte' (this ritornello is repeated several times), as in Peri's *Euridice*.[12]

Corteccia (1502–71) continued to contribute to stage music for Florentine entertainments. He provided intermedi for two comedies by Francesco d'Ambra: five of them for *Il furto*, staged in 1544; and three out of six (the third, fourth, and sixth) for *La cofanaria*, staged in 1565. Those for the *Furto* are extant, but on a more modest scale than the intermedi for 1539; for the *Cofanaria* all Corteccia's music (including that for the sixth and last intermedio) is lost, though some of the music for the first and fifth intermedi by Striggio has survived. (The composer Alessandro Striggio, the elder, was the father of Monteverdi's librettist of the same name.) For the development of the finale, then, we must at this point bid farewell to Corteccia, which, however, in no way diminishes the stature of the 1539 intermedi or their influence on subsequent stage music.[13]

Two sets of intermedi seem to derive from those of 1539, namely the festivities at Lyons in 1548 and at Naples in 1558. Some of the connections are thematic, some structural. At Florence the proceedings were opened by Dawn (first intermedio) and concluded by Night (sixth intermedio). At Lyons a set of eight intermedi opened (first intermedio) and closed (eighth intermedio) similarly. Between these two framing-points such familiar figures and topics as Apollo (second and seventh intermedi) and the Golden Age

[12] Ed. Howard Mayer Brown (RRMBE 36–7; Madison, Wis., 1981), 187.

[13] Concerning the intermedi for *Furto*, cf. F. Ghisi (ed.), *Feste musicali della Firenze medicea* (Florence, 1939; repr. Bologna, 1969), 65–73; Osthoff, *Theatergesang*, i. 342, ii. 110–21; *Nuovo Vogel*, no. 627; Francesco Corteccia, *Collected Secular Works*, ed. Frank A. D'Accone, viii (CMM 32; Rome, 1981), p. xxvi; Pirrotta, *Music and Theatre*, 158 n. 69. Concerning the intermedi for *Cofanaria*, cf. Osthoff, *Theatergesang*, i. 342–6, ii. 122–31; Pirrotta, 174, 176–82, and below, Ch. 7. Howard M. Brown's 'A Typology of Francesco Corteccia's Madrigals', in J. Caldwell *et al.* (eds.), *Well Enchanting Skill*, 3–28, appeared after the completion of this chapter. It greatly adds to our knowledge of the dramatic destination of the possibly theatrical madrigals of Corteccia.

(sixth intermedio) appear again. At Naples a set of four intermedi punctuated a comedy: again the prologue involved both Dawn and Apollo, and the postlude Night. Such topical connections are not surprising since both the celebrations at Lyons and at Naples had artistic and dynastic bonds with Tuscan towns (Florence and Siena). Unfortunately, practically no music (except a small piece for the third Neapolitan intermedio) survives, but the extant descriptions and publications of the plays performed permit a few deductions about the function and time-dimension of the relevant intermedi.

The Lyons intermedi, framing Bibbiena's five-act comedy *La calandria*, are more sumptuous, described in more detail, and more important for the history of stage music and of the finale.[14] The surviving sources induce the judgement that more music and more time is allotted to the intermedi. In other words, the framework begins to rival the play thus framed. The comedy has two numbers for a prelude (Dawn, Apollo), and two for a finale (Apollo, Night), the latter procedure obviously copied from Corteccia's postlude of 1539. And between the acts, the Ages of Iron, Brass, Silver, and Gold are enacted: their spirits appear on the stage, each accompanied by three appropriate allegorical figures. The Age of Iron is flanked by Cruelty, Avarice, and Envy; that of Gold by Peace, Justice, and Religion.

The Neapolitan intermedi framed a performance of Piccolomini's five-act play *Alessandro*. Whereas at Lyons the Italian colony had celebrated the entry of the King of France, at Naples the Marchioness del Vasto honoured the departure of a mere vicereine. Consequently, the presentation was less sumptuous and the comedy framed by only four intermedi, namely two interludes in addition to a prelude and a finale (consisting of a single number). Incidentally, on neither occasion was an original play performed; it seemed quite appropriate to revive existing dramas such as the *Calandria* (Urbino, 1513) or the *Alessandro* (Siena, 1544), providing them with new intermedi according to the available local resources. Another point of interest from the perspective of early opera is that Scipione della Palla, who was involved both as actor and composer in the Neapolitan presentation, was Caccini's teacher.[15]

THE PASTORAL

In addition to the intermedi, inserted between the acts of a spoken comedy, we must also consider plays where music forms an integral part of the drama

---

[14] Concerning Lyons see the Introduction to this chapter. Cf. also Angelo Solerti, 'La rappresentazione della *Calandria* a Lione nel 1548', *Raccolta di studii critici dedicata ad Alessandro D'Ancona* (Florence, 1901), 693–9; Brown, *Sixteenth-Century Instrumentation*, 94–6; Pirrotta, *Music and Theatre*, 169–71; F. Dobbins, *Music in Renaissance Lyons* (Oxford, 1992), 113–16.

[15] Cf. Carol MacClintock, *Giaches de Wert* (MSD 17; Rome, 1966), 167; Alessandro Piccolomini, *Alessandro*, ed. F. Cerreta (Siena, 1966); Pirrotta, *Music and Theatre*, 198–200; *New Grove*, s.v. 'Delle Palle'; *MGG*, xvii, s.v. 'Palla'.

and does not function merely as an interlude. The relevant dramatic genre, leading to the birth of opera, was the pastoral, whose cast consisted mainly of 'pastori e ninfe'. But these shepherds and nymphs were not humble, lowly folk, notwithstanding Trissino;[16] as a rule they spoke poetic verse as if it were their natural tongue. The place of action, suggested on the stage, was not the palace of tragedy or the ordinary house of comedy; rather it was the grove (or meadow or grotto) of the pastoral.[17] Not only did these shepherds sing verse at certain lyrical stations of the plot, they broke into song with an ease that assumed music to be one of their customary skills. It is these references to songs and musical instruments that form a link between various forms of pastoral literature, extant from antiquity and the Renaissance, and hence establish the pastoral as one of the most important ancestors, if not the ancestor of opera.

This is not the place to trace the genealogy of pastorals;[18] suffice it to say that for many and obvious reasons (such as the education of schoolboys) a reading knowledge of Latin was more common (and certainly more useful to courtiers) than that of Greek, and it is to the *Eclogues* and *Georgics* of Virgil, rather than to the *Idylls* of Theocritus that we must look as the fountain-heads of the plots encountered in the sixteenth and early seventeenth centuries. Nor should it be thought that the vogue for pastoral was restricted to dramatists or librettists. Some of the most influential chefs-d'œuvre of pastoral literature were romances or novels. But whether narrative or dramatic, whether the title-page bore the label 'Arcadia', 'Eclogue', 'Pastorale', or 'Favola', all these works were populated by shepherds.

It is difficult to account for the continuity of this bucolic, idyllic note, which extends from Poliziano to Rinuccini and Striggio, and from them to the pastoral operas of Gluck, Haydn, and Mozart. The singing and piping of shepherds, the rustling of leaves and brooks, the echoes of caves and grottoes seem to act as a permanent background to the unfolding of actions, whether they be mythological, historical, or freely invented. Of course, the historian of literature and of music must record the tides of fashion without necessarily being able to account for them, leaving that task to psychologists, sociologists, and historians of taste. Obviously, no single factor can be the cause of a phenomenon extending over three centuries (perhaps even a longer period). To speak of a 'return to nature', in the manner of Rousseau, would be simplistic. The shepherds and nymphs are far from being humble country folk, and the artificiality of the pastoral pretence is evident to any

---

[16] Cf. above, Ch. 3.

[17] Cf. again above, Ch. 3.

[18] Giosuè Carducci, *Su l'Aminta di Torquato Tasso* (Florence, 1896); Walter Wilson Greg, *Pastoral Poetry and Pastoral Drama* (London, 1906; repr. New York, 1959); William Empson, *Some Versions of Pastoral* (London, 1935; repr. 1950); Jacopo Sannazaro, *Opere*, ed. Alfredo Mauro (Scrittori d'Italia, 220; Bari, 1961); Sannazaro, *Arcadia and Piscatorial Eclogues*, trans. Ralph Nash (Detroit, 1966); Osthoff, *Theatergesang*; Helen Cooper, *Pastoral: Medieval into Renaissance* (Cambridge, 1977); H. Jung, *Pastorale*; Pirrotta, *Music and Theatre*.

student of dramatic literature. Perhaps escapism offers a more likely motive for the pleasure with which courtiers contemplated the noble grandeur and chaste purity with which affairs, amorous and otherwise, were conducted. A public that knew all about ruthless struggles for power, about greedy haggling over the size of a dowry, may have enjoyed occasional repose in contemplating idyllic idealism and love, pure and noble.

However that may be, the natural speech of the shepherds, who pronounced and articulated the *lieto fine* of these plays, was verse, and at the emotional climaxes they broke into song. It is the fact that lyrics were a basic ingredient of the pastoral that distinguishes it from other genres, and establishes such a work as Sannazaro's *Arcadia* as the ancestor of similar works by Sidney, Cervantes, and D'Urfé. And Sannazaro's *Arcadia*, although not a play in itself, influenced plays,[19] and was in turn affected by a romance of the fourteenth century, namely Boccaccio's *Ameto*. But before proceeding to a discussion of sixteenth-century pastoral plays, culminating in the well-known works of Tasso and Guarini, it will be useful to offer a chronological chart of the more influential pastorals, whether narrative or dramatic (see Table 4.2).[20]

What the non-dramatic works in Table 4.2 have in common is a quasi-dramatic element, largely due to the lyrics with which they are interspersed. Spenser's *Calendar*, of course, consists entirely of eclogues, modelled on Theocritus and Virgil, so the dialogue, bordering on the dramatic, is never far away. But even in prose romances or pastorals the prose is rather delightfully interrupted, lovers of poetry and music would say, by eclogues and other forms of verse, which elevate the prose to the condition of music, but which also shift from the mode of narration to that of representation. (The very term 'representation' reminds us of such concepts as 'rappresentazione' and 'stile rappresentativo' in the prehistory and early history of opera.) The pastoral idylls of Montemayor, Sidney,[21] and D'Urfé have a theatrical quality about them, just as the slow movement in Beethoven's Pastoral Symphony is an unmistakable 'scena'. It is therefore right and proper that we should return from the pastoral in general to pastoral plays, namely the dramas associated in one way or another with Ferrara: *Egle*, *Sacrificio*, *Aminta*, and *Pastor fido*.[22]

---

[19] It probably bequeathed to Shakespeare the name 'Ophelia', strikingly similar to that of Sannazaro's shepherd 'Ofelio'.

[20] For dramatic pastorals the place of performance is indicated.

[21] Sidney's *Arcadia* survives in two versions: the *Old Arcadia*, completed in 1581, and the *New Arcadia*, left incomplete at Sidney's death in 1586. No new songs were added to the *New Arcadia*, and it is in the eclogues and other lyrics that the quasi-dramatic element is centred. Cf. Sidney, *The Countess of Pembroke's Arcadia*, ed. J. Robertson (Oxford, 1973).

[22] Space forbids a discussion of *Tirsi*, an early eclogue whose stanzas were 'presented on the stage in a pastoral manner' (*pastoralmente recitate*) by Castiglione before the Duchess of Urbino in 1506. Music for a lament is extant, but no specific music for the finale, a moresca, is known. Cf. Osthoff, *Theatergesang*, i. 150 3 and ii. 60 3. Concerning the moresca, cf. n. 9 above.

TABLE 4.2. *Pastorals, 1341 – 1637*

Date	Title	Author	Place	Genre
1341/2	Ameto	Boccaccio	—	prose romance interspersed with verses
c.1480	Orfeo	Poliziano	Mantua	drama
c.1485	Orphei tragoedia	?	?Ferrara	drama
1487	Cefalo	Correggio	Ferrara	drama
1504	Arcadia	Sannazaro	—	prose pastoral interspersed with eclogues
1506	Tirsi	Castiglione	Urbino	drama
1545	Egle	Cinthio	Ferrara	drama
1554	Sacrificio	Beccari	Ferrara	drama
c.1559	Diana	Montemayor	—	prose pastoral interspersed with verses
1573	Aminta	Tasso	Ferrara	drama
1579	Shepherds' Calendar	Spenser	—	eclogues
1581	Old Arcadia	Sidney	—	prose romance interspersed with poems and eclogues
1585	Galatea	Cervantes	—	pastoral novel interspersed with verses
1585	Sacrificio[a]	Beccari	Ferrara	drama
1589	Pastor fido[b]	Guarini	—	drama
1598	Pastor fido	Guarini	Mantua	drama
1604	Pastor fidus[c]	?	Cambridge	drama
1608	Faithful Shepherdess	Fletcher	London	drama
1627	Astrée	D'Urfé	—	prose romance (1607–27), interspersed with madrigals and sonnets
1637	Sad Shepherd[d]	Jonson	—	drama

[a] Revival with Guarini in cast.
[b] Published, but not staged.
[c] Latin translation of Guarini.
[d] Left incomplete at Jonson's death in 1637.

G. B. Giraldi (usually called 'Cinthio') staged his *Egle* at Ferrara in 1545.[23] The music by Antonio dal Cornetto[24] is lost, but the extant verbal text permits a few observations. Cinthio called his play a 'satira', and *fabula satyrica* is a synonym for pastoral or tragicomedy, as we have seen. Indeed satyrs (and other followers of Bacchus or Pan) and their appetite for attractive nymphs (which smacks more of the flesh than of the spirit) are an important part of the cast of a typical pastoral. Aristeo and his attendant Mopso in Poliziano's *Orfeo* represent gross desire, which leads to Euridice's flight and death. The contrast between gentle (and genteel) shepherds and nymphs and the more brutal representations of the flesh is still to be perceived in Shakespeare and Mozart: Caliban vs. Ferdinand and Miranda, Monostatos vs. Tamino and Pamina. Such opposition between permissible and illicit love points to the *Pastor fido* and the operatic plots of the seventeenth century. As far as satyrs go, the *Egle* of 1545 had been anticipated in the quattrocento. In *Orphei tragoedia* (the anonymous *rifacimento* of *c.*1485) a satyr had been introduced into Poliziano's plot; and in Correggio's *Cefalo* (presented at Ferrara in 1487) one of the acts concluded with a chorus of satyrs.[25] Speaking of the conclusion of acts, it is notable that the *Egle* consists of blank verse, though at the end of the acts the chorus sings in rhymed verse. This scheme, together with a plot involving satyrs and little satyrs (*satiri e satirini*) and leading to a *lieto fine*, points decidedly in the direction of the finale we encounter with *Dafne* in 1598 and thereafter. But the influence of the *Egle* was limited. In the annals of theatrical history Cinthio is remembered for his tragedies and for his *Hecatommithi*, which provided plots for Elizabethan and Jacobean playwrights, not least for Shakespeare's *Othello*. Still, the *Egle* paved the way for the *Sacrificio*, and was acknowledged to have done so.

Agostino Beccari's *Sacrificio* was twice performed at Ferrara in 1554, published in 1555, and revived and reprinted in 1587 (at which revival Guarini was a member of the cast). Probably Beccari's fame among the authors of Italian pastorals of the sixteenth century is largely based on the lavish praise bestowed on him by Guarini who—in his defence of the *Pastor fido* and of the genre of tragicomedy in general—calls on Beccari as a key witness. In addition, historians of early opera and stage music (Solerti, Einstein, Schering, Osthoff) have paid attention to the *Sacrificio* because it is one of the few plays for which two musical excerpts have survived, namely, the sacrificial scene from Act III as well as the finale.[26] As Carducci aptly

---

[23] Cf. Carducci, *Su l'Aminta*, 54 ff; Osthoff, *Theatergesang*, i. 151, 312.

[24] Such generic names as 'dal Cornetto' and 'dàlla Viola' (the composer of the *Sacrificio*, discussed below) appear often as the appellations of musicians in the archives of Ferrara and other Italian towns.

[25] Cf. Antonia Tissoni Benvenuti (ed.), *Teatro del Quattrocento: Le corti padane* (Turin, 1983), 187, 238.

[26] The best sketch of Beccari remains Carducci, *Su l'Aminta*, 57 61. Carducci, a poet himself, had a discriminating ear for the quality of verse. He was also a pioneer of Italian literary history. Cf. also Angelo Solerti, *Gli albori del melodramma*, 3 vols. (Milan, 1904 5; repr. 1969 and 1976), i. 12 ff.; Osthoff, *Theatergesang*, i. 312 17 (315 17 on the finale), ii. 84 9 (87 9 on the finale); H. Jung, *Pastorale*, 41, 269.

remarks, lovers of poetry will not be struck by the exquisite beauty of Beccari's verse, but his plot and diction—obviously influenced by Virgil's eclogues and Ovid's pastoral passages—are both fashionable and elegant. (An acute assessment of public taste remains, in the short term, a more decisive cause for success in the theatre than poetic stature.) The plot involves three nymphs, three swains, the obligatory satyr, and the festive strains of a sacrifice (*sacrificio*) to Pan. It all ends happily 'to praise the happy day' (*lodar felice giorno*), to quote from the final canzone, couched in versi toscani and set to music in four parts by Alfonso dalla Viola. It is not clear how these parts were performed, whether by a soloist accompanied by the other three parts instrumentally, or by a vocal ensemble. Osthoff, who provided an accurate transcription of the music as well as a thoughtful analysis of it, considers an entirely vocal performance more likely. Certainly, the music is decidedly syllabic, homophonic, and chordal, more akin to Verdelot's 'O dolce notte' than to his 'Quanto sia lieto', and to Corteccia's 'Bacco, Bacco'. The chordal character of Alfonso dalla Viola's music is quite pronounced: all chords—with one or two insignificant exceptions—are in root position, and move in a most simple and artless manner. These unsophisticated and undemanding pieces of Verdelot, Corteccia, and Alfonso are not typical madrigals; they are theatre music, and point the way to the homophony of opera, where no counterpoint interferes with the intelligibility of the words.

Unfortunately, most incidental and theatrical music by Alfonso dalla Viola is no longer extant. With the exception of the two numbers for the *Sacrificio*, just discussed, the following scores, all for Ferrara (where Alfonso was active until *c*.1573) seem to be lost, namely music for

1. the intermedi for a banquet given for Ercole d'Este and his bride Renée of France, 1529;
2. the tragedy *Orbecche*, by Cinthio (or Cintio), 1541;
3. the pastoral *L'Aretusa*, by A. Lollio, 1563;
4. the pastoral *Lo sfortunato*, by A. Argenti, 1567.

It is interesting that the description of the 1529 intermedi indicates that the proceedings concluded with a moresca. We have encountered this term in connection with the Bacchanalian finales of Poliziano (1480) and the Florentine intermedi (1539), and with Castiglione's pastoral eclogue (Urbino, 1506). But the term also provides, as we have seen, the title for the merry and festive strains that conclude Monteverdi's *Orfeo* score of 1609. It will come as no surprise to meet the term again later in connection with pastorals such as the *Pastor fido* (Mantua, 1598) or operas such as *Anima e corpo* (Rome, 1600).[27]

---

[27] For the Ferrara intermedi of 1529 see Brown, 'Cook's Tour'. For Alfonso dalla Viola in general, see (besides Osthoff already cited) the dictionary articles by Sartori in *MGG* on 'Viola'; by Haar on

The lack of extant music is equally responsible for the gap between the *Sacrificio* of 1554 and the *Aminta* of 1573. Of the Florentine intermedi of 1565 only two pieces of music survive and neither of them gives a complete intermedio or occurs at the end of the intermedio: in other words, they do not constitute an end-of-act finale. From the descriptions, however, we gather that the resources employed must have been even more sumptuous than they were in 1539 and 1548. The chorus from the first intermedio (music extant) was scored for eight vocal parts, accompanied by a goodly consort of wind and string instruments. And the final chorus of the sixth intermedio (music not extant) was sung by eight voices, accompanying dancing, but its refrain, 'as though to reawaken the souls of the audience, was played and sung with renewed gaiety by all'. The accompanying instruments, played, incidentally, by Pan and nine satyrs, are described as 'pastoral'.[28]

To survey the history of the pastoral in the later sixteenth century without mention of Tasso's *Aminta* of 1573 would seem perverse. Needless to say, Tasso was a greater poet than Cinthio or Beccari before him, or his successor and imitator Guarini. Nor was Tasso's genius restricted to his poetic gifts, for he was no mean playwright, and if the *Pastor fido* proved to be, for a few decades, more popular than the *Aminta*, this is more of a reflection on the taste of the early seventeenth century than an indication—*sub specie aeternitatis*—of the enduring influence of *Aminta* on pastoral and quasi-pastoral plays from the age of Shakespeare to that of Rousseau. It is, for instance, thought that the poetic speech of Berowne from *Love's Labour's Lost* (IV. iii)

> But love, first learnèd in a lady's eyes,
> Lives not alone immurèd in the brain,
>
> . . . .
>
> A lover's eyes will gaze an eagle blind.
>
> . . . .
>
> From women's eyes this doctrine I derive:
> They sparkle still the right Promethean fire;
> They are the books, the arts, the academes . . .

owes not a little to the chorus that concludes Act II of *Aminta*:

> Amor, leggan pur gli altri
> le socratiche carte,
> Ch'io in due begli occhi apprenderò quest'arte . . .

'Dalla Viola' in *New Grove*. Cf. also Maria Antonella Balsano, *L'Ariosto: la musica, i musicisti: quattro studi e sette madrigali ariosteschi* (Quaderni della Rivista italiana di musicologia, 5; Florence, 1981), 53, 67, 73, 79–80, 91–2, 93–4, 104–6; Haar, *Essays on Italian Poetry*, 60 *et passim*. We cannot be certain that Gian Pietro della Viola, who provided the lost music for *Dafne* (or *Febo e Feton*) at Mantua in 1486, was related to Alfonso dalla Viola or his forebears; cf. Pirrotta, *Music and Theatre*, 73, 94 n. 47; Tissoni Benvenuti, *Quattrocento*, 45–73.

[28] Cf. above, n. 13 for bibliographical details.

Love, let others read
the pages of Socrates [the *Symposium* of Plato]
For I shall learn this art from two beautiful eyes ...

But there's the rub for the music historian: neither Tasso's nor Shakespeare's verse requires the collaboration of music. Both passages are intellectually and aurally self-sufficient, they sparkle still the right Promethean fire without the assistance of any other art. We may also note in passing that Tasso's play would be too long to be set to continuous music, in the manner of *Dafne* or *Euridice*, for it runs to about 2,000 lines, while the average early libretto numbers between 400 and 1,100 lines.[29]

THE LATER SIXTEENTH CENTURY

On the other hand, choruses of plays were at times set to music in the sixteenth century, and in that case they provided a musical finale to a spoken act. Twelve years after the *Aminta* was staged on a little island in the River Po near Ferrara, Vicenza inaugurated its Palladian theatre, the Teatro Olimpico, with a performance of *Edipo tiranno*, a refashioning of Sophocles' *Oedipus Rex* in Italian verse. And for this performance of 1585 the local Academy, the Accademia Olimpica, commissioned no less a composer than Andrea Gabrieli to set to music the choruses. In the history of the finale, then, these four end-of-act choruses, printed at Venice in 1588, are an important milestone of the genre.

The first two aspects to notice about these Gabrieli finales are their vocal scoring and their time-dimension. They are planned for fifteen singers, not for eight (as is the extant Corteccia finale of 1539 and the lost Corteccia finale of 1565). Thus the Vicenza production boasted more ample vocal resources, though not necessarily larger sonorities since Gabrieli's fifteen singers sang *a cappella*, without instrumental doubling. On the other hand, the greater number of singers permitted greater variations, and therefore more striking contrasts of texture. Let us, for instance, consider the chorus at the end of Act I, consisting of nineteen sections, varying from a short solo for a single voice (bars 48–54) to tutti sonorities for six vocal parts (bars 124–59, and the concluding bars 349–88). Between these two extremes we encounter choral passages for two, three, four, and five parts. Gabrieli achieves variety not only by interspersing choral with solo singing, but also by employing different voice-ranges. The choral passages for two vocal parts are sometimes scored for cantus and altus, sometimes for tenor and bassus (bars 223–43 and 259–79). With a total complement of fifteen singers, we may safely assume that between two and three singers were assigned to

---

[29] Cf. Ch. 3 about the length of librettos.

each vocal part, except when the composer specifies solo performance. These textural alternations must have exercised a powerful influence on the concertato finale that Cavalieri composed in 1589 for the Florentine intermedi of that year, where an initial and final tutti frame eighteen sections in which tutti and concertino fragments alternate, as we shall see.[30]

The variety Gabrieli's nineteen sections had to offer in texture and pitch also made it possible for him to erect a structure occupying a considerably longer span of time: his final tutti *a 6* from the chorus at the end of Act I (bars 349–88) is as long as the entire finales of Verdelot, Corteccia, and Alfonso dalla Viola, discussed previously. The difference in the time-dimensions is stupendous. It is as striking as the difference in scale between the symphonies of the late eighteenth century and the *Eroica*. Again Gabrieli points the way to Cavalieri's finale of 1589, which runs to 250 bars. That Gabrieli exercised so powerful an influence in spite of the fact that the choruses for the tragedy *Edipo* could hardly be claimed to be in the mainstream of intermedi, pastorals, and comedies (that is to say, the principal channels of stage music in the sixteenth century) is not surprising. Andrea Gabrieli was, after all, a musician of greater stature, renown, and influence than his predecessors Corteccia and Striggio, and his successor Cavalieri. And it took a musician of stature and imagination to alternate sections scored for five and six parts with portions composed for one or two parts, and to perceive the potential benefit of such a procedure for the possibility of greatly expanding the time-dimension of a musical structure, not interrupted by spoken dialogue. Of course it would be absurd to claim that Willaert or Gabrieli or any single Venetian composer 'invented' such techniques, which inevitably lead to the Baroque concerto, just as it would be simplistic to say that Haydn (or whoever) invented the string quartet. And yet, as far as national and international influence goes, it is no overstatement to observe that Andrea Gabrieli (and his nephew Giovanni) employed their innovatory textural and structural techniques so successfully (and with such effect on the Baroque concertato and concerto) that to compare their influence with that of Haydn on subsequent composers in the genre of the string quartet seems perfectly in order.

But we cannot leave the *Edipo* of 1585 without clarifying two points, first the difference between final chorus and intermedio, and secondly the different roles assigned to music in comedy and tragicomedy on the one hand, and tragedy on the other.[31]

---

[30] Some scholars doubt the influence of the 1585 choruses on the 1589 finale. True, the choruses were not published till 1588. But circulation in manuscript in northern Italy between 1585 and 1589 seems to me quite likely, particularly in circles interested in stage music.

[31] Discussion of Andrea Gabrieli's music must be based on Schrade's edition, *La Représentation d'Edipo Tiranno au Teatro Olimpico (Vicence 1585)* (Le chœur des muses; Paris, 1960), particularly on the ample historical introduction (pp. 11–77) that precedes the edition of the Italian verse translation (pp. 83–156), and of the music proper (pp. 157–246). More recently much information concerning the history of the

The difficulty about the distinction between end-of-act choruses and end-of-act intermedi is that Italian humanists with their clever glosses on Aristotle's *Poetics*, and their sharply drawn definitions, paint a highly ordered and systematic picture that seems at variance with practice, in so far as we can judge that practice from its few surviving specimens. Who, after all, would dare to characterize the plays of Shakespeare or Molière from contemporary treatises on drama? Or the vocal polyphony of Lassus or Byrd from the manuals of Zarlino? Or late Romanticism from the polemics of Wagner and Hanslick? However that may be, Italian humanists of the sixteenth century usually state in their treatises that tragedies require choruses, while other plays (notably comedies) demand instead intermedi. Furthermore these said intermedi differ from the choruses in sonority by the admixture of instruments, and dramatically by the addition of jollity (if not outright jesting).[32]

In the first half of the century, Daniello, in his *Poetica* of 1536, divides the dramatic genres:

The choruses of a tragedy take the part of the just ... who have suffered unreservedly ... In comedies choruses are no longer used. In their place ... between one act and the next instrumental music (*suoni*), songs (*canti*), merry dances (*moresche*), and jesting are customarily mingled.[33]

In other words, the vocal performance of the tragic chorus is supplanted by a jolly intermedio in which the music made by singers (*cantori*) is supplemented by the playing of instrumentalists (*suonatori*). Also, whereas the chorus of a tragedy deals with the fate of the protagonists, no connection between intermedio and the main action is specified.

At the end of the century little has changed, except that the genre of tragedy is contrasted not only with comedy but also with the pastoral.

theatre and of music, as they bear on this work, has been added by Alberto Gallo, *La prima rappresentazione al Teatro Olimpico: Con i progetti e le relazioni dei contemporanei* (Archivio del teatro italiano, 6; Milan, 1973), and Pirrotta, 'I cori per l' "Edipo Tiranno"', in Degrada (ed.), *Andrea Gabrieli*, 273–92. Pirrotta makes many perceptive remarks about Gabrieli's musical achievements in spite of the restrictions of a syllabic, homophonic style. For a discussion of the role of music in tragedy, see Schrade, *Tragedy in the Art of Music* (Cambridge, Mass., 1964); to which Slim, 'Coro', and Margaret Murata, 'Classical Tragedy in the History of Early Opera in Rome', *EMH* 4 (1984), 101–34, add instructive musical examples from Italian stage music of the 16th and 17th cc. Views on 'prolongation' and 'time-scale' of stage music of the Renaissance were aired extensively at the New England Conference on Renaissance Studies in 1945, when the speakers included Einstein, Schrade, and Sternfeld. Some of the views appeared subsequently in the aforementioned publications of Schrade and in Sternfeld, *Music in Shakespearean Tragedy* (London and New York, 1963; 2nd edn., 1967), where the relative roles of spoken verse declamation and music within the tradition of tragedy are considered at greater leisure.

[32] The best surveys of the treatises are Bernard Weinberg's *A History of Literary Criticism in the Italian Renaissance*, 2 vols. (Chicago, 1961); and his magisterial *Trattati*. Individual treatises of particular usefulness for the music historian are Daniello's *Poetica* (1536); Toscanella's *Precetti* (1562), and A. Ingegneri's *Discorso* (1598). For the purposes of the present chapter they have been checked in the original editions, not in modern reprints.

[33] *Della poetica*, p. 36; ed. Weinberg, *Trattati*, i. 252.

Angelo Ingegneri, who also directed the performance of the *Edipo tiranno* at Vicenza in 1585, wrote in his *Discourse* ('Discorso') *on Stage Music* of 1598:

... intermedi give wide berth to tragedies, whereas in pastorals and comedies they are not only acceptable but are a considerable adornment ... Where there is a chorus [that is, in a tragedy] let it be sung simply. But where the chorus [functions as] an intermedio ... it is necessary to employ more elaborate singing, and not a bad idea to put instrumentalists behind the scene.[34]

How do these treatises square with the extant music? Let us first consider the *Edipo* of 1585, where Ingegneri's ideas were carefully considered and in part obeyed. The choruses are certainly 'simple', that is, syllabic and homophonic, and it is obvious that Gabrieli curtailed his musical expertise in order to ensure audibility and intelligibility of the words. He also refrained from employing instruments, and had his 'cantori' perform *a cappella*. Furthermore, the chorus does not always sing. When it (or the leader of the chorus) engages in dialogue with the protagonists, the verse is spoken; when, on the other hand, the chorus is alone on the stage, it sings, and Gabrieli has provided choruses as postludes to the first four acts.[35] On the other hand, the chorus at the conclusion of Act V did not receive a musical setting, perhaps because the chorus was not alone on the stage, perhaps because Ingegneri felt that the final chorus, with its extreme brevity and stern moral lesson, was not amenable to musical setting: it is only fourteen lines long and lacks the rhetorical *élan* of the end-of-act first chorus, which runs to 114 lines and embraces a variety of emotions, culminating in a call to Bacchus (lines 98–107), which Gabrieli sets as a tutti *a 6*.[36] What is surprising, though, is that despite Ingegneri's condemnation of intermedi for tragedies, the *Edipo* of 1585 was not only punctuated by choral interludes *a cappella* between the acts, but additionally by intermedi composed by one Marc'Antonio Pordenone, and scored for voices and instruments.[37] Neither the text nor the music is extant, but the very existence of these intermedi indicates that the public's taste for greater variety of sonority and pace was probably more important than the Aristotelian fastidiousness of the treatises.

Before proceeding to the intermedi of 1589, it may be as well to review briefly the presence or absence of choral conclusions in plays between *c.*1480 and 1585, that is, those discussed so far in this and the preceding chapter. First let us be clear that all the plays reviewed are comedies or pastorals, regardless of what they are called on the title-page (if any classification appears there). Even the anonymous *Orphei tragoedia* conceals a fabula satyrica behind its title. And, to leap some decades ahead, even Monteverdi's and

---

[34] pp. 483, 496, and 537 of the 1738 reprint.

[35] Schrade, *Edipo*, 100 (text) and 161–83 (music); 114 and 185–210, 130 and 211–30, 143 and 231–46.

[36] Cf. ibid. 100–2 and 156 for the verbal texts of the first and fifth choruses; cf. also pp. 58, 60, 68–9 for the views of Ingegneri and the poet Giustiniani on the musical role of the chorus.

[37] Ibid. 66.

Rinuccini's *Arianna* of 1608, although labelled as 'tragedia' on the libretto, is a pastorale, with its chorus of fishermen and its Bacchic *lieto fine*. The only true tragedy in this entire account is *Edipo*, and that seems to be due to the academic concern with the tragedies of Sophocles; but the tragic grandeur of Sophocles is quite atypical of the history of Italian stage music and early opera. Similarly, a caveat must be entered (or rather reiterated) concerning the term 'chorus' (*coro*): it may refer to an ensemble of soloists *a cappella* (Verdelot), or a chamber choir *a cappella*, or any vocal ensemble, whether or not doubled or supported by instruments. The size of the vocal ensemble is irrelevant to the possibility of concertato contrasts between one voice and a responsorial chorus of two or three other voices. Four-part madrigals by Verdelot or three-part madrigals by Festa from the early sixteenth century, and Monteverdi's famous *Lamento della ninfa* (text by Rinuccini) from the seventeenth century testify to that. Broadly speaking, then, we may say that the number of choruses acting as finales to individual acts or scenes, if not the entire play, increases steadily. The development of the 1480s seems to be symptomatic: one chorus in Poliziano leads to two in *Orphei tragoedia* and to five in *Cefalo*. There is no reason to believe that instrumental accompaniment and dancing did not partner the singing from the very beginning of Italian stage music. The Verdelot intermedi for Machiavelli's comedies are atypical in this respect: they are 'madrigalian' interludes; but with the 1539 intermedi and their final Bacchic chorus we are back to the festive conclusion in which scenery, singing, playing, and dancing combine to delight the audience and encourage it to applaud (regardless of the fate of the protagonist). Finally, if any general tendencies can be discerned from such a small statistical sample, one may say that on the whole the choruses get longer, the tutti portions tend to be larger than the concertino, and the number of parts and singers per part increase. All of which seems the right preamble to a discussion of the Florentine intermedi of 1589.

The wedding of 1589, which was celebrated by these extensive festivities, was of considerable importance. The marriage of Ferdinando de' Medici to Christine (or 'Cristiana', as she is called in the sixth intermedio) of Lorraine had obvious strategic, political, financial, and dynastic aspects. In fact, a reader unfamiliar with the genealogy of the Medici should consult a reliable reference work,[38] since a knowledge of the family trees of the ruling families of Austria, Spain, and France, as well as of Florence, explains the strategic value of the intermedi of 1539, 1548, and 1565, among others. Suffice it to say that when Cosimo (whose wedding in 1539 has been discussed earlier) died in 1574, he was succeeded by his son Francesco, whose death in 1587 caused his brother to become Grand Duke of Tuscany. The external alliance decided upon for the Medici (who have sometimes been called the bankers

[38]   e.g. Adriano Cappelli's *Cronologia, cronografia e calendario perpetuo* (3rd edn., Milan, 1969); or standard reference works such as the *Cambridge Modern History* and the *New Cambridge Modern History*.

of Europe) was with the house of France. Christine was the granddaughter of Henri II and of Caterina de' Medici (whose entry into Lyons in 1548 has also been discussed) and the niece of Henri III. Through her grandmother, then, she was descended from another branch of the Medici family, which was neither a disadvantage nor unusual in the chess game of dynastic marriages of the Renaissance.[39]

Several aspects strike the historian of opera who studies these intermedi: the librettists and composers involved (which included Rinuccini, Cavalieri, Caccini, and Peri), the subject-matter, the methods of construction employed in the finale, and—last but not least—the time-dimension of the spectacle and consequently of the music. Certainly the sheer bulk of the entertainment is unprecedented in the annals of Italian stage music. Various estimates have been made of the combined length of Bargagli's five-act comedy *La pellegrina* and the six intermedi that frame the play,[40] and reports of seven hours have been mooted. This may be exaggerated, but those of us who attended the concert performance (arranged by the BBC at St John's, Smith Square, London on 17 September 1979) can attest to the fact that the singing and playing of the music for the intermedi, without the delays engendered by scenic staging, took considerably more time than one hour. The sixth and last intermedio alone occupies about fifteen minutes; it is composed of six component parts (see Table 4.3). It is not only the sheer length of 475 bars of continuous music that is impressive, but also the great variety of sonorities displayed by these five sections of the finale. They range from an instrumental overture (no. 1*a*) and an accompanied solo song (no. 3) to a chorus in thirty parts, performed by sixty singers with some instrumental doubling (no. 4), to the climax of the sixth intermedio and of the entire entertainment, Cavalieri's 'ballo' (no. 5). This comprises 250 bars, divided into twenty-one subsections plus coda, and displays the maximum of vocal and instrumental sound available, symbolizing the power of the Medici, who had arranged to have the spectacle mounted. The stage direction reads: 'Questo ballo fù cantato da tutte le voci e sonato da tutti gli strumenti sudetti [*sic*]' (this dance was sung by all the voices and played by all the aforesaid instruments). This implies a tutti of sixty voices and twenty-five to thirty instruments. The construction of this final section, the finale to the finale, in its length and complexity obviously influenced by

---

[39] Cf. Frances A. Yates, *The Valois Tapestries* (Studies of the Warburg Institute, 23; London, 1959), for a characterization of Caterina de' Medici as a 'politique', i.e. a queen mother whose preoccupations explain much about the role of the 1589 intermedi as contributing to the pro-French, anti-Spanish policy of Ferdinando de' Medici. Christine of Lorraine was Caterina's favourite granddaughter, and the Valois tapestries now hang in the Uffizi in Florence as the result of the 1589 wedding.

[40] At last made available in an edn. with adequate commentary by F. Cerreta in 1971, whose edn. of Piccolomini's *Alessandro,* another Sienese play, was noted earlier. Another edn., useful for the comparison it affords with other comedies of the 16th c., is included in the paperback anthology, ed. Nino Borsellino, *Commedie del Cinquento,* 2 vols. (Milan, 1962–7).

TABLE 4.3. *Sixth intermedio, 1589*

Page references are to Walker, *Musique des intermèdes*

Section	Incipit	No. of parts	Page of score	Page of Introduction	No. of bars
1a	Dal vago e bel sereno (instrumental, 'senza voce')	a 6	112	li	64
1b	Dal vago e bel sereno (repeated with voices: 'con le voci raddoppiate')	a 6	112	li	64
2	O qual resplende nube	a 6	117	lii	26
3	Godi turba mortal (solo with four accompanying parts)	a 5	120	liii	17
4	O fortunato giorno (60 singers)	a 30	122	liii	54
5	O che nuovo miracolo (tutti a 5, interspersed with concertini a 3)	a 5	140	liv	250

Gabrieli's precedent, will be considered later. But first it is useful to cast a cursory glance at the subject-matter.

All six intermedi are unified by a common theme, the power and glory of music. The sixth intermedio deals with a myth, as told in Plato's *Laws*, namely the descent of Harmony and Rhythm, a gift of the gods to the mortals on earth, who through dance and song find relief from their toils. A rather Platonic philosophical theme, as one would expect from the intellectual mentors of the 1589 intermedi, namely Bardi and Mei, and one not unrelated to the allegorical interpretation of the Orpheus topic, as treated from Boethius to Monteverdi and beyond. But as in Poliziano and Monteverdi, the story is not told in bald philosophical terms, but rather appears in pastoral garb.

Already in the first chorus (no. 1b), the immortals from heaven exhort the mortals on earth:

> Movian liete carole
> In questo dì giocondo
> Per arrichir, per adornar il mondo.[41]
>
> Let us move in happy dances
> On this joyful day
> To enrich and adorn the earth.

[41] D. P. Walker (ed.), *Musique des intermèdes de 'La Pellegrina'* (Les Fêtes du mariage de Ferdinand de Médicis et de Christine de Lorraine, i; Paris, 1963; repr. 1986), pp. li, 114 (bar 28), 115 (bar 46). Cf. also Alois M. Nagler, *Theatre Festivals of the Medici, 1539–1637* (New Haven, Conn., 1964), 89, and plates 61–3, for a detailed description of action and decor.

This recipe for pastoral dances (*carole*) becomes more emphatic by repetition (bars 28–45 and 46–64). The immortals who descend on clouds to earth not only include Rhythm, Harmony, the Graces, and the Muses, but also Apollo and Bacchus. Certainly, the presence of the God of Wine and Merriment invites the audience to expect a pastoral *lieto fine*: lured by the chant of the Muses, twenty mortal pairs, attired in rustic dress and with rustic instruments, appear on the stage and admire the beautiful clouds (and the gods and spirits they have brought to the earth). Their song (no. 2) speaks of shepherds and nymphs:

> Accorrete pastori,
> E voi vezzose e liete
> Belle. ninfe accorrete . . .

> Come swiftly here, shepherds,
> And you graceful and joyful
> Beautiful nymphs come swiftly . . .

Here again repetitive devices of rhetoric, such as 'accorrete' in the first and third lines, enhance the exhortation to jubilation. This theme is taken up at the highest level when the king of the gods, Jove, commands the mortals to rejoice (no. 3). The anaphora of the opening word 'Godi' (rejoice) is another rhetorical emphasis:

> Godi turba mortal, felice e lieto,
> Godi di tanto dono,
> E col canto e col suono:
> I faticosi tuoi travagli acqueta.

> Rejoice mortal crowd, happy and glad,
> Rejoice in such a gift,
> And with singing and playing:
> Find relief from your weary toils.

Two aspects of Jove's solo are worth noting. First, the advice to find respite from toil by singing and playing is remarkably similar to the definition of intermedi, suitable for comedies, given by Daniello in 1536 (*suoni, canti*).[42] Secondly, Jove's song, sung by the castrato Gualfreducci, is an unashamed virtuoso solo, unencumbered by the syllabic procedure intended to facilitate comprehension of the verbal texts. Various melismas give the performer a chance to display his prowess, notably twenty notes on the word *suono* (instrumental music) and thirty-two notes on *acqueta* (respite, relief). Of course, with such vocal virtuosi as Gualfreducci, Vittoria Archilei, Caccini, and Peri in the cast, unimpeded by Sophoclean tragedy or Ingegneri's ideas about the role of music in tragedy, Cavalieri (the composer of no. 3) did not labour under the handicaps that shackled Gabrieli at Vicenza. Throughout the

---

[42] Cf. discussion of Daniello above.

sixth intermedio we witness a dialogue, a concertato between two ensembles:
the divine group descending from heaven, and the mortal shepherds and
nymphs on this earth. The latter sing simply and syllabically, but the
heavenly crowd behaves at times unusually, in a manner associated with a
concertino of soloists.

The next piece, no. 4, is by contrast a huge ripieno or tutti, performed
by sixty singers—as large a chorus as we have encountered heretofore. The
thirty parts are divided into seven sub-choirs: sometimes the phrases are
tossed back and forth antiphonally between these, sometimes they sing
together in block chords. But certainly the singing is characterized by
syllabic style, prevailing in most stage music throughout the century.

This brings us to no. 5, the final 'ballo', which, like no. 3, was composed
by Cavalieri, and was easily the most popular piece of these entire 1589
intermedi. Before investigating its poetic and musical characteristics, a word
must be said about its subject-matter. The text consists of sixty-eight lines,[43]
a protracted dialogue between immortals (gods, the spirits of harmony and
rhythm, the graces, the muses) and mortals. The latter, being in the majority,
provide the opening (ll. 1–6, subsection 1) and closing (ll. 55–60, subsection
21) tutti, followed by a tutti coda (ll. 61–8). The standard personnel of the
pastoral makes its appearance in this coda, recalling the shepherds and
nymphs quoted above (from section no. 2):

> Portin Ninfe e Pastori
> Del Arno al ciel gl'onori
>
> Nymphs and shepherds carry the honour
> Of the River Arno to heaven
> (Walker, p. lv; cf. also p. lii)

Between the opening and closing tutti (subsections 1 and 21) the dialogue
between mortals and immortals is carried on, in which another favourite
topic of the pastoral reappears, namely the Golden Age:

> [mortals]   Tornerà d'auro il secolo?
> [immortals] Tornerà 'l secol d'oro ...
>
> Will the Golden Age return?
> The Age of Gold will return ...
> (Walker, p. liv)

To turn from the subject-matter of the finale to its poetic and musical
construction, one notes—first of all—that the opening and closing tutti are
characteristic of the simple, square dance tunes associated with octosyllabic
verse. Several variants of the incipit of Cavalieri's 'ballo' have already been
quoted, namely, that employed in 1589 (Ex. 4.1b), a simplified version of it

---

[43] Cf. Walker, pp. liv–lvi. Subsequent references to Walker will mostly be given in the main text in
parentheses.

which reduces pseudo-polyphony to homophony (Ex. 4.1*c*), and that transmitted in Caroso's dance manual of 1600 (Ex. 4.1*d*). Both melody and bass proved extremely popular and appeared in various guises in anthologies as well as in the works of individual composers. Among the latter we may name Banchieri, Frescobaldi, and Viadana; and, apart from natives of Italy, Sweelinck and the expatriate Peter Phillips. Sometimes the piece is labelled 'Aria di Firenze [or 'Fiorenza']', referring to Florence; sometimes 'Aria del Granduca', referring to Ferdinando de' Medici, Grand Duke of Tuscany; at other times 'Laura suave [soave]', literally 'Sweet Laura'. The reason for this last heading is not clear. It has been surmised that the cause may be that the name of the librettist was Laura Lucchesini, although the tag or incipit 'Laura soave' appears in earlier anthologies, not connected with the 1589 intermedi or their music.[44]

The music was not only popular, but its gestation preceded the text, and the words were written to fit the music:

La musica di questo ballo, & il ballo stesso fù del Sig. Emilio de' Cavalieri e le parole furno fatto dopo l'aria dalla Sig. Laura Lucchesini de' Guidiccioni ...

(Walker, p. lvi).

The music of this dance and the choreography itself were by Signor Emilio de' Cavalieri, and the words were written, after the music of the dance [had been completed], by Signora Laura Lucchesini de' Guidiccioni.

In other words, primary importance was attached to choreography and music, and the text was produced afterwards ('dopo l'aria') to conform with the musical requirements. We shall encounter this primacy of dance and music over the words again in connection with the performance of the *Pastor fido* at Mantua in 1598. In fact, some evidence suggests that at Florence in 1589 the librettist did not simply invent words to suit the 'aria', but quite likely she adapted and rearranged a pre-existent text, and Cavalieri may have similarly reworked a musical skeleton, already available. Recently John W. Hill discovered a sacred text in a Florentine manuscript, which in content, syllabic structure, and metre is so remarkably similar to the 1589 finale that it inevitably suggests that one text derives from the other.[45] In the sacred text we have a dialogue, a concertato between mortals (tutti) and angels (concertino), whereas in Cavalieri's 'ballo' the exchanges take place between shepherds and nymphs (tutti) and the gods and their attendant spirits (concertino). From a quotation of six lines from the opening tutti in

[44] The most extensive coverage of this multifarious subject is provided by Warren Kirkendale, *L'Aria di Fiorenza* (Florence, 1972). Addenda and corrigenda are supplied in Caroso, *Nobiltà*, ed. Sutton and Walker, and John W. Hill, ' "O che nuovo miracolo!": A New Hypothesis about the "Aria di Fiorenza" ', in Della Seta and Piperno (eds.), *In Cantu*, 283 322. Hill's discovery of a probable sacred model for the 1589 finale is of considerable importance. Cf. also Harry B. Lincoln, *The Italian Madrigal and Related Repertories: Indexes to Printed Collections, 1500–1600* (New Haven, Conn., 1988), s.v. 'Laura soave'.

[45] See n. 44.

both versions it will be seen that in the secular variant the glory of Hymen, Venus, and various spirits is substituted for the Blessed Virgin and her angels:

O che nuovo miracolo!	1	O che nuovo miracolo!
Ecco, ch'in terra scendono,	2	Ecco, ch'in terra scendono,
Celest[e] alto spettacolo,	3	Celest[e] alto spettacolo,
Gl'angeli, che risplendono,	4	Gli dei ch'il mond'accendono:
Ecco la santa Vergine	5	Ecc[o] Imene[o] e Venere
Col piè le nub[i] or premere.	6	Col piè la terr[a] or premere.

O what unheard-of miracle!	1	
Here are, descending to earth	2	
(Celestial and sublime spectacle),	3	
The angels who provide splendour.	4	The gods who illumine the world:
Here is the blessed Virgin,	5	Here are Hymen and Venus,
Her feet treading the clouds.	6	Their feet treading the ground.

Poetically, such rhyme words as *spettácolo* and *mirácolo* or *Vènere* and *prèmere*, with their accent on the antepenultimate syllable, give the tutti a sdrucciolo rhythm, and indeed the opening tutti just quoted (ll. 1–6; Walker, p. 140, bars 1–24) and the closing tutti (ll. 55–60; Walker, p. 152, bars 206–28) are settenari sdruccioli, producing octosyllabic verse, as will be seen from a syllabic count of the opening three lines, which are common to the sacred and secular texts:

O	che	nuo-	vo	mi-	ra-	co-	lo!
Ec-	co,	ch'in	ter-	ra	scen-	do-	no,
Ce-	lest'	al-	to	spet-	ta-	co-	lo..

Both 'O che nuovo miracolo' (ll. 1–6) and 'Le querc[ie] hor mel distillono' (ll. 55–60) are cast in the same octosyllabic mould and can therefore be sung to the same music. This is precisely what happens in Cavalieri's finale: the two subsections are treated as two stanzas, sung to the 'Aria di Firenze'. (They could also be sung to any other octosyllabic music, which would equally well fit verse arranged in ottonari piani or in settenari sdruccioli.)

The contrast between the opening tutti and the concertino that succeeds it (ll. 7–12) is striking. The concertino reduces the texture from five to three parts, and—what is more noticeable—the sonority from sixty singers and twenty-odd instrumentalists to three soloists, accompanied by two guitars and a tambourine ('un cembalino adornato di sonagli'). The absence of bass voices or instruments from this ensemble of three sopranos is conspicuous. The contrast also extends to the musical rhythm, the syllabic count, the incidence of pseudo-polyphony, and the choreography. The tutti is performed by the entire corps de ballet, whereas the trio is danced by the three soloists only. Apart from the 'canto' (highest part) in the opening two lines, the tutti proceeds by and large in block chords, while the concertino consistently staggers its entries (bars 25, 30, 39, 44, 49). There is also a switch from quadruple time to triple time, and from lines of eight syllables to lines of eleven and seven syllables. To demonstrate this last point it is only necessary to quote the opening lines of the concertino, cast in versi toscani, that is a mixture of endecasillabi piani and settenari piani:

> Del grand' he- roe   che con be-ni-gna leg-ge
> He- trur'   af- fren'   e   reg- ge
> U- dit'   ha Giov' in   cie- lo
>
> To the mighty hero, who with benign rule
> Governs and reigns Etruria,
> Jove in heaven has listened

Since the young Peri was among the composers and singers present at Florence in 1589, it may be well to quote the musical opening of this concertino (Ex. 4.2*a*), since it bears a resemblance to the concertino of the finale of Peri's *Euridice*, written in 1600 (Ex. 4.2*b*), which also contrasts a trio of sopranos with the main five-part tutti, and which sounds—at least to some ears—like a G minor variation of Cavalieri's G major:

Ex. 4.2*a*. Cavalieri, concertino section of 'O che nuovo miracolo'

Ex. 4.2*b*. Peri, concertino section of finale of *Euridice*

se fre - gia - - - t'il crin d'al - lo - ro,

se fre - gia - - - t'il crin d'al - lo - ro,

se fre - gia - - t'il crin d'al - lo - ro

511

bel te - so - ro rec' al sen gem - ma - ta li - ra,

bel te - so - ro rec' al sen gem - ma - ta li - ra,

bel te - so - ro rec' al sen gem - ma - ta li - ra,

> Se fregiat'il crin d'alloro,
> Bel tesoro
> Rec'al sen gemmata lira . . .
>
> When, his hair wreathed in laurel,
> He holds the beautiful treasure
> To his breast, the jewelled lyre . . .

At the start of the 'ballo' Cavalieri contrasts a full tutti, consisting of six component parts (bars 1–24: AABCDD), with a complete concertino (bars 25–54: aaba'cc). These two complete statements are contrasted in a variety of ways, as we have seen, time signature being one of them (quadruple time versus triple or compound triple time). For a considerable time thereafter (bars 55–205) the composer presents his audience only with alternating snatches of tutti and concertino, also contrasting in time signature. These fragmentary references to the opening statement remind the modern listener of the formal design of an eighteenth-century concerto, where the opening ritornello is not restated in full until the end of the movement. In our 'ballo', too, the complete tutti does not reappear until the end (bars 206–29), followed by a tutti coda (bars 229–50).

In Table 4.4 the full statements of opening tutti and concertino (subsections 1 and 2) and the full tutti at the end (subsection 21 and coda) are summarized. So are three sets of alternating fragments that intervene between these framing 'ritornellos'.

TABLE 4.4. *Design of the sixth intermedio,* 1589

Walker: page	bars	subsection		tutti		concertino	time signature
140	1–24	1		AABCDD			4/4
141	25–54		2			aaba'cc	6/4
142	55–62	3		AA			4/4
143	63–73		4			aa	6/4
143	74–7	5			B		4/4
144	78–87		6			ba'	6/4
144	88–95	7			DD		4/4
145	96–106		8			cc	6/4
145	107–14	9		AA			3/2
146	115–25		10			aa	4/4
146	126–9	11			B		3/2
147	130–9		12			ba'	4/4
147	140–7	13			DD		3/2
148	148–58		14			cc	4/4
148	159–66	15		AA			6/4
148	167–75		16			aa	3/2
149	176–9	17			B		6/4
150	180–8		18			ba'	3/2
150	189–96	19			DD		6/4
151	197–205		20			cc	3/2
152	206–29	21		AABCDD			4/4
153	229–50	Coda					6/4

It is fitting that our survey of Italian stage music, preceding the establishment of opera proper, should conclude with Guarini's *Pastor fido.* It can be stated without exaggeration that it is probably the most successful stage play originating in the sixteenth century, but extending in influence far beyond that period. Entire volumes have been written about the vogue of Guarini's pastoral in countries other than Italy, for instance in Germany and England, and even in the eighteenth century we have tokens of its perennial fashion in Handel's opera of the same title (London, 1712, libretto adapted by G. Rossi) and that of Salieri (Vienna, 1789, adapted by Da Ponte). It is difficult to account for this extraordinary popularity. The *Aminta* by Tasso was written by a greater poet, but it seems that it was the prolixity and sentimentality of Guarini that appealed to the many if not the few. Certainly excerpts from his play as well as other lyrics by him have inspired countless composers, not least of them Monteverdi. (In reference works listing Italian secular compositions there are more entries for Guarini than for Tasso or Rinuccini or Marino.) The prolixity of the *Pastor fido* is obvious. Tasso's *Aminta* was some 2,100 lines long, and, as we have remarked, even that modest dimension established it as a spoken play as opposed to a libretto intended for continuous music. Guarini's pastoral, by comparison, comprises some 6,800 lines and is therefore even more unmistakably a play, primarily spoken, even if a few scenes contain choral elements, as we shall see. Considerable expansion of the time-dimension of the drama was achieved by Guarini by greatly increasing the number of actors in the cast, particularly by introducing another pair of lovers, Silvio and Dorinda, whose affairs provided further complications and additional scenes. (The five acts of the play are subdivided into a total of thirty-nine scenes, but by contrast in Tasso's *Aminta* the five acts are split into ten scenes.) By and large the plays and pastorals from Poliziano to Tasso had preserved the Aristotelian 'unity of action' by concentrating on a single pair of lovers, whether they be called Orfeo and Euridice, or Aminta and Silvia. Rivals for the favours of the nymph or shepherdess (Aristeo in *Orfeo*, Satiro in *Aminta*) were distinctly secondary, both in dramatic importance and in the amount of lines allotted to them. But in the *Pastor fido*, Silvio and Dorinda occupy a good deal of the space of the action. (Whether or not such an expansion violated the canons of Aristotle's *Poetics* was discussed in connection with the development of the operatic libretto in the seventeenth century, as will be seen in a later chapter.)

However that may be, three scenes from the *Pastor fido* call for the assistance of music by virtue of choral interventions. These are the 'ballo della cieca' (blindman's buff) in III. ii; the chorus of hunters and shepherds in IV. vi; and the finale of the play, involving a chorus of shepherds, in V. ix–x. Of these the 'ballo della cieca' is particularly interesting because of the analogies it provides to several of the finales from Poliziano to Monteverdi. This intermedio-like insertion into Guarini's third act has more lines allotted to the chorus than to individual characters, and cannot make its effect without choreographic and musical implementation; no wonder it survives in music by such diverse composers as Gastoldi, Ghizzolo, Brognonico, and Casentini (in addition to the lost settings of Luzzaschi and Cavalieri). Two points are worth recording here. First, the dance patterns, and the music to accompany that dance, preceded the words. To quote Guarini himself: 'sotto le note di quella musica il poeta fe' le parole' (under the notes of the music the poet put [fitted] the words). This procedure is reminiscent of that observed for the finale of the 1589 intermedi. Secondly, the nature and accents of the music required greater metrical variety than the mixture of the endecasillabi and settenari prevalent throughout most of this pastoral, and Guarini was thus forced to produce a 'diversità dei versi, ora di cinque sillabe ... ora di otto ...' (diversity of verses, now of five ... now of eight syllables) in order to suit the needs of the music. Thus we again encounter octosyllabic verse, which plays such a prominent role in the history of the finale and other musical interludes.[46]

The finale is punctuated by a refrain of five lines, pronounced by a chorus of shepherds six times, and repeated by a chorus of shepherds and a heavenly chorus, in the sixth and final intermedio that concluded the performance of the *Pastor fido* at Mantua in 1598.[47] When speaking of Gastoldi's setting of the 'ballo della cieca' or the six intermedi that framed the pastoral and concluded it by echoing and extending the choral refrain of the finale, it is as well to speak of a specific performance, namely that given at Mantua on 22 November 1598, of which we have an extensive printed account. The chronology of the *Pastor fido* is unusually complicated. Apparently the play circulated in manuscript in the 1580s, and although the first editions bear the date 1590, some copies seem to have been distributed as early as 1589. But the subsequent history of performances is fairly uncertain. Several times an attempt was made to stage the play, but we cannot be sure that it was carried out before 1598. The first performance may have taken place at Siena in 1593, or at Crema in 1595–6, or at Roncilione in 1596, but specific records concerning the 'ballo della cieca' and the intermedi are only available for the Mantuan performance of 1598, attended by Margaret of Austria (by then wife of Philip III of Spain) and Archduke Albert of Habsburg. Certainly the Mantuan performance was a sumptuous one, and, as in the case of the Florentine celebrations of 1589, the greatest amount of vocal and instrumental music occurred not in the play itself but in the intermedi that framed the five acts. For instance, in the last intermedio the abovementioned choral refrain ('Vieni, santo Imeneo') is first sung by the chorus of shepherds on the stage, presumably accompanied by the stage orchestra, and then taken up by a celestial chorus, appearing on clouds in the sky, with their own instruments ('con strumenti da sonar in mano'); this is followed by other music and dance ('lieti suoni, et balli'), involving

---

[46] Guarini, *Opere*, ed. Marzino Guglielminetti (2nd edn., Turin, 1971), 562; *Il Pastor fido*, ed. Ettore Bonora (Grande Universale Mursia, 28; Milan, 1977), 116. Concerning the settings by Gastoldi and others cf. *Nuovo Vogel*, nos. 427, 498, 1114, 1193; also Iain Fenlon, 'Music and Spectacle at the Gonzaga Court', *PRMA* 103 (1976/7), 90–105.

[47] Cf. the edn. by Guglielminetti, 711–16; by Bonora, 265–70; ll. 1460–4, 1476–80, 1505–9, 1574–8, 1598–1602 of Act V. Concerning the intermedi, cf. Achille Neri, 'Gli intermezzi del Pastor fido', *GSLI* 11 (1888), 405–15, in general, and particularly p. 406 about the return of the choral refrain in the sixth intermedio.

percussion and other instruments ('col timpano, et altri strumenti'), and ending up with a moresca, which so often concluded pastorals, as in the case of Castiglione's *Tirsi* of 1506. The entire Mantuan performance tended to emphasize the importance of the pastoral, of the *lieto fine*, and of the choral finale, all of which had been steadily increasing in stature in the course of the century. But although Guarini had been active at Ferrara (as had Tasso and others before him), and although this spectacular performance of the *Pastor fido* took place at Mantua, it was at Florence that the various roots of opera finally bore fruit. But that—as the saying goes—is another chapter.

5

The Operatic Finale

CONTINUOUS ACTION AND THE FIVEFOLD DIVISION

Having considered spoken plays, punctuated by musical interludes, we now proceed to an examination of the finale in a genre sung from beginning to end: namely, the early operas performed at Florence, Mantua, and Rome in the decade 1598–1608. In view of the paucity of extant librettos and scores, we are fortunate in being able to deal with quite a few sources that have survived. Nine works, for all of which we have either libretto or score, and for most of them both, are listed in Table 5.1.[1]

TABLE 5.1. *Early operas with extant score or libretto*

Date	Place	Title	Composer	Librettist	Date of publication of score
carnival 1598	Florence	*Dafne*	Peri	Rinuccini	—
Feb. 1600	Rome	*Anima e corpo*	Cavalieri	Manni	1600
Oct. 1600	Florence	*Euridice*	Peri	Rinuccini	1601
Oct. 1600	Florence	*Cefalo*	Caccini[a]	Chiabrera	—
1602	Florence	*Euridice*	Caccini	Rinuccini	1600
1606	Rome	*Eumelio*	Agazzari	De Cupis and Tirletti	1606
1607	Mantua	*Orfeo*	Monteverdi	Striggio	1609
carnival 1608	Mantua	*Dafne*	Gagliano	Rinuccini	1608
May 1608	Mantua	*Arianna*	Monteverdi	Rinuccini	—

[a] With contributions by Venturi, Bati, and Strozzi.

The first problem to confront us in connection with some pilot works, namely those of Rinuccini, is the absence of any division into acts or scenes, either in the libretto or the score. Due to the lack of such articulation, Solerti, the early and meritorious editor of these dramas, supplied scene-division,

[1] Concerning Chiabrera's *Il rapimento di Cefalo*, performed at Florence three days after Rinuccini's *Euridice*, cf. n. 15 below.

which he derived from such factors as arrivals and departures of characters
from the scene. These square-bracketed scene-divisions of Solerti have been
perpetuated by most subsequent editors, such as Hanning and others. Solerti
has six scenes for *Dafne*, six for *Euridice*, and eight for *Arianna*. The trouble
with this numbering is that, in overall dramatic terms, it does not make sense,
primarily because it does not take into account the articulating role of the
chorus at the end of scenes. This is why Howard Brown, in his edition of
Euridice, starts his fifth scene with the return from the underworld to the
upper world, but does not start a sixth scene when Orpheus and Eurydice
join the other characters.[2] This latter event is, of course, an important
subdivision of the action, one would not hesitate to call it Act V, scene ii if
the main divisions were termed 'acts' rather than 'scenes'. But as point of
punctuation, the arrival of Orpheus is less important than the shift from
the lower to the upper world; and there is no chorus to herald the arrival
of the happy couple, or to conclude the previous scene.

Before approaching Rinuccini's librettos in general, and that of *Dafne* in
particular, three questions need to be addressed. First, in which way, if any,
were the plays of the ancient Greeks and Romans subdivided? Secondly,
how did Renaissance humanists think that these ancient plays were organized?
And last, what was the manner in which drama was presented at the turn
of the sixteenth and seventeenth centuries? Unfortunately, most of us have
experienced our first Shakespeare play or Monteverdi opera with acts, curtains, and intervals. Only gradually has modern scholarship become aware
of the fact that this mode of presentation is not necessarily indigenous to
the original texts, and that the division into five acts frequently represents
an imposition by editors, practised for centuries. To start with Shakespeare,
we may note that none of his plays printed during his lifetime displayed
the now customary division into five acts.[3] His dramas were written and at
first printed in an unbroken continuity. The same applies to most early
operas, at least to those operas written by humanist librettists. For instance,
it is now usually thought that Monteverdi's *Orfeo* was performed as a single,
continuous action, without intervals or curtains between the acts. And
similarly, a continuous mode of stage presentation is assumed for *Dafne*,
Euridice, and *Arianna*. In the case of *Arianna*, a libretto of over 1,100 lines
would scarcely have allowed for an interval.[4] At the same time, Striggio's
Orfeo and the three librettos by Rinuccini, just mentioned, seem to fall into
five episodes or 'acts', at the end of which a chorus functions as a conspicuous
and audible point of division, with the final 'coro' or 'ballo' (or both) acting as

---

[2] *Euridice*, 147, 166; Solerti, *Albori*, ii. 135, 138; Hanning, *Music's Power*, 289, 292.

[3] This applies to all the so-called good quartos, except that of *Othello*, printed posthumously in 1622.
Cf. Henry L. Snuggs, *Shakespeare and Five Acts* (New York, 1960), with a good digest of previous
scholarship, including that of Dr Johnson in the 18th c.

[4] Cf. Whenham, *Monteverdi: Orfeo*, 42, with reference to Nino Pirrotta, *Music and Culture in Italy from
the Middle Ages to the Baroque* (Studies in the History of Music, 1; Cambridge, Mass., 1984), 254.

the finale. Why five 'scenes' or 'acts', and not six or eight, as in Solerti's misleading edition? The answer lies neither in Aristotle's *Poetics* nor the so-called Aristotelian 'unities' of time, place, and action, but in a short sentence in Horace's widely read *Ars poetica* (189–90):

A play that wants to be in demand and to be revived must not be shorter or longer than five acts.[5]

On the basis of this passage and certain remarks by later authors (notably Donatus), Renaissance editors tended to impose a division into five acts upon the plays of Plautus, Terence, and other authors. But we must remember that these divisions, implying intervals between acts, do not occur in the original texts and that most classical scholars agree that 'continuous performance, which is the negation of act-division, was the rule for ancient drama from Aeschylus to Terence'.[6]

Before examining the fivefold articulation of the librettos of Rinuccini and his followers, a word of warning must be entered. Not all the early operas listed in Table 5.1 fall into five subdivisions. Two of them, Cavalieri's *Anima e corpo* of 1600 and Agazzari's *Eumelio* of 1606, have three acts. And indeed, in the later seventeenth century, certainly in Venetian opera after 1640, three rather than five acts become the rule. It is difficult to say why this is so. Perhaps the speed at which music moved favoured fewer subdivisions of the action. Also, the humanistic ambition to follow the supposed laws of the ancients became less pronounced, and vernacular models became more influential. These models were not concerned with classical learning or 'Horace's law' but rather with stage-worthiness. One thinks here of the Italian *commedia dell'arte*[7] and Spanish comedies. But certainly at the birth of opera the fivefold subdivision looms large in the work of Rinuccini, who must be reckoned to be the most influential librettist of the period.

DAFNE

Perhaps this will be clearer when we consider detailed investigations of Rinuccini's *Dafne* (set to music by Peri and Gagliano), his *Euridice* (set to

---

[5] Cf. D. A. Russell and M. Winterbottom, *Ancient Literary Criticism: The Principal Texts in New Translation* (Oxford, 1972), 284; W. Beare, *The Roman Stage* (3rd rev. edn., London, 1964), 196.

[6] Cf. Beare, *Roman Stage*, 217; also quoted by Murata, 'Classical Tragedy', 107 n. 20; cf. also Pirrotta, *Music and Theatre*, 46, on the introduction of five-act division into editions of Plautus. One exception to the 'continuous performance without act-division' seems to be provided by the Greek comedies of Menander. Some scholars think that, apart from Menander's comedies (not known in the Renaissance), and leaving aside the question of a 'continuous' performance, the fivefold division of ancient dramas may be discernible by the positioning of the choral passages.

[7] The scenarios of *commedia dell'arte*, in three acts, published in Flaminio Scala's *Teatro delle favole rappresentative* (Venice, 1611), are typical. Cf. C. Jannaco, *Il Seicento* (Storia letteraria d'Italia; 2nd edn., Milan, 1966), 296 *et passim*.

music by Peri and Caccini), his *Arianna* (set to music by Monteverdi), and Striggio's *Orfeo* (greatly influenced by Rinuccini, and also set to music by Monteverdi). It will be seen that in these librettos, which demonstrate the dramatic and musical imagination of Rinuccini, the end-of-act choruses tell the audience, in lieu of the curtain of the modern proscenium theatre, that an important portion of the action, or the entire action, has come to a close. We have, of course, seen intermedi or choruses (or both) function in similar fashion in works of the sixteenth century, discussed in Chapter 4. But in early opera the unbroken dramatic continuity is enhanced by the continuity of the music. From this it follows that the finale will be perceived as such primarily by its length, its sonority, and its positioning, rather than by the switch from spoken recitation to music. Most Rinuccini finales are characterized by ample time-span, strophic construction, and frequently by the presence of octosyllabic metres. None of these features is restricted to finales, or to end-of-act choruses. Large chunks of music, as opposed to recitative, may occur within the act; and so may ottonari and other metres to contrast with the more ubiquitous versi toscani. And, naturally, strophic construction, one of the main springs of lyrical expression, applies to choruses and solo songs throughout any opera. Yet, if one opened an early libretto at random and encountered a piece organized into eight stanzas, it would not be a bad guess to suspect the passage of being a 'finale', the conclusion of the final scene or act, a chorus of glad tidings that informs the audience that the show is over. It is precisely in eight stanzas, in ottonari and quaternari, that Rinuccini concludes his first operas, *Dafne* and *Euridice*.

In the charts of *Dafne* and other operas given in Tables 5.2–4, it will be easier to survey the material if it is condensed by abbreviation.[8] It will be seen from Table 5.2 that *Dafne*, Rinuccini's first experiment (*prova*) in operatic construction, has closing choruses for all but one of its five scenes; and even the fourth scene, in its expansion of 1608 (set by Gagliano), ended with a choral concertato. As to the finale proper, ll. 398–445, it is by far the longest piece of verse, has the most stanzas, and introduces lines of eight and four syllables into the genre of the operatic finale. In doing so the poet was aware of dramatic precedents (from Poliziano to the intermedi of 1589) and of poetic models (Chiabrera). Still, the fact that three of the four closing choruses employ ottonari must be reckoned to be a major innovation on the librettist's part. As far as the music of the final chorus goes, we have a brief manuscript excerpt for 'Bella ninfa fuggitiva', notated on two staves, vocal line and bass (Ex. 5.1), and the five-part choral concertato of Gagliano's

---

[8] Line-numbers follow the customary arrangement of Solerti, Hanning, and others. But numerals with a prime indicate lines that do not occur in the original libretto, but in a revision or expansion, e.g. in *Dafne*, ll. 371' 90' refers to Gagliano's expansion of 1608; and in *Orfeo*, ll. 645' 56' refers to the text of Monteverdi's score of 1609 (not the libretto of 1607). Metres are abbreviated by numerals: 11+7 = versi toscani, 11 = endecasillabi, 7 = settenari, 8 = ottonari, 8+4 = ottonari and quaternari.

TABLE 5.2. *Concluding choruses of* Dafne[a]

Scene	Lines	Text	Structure and metre
1	67–90	Almo dio ch'il carro ardente	4 six-line stanzas; metre '8'
2	159–93	Nud'arcier chi l'arco tendi	5 seven-line stanzas; metre '8'
3	276–303	Non si nasconde in selva	4 seven-line stanzas; metre '11+7' (corresponds to scenes 3–4 of Solerti)
4	371'–90'	Piangete, O Ninfe, e con voi pianga Amore[b]	irregular; metre '11+7'
5	398–445	Bella ninfa fuggitiva	8 six-line stanzas; metre '8+4'

[a] Text and music of these choruses will be found Gagliano, *Dafne*, ed. Erber, 12, 20, 31, 37, 47; text in Hanning, *Music's Power*, 248, 251, 255, 266, 258; Solerti, *Albori*, ii. 80, 84, 91, 95, 97.
[b] No concluding chorus for messenger scene in original libretto, but in expansion for Gagliano, 1608, concertato *a 1*, *a 2*, and *a 3*, with choral refrain and several lines *a 5* (ll. 383', 384'–7', 390').

version of 1608 (Ex. 5.2*a*). The former is attributed, in the Brussels manuscript, to Jacopo Corsi, the patron and presenter of *Dafne*. It has been surmised that this may represent a reduction of a homophonic chorus. This may be so, but the piece strikes one as too simple and unimpressive to serve as many as eight successive stanzas. Moreover, it does not seem suitable, without considerable modification and elaboration, to provide a contrast, in sonority and vocal style, with the opening tutti: an opposition as we encountered it in the intermedi of 1589, and as it is found Peri's *Euridice* of 1600 and in Gagliano's *Dafne* of 1608.[9] These extant printed scores of *Euridice* and *Dafne* throw the opening massive five-part tutti into textural relief by allotting other stanzas to a concertino of three high voices (without vocal bass). In the case of Gagliano's *Dafne*, the concertino stanza offers a strikingly different variation of the tutti: the melodic and harmonic skeleton is clearly recognizable, but the melismas allotted to the solo singers provide an obvious foil for the syllabic style of the tutti (note the thirty-one notes given to the second syllable of *celesti* in Ex. 5.2*b*). Also, both *Euridice* and *Dafne* have instrumental ritornellos in triple time for part of the finale (Ex. 5.2*c*); these contrast with the duple (or quadruple) time of the stanzas, all of which are sung.

[9] For the version attributed to Corsi, cf. W. V. Porter, 'Peri's and Corsi's *Dafne*', *JAMS* 18 (1965), 170–96, esp. p. 183; also Hanning, *Music's Power*, 142–4. For the Gagliano finale of 1608, cf. facs. of the original score (Bologna, 1970), 52–5; Robert Eitner (ed.), *Die Oper* (Publikationen älterer praktischer und theoretischer Musikwerke, 10; Leipzig, 1881), 114–17; *Dafne*, ed. James Erber (London: Cathedral Music, 1978), 47–9.

Text of tutti stanza, ll. 398–403 (Ex.5.2a)

Bella ninfa fuggitiva,	Lovely, fugitive nymph,
Sciolt'e priva	Deprived and freed
Del mortal tuo nobil velo,	From thy mortal, noble veil,
Godi pur pianta novella,	Rejoice, young plant,
Casta e bella,	Chaste and beautiful,
Cara al modo e cara al cielo.	Dear to the world and dear to heaven.

Text of concertino stanza, ll. 404–6 (Ex. 5.2b)

Tu non curi e nembi e tuoni,	Thou art not disturbed by rain or thunder,
Tu coroni	Thou crownest
Cigni, regi, e dei celesti . . .	Swans [i.e. poets], kings, and celestial gods . . .

One's guess is that the excerpt preserved in the Brussels manuscript and attributed to Corsi (Ex. 5.1) represents an early attempt to provide a suitable setting for the six-line stanzas (ll. 398–445). At some time between 1598 and 1600 Peri probably wrote a musically more adequate and varied concertato, not radically different from the finales in the extant scores of *Dafne* and *Euridice*. It is interesting that harmonically both Corsi's and Gagliano's stanzas (Exx. 5.1 and 5.2a) cadence on F major (Corsi, first statement of l. 403, *cara al cielo*; Gagliano, l. 401, *pianta novella*) but then conclude with a repetition of the sixth and last line of the stanza, cadencing on G minor (to use modern terminology). It is, in fact, curious how frequently the small circle of composers, resident in Florence, when setting the same lines of Rinuccini to music, employ the same pitch and similar harmonic turns.[10]

In terms of dramatic construction, the finale of Rinuccini's *Dafne* must wrestle with particular difficulties to achieve its obligatory *lieto fine*. In the case of the Orpheus plot the poet radically changed the story in 1600, as we have seen, but the 1598 opera does not conclude with a happily united couple, Apollo and Daphne: Ovid is too closely reflected (in spite of some modifications). Of course, the metamorphosis of Daphne into the laurel, with which poets and kings are crowned, has attracted librettists and composers from Peri to Strauss. In the case of Peri and Rinuccini the 'happy' note of the *lieto fine* is reached by having Apollo shift from his lament about the loss of the beloved (ll. 371–8) to a hymn of praise for the glories of the laurel, impervious to heat or frost (*o fiamma o gelo*), fit for the brows of great poets and sovereign monarchs (ll. 379–97). This forms a suitable transition to the finale proper, 'Bella ninfa fuggitiva' (ll. 398–445), which praises in addition to the beautiful nymph and the distinction of the laurel also the happiness of love. But this latter staple of operatic lore is never

---

[10] In regard to Peri's and Caccini's *Euridice* cf. Hanning, 144–5, concerning the finale; and Robert M. Haas, *Die Musik des Barocks* (Potsdam, 1929; repr. 1949), 37, concerning Orpheus' solo, preceding the finale.

Ex. 5.1. Corsi, final chorus of *Dafne*

The vertical lines extending beyond the staves indicate the conclusions of the six lines of the stanza.

consummated in the opera: it is achieved only in the indirect, metaphoric manner, so apposite to the poetic imagination, 'music' in the original Greek sense of the word.[11]

---

[11] For a sensitive comparison of the plots of Ovid and Rinuccini, see Barbara Russano Hanning, 'Glorious Apollo: Poetic and Political Themes in the First Opera', *Renaissance Quarterly*, 32 (1979), 485–513. Concerning the chronology of the libretto see Sternfeld, 'First Printed Opera Libretto'.

Ex. 5.2*a*. Gagliano, opening section of final chorus of *Dafne*

Ex. 5.2*b*. Gagliano, concertino section of final chorus of *Dafne*

Ex. 5.2*c*. Gagliano, instrumental ritornello in final chorus of *Dafne*

EURIDICE

It is only when we consult the scores of the first operas that we are able to supplement the information vouchsafed in the librettos. The latter show the positioning of the end-of-scene choruses and their strophic construction. But the mode of operation of a concertato, and other details of performance, must be gathered mostly from the extant music and the invaluable rubrics printed with these scores. It is clear that all five choruses of *Euridice*, summarized in Table 5.3, employ the contrast between a tutti (*a 5* or *a 4*) and variously scored concertino sections (*a 1* or *a 3*). Whether the choral refrain precedes the stanza (as in scene 1) or follows it (scene 2) is a matter of choice. The most intricate interplay occurs, as one would expect, at the end of the final scene: here the rubrics indicate not only tutti vs. concertino, but also singing vs. playing, dancing vs. non-dancing, and corps de ballet vs. solo dancing. Keeping in mind various remarks printed in Cavalieri's score of 1600 and Gagliano's score of 1608, we may assume a complement of twelve to fifteen singers in *Euridice*. Thus the contrast in sonority and texture in the finale between a tutti *a 5* and a concertino *a 3* would be considerable. Equally pronounced would be the difference between types of choreography: on the one hand the tutti (i.e. the entire corps de ballet) performing more slowly in quadruple time (perhaps in the manner of a pavan); on the other the dancing of two soloists during the instrumental ritornellos in quicker steps in triple time (perhaps in the manner of a galliard).

Peri's rubrics for the finale are not very detailed: for the tutti (l. 743) we are told that they all dance ('tutti . . . ballano'), whereas the ritornello is danced only by two soloists ('ballato da due soli del coro'). But fortunately we have a similar contrast between choral tutti and instrumental ritornello in the finale of Cavalieri's *Anima e corpo*, and in this case the remarks about the performance (*avvertimenti*) that preface the score are more explicit:

The finale may be performed in two ways: either with choreography (*con un ballo*) or without . . . If one wants to finish with dancing, one begins to sing 'Chiostri altissimi e stellati' [tutti *a 5*]. At this point the corps de ballet (*il ballo*) starts slowly (*in riverenza e continenza, e poi seguino altri passi gravi*) . . . During the instrumental ritornellos four solo dancers, performing exquisitely, execute a dance with leaps and there is no singing (*senza cantare*). And so forth through all the stanzas . . . And the four solo dancers (*quattro maestri*) may vary their steps, one time a galliard . . . one time a courante.[12]

In the simpler plan of *Anima e corpo*, then, several vocal tuttis *a 5* (notated on five staves plus basso continuo) alternate with instrumental ritornellos of a smaller texture (notated on three staves plus basso continuo). The former are

---

[12] For the complete Italian text, see Solerti, *Origini*, 10 11. I have translated 'fine' as 'finale'. Neither of these words exists as a technical term in the early 17th c., which created the finale, but did not define it. 'Riverenze', 'continenze', and 'passi gravi' are standard Italian dance steps.

TABLE 5.3. *Concluding choruses of* Euridice[a]

Scene	Lines	Text	Structure and metre
1	85–100	Al canto, al ballo, all'ombre, al prato adorno	4 four-line stanzas; metre '11 + 7'; 3 stanzas *a 1* (bars 199, 235, 270) framed by 4 refrains *a 5* (bars 175, 211, 246, 283)
2	265–92	Sospirate aure celesti	7 four-line stanzas; metre '8'; 7 stanzas (nos. 1–5 *a 1*; nos. 6–7 *a 3*) concluded by 7 refrains *a 5* (bars 543, 560, 570, 560, 570, 602, 602). Metrically, the first refrain repeats the last 2 ll. of the first stanza (bars 535, 543); but usually the refrain concludes without forming part of the stanza, hence its absence from the line numbers of Hanning and Solerti; similarly, when successive stanzas are fitted to the same music, it is necessary to repeat numerals in the bar-numbering of Brown.
3	372–89	Se de boschi i verdi onori	3 six-line stanzas; metre '8'; 3 stanzas *a 5* (bars 218, 233, 248) in '8'; followed by a stanza *a 1* (bar 264) in '11 + 7' whose last line is repeated *a 5* (bars 281, 285). Thus this end-of-scene finale also concludes as a 'coro'.
4	554–83	Poi che gl'eterni imperi	5 six-line stanzas; metre '7'; 4 stanzas *a 4* (bars 565, 579, 607, 621), 1 stanza *a 1* (bar 596)
5	743–90	Biondo arcier che d'alto monte	8 six-line stanzas; metre '8 + 4'; interplay between 3 component parts: (*a*) choral tutti *a 5*, danced by entire corps de ballet, which provides 6 stanzas (bars 453, 485, 525, 557, 597, 629); (*b*) instrumental ritornello, danced by 2 soloists, repeated *ad libitum* (e.g. bars 475, 547, 619 in Brown); (*c*) concertino *a 3*, for high voices without vocal bass, not danced, which provides stanzas 3 and 6 (bars 507, 579).

[a] Text and music will be found in Peri, *Euridice*, ed. Brown, 31, 76, 99, 140, 183; text in Hanning, *Music's Power*, 273, 279, 283, 288, 294; Solerti, *Albori*, ii. 118, 124, 128, 134, 141.

in duple time and slow, the latter in triple time and quick. (Both the galliard and the courante, given as examples, are typically in triple time.) The dancers of the large corps de ballet impress by their stately intertwining (*con trecciate*), the solo dancers by their virtuosity. Thus the tutti–concertino contrast applies to the choreography as well as to the music. Since *Anima e corpo* was performed in February 1600 and *Euridice* in October of that year, it seems reasonable to annotate the slender rubrics of Peri's score with those of Cavalieri. But there was nothing sparse about Peri's musical means, where the vocal tutti is contrasted with a vocal concertino as well as with a ritornello. And yet this wealth of resources never obscures the difference between the expressive solo singing that precedes the finale and the ample sonority of the closing chorus. Rinuccini seems to have been particularly intent on providing the composer with such a plan: in *Dafne*, as we have seen, Apollo's lament and hymn to the laurel usher in the 'Bella ninfa' finale; and in *Euridice* Orpheus' attractive and melodic 'Gioite al canto mio' (a modified strophic song) precedes the choral stanza 'Biondo arcier', where all sing and dance. Later librettists were influenced by Rinuccini, and when Striggio wrote *Orfeo* for Monteverdi, he was careful to have in his 1607 libretto an impressive example of solo singing before the finale, namely Orpheus' lament, to which Monteverdi, in the 1609 score, added the virtuoso duet between Orpheus and Apollo. (Neither one of these two pieces can be written off as 'tedious recitative'.)

There is no need to analyse again the manner in which Rinuccini brings about the *lieto fine* in *Euridice*. It is inevitably a matter extensively discussed in Ch. 1 and indeed throughout this monograph, since it invites comparisons with other treatments of the Orpheus plot. But at this point it will be more useful to examine the fivefold division in Striggio's and Monteverdi's *Orfeo*.

ORFEO

Both the libretto of 1607 and the score of 1609 are quite explicit about the number of units (whether they be called 'scenes' or 'acts') that make up the entire action. There are five acts, no more, no less, as Horace had decreed, and as the good humanists of the Accademia degli Invaghiti—who made the arrangements for the performance *Orfeo*—knew well. (It is useful to remember that *Euridice* and *Arianna* were commissioned for courtly weddings, while *Orfeo* was a carnival entertainment, arranged by the Mantuan academy for no particular political or dynastic event.) The subdivision into five acts is quite clear in the score, where each page has a running-head such as 'Atto primo' or 'Atto quinto'. Then there are rubrics indicating the end of each act. Moreover, on the last page of the score (p. 100) there is a table of contents (*tavola*), listing all acts with their respective page-numbers. Finally, at the end of each act there is always a section entitled 'coro', and at least a portion of it is a tutti scored for five vocal parts. Indeed, the choruses of nymphs and shepherds, which in pastoral style conclude Acts I–II and V, and the choruses of the spirits of the underworld, which conclude Acts III and IV, are specifically mentioned in the cast-list (*personaggi*) that precedes the score. In fact, this list carefully distinguishes between two pastoral choruses, one of singers and another of dancers 'who performed the final moresca' (*che fecero la moresca nel fine*). Indeed, this final instrumental moresca is the last piece of music to be printed in the score, as is the instrumental ritornello in the finale of *Euridice*. The fivefold division, then, is spelt out in *Orfeo*, and not left to the intuition of modern editors, from Solerti onwards. This, of course, in no way interferes with the continuous action that starts when the curtain reveals the scene, that is, after the opening toccata, and unfolds, without break, until the moresca brings the finale to a close.

In contemplating the chart given in Table 5.4, and comparing it with that for *Euridice* (Table 5.3), there are, as one would expect, some striking similarities, for instance in regard to concertato procedure and the employment of five-part tutti. But there are also differences: ottonari are less conspicuous as metrical 'markers' for end-of-scene choruses, and strophic construction is less to the fore. But even more pronounced is the different manner in which the composer has treated the libretto: there is not a single act where Monteverdi, in one way or another, does not interfere with Striggio's concluding choruses. He either omits groups of lines, or reduces three stanzas to one, or—in the case of Act V—substitutes an entirely different finale. One is tempted to extrapolate from this procedure two hypotheses: first, that Monteverdi had a will and temperament of his own. Secondly, in each case the concluding 'coro' set to music by the composer is shorter than Striggio's text, and one is inclined to think that Monteverdi's sense of timing was crucially involved in these decisions. He is unwilling to linger at the dramatic climax, even if he misses some musical opportunities.

We do not know who provided the text for the altered fifth act, but considerations of rhymed pairs of verses and other stylistic traits make it unlikely that Striggio wrote the new section of Act V. Both Rinuccini (who was in Mantua in 1608) and Ferdinando Gonzaga have been suggested as likely authors, but whoever it was must have looked at Rinuccini's extant librettos.[13]

Among the many remarkable aspects of this choral finale, besides its brevity (already discussed), are: the absence of concertato technique, the presence of the metre of ottonari; the employment of the dramatic device of *deus ex machina*; and—last but not least—the fact that Orpheus finds his ultimate contentment in being translated to heaven rather than being reunited with his beloved. All these elements of musical, poetic, and dramatic style

---

[13] Cf. Hanning, *Music's Power*, 129–30; Arnold and Fortune, *New Monteverdi Companion*, 264.

TABLE 5.4. *Concluding choruses of* Orfeo[a]

Act	Lines	Text	Structure and metre
I	125–51	Alcun non sia che disperato in preda	Irregular; metre '11+7'; 1609 score: ll. 137–51 omitted; concertato: l. 125 *a 2*, l. 128 *a 3*, l. 131 *a 2*, l. 133 *a 5*.
II	271–314	Chi ne consola ahi lassi ll. 298–314 omitted; concertato	Irregular; metre '11+7'; 1609 score: with 2-line choral refrain (ll. 283, 296): l. 271 *a 2*, l. 283 *a 5*, l. 285 *a 2*, l. 296 *a 5*.
III	412–41	Nulla impresa per huom si tenta in vano	3 ten-line stanzas; metre '11+7'; 1609 score: ll. 422–41 omitted; throughout extant music: tutti *a 5*.
IV	549–62	E la virtute un raggio ll. 555–8 omitted; throughout extant	Irregular; metre '11+7'; 1609 score: music: tutti *a 5*.
V	617–78 (libretto)	Evohè, padre Lieo	These 62 lines (not in score) consist of (*a*) 5 seven-line framing stanzas, metre '8+4' (ll. 617, 632, 644, 661, 672); 35 ll.; probably intended for tutti *a 5*; (*b*) an additional 27 lines, metre '11+7'; probably intended for concertino (e.g.: l. 624 *a 1*, l. 630 *a 2*, l. 639 *a 1*, etc.).
V	645'–56' (score)	Vanne, Orfeo, felice a pieno	These 12 lines (not in libretto) consist of 2 six-line stanzas, metre '8'; vocal tutti *a 5* throughout, followed by an instrumental moresca.

[a] Text and music will be found in facsimile, 20, 42, 79, 84,—, 98; text in Hanning, *Music's Power*, 309, 313, 318, 322, 324, (329); Solerti, *Albori*, ii. 251, 262, 268, 271, (272) (the line-numbering is occasionally faulty).

could be treated in separate monographs and are touched upon at various points in the present work. But they must be briefly considered in this chapter.

Musically, the revised text does not give the concluding chorus the space to employ concertato technique: the tutti *a 5* for the first stanza is repeated for the second stanza. There is no room for the insertion of a concertino contrast. The difference in time-dimension between this concluding chorus and that of *Euridice*, or Striggio's libretto of 1607, is obvious. But there is also a difference of tone. Both Rinuccini's and Striggio's concluding choruses are joyous and pagan: one addresses Apollo, the other Bacchus. But the Monteverdi score closes on a serious, moralizing note, with an echo of the Psalms. This is neither amorous nor bibulous, but severely Neoplatonic (if not a Christian allegory). The jollity associated with a *lieto fine* does not arrive until the two choral stanzas have been completed, when they are succeeded by the customary final dance, the moresca. Most students of Monteverdi surmise that in the Dionysian merriness of this moresca something of the spirit of Striggio's (and Poliziano's) Bacchanalian finale survives. In any event, it certainly brings this entertainment for the courtiers of the Academy of the Invaghiti to a conventional and expected conclusion. It is interesting that the contrast between duple and triple time, which we observed in Peri and Gagliano, also pertains here: the tutti chorus sings in duple time, and the instrumental moresca is in triple time (in most modern editions it is notated in compound time, such as 6/4 or 6/2). Osthoff has noted some similarity between this concluding number of *Orfeo* and the jolly drinking-song of Charon in Landi's *Morte d'Orfeo* of 1619. He also rightly reminds us that this juxtaposition of the Apollonian and Dionysian spheres is anticipated in both ancient and Neoplatonic sources.[14]

If the absence of vocal concertino contrasts in the concluding chorus of Monteverdi's score is uncharacteristic of the early finale and of this composer's favourite procedures, the fact that the chorus is a setting of ottonari attests to the influence of Rinuccini and the Florentine tradition. Octosyllabic verse plays a prominent role in the finales of Poliziano, the intermedi of 1539, and those of 1589, as we have seen in Chapters 3 and 4. It is therefore not surprising that Rinuccini used this metre conspicuously in the final choruses of *Dafne* and *Euridice*. It is not that other poets were unfamiliar with the use of ottonari or Poliziano's employment of this verse-form in his *Orfeo*. Chiabrera, in his *Le maniere de' versi toscani* (1599), quotes Poliziano's finale and uses the metre in his own lyrical poems. But it was Rinuccini who pioneered the introduction of octosyllabic verse for the finale of the operatic libretto, and after a few years other librettists, notably Chiabrera and Striggio, followed his example. (The shorter octosyllabic line is, of course, more suitable for a full-fledged musical setting than the longer hendecasyllabic line, firmly established for spoken recitation, and continuing to serve for recitative and parlando.) It is historically relevant that both Striggio's libretto and Monteverdi's score employ the more conventional endecasillabi in the concluding choruses for the first four acts, but both librettist and composer have recourse to ottonari for their respective versions of Act V. But the case of Chiabrera shows the influence of Rinuccini's librettos even more clearly. In 1600, when writing *Rapimento di Cefalo*, Chiabrera

---

[14] Osthoff, 'Contro le legge', 62–5.

employed the conventional versi toscani (i.e. 11+7) for the finale,[15] but in his later librettos, for example *Galatea* (1608/14) and *Orfeo dolente* (1608/16), octosyllabic verse provided the conclusion.[16] When we consider that ottonari are also encountered in other operas of the period, it will be seen how influential Rinuccini's finale formula was. He tried it in *Dafne*, and with the success of *Euridice* it became established as an operatic tradition.

We may note in passing that the choral concertatos placed at the end of the fifth act of Monteverdi's *Arianna* of 1608, and of Landi's *Morte d'Orfeo* of 1619, also employ ottonari prominently (though not exclusively), in a manner analogous to Striggio's finale of 1607. The *Arianna* finale[17] consists of a concertato of forty-seven lines (1068–79) where the opening chorus is composed of two six-line stanzas, cast in the same mould of octosyllabic lines and half-lines, 8–4–8–8–4–8, as the finales of *Dafne* and *Euridice*. The *Morte d'Orfeo* finale[18] employs a concertato of seventy-one lines where the closing chorus of gods and shepherds opens with four and concludes with five ottonari (lines 864–7 and 875–9). At this point we may give two examples of music fitting octosyllabic texts, which—incidentally—also provide a basis of comparison for the tunes and basses quoted in Chapter 4. The first example is from the final chorus of Monteverdi's *Orfeo* (Ex. 5.3*a*), the second from the final chorus of Landi's *Morte d'Orfeo* (Ex. 5.3*b*). The five vocal parts of Monteverdi and the eight vocal parts (plus basso continuo) of Landi do not conceal a basically homophonic and syllabic structure. (In both cases only the outer parts are given.)

*Monteverdi, Orfeo, l. 645′, text of Ex. 5.3*a

Vanne, Orfeo, felice a pieno	Go, Orpheus, fully happy
A goder celeste onore . . .	To enjoy celestial honour . . .

*Landi, Morte d'Orfeo, l. 875, text of Ex. 5.3*b

Fortunato semideo	Fortunate demigod
Che col pregio del tuo canto . . .	Who with the excellence of thy song . . .

[15] Chiabrera's libretto, based on the same Ovidian myth as the earlier *Cefalo* of Correggio, is reprinted in Solerti, *Albori*, iii. 9 58. The music was largely by Caccini, but also with contributions by Bati, Strozzi, and Venturi. Most of it is lost, but two numbers by Caccini, including the finale, survive. Cf. *Nuove musiche* [1602], ed. H. Wiley Hitchcock (RRMBE, 9; Madison, Wis., 2nd corr. pr., 1982), 20, 28, 101, 137, 142 (re p. 111).

[16] Cf. Sternfeld, 'The "Occasional" Element in the Choral Finale from Poliziano to Rinuccini', in Marc Honegger *et al.* (eds.), *La Musique et le rite sacré et profane: Actes du XIIIᵉ Congrès de la Société Internationale de Musicologie, Strasbourg, 29 août–3 septembre 1982*, 2 vols. (Strasburg, 1986), i. 371 6, for further discussion, and a chronological list of ottonari finales up to Landi's *Morte d'Orfeo* of 1619. Cf. also Hanning, 'Chiabrera', in *New Grove*; and her *Music's Power*.

[17] Solerti, *Albori*, ii. 185 7, ll. 1068 1114. This is the fifth end-of-scene (or end-of-act) chorus in the libretto. The first four scenes are concluded as follows: scene 1, ll. 298 ff. (Solerti, p. 159); scene 2, ll. 458 ff. (p. 164); scene 3, ll. 619 ff. (p. 170); scene 4, ll. 909 ff. (p. 180).

[18] Solerti, *Albori*, iii. 334 7, ll. 809 79.

Ex. 5.3*a*. Monteverdi, from final chorus of *Orfeo*

Ex. 5.3*b*. Landi, from final chorus of *Morte d'Orfeo*

Before considering the dramatic technique and devices employed by Striggio and Monteverdi, it might be as well to examine other instances of concertato and ottonari in operas earlier than *Orfeo*. Obvious points of comparison are offered by *Anima e corpo* (1600) and *Eumelio* (1606). Both are preserved in printed scores that divide the action clearly and explicitly into acts, as in the case of *Orfeo*, but into three (not five) acts: both seem to be closer to the live tradition of the theatre than the canons of humanistic and neo-Aristotelian erudition. In *Anima* the conclusion of each act is marked by a chorus, as one would expect. That concluding the first act is in versi toscani (11+7) and scored for four vocal parts plus basso continuo, punctuated by instrumental ritornellos.[19] There is little variation of texture, except the concertato contrast between a vocal tutti *a 4* (plus basso continuo) and instrumental ritornellos *a 3* (plus basso continuo). The concluding chorus for the second act (no. 54) is again in versi toscani, but the concertato procedure is more extensive, mingling sections for one, two, and four vocal parts (plus basso continuo), as well as employing echo technique. For the completion of the third act, the finale, the score offers two alternatives (nos. 90 and 91). The second of these (no. 91) has already been discussed briefly, comparing its choreography with that in the finale of *Euridice*. But we must search both finales for their employment of concertato and octosyllabic verse. Both are almost entirely composed of ottonari. The finale for singing only (no. 90) consists of eight lines, of which the first seven are ottonari, and the eighth an endecasillabo (sung by four vocal parts, and echoed by eight). The finale for singing and dancing (no. 91) consists of six stanzas of six lines each, all thirty-six lines being ottonari. Contrasts of texture in both finales are slight. In that for singing only, it is restricted to the repetition of the last line as an echo for eight vocal parts, which with its ample sonority confirms and concludes the piece, otherwise scored for four vocal parts. (All sections of no. 90, as well as of no. 91, have their separately printed basso continuo.) In the alternative finale (no. 91), discussed earlier, concertato procedure is restricted to the contrast between the vocal tutti *a 5* and the instrumental ritornellos *a 3*. But, then, one suspects that the concurrent opposition between corps de ballet and solo dancing introduces considerable variety of another sort. To what extent Cavalieri in 1600 was influenced by the precedent of *Dafne* (1598) is difficult to say. Both concertato and octosyllabic verse had been employed by Cavalieri himself for the finale of 1589. Suffice it to say that he and Peri acted as models for Monteverdi in 1607.

Certainly, Cavalieri's *Anima* and Peri's *Euridice* must have influenced Agazzari's *Eumelio* of 1606. Three-act structure and religious allegory suggest the former, and the very plot of *Eumelio* is a thinly disguised modification of the latter, as has been stated before. Both in terms of concertato and of metrical procedures, the finale of *Eumelio* is closer to *Dafne* and *Euridice* than to either *Anima* or *Orfeo*. Of the choruses that conclude the three acts of

---

[19] No. 15 in the printed score (and in the libretto, printed at the end of the score). This valuable source is available in facs. edns. of 1912 and 1967, the latter with a postscript by M. Baroni. The same numbers, applying to score-cum-libretto, are also used by Solerti in his *Origini*, 18 39, where the libretto is reprinted.

Eumelio, only the third displays an unmistakable vocal concertato.[20] It consists of three component parts, the first of which acts as a choral ritornello, scored for eight vocal parts. (If a basso continuo underpinned this, which seems not unlikely, it is not notated in the score, pp. 33–4.) This first tutti is succeeded by a concertino for two vocal parts (plus notated basso continuo, p. 35), at the end of which a rubric indicates that the opening tutti is to be repeated. Then follows another concertino for two vocal parts (plus notated basso continuo, pp. 35–6), again succeeded by the direction that the opening tutti is to be heard again. Metrically the resemblance to the *Euridice* finale is unmistakable, since both the tutti ritornello and the two concertinos are couched in the same mixture of octosyllabic full and half-lines (8–4–8–8–4–8) as were the finales of *Dafne* and *Euridice* (also used subsequently in the *Arianna* finale of 1608). By contrast, the choruses concluding Acts I and II are in settenari. Either settenari or endecasillabi, or a mixture of the two (versi toscani) were, of course, traditional in librettos of the period. They appear, for instance, at the end of the five acts of Chiabrera's *Cefalo*, and—as we have seen—at the conclusion of the first four acts of *Orfeo*. The deliberate switch to ottonari and to vocal concertato in the *Eumelio* finale is a further indication of the influence provided by Rinuccini and Peri.

DEUS EX MACHINA AND APOTHEOSIS

The crucial difference between Striggio's libretto and Monteverdi's score hinges on the intervention of Apollo. As we have seen in Chapters 1 and 3, the ancient device of *deus ex machina* basically affects the conclusions of Monteverdi and Stravinsky. It is the 'appearance', the 'epiphany', of Apollo that suddenly and unexpectedly moves us from beholding Orpheus' misery to witnessing his triumph and immortality. Such sudden shifts are eminently characteristic of early Baroque drama, which presupposes a fondness of and delight in the miracles of stagecraft. Sudden revelations occur in Stravinsky's ballets with finely judged theatrical effects, *vide* the appearance of the puppet's ghost at the end of *Petrouchka*, or Orpheus' lyre raised heavenwards in *Orpheus*. Whether the machine in question is a pulley with which a cloud (or a god on a cloud) is hoisted on to the stage,[21] or magic lantern, or a more

[20] In the case of *Eumelio*, where no modern facsimile or transcription has been published, it is best to refer to the pages of the printed score of 1606, and a later libretto printed for a performance at Amelia in 1614 (with inserted intermedi). Both of these sources are extant at the Biblioteca di Santa Cecilia at Rome (I-Rsc) and have been consulted for this chapter. Act I concludes with a chorus for eight vocal parts (score, pp. 11–14), Act II with one for five vocal parts (score, pp. 21–2); the finale appears on pp. 33–6 of the score and pp. 63–4 of the libretto.

[21] Machines are mentioned in Aristotle's *Poetics* (1454[b]); cf. the translation in Russell and Winterbottom, *Ancient Literary Criticism*, 111; see also the article on *deus ex machina* in the forthcoming *New Grove Dictionary of Opera*.

modern device of projection does not matter. What is of the essence is the sudden and at times arbitrary manner in which the action and atmosphere shift from tragedy and defeat to triumph and jubilation.

In the case of Monteverdi, the rubric in the score 'Apollo descende in una nuvola cantando' (Apollo descends in a cloud, singing) obviously refers to stage machinery, whereas Stravinsky's 'Apollo appears. He wrests the lyre from Orpheus and raises his song heavenwards' refers to miraculous movement, whether performed or projected (or imagined, as in a concert performance). Such wondrous events are by their very nature supernatural, but in the theatrical tradition they also usually fall outside the boundaries of the reasonable and/or probable. Perhaps we can clarify this by reference to divine involvements that do not satisfy the criteria of the *deus ex machina* device. In *Euridice*, the model for *Orfeo* in ways more than one, gods and goddesses also partake of the action, as they usually do in a mythological libretto. In Rinuccini's third scene we learn that Venus descends on a chariot from heaven to console and counsel Orpheus. This event is certainly comparable to Apollo's descent on a cloud in *Orfeo*, but note that in *Euridice* the descent does not involve stage machinery but is merely narrated by Arcetro. In the fourth scene of *Euridice*, the actual dialogue between Venus and Orpheus takes place, reminding students of early opera of the comparable dialogue between Speranza (the spirit of Hope) and Orpheus in *Orfeo*, where Speranza functions somewhat similarly to Rinuccini's Venus.[22] But students of the theatre would hardly consider Venus fulfilling the role of a *dea ex machina* in *Euridice*. It is not only that no *machina* is required to hoist her on to the stage: her advice to Orpheus is too reasonable, and the change in the course of action is not sufficiently sudden and spectacular. Orpheus could proceed to the underworld without the advice of Venus, and in some operas he does; it would also be unnatural and improbable if he were not to use his song to lend eloquence to his plea. Indeed, the entire action of Rinuccini, with no condition attached to the restitution of Euridice, remains more within the bounds of a reasonable tale than other treatments of the same plot. Similarly, to leap some centuries, the employment of a magic potion in *Tristan und Isolde* is a convenient stage symbol for what happens in the minds of the protagonists, but it is not indispensable. No love potion is administered in *Pelléas et Mélisande*, and the fatal passion prevails nevertheless. On the other hand, the intervention of Apollo in Monteverdi's *Orfeo* is obligatory for the reversal of fortune in the course of the action. The god of sun and light crucially changes the mind and purpose of Orpheus. The god's advice runs counter to the tale of devoted love, transmitted in Ovid and other sources, and the acceptance of his counsel by Orpheus generates dramatic and psychological surprise of some magnitude.

---

[22] In both cases the dialogue starts with the same word, 'scorto' (escorted, led): 'Scorto da immortal guida' ('Led by an immortal guide', *Euridice*, l. 398); 'Scorto da te, mio nume Speranza' ('Led by thee, my goddess Hope', *Orfeo*, l. 315).

We have already discussed, in Chapter 3, the vital way in which the *deus ex machina* technique affects plot and finale with reference to Correggio's *Cefalo* (1487) and Gluck's *Echo et Narcisse* (1779). In *Cefalo* it is the goddess Diana and in *Echo* the god Amor who suddenly and spectacularly wrench the plot from misery to happiness. Needless to say, whether we deal with Correggio in the fifteenth century, Monteverdi in the seventeenth, or Gluck in the eighteenth, we recognize the potent influence of ancient drama, notably of Euripides, where such miraculous appearances of gods ('theophanies') occur in the majority of his extant plays. That such changes brought about by the intervention of an unpredictable *deus ex machina* would be attractive to Baroque composers stands to reason. The sudden *lieto fine* would present opportunities for engendering variety: in tempo, in vocal style, in instrumentation, in fact in every facet of music used to lend expressiveness to the drama. For the cognoscenti in Monteverdi's audience, the intervention of Apollo could not but have had allegorical and Neoplatonic implications. But for many it must have been a disappointment that the *deus ex machina* did not reunite the lovers, as did Diana in Correggio's *Cefalo*, and as Amor was to do in countless operas up to Gluck's *Echo*.

This brings us to the other dramatic crux of Monteverdi's finale, which might be summed up in the term 'apotheosis': the transfer to the company of the gods, to their habitat (whether it be Olympus or the starry firmament), and the happiness found in that transfer. Here again we deal with an aspect of the finale that was not likely to please 'the million', being 'caviare to the general'. To an artist, and to the artistic mind, the sublimation and subtlety inherent in the conclusions of *Dafne* and *Orfeo* made sense: the laurel will be for ever the emblem of great and timeless poetry, and the translation of the divine singer from this vale of mortality to the place where the immortals dwell is just and right. No doubt, to dramatists such as Rinuccini and Monteverdi (and Monteverdi's views on drama must have influenced the Apollo scene) the merit of such finales was obvious. And in a way we may gauge their success as artists by the degree to which they were able to carry the fickle and frivolous section of their audience with them, and to the extent to which their procedure influenced their successors.

LATER DEVELOPMENTS

Early operas, functioning as models in the course of the seventeenth century and beyond, offer the historian a valuable means of assessing the importance of these first pilot works. These latter tended to be written for special occasions, and the festive and lavish display of all available resources was certainly among the *raisons d'être* of their gestation. To start with the choral finale (whether or not modified and prolongated by the insertion of concertino episodes), this type of conclusion was both festive and effective. Its efficacy was both social and formal: it stressed the resources and munificence of the aristocratic patron, and it signalled to the audience that the entertainment had come to a close. Until Venetian opera came of age (and certainly by the 1640s it overshadowed all other developments) Florentine, Mantuan, and Roman opera continued to employ the choral finale in the first half of the century. This is particularly true of Roman opera, patronized by the princes and institutions of the church in a manner quite analogous to the dukes and academies of northern Italy. Reference has already been made to tutti choruses in five parts in *Anima e corpo*, and in eight parts in *Eumelio* and in *Morte d'Orfeo*. To these should be added the extensive concertato finale of Landi's *Sant'Alessio* (first version 1631, revised 1634, printed score 1634). As in the case of *Anima* (alternative finale, no. 91), of *Euridice*, and of *Orfeo*, the finale of *Alessio* involves both singing and dancing: an instrumental ballet of Virtues, notated on five staves, is interposed four times between various vocal textures, which extend from a single vocal line (Religion) with bass to ensembles of four vocal parts with bass and of eight vocal parts, accompanied by instruments notated on five staves. The variety affects not only sonority and texture, but also—as one would expect—vocal style. Religion finishes her solo with a coloratura flourish of nearly fifty notes on the word 'canto', whereas the choruses stay predictably syllabic as well as homophonic.[23]

Finales involving such vocal, instrumental, and choreographic resources presuppose as a rule an institution able to provide the necessary means. And indeed the prominent examples of extensive choral finales from the later periods usually involve court patronage. The most prominent instances that spring to mind are works of Lully in the seventeenth and of Gluck in the eighteenth century. At the court of Louis XIV, Lully presided over a well-trained orchestra, chorus, and corps de ballet. Drawing on the native French tradition of the ballet de cour as well as on Roman opera imported into France by Mazarin, he also wished to please his royal master by a finale-divertissement in which his splendid orchestra provided both scope for dancing and, at times, accompanied the chorus. It is significant that his first two *tragédies lyriques*, namely *Cadmus* of 1673 and *Alceste* of 1674, provide both the humanistic and mythological subject-matter and the concertato finale associated with the birth of opera. In *Cadmus* the choral refrain is contrasted with concertino episodes for Jupiter, Venus, and Pallas; and in *Alceste* the repetitions of the triumphal chorus 'Aimez, en paix' enclose similar episodes for Straton and Cephise. Nor should we neglect the chorus of muses and shepherds that celebrates the descent of Apollo as well as the

---

[23] For the text of this finale, which employs lines of 5, 8, and 11 syllables, cf. Andrea Della Corte, *Drammi per musica*, 2 vols. (Turin, 1958), i. 263 5; musical excerpts in H. Goldschmidt, *Studien zur Geschichte der italienischen Oper im 17. Jahrhundert*, 2 vols. (Leipzig, 1901 4; repr. 1967), 237 51; the printed score, available in facsimile, gives the finale on pp. 155 82.

triumph of Hercules, Admetus, and Alcestis, since it cannot but remind us of the role played by Apollo in Peri, Monteverdi, and Stravinsky. The international influence of Lully's success was so immediate and widespread that to chronicle it here would be impossible. But not even the most cursory sketch of the choral finale could fail to mention Gluck, who in so many ways acts as a Janus-figure, summarizing earlier opera and pointing as well to future developments (e.g. Mozart).

As far as giving the chorus ample scope, no better examples could be found than Gluck's first two reform operas written on Italian librettos by Calzabigi, and later revised, with French texts, for presentation at Paris. Both at the Habsburg and at the Bourbon courts, Gluck could draw on a wealth of musical and choreographic resources. In *Orfeo* (Italian version, 1762) we are closest to early opera and its mingling of tutti, concertino, and 'ballo'. Gluck's finale is 384 bars long and consists of an opening orchestral ritornello, four orchestral dances ('balli'), and three choral ritornelli, punctuated by three concertino episodes. In this finale it is the divine intervention of Amor that prevents a tragic ending. In *Alceste* (Italian version, 1767) Apollo performs this same essential function, and the event is duly celebrated by the obligatory *lieto fine* chorus. But for good measure Gluck gives the chorus more ample scope in the penultimate number, a great concertato mourning the tragic events before the reversal of fortune: the chorus sings 'Piangi o patria' four times, punctuated by three concertino episodes. (Put differently, Gluck presents us both with a *fine tragico* and a *lieto fine*.) Naturally, Gluck did not neglect the choral finale when he composed new operas for the Parisian court, to establish himself as the successor of Lully and Rameau. His *Iphigénie en Aulide* (1774) follows the choreography of the great chaconne with a final chorus: in the first version of 1774 the priest Calchas announces the happy turn of events, whereas in the revision of 1775 the goddess Diana herself intervenes, but in *Iphigénie en Tauride* (1779) Diana brings about the peripeteia with appropriate dramatic cogency framed by the final chorus.[24]

But a different type of finale grew up in the Venetian opera-houses, a novel type of secular institution that was bound to affect all aspects of the genre. Venice boasted four such theatres by 1641, and six by the end of the century. The resultant shift from festive productions for special occasions to a system where several theatres, in the same city, produced more than one opera each year, and paid for these productions by the rental of boxes and the sale of tickets of admission, has often been described. One of the many results of this shift was a greater emphasis on solo singing, and on the fate

---

[24] I have dealt with various aspects of Gluck's choral finales in greater detail: cf. 'Expression and Revision in Gluck's *Orfeo* and *Alceste*', in Jack Westrup (ed.), *Essays Presented to Egon Wellesz* (Oxford, 1966); repr. Hortschansky (ed.), *Gluck*, 172–99; 'Des intermèdes à l'opéra: la technique du finale', in Jean Jacquot and Elie Konigson (eds.), *Les Fêtes de la Renaissance*, iii (Paris, 1975), 267–80; 'Gluck's Operas and Italian Tradition', *Chigiana*, 29–30 (1972–3), 275–81.

of the characters, portrayed by the most prominent soloists, the 'stars'. In fact, the modern operatic star system, with its emphasis on the 'divo' and the 'diva', may be said to begin with Venetian opera. However that may be, the chorus plays a much reduced role in the average Venetian opera of the seventeenth century, and as a result we frequently encounter as finale a love duet, not a chorus or a choral concertato with ballo. To put the matter differently, the *lieto fine* is articulated by the protagonists themselves, not by a chorus congratulating or exhorting them, or expressing gratitude to the divinity who has brought about this happiness. In fact, the intervention of gods and goddesses, though still met in Lully, Gluck, and Stravinsky, becomes increasingly rare in operatic plots. In so-called 'historical' operas, magnanimous kings tend to supersede gods. As to the love duet as the preferred finale formula in Venetian opera, it will be most convenient to examine, from the corpus of extant works, the two Venetian operas of Monteverdi and some of the more numerous surviving works of Cavalli written from 1640 on. It must be remembered that Venetian opera created not only professional opera composers, but also professional librettists, who deliberately inserted arias and duets in which singers could display their expertise and virtuosity. (The favourite ensemble of seventeenth-century opera is the duet, whether amatory or otherwise).

Both questions of date and of authenticity in regard to Monteverdi's last two extant operas have vexed music historians for some time. But the consensus of scholarship, following Osthoff, Curtis, and others, seems to dispose of the differences between printed librettos and manuscript scores by assigning the first performance of *Ulisse* to the year 1640 and *Poppea* to the year 1643 (that is, the season from 26 December 1642 to the end of the carnival, 1643). Most scholars accept the love duet between Ulysses and Penelope, which concludes the score of *Ulisse*, as by Monteverdi. On the other hand, the famous and beautiful love duet between Nero and Poppaea that concludes the extant manuscript scores, but does not occur in the libretto, is now sometimes credited to Sacrati (text by Ferrari).[25] But it does not matter who wrote the music, as long as we know that both extant manuscript versions (in Venice and Naples) end with a love duet, and that the opera was performed in that manner in the middle of the seventeenth century, even if some other composer completed the portions of the score left unfinished by Monteverdi. Both *Ulisse* and *Poppea* must have undergone considerable revision before the extant manuscript scores were copied. And in both instances the later Venetian tradition seems to have superseded the

---

[25] The incredibly complicated transmission of scenario, librettos, and manuscript scores is summarized in Alan Curtis, 'La Poppea Impasticciata, or Who Wrote the Music to *L'Incoronazione* (1643)?' *JAMS* 42 (1989), 23–54, with reference to Paolo Fabbri, *Monteverdi* (Turin, 1985), and Alessandra Chiarelli, ' "L'incoronazione di Poppea" o "Il Nerone", problemi di filologia testuale', *RIM* 9 (1974), 117–51. Some scholars ascribe the duet to Monteverdi, others to Sacrati, others to Ferrari. Cf. Ellen Rosand, *Opera in Seventeenth-Century Venice: The Creation of a Genre* (Berkeley, Calif., 1991), 336.

earlier humanistic traditions of Florence and Mantua. The libretto of *Ulisse* is divided into five acts, but the extant score (in Vienna) falls into three acts. Similarly, the plans for the finale of *Poppea* seem to have included a 'coro d'amori' (a chorus of the spirits of love, who attended the god Amor), but no music for such a chorus survives in the Venetian score.[26] On the other hand, the Neapolitan score preserves an interesting older type of finale, a choral concertato of about 190 bars, followed by the more modern love duet in the Venetian style.

When we proceed to the numerous scores of Monteverdi's pupil Cavalli from 1640 on, we have numerically a better base for generalizations, but we also deal with a composer who more decisively affected the development of the genre of opera in the seventeenth century. In his works the love duet frequently functions as finale, though there are exceptions to this rule as well. For instance, in *Apollo e Dafne*, where Daphne is transformed into a laurel tree, as we know, no amatory duo concludes the proceedings; similarly, when Cavalli worked for Paris (*Ercole amante*), with its established choral tradition, he adjusted the finale to that. But in many of Cavalli's operas, notably those that established his fame between 1641 and 1651 (mostly to librettos by Faustini, a professional librettist), the concluding ensemble is a duet of lovers (to which sometimes by way of extension a trio or a quartet is added). The music sounds like music for soloists, not homophonic choral music, although a happy ensemble for two soloists is rarely free from consecutive thirds and sixths. But whereas the music of the choral finales sounds festive and seems to indicate a formal conclusion, Cavalli's finale duets—with their shapely solo melodies—sound sensuous. Happiness is expressed not by increased sonority and dense texture, but by 'catchy', chirpy tunes and the occasional expressive melisma, underpinned by a tiny bit of imitation between the voices. Good examples of such duets occur in *Ormindo* (1644) and *Rosinda* (1651), both to librettos by Faustini.[27]

In metrical matters, too, the finale of Venetian and other later operas differed from the formula that had proved so successful in the early works in that octosyllabic verse was not necessarily favoured. Venetian librettists tended to interrupt the flow of recitative by rhymed lyrics in lines of less than eleven syllables (often ottonari, settenari, or senari). And such lyrics, functioning in the score as 'closed' numbers, increasingly punctuated the flow of 'open' recitative in the course of the century. Thus these lyrics provided both musical and prosodic variety. Doni articulates this need for metrical change. He distinguishes between long lines ('versi lunghi', e.g. endecasillabi)

---

[26] Cf. Curtis, 'Poppea', 34; Malipiero's edn. of *Poppea*, 232, 242, 243–6, 272–80. Curtis has followed his article with a new edition of *Poppea* (London: Novello, 1989); the present writer offers a more detailed discussion of the *Poppea* finale in a review in *JRMA* 116 (1991), 307–11.

[27] For modern edns., cf. Leppard's edn. of *Ormindo* (London: Faber, 1969), 213–15 (in the original manuscript in the Biblioteca Marciana, Venice, fos. 200–202); Sternfeld, 'Des intermèdes à l'opéra', 275–8.

and lines of medium length ('versi mezzani', e.g. ottonari, settenari, senari). He then advises that in stage music

after thirty long lines it would be as well to have ten or twelve lines of medium length of this or that kind, according to the subject-matter, primarily settenari for serious or a variety of other matters . . . and also ottonari for some pleasant and very cheerful matters [*e gli ottonari in alcune leggiere, e molto allegre*].[28]

Lines of even numbers of syllables (e.g. octosyllabic or hexasyllabic verse), with their regularly recurring accents, do provide lyrical islands in the course of both early and Venetian opera. The regularity of accents made them apt for singing and dancing (notions never far away from the closed numbers of seventeenth-century opera), but after 1640 or so they were not restricted to finales, and finales were no longer necessarily cast in ottonari. On the other hand, the principle of metrical variety, which had influenced Rinuccini's finale formula, continued to hold its sway over the operatic libretto.

DRAMATIC STRUCTURE

The musical and prosodic elements employed in the finale were of course dictated by the shaping of the plot, since both voice and verse had to correspond to the mood, the subject-matter, and the milieu with which the action concluded. In the case of such plots as those involving Orpheus, Ariadne, Echo, or Alcestis, the manner in which the *lieto fine* was reached differed considerably over the decades. *Euridice* and *Orfeo* were rather short operas, lasting less than two hours, with a limited cast that included only one pair of lovers. It was the happiness or misery of that pair (or at least of one of the protagonists) that dominated most of the action. The three obvious possibilities in such dramatic situations were to leave the couple at the end happily united (Rinuccini–Peri), to forget about the protagonists and provide a bacchanalian finale (Striggio), or to have the lover leave the beloved behind and join the gods (Monteverdi). But in the course of the century, as opera became a standardized entertainment, both the size of the cast and number of possible dramatic complications expanded, with a consequent increase in the length of the libretto and the score. Intrigues and disguises invaded the plot, and the single couple formed part of an ensemble of three or four lovers; and what with attendants and confidants, three couples might be happily united at the end of the opera.

It may readily be seen that an expansion of the cast and of the element of intrigue are essential to the change from the simple plots of Daphne and Orpheus to the compound plots of Venetian and Neapolitan opera. In the case of the myth of Orpheus the entering wedge is provided by Aristaeus,

---

[28] Ch. VII of *Trattato della musica scenica*; Doni, *Lyra*, ii. 19; repr. Solerti, *Origini*, 207.

a rival of Orpheus for the love of Eurydice. He occurs in Virgil, and with his impeccable classical pedigree he appears in the prehistory and history of opera from Poliziano to Birtwistle. In Poliziano he plays a minor role at the beginning of the action and is forgotten after Euridice's death; in Rinuccini's and Striggio's librettos he is entirely omitted. But in Luigi Rossi's *Orfeo* (a fundamentally Roman opera, first performed at Paris in 1647) his love for Euridice provides occasion for incident and intrigue, and we shall encounter him again in the multiple plots of some later operas. But these, as a rule, have more than one couple in the plot, as we have said. Such multiple pairs of lovers, of course, are not restricted to opera. We meet them in sixteenth-century drama, such as Shakespeare's *Midsummer Night's Dream* or, nearer to Italian stage music, in Guarini's *Pastor fido*. It is interesting that Busenello, who functioned as librettist for late Monteverdi and Cavalli, felt obliged to apologize for introducing additional love affairs into his plot. He does so in the preface of his *Amori d'Apollo e di Dafne* (Cavalli, 1641; libretto printed 1656): in addition to Daphne and Apollo he introduces Procris and Cephalus, as well as Aurora and Tithonus. This, Busenello feels, may induce some critics to fear that the unity of action ('unità della favola') was being damaged by such multifarious love affairs ('duplicità degl'amori'). But he justifies his procedure by reference to the *Pastor fido*, where the love of Mirtillo and Amarilli is paralleled by that of Silvio and Dorinda.

The reference to the 'unity of action' reminds us of the so-called Aristotelian unities of time, place, and action; and the whole set of rules and conventions so rigidly rehearsed by the classicists and neo-Aristotelians of the seventeenth century in Western Europe in general, and in France in particular. Aristotle says very little, if anything, about the unities of time and place, just as Horace probably never realized that a single sentence of his would spawn such great numbers of five-act dramas and operas. But whether justified by the precedent of ancient drama or not, literary critics of the seventeenth century believed in these rules, and the French *tragédie classique* followed them, and—in the wake of the success of Lully—influenced some operatic librettos. This applies to the 'unities' as well as to the 'fivefold division'. As far as the unities go, even earlier opera with its changes from upper to underworld, for instance, was always closer to the live theatre in England (Shakespeare), Spain (Lope, Calderón), and Italy itself (*commedia dell'arte*) than to French *tragédie classique*. And in Venetian opera the intercourse between mortals and immortals, demigods, demons, and ghosts made unity of place as difficult, as unity of action was endangered by a constant quest for novelty of plot and dramatic variety.

In regard to act-division, too, Venetian opera had more affinities with theatrical tradition than with humanistic learning. Certainly, the majority of operas after 1640 are divided into three acts, rather than into five acts or five scenes. The case of Monteverdi's *Ulisse* has already been mentioned:

the printed libretto is in five acts, but Monteverdi's manuscript score is in three acts. The latter is characteristic of later developments, including the eighteenth century. But there are exceptions to this rule. Lully's *tragédies lyriques* are all in five acts, and following their great success, and the general respect in which Corneille, Racine, and Quinault (Lully's librettist) were held, several Italian librettists at the turn of the seventeenth and eighteenth centuries experimentally revived the fivefold division. Among them were Girolamo Frigimelica-Roberti, who wrote eleven librettos in five acts (set to music by Pollarolo, A. Scarlatti, Caldara, and others), and Apostolo Zeno, who more often divided his *drammi* into three acts but nevertheless experimented fourteen times with the fivefold division (set to music by Pollarolo, Gasparini, Caldara, and others). With both these poets and several of their contemporaries the five-act structure is merely a tell-tale of the general influence of the *tragédie classique*, which naturally also affected the subject-matter of these librettos. But the general predominance of the three-act form is nevertheless attested by Metastasio's *drammi per musica*, probably the texts most frequently set to music in the history of opera, all of which are cast in three acts, although in their lofty and serious tone they by no means ignore the reforms of Zeno and the achievements of his French models.[29] Regarding the earlier seventeenth century, Table 5.5 shows several tendencies. First, the early existence of the three-act form in Roman opera, which seemed more ready to respond to native and Spanish theatrical precedents (1600 *Anima*, 1606, 1613, 1632, 1633). It also demonstrates the general ascendancy of this type of organization in Venetian opera (starting 1637), but examples of threefold division there are so plentiful that no extensive documentation of this has been deemed necessary. On the other hand, the survival, sparse as it was, of operas cast in five acts seemed worth recording. It is interesting to observe that for Venetian operas in that form we frequently depend on librettos and scenarios, since no extant scores survive. The third column also includes operas with no division into acts or scenes, provided end-of-scene choruses and other considerations indicate the traditional, humanistic fivefold division.

SIMPLE VERSUS MULTIPLE PLOTS

Ultimately, though, the main difference between early opera and later developments hinged less on act-division than on the contrast between simple and multiple plots, and the nature of the happiness at which the conclusion

---

[29] For a discussion of the influence of *tragédie classique* on Italian opera see three publications by Reinhard Strohm: *Die italienische Oper im 18. Jahrhundert* (Taschenbücher zur Musikwissenschaft, 25; Wilhelmshaven, 1979) (of which a revised English edn. is in course of preparation); 'Die Tragedia per Musica als Repertoirestück: Zwei Hamburger Opern von G. M. Orlandini', *HJMw* 5 (1981), 37–54; ' "Tragédie" into "Dramma per musica" ', *Informazioni e studi vivaldiani*, 9 (1988), 14–25; 10 (1989), 57–102; 11 (1990), 11–26; 12 (1991), 47–75.

of the drama arrives. In the following survey of Orpheus operas after Peri and Monteverdi, the accent will therefore be on the presence or absence of a single pair of lovers, and of the happy reunion of the couple (or couples).

TABLE 5.5. *Division into three and five acts*

Date	Title	Number of acts	Librettist	Composer
1598	*Dafne*[a]	[5]	Rinuccini	Peri
Feb. 1600	*Anima e corpo*	3	?Manni	Cavalieri
Oct. 1600	*Euridice*	[5]	Rinuccini	Peri
Oct. 1600	*Cefalo*[a]	5	Chiabrera	Caccini[b]
1606	*Eumelio*	3	De Cupis and Tirletti	Agazzari
1607	*Orfeo*	5	Striggio	Monteverdi
1608	*Arianna*[a]	[5]	Rinuccini	Monteverdi
1613	*David musicus*[c]	3	Donati	Catalani
1619	*Morte d'Orfeo*	5	?Landi	Landi
1626	*Catena d'Adone*	5	Tronsarelli	Mazzocchi
1627	*Dafne*[c]	5	Opitz	Schütz
1632	*Sant'Alessio*	3	Rospigliosi	Landi
1633	*Erminia*	3	Rospigliosi	M. Rossi
1637	*Andromeda*[c]	3	Ferrari	Manelli
1638	*Maga fulminata*[c]	3	Ferrari	Manelli
1638	*Nozze di Teti*	3	Persiani	Cavalli
1639	*Delia*[c]	3	Strozzi	Manelli
1639	*Adone*[c]	5	Vendramin	Manelli
1640	*Ritorno d'Ulisse*[d]	5	Badoaro	Monteverdi
1640	*Apollo e Dafne*	3	Busenello	Cavalli
1641	*Didone*	3	Busenello	Cavalli
1641	*Finta pazza*	3	Strozzi	Sacrati
1641	*Nozze d'Enea*[c]	5	anonymous	Monteverdi
1642	*Amore innamorato*[c]	5	Fusconi	Cavalli
1642	*Poppea*	3	Busenello	Monteverdi
1644	*Ulisse errante*[c]	5	Badoaro	Sacrati
1646	*Giulio Cesare*[c]	5	Busenello	Cavalli?

[a] Only excerpts extant.
[b] With contributions by other composers.
[c] Score not extant.
[d] Score in three acts.

Landi's *Morte d'Orfeo*, the choral finale of which has already been discussed, is a curious work. Its score, printed at Venice in 1619, is extant, but we do not know for which occasion it was performed, or who wrote the libretto (perhaps Landi himself). Internal evidence suggests that the author knew the scores of Peri and Monteverdi: it is a mythological opera, subdivided into five acts, and ends with the apotheosis of Orpheus. The action, which begins after the death of Eurydice, deals more with Bacchus and the Bacchic women than with the protagonist's beloved. But Eurydice appears in one scene preceding the finale. Her shade (*ombra*) comes upon the stage, and, having drunk from the river Lethe, she has forgotten Orpheus so completely that she neither recognizes him nor reciprocates his desire for reunion. Only after this bitter disappointment does our hero accept the advice of Mercury, and lets the latter lead him to Jove and the gods. Such apotheosis, or 'stellification', reminds us inevitably of Monteverdi; and, as in Rinuccini and Monteverdi, no rivalry (Aristaeus) or second couple interferes with the dramatic concentration on Orpheus' love for Eurydice. The term 'stellification' is used by the poet John Ashbery in a text set to music by Elliott Carter in 1978, and in Table 5.6 the various compositions referred to in the remainder of this chapter are listed in chronological order.[30]

TABLE 5.6. *The Orpheus myth after Rinuccini and Monteverdi, 1619–1986*

Date	Place	Composer and Title	Librettist
1619	?Rome	Landi, *Morte d'Orfeo*	?Landi
1647	Paris	Luigi Rossi, *Orfeo*	Buti
1672	Venice	Sartorio, *Orfeo*	Aureli
1698	Brunswick	Keiser, *Orpheus*	Bressand
1715	Vienna	Fux, *Orfeo*	Pariati
1750	Vienna	Wagenseil, *Euridice*	?
1762	Vienna	Gluck, *Orfeo*	Calzabigi
1791	[London]	Haydn, *L'anima del filosofo ossia Orfeo ed Euridice*	Badini
1827	[Paris]	Berlioz, *Mort d'Orphée* (cantata)	Berton
1858	Paris	Offenbach, *Orphée*	Crémieux and Halévy
1948	New York	Stravinsky, *Orpheus* (ballet)	Balanchine
1950	[Paris]	Auric, *Orphée* (film)	Cocteau
1978	[New York]	Carter, *Syringa* (cantata)	Ashbery
1984	Boston	Tippett, *Mask of Time* (oratorio)	Rilke[a]
1986	London	Birtwistle, *Mask of Orpheus*	Zinovieff

[a] Section 9.1, 'The Severed Head', after Rilke's *Sonette an Orpheus*.

[30] This chart is less detailed than Table 1 of Ch. 1; however, it extends into the 20th c.

Apotheosis also provides the denouement of Rossi's *Orfeo* of 1647. The Bacchic women are ready to destroy Orpheus (as they had been in Poliziano, Striggio, and Landi), but Jupiter intervenes—a true *deus ex machina*—and decrees the immortality of the divine singer and his song.[31] It is difficult to believe that Rossi and his librettist did not know the scores of their predecessors, Monteverdi and Landi, and probably also of Peri. On the other hand, this work also shows itself to be of the 1640s: it is in three acts and the plot accommodates complications to which a single pair of lovers is ill suited. As mentioned earlier, it is the rivalry between Orpheus and Aristaeus for the favour of Eurydice, and the championing of their respective causes by Juno and Venus, that provides the necessary intrigues and changes of fortune. At one point Venus, disguised as a fortune-teller, endeavours to assist the cause of Aristaeus. Certainly, rivalries and enlargements of the cast to more than two lovers continued to be used in subsequent librettos. But apotheosis rather than a happily united couple did not, on the whole, seem to suit the operatic boards, and, with the exception of Keiser's German opera of 1698, it is the bringing together of lovers that the finales of mythological operas of the seventeenth and eighteenth centuries primarily aim at. (Cantatas and ballets of the nineteenth and twentieth centuries are another matter.)

Certainly, the figure of Aristaeus proved useful in the operas of Sartorio, Fux, and Wagenseil, in all of which he contributes to the prolongation of the plot. But it must be owned that the love of Orpheus and Eurydice remains curiously unfulfilled in Sartorio's successful *Orfeo* of 1672. Its librettist, Aureli, presents us with the customary two couples of the second half of the century: Orpheus and Eurydice, Aristaeus and Autonoe.[32] This provides the opportunities for jealousy between Orpheus and Aristaeus, as one would expect. But the conclusion of the drama is odd indeed. After Orpheus has looked back and lost Eurydice a second time, he first laments her loss, and then, in misogynist manner, renounces all women. But in the last three scenes neither he nor Eurydice appears. Instead the dramatic knot is untied by bringing Aristaeus back to his true love, Autonoe, and the finale proper (*scena ultima*) is sung by five characters: Aristaeus and Autonoe (who are happily united); Thetys and her son Achilles (where Thetys is happy to spirit Achilles safely away from the dangers of the Trojan war); and the old nurse Erinda. Thus the compound plot permits the finale to include a love duet, but notwithstanding the title and the expectation of the audience, it is performed by the wrong (or at least secondary) couple. The second loss of Eurydice and the second lament of Orpheus are reminiscent of Monteverdi,

---

[31] Cf. Goldschmidt, *Studien*, 79–85, 299–311; Henry Prunières, *L'Opéra italien en France avant Lully* (Paris, 1913), 109–10.

[32] Score and libretto are available in facs., ed. E. Rosand (Drammaturgia musicale veneta, 6; Milan, 1983). The numbering of the scenes in libretto and score does not always agree.

whose score must still have been known in the later seventeenth century,[33] but the happiness of Aristaeus and his beloved harks back more to the finale of Peri. How perverse, though, that to achieve the final love duet, the librettist had to pair off the rival of Orpheus, Aristaeus, with the girl to whom he should have been faithful in the first place! Perhaps it was the constant desire for novelty in the Venetian repertory that produced such unexpected variations. No such irregularities, however, occur in the next three Orpheus operas to be chronicled here, since these were written for courtly occasions, and there the happiness of the main couple was to be taken for granted. These festive works, entitled 'componimento' or 'festa teatrale', differ from the ordinary *dramma per musica* by their frankly occasional nature.

For instance, in Fux's *Orfeo ed Euridice*, written for the birthday of the Habsburg emperor in 1715, the finale conspicuously draws an analogy between Jove's birthday and that of the emperor. Clearly, on such an occasion the hero and heroine of the myth (and the title) must be united. But since a slight amount of complication and rivalry is *de rigueur*, the beauty of Eurydice receives attention not only from the obligatory Aristaeus, but also from the king of the underworld, Pluto. So in this compound plot, the second couple, happily rejoined, are Pluto and Proserpina. A chastening god of love ('Amore pudico') sees to it that Proserpina's jealousy of Eurydice proves groundless.

Several features of Fux's opera are new, compared with Monteverdi, Landi, Rossi, and Sartorio: for the first time since 1600 Orpheus and Eurydice are happily reunited at the end of the opera, as they are in Rinuccini. And, again as in Rinuccini, Pluto's release of Eurydice is unconditional; there is no second loss (and no second lament). There is no doubt that Rinuccini's libretto was known to poets and theorists throughout the eighteenth century: traces of the 1600 libretto are to be detected from Fux to Haydn.[34] Another feature that distinguishes Fux's *Orfeo* from the average Venetian or Neapolitan opera is the prominent employment of the chorus, which adds variety to a diet of solo singing. Of the twenty-four numbers of the score, three are choral: no. 6, a 'coro d'amori' (spirits of love, attendant on Amor), no. 19, a 'coro d'ombre infernali' (spirits of the underworld, attendant on Pluto), and no. 23, a final chorus that concludes the opera and is repeated after a concertino episode for Amor, no. 24. This

---

[33] One fingerprint of Monteverdi's influence is perhaps the phrase with which Orpheus pleads with the underworld, 'return to me *(rendetemi)* my beloved'. In several variations, the phrase, emphatically repeated, appears in musical fashionings of the Orpheus story: three times in Monteverdi's *Orfeo* ('rendetemi 'l mio ben', l. 411, facs., p. 68); twice in Cavalli's *Egisto*, where, in a mad scene, the hero imagines himself to be Orpheus ('rendetemi, rendetemi Euridice'); twice in Rossi's *Orfeo* ('rendetemi . . . l'amato bene'; Goldschmidt, *Studien*, 309); and twice in Sartorio's *Orfeo* ('rendetemi Euridice', score, fo. 81ᵛ).

[34] Cf. J. H. van der Meer, *J. J. Fux als Opernkomponist*, 2 vols. (Bilthoven, 1961), 130 *et passim*; also the facs. edn. of the score in the series Italian Opera, 1640–1770, ed. H. M. Brown, vol. 19. Wagenseil's *Euridice* is reproduced in the same series, vol. 75, ed. E. Weimer.

final dismissal of the audience (*licenza*) is preceded by a love duet for Orpheus and Eurydice, no. 22. We have here, then, as in the Neapolitan score of Monteverdi's *Poppea*, two types of finale following each other. This conspicuous employment of the chorus may be partly due to the influence of Lully, but there also existed at the Habsburg court a native choral tradition, which Fux passed on to his pupil and successor, Wagenseil, and eventually to Gluck. (To the average music student Fux, after all, is known as a composer of church music and a teacher of counterpoint.)

The chorus also plays a prominent part in the finale of Wagenseil's *Euridice*, a pasticcio to which several other composers contributed arias, among them Hasse, Holzbauer, and Jommelli. No fewer than seven choruses are to be found in the last thirty-seven pages of the score,[35] which points forward to Gluck rather than conforming to the norms of Metastasian opera. The work was performed at Vienna in 1750, for the name-day ('giorno onomastico') of Maria Anna of Habsburg, and, as one would expect, the rivalry between Orpheus and Aristaeus prolongs the action, but does not interfere with the expected *lieto fine*, where Orpheus is reunited with Eurydice, and Aristaeus with his beloved (here called 'Egeria', not 'Autonoe', as in Sartorio). In fact, Rinuccini–Peri are recalled not only in what may be called the 'happy couple' formula, but there is also no interdict against looking back and no second loss. What is more, in the preface and synopsis ('argomento') the anonymous librettist apologizes for his departure from the classical plot in order to avoid 'un fine troppo tragico'. Even the title *Euridice* is more reminiscent of Rinuccini than of Striggio.

Gluck's *Orfeo* of 1762 was, like Wagenseil's opera, a 'festa teatrale', occasioned by the court calendar of Vienna, in this case the name-day of the Habsburg emperor. Its cardinal importance in the history of opera has been long recognized and described in considerable detail several times.[36] The importance of the Gluckian 'reform' for our purposes is the 'noble simplicity' of Calzabigi's and Gluck's design. Winckelmann's conception of the antique as 'edle Einfalt und stille Größe' (noble simplicity and quiet grandeur) dominated the later eighteenth century. Certainly, the style of *Orfeo* (and also of *Alceste* of 1767) exemplify Winckelmann's notions of Greek art as noble, serene, and—last but not least—simple. Applied to the Orpheus plot, this meant for Gluck a return to the single couple of Rinuccini. Gone was Aristaeus, his jealousy, his intrigues, and his Autonoe (or Egeria). This simplification and the consequent loss of the compound plot provided—on the other hand—time for a more extensive portrayal of the terror of the underworld and of the bliss of Elysium. It also permitted the eloquence of the second loss of Eurydice and Orpheus' subsequent lament, an aspect of

[35] Concerning the facs., see n. 34.

[36] A good summary of modern scholarship on Gluck will be found in Klaus Hortschansky (ed.), *Gluck und die Opernreform* (Wege der Forschung, 163; Darmstadt, 1989).

Ovid and Virgil ignored by Rinuccini, Fux, and Wagenseil. Simplicity is also at the heart of Gluck's dramatic contrasts of sonorities: the divine solo singer versus the chorus, Orpheus' lyre versus the orchestra of the furies. The importance of the chorus throughout the opera, and particularly in the extensive concertato finale, already described, was of course influenced by Lully and Rameau, but also by the Austrian tradition, as exemplified by Fux and Wagenseil. There are several traces of Rinuccini, of which we may mention two: a preface that apologizes for having departed from the denouement of the classical sources to arrive at a *lieto fine* ('ho dovuto cambiar la catastrofe'); and the fact that Orpheus finds happiness not in apotheosis but in reunion with his beloved.

We cannot leave the topic of Gluck, of which we have hardly scratched the surface, without reference to his *Alceste*, because his second Viennese reform opera also illustrates the contrast between the multiple plots of Italian opera from Faustini to Metastasio and single pairs of lovers, usually imitating classical precedent and influenced by neo-Aristotelian ideas of the unity of action. The main classical source of the Alcestis plot (Euripides) has only one pair of lovers, but Venetian opera (Ziani–Aureli, 1660) expanded and complicated the action by the introduction of a second pair. This tradition was continued by various operas with various titles (*Alceste, Admeto, Alcide,* etc.), which in several ways were indebted to the Venetian tradition. Of these we may quote the operas of Strungk (1693), Draghi (1699), Schürmann (1719), and Handel (1727) as examples. Opposed to this multiplicity of lovers and complications is the more classicistic *Alceste* of Lully and Quinault (1674), which not only restricts the action to the single pair of Alcestis and Admetus, but which is in many ways related to the early humanistic court operas (choral finale, act-division, *deus ex machina,* etc.). Both Gluck and Calzabigi knew Lully's *tragédie lyrique,* and their *Alceste* of 1767, with its simple plot and its choral finale, exercised a crucial influence on subsequent treatment of the Alcestis plot, notably the operas of Guglielmi and Schweitzer in the eighteenth century, and of Wellesz and Talma in the twentieth.[37]

Haydn's opera *L'anima del filosofo ossia Orfeo ed Euridice* (The soul of the philosopher, or Orpheus and Eurydice) was intended for performance in London in 1791, but never staged or completed.[38] Still, the extant excerpts are sufficiently substantial to warrant several conclusions about the work and

[37] For further discussion of the Alcestis plot from 1660 to 1962, cf. A. A. Abert in Hortschansky (ed.), *Gluck,* 50–82; Sternfeld, 'Deus ex machina', *New Grove Dictionary of Opera* (in press); classical and operatic dictionaries s.v. 'Admetus', 'Alcestis', etc.

[38] Cf. H. Wirth's edn. in Haydn's *Werke,* ser. 25, vol. 13 (1974); Silke Leopold, 'Haydn und die Tradition der Orpheus-Opern', *Musica,* 36 (1982), 131–5; Curtis Price, 'Italian Opera and Arson in Late 18th-Century London', *JAMS* 42 (1989), 55–107, esp. 60, 88, 96, 99. Silke Leopold has also kindly put at my disposal the typescript of an article, unpublished as of June 1989, entitled 'Haydn: L'anima del filosofo ossia Orfeo ed Euridice'. I am much indebted to Leopold for sharing her thoughts and researches with me; most of our thoughts about Haydn's finale coincide.

its finale. Although reference to Aristaeus (here misnamed 'Arideo') and his love for Eurydice occurs at the beginning of the opera, he himself is not a member of the small cast, and his role is even less important than it was in Poliziano. Haydn and his librettist Badini return effectively to the simple plot of Peri–Rinuccini, as Gluck had done some thirty years earlier. That Badini must have studied Rinuccini's libretto becomes clear from the fact that eleven lines from the underworld scene of 1600 reappear in Haydn's opera.[39]

The conclusion of the opera, as preserved in the most comprehensive extant score (the version now at Paris) is strange and tragic indeed. After Orpheus has lost Eurydice a second time and lamented his misfortune, he encounters the Bacchic women and renounces them in misogynist fashion; they poison him, but are themselves punished and drowned due to a storm. The chorus, which has played a conspicuous role throughout the opera, thus concludes the score in a number that displays Haydn's orchestral and choral mastery. But such a *fine tragico* both for Orpheus and the Bacchic women runs counter to what we know about librettos of the eighteenth century in general, and Haydn's late operas in particular. Leopold has suggested that only the choral portions of the work's conclusion are extant, and that the original plan (whether completed or not) had Genio (genius) function as a *deus ex machina* and bring about the inevitable *lieto fine*. Genio preaches the virtues of self-control and moderation, of the 'philosophy' alluded to in Haydn's title, and also stressed in Mozart's *Zauberflöte* (which dates from the same year, 1791), and in Terrasson's *Sethos* (discussed in Ch. 1); in fact all these works of the eighteenth century are related to the Neoplatonic moderation that Apollo recommends to Orpheus in Monteverdi. But just what kind of finale the exhortations of Genio would have led to is difficult to say: it may have been a happy reunion of Orpheus and Eurydice, corresponding to the completion of the trials of Tamino and Pamina in Mozart, or it may have been an apotheosis, reminiscent of a few seventeenth-century operas. And with such (and other) unresolved questions we must take leave of this merest sketch of the finale, as exemplified in the Orpheus operas of the seventeenth and eighteenth centuries. Whether the plots are simple or compound, most of them show familiarity with Rinuccini's and Peri's model, which was not only known to such observers of the operatic genre as Algarotti, Arteaga, and Burney,[40] but also studied and emulated by the librettists who served the composers of the eighteenth century from Fux to Haydn.

---

[39] Cf. Solerti, *Albori*, ii. 133 4, ll. 543 53; Wirth's edn., 217; no libretto for Haydn's opera is extant; we depend on three manuscript copies of the score now in Berlin (autograph), Budapest, and Paris.

[40] Algarotti, *Saggio* (1755); Arteaga, *Rivoluzioni* (1783 5), i. 190; Burney, *History* (1776 89), iv. 23 7; cf. also the entry on 'Rinuccini' in *Nuovo Vogel*, iii. 22.

THE IMMORTALITY OF MUSIC

No doubt there were many reasons for this. When Arteaga opined that Rinuccini's libretto was the best written in Italy ('il migliore scritto in Italia') up to the time of Metastasio, he was judging him, as we are, for his valour as a poet, for the 'singability' of his verse, and for the imaginative way with which he positioned the lyrical stations within the dramatic structure. The concluding such station is, of course, the finale, the summing up with which the audience is left, and in this regard the final impression created by the finales of Peri and Monteverdi are different indeed. In Rinuccini–Peri (as in Gluck) the majority of listeners thinks of Orpheus as a lover, faithful beyond death, and rewarded by the gods with happiness and reunion with his beloved. This emphasis on love, this particular way of untying the knot and arriving at the *lieto fine*, undoubtedly appealed to librettists, composers, and audiences of the seventeenth and eighteenth centuries, and was one of the main causes for the popularity and influence of Rinuccini's libretto up to Gluck and Haydn. On the other hand, Monteverdi's finale dismisses us with another impression: it concentrates not on the amorous union of the protagonists and the happiness they bring each other; rather, it stresses the excellence and exquisiteness of Orpheus' art, and of poetry and music in general, of 'singen und sagen', of 'voice and verse'. It is the victory of the creative artist, of the 'maker' of song, that brings him as his reward immortality. Such an interpretation would obviously be attractive to poets and composers, and indeed to anyone endowed with artistic sensitivity and imagination, but would hardly fit the expectations of the aristocratic patrons and audiences, so prominent until the Congress of Vienna.

The apotheosis of Orpheus, as suggested by Monteverdi, appears only occasionally in the operas of the two centuries immediately succeeding him. True, we encounter it in Landi and Rossi, and in both these instances it may be influenced by an ancient source, such as Hyginus, as well as by Monteverdi. But the accounts of antiquity give intimations of immortality not only by the transfer of Orpheus or his lyre to heaven. As we have seen in Chapter 1, both Ovid and Hyginus relate another wondrous event. After Orpheus has been killed by the Bacchic women, his head and lyre—floating on the river—lament. Now, that the severed head should sing or speak, and that the lyre should sound without Orpheus playing it, is miraculous, and must, to the poetic and allegorical mind, be another token of the permanence, of the immortality, of music. This aspect of the myth, the severed head and lyre floating and sounding, is difficult to depict on the stage and appears only rarely in opera and ballet. But in Keiser's *Orpheus* of 1698[41] head and lyre float on the river Hebrus, as they do in Hyginus, producing

    [41] Cf. Klaus Zelm, *Die Opern Reinhard Keisers* (Munich and Salzburg, 1975); Leopold, 'Haydn', 133.

their astounding and symbolic sonorities. On the whole, though, the episode of head and lyre is more likely to occur in poetry, and in cantatas and oratorios based on such poetry. One thinks of Rilke's *Sonette an Orpheus*, of Berlioz's *Mort d'Orphée* of 1827, and of Tippett's 'Severed Head' (based on Rilke) in the *Mask of Time* of 1984. Both in Berlioz and Tippett, the 'miracle on the river Hebrus' is not followed by apotheosis or 'stellification' (Carter–Ashbery, 1978). On the other hand, in Stravinsky it is only apotheosis that testifies to the immortality of music, and it is just the lyre, not Orpheus himself, that is translated to heaven. But both these miracles make manifest the permanence, the continuity, of music beyond death, and both of them—in terms of instrumentation—are often represented by the sound of the harp and soft strings. That the harp should be used to indicate the lyre (or kithara) of the ancients is not surprising. It certainly plays a prominent role in treatments of the Orpheus plot by Monteverdi, Gluck, Haydn, Berlioz, and Stravinsky, to name but a few examples.

The contrast in Monteverdi between the louder orchestra (which includes trombones and cornetts) associated with the underworld and the soft strings in general, and the harp in particular, associated with Orpheus and his pastoral companions, has often been commented upon. The performance rubrics, at the beginning and end of the underworld scenes, make clear the instrumentational contrast between the world of Charon and Pluto and the gentle lyre of Orpheus. At the beginning trombones, cornetts, regals, etc. start to sound (*entrano*), and viols, harpsichords, etc. are silent (*tacciono*). At the conclusion of the infernal scenes it is the trombones, cornetts, and regals that fall silent, and the viols, harpsichords, and harps that start to play (*entrano a sonare*). And the double harp provides a prominent obbligato accompaniment to Orpheus' plea to Charon (third stanza).[42]

In Gluck's opera the harp plays a prominent role in the small concertino orchestra that symbolizes the power of Orpheus' music, accompanies his singing, and contrasts with the main orchestra (including cornetts and other loud instruments), which accompanies the furies. This is the one score that, in one revision or another, remained in repertory ever since its first performance. It is a fair assumption that Gluck's use of the harp to portray the lyre of Orpheus was known to Haydn, Berlioz, and Stravinsky; and also—*mirabile dictu*—to Beethoven, whose Fourth Piano Concerto (slow movement) shows how the soloist pleads successfully with a grim and opposing tutti.[43] That Beethoven should use the piano, to which he felt particularly close, rather than the harp, is readily understandable. In fact, when a soloist, representing

---

[42] For the complete Italian text of these performance rubrics, cf. Whenham, *Monteverdi: Orfeo*, 142; also facs. of 1609 score, pp. 10–11, 47 (bottom), 58, 88.

[43] The comparison between Beethoven's slow movement and Gluck's underworld scene was probably first made by A. B. Marx, not by Liszt; cf. Owen Jander, 'Beethoven's "Orpheus in Hades": The *Andante con moto* of the Fourth Piano Concerto', *19th Century Music*, 8 (1985), 195–212.

the forces of light, gains victory over opposing forces, various timbres have
been used: Mozart's Tamino, another Orpheus, prevails with a flute, Papageno
with a glockenspiel, and Tippett occasionally employs the xylophone.

But to return to the harp after Gluck, we may note its employment in
Haydn, Berlioz, and Stravinsky. To leap from Haydn to Stravinsky seems to
create a chronological gap of surprising magnitude. (Berlioz's cantata, though
of historical importance, is too rarely performed to matter.) But it must be
admitted that the nineteenth century did not provide a climate propitious
for mythological operas in general, or new treatments of the Orpheus plot
in particular. Offenbach used the myth cleverly to satirize contemporary
Parisian society (and was in turn satirized by Saint-Saëns in the *Carnaval
des animaux*), but the basic outlines of the action, whether concluded by a *lieto
fine* in the manner of Peri or of Monteverdi, did not seem to appeal to the
Romanticist imagination. The twentieth century was more sympathetic to
the archetypal aspects of the plot, but either the operas were not completed
or failed to obtain a lasting hold on the repertory.[44] Considering the employment of the harp as a symbol of Orpheus' lyre, its prominent positioning
within the dramatic structure differs considerably. In Monteverdi and
Gluck it occurs in the central acts, when the divine singer pleads with the
underworld: the third of five acts in Monteverdi, the second of three in
Gluck. In Haydn, on the other hand, it is the opening act that introduces
Orpheus rescuing Eurydice in an accompanied recitative, where the
orchestral fabric is restricted to harp and pizzicato strings.[45] Berlioz, in his
cantata, limits his tale to the death of Orpheus, and achieves one of his
most striking effects in an orchestral postlude, where above the gentle
waters of the river Hebrus Orpheus' lyre can be heard vibrating in the
breeze ('Le vent fait vibrer ... la harpe d'Orphée'), represented by harp
arpeggios above chromatic string chords.[46] It is unlikely that Stravinsky
knew Berlioz's cantata of 1827, but he certainly knew the scores of
Monteverdi and Gluck. And it was a dramatic masterstroke that in his
ballet he transferred the concertato between harp and tutti from the centre
of the action to its conclusion: in the final section ('Orpheus' Apotheosis')[47]
the double and triple forte of the tutti is succeeded by harp and strings, *vivace*
by *lento sostenuto*. This placement of the triumph of the soloist at the end of
the action is here facilitated by the fact, already mentioned, that the apotheosis applies not to the singer, as in Monteverdi, but to the instrument that
accompanies and symbolizes his song and his art, his 'maîtrise'.

---

[44] Cf. A. Joly-Segalen and A. Schaeffner (eds.), *Segalen et Debussy* (Monaco, 1961); Rollo Myers, 'The
Opera that never was: Debussy's Collaboration with Victor Segalen in the Preparation of *Orphée*', *MQ*
64 (1978), 495 506; Hans Knoch, *Orpheus und Eurydike: Der antike Sagenstoff in den Opern von Darius Milhaud
und Ernst Krenek* (Kölner Beiträge zur Musikforschung, 91; Regensburg, 1977).

[45] Cf. Wirth's edn., p. 46.

[46] Cf. facs. of score (Paris, 1930), 80.

[47] Miniature score (London, 1948), 57 9.

Stravinsky's ballet, first performed in 1948, and one of the works of his neoclassical phase, rightly admired ever since, raises questions as to its antecedents and its meaning. The two main influences are obviously Gluck and Monteverdi. Little needs to be said about Stravinsky's acquaintance with Gluck, whose score is readily available to any student of music or opera or composition. Monteverdi may at first seem less likely to be included among his neoclassical or neo-Baroque models, but it is usually thought that the composer first heard a version of Monteverdi's *Orfeo* at St Petersburg in 1905, probably based on the revival of Vincent d'Indy.[48] However that may be, in the decades preceding the Second World War, Stravinsky certainly had opportunity to study the editions of Malipiero (published in 1923 and 1931), apart from the championing of the works of Monteverdi by Nadia Boulanger (who in turn introduced so many English-speaking composers to Stravinsky's Apollonian art). As to the meaning of the ballet's finale, clearly the quiet manner in which harp and strings prevail is a metaphor, an allegory beyond its mere sonority. This was best expressed by the composer when he played the apotheosis to Nicolas Nabokov on the piano, a few months before the world première:

Here in the Epilogue it sounds like a kind of . . . compulsion, like something unable to stop . . . Orpheus is dead, the song is gone, but the accompaniment goes on.[49]

Clearly, it is the fact that the accompaniment, that the music, 'goes on' that matters; that is the message conveyed by the sonority of the plucked strings of the harp: Apollonian order achieves victory over chaos and destruction. The victory of Orpheus' lyre over death becomes a metaphor for the gospel of the permanence of music. True, the *lieto fine*, as we have seen in Chapter 3, is sometimes viewed as a mere convention. (Some observers regard its appearance at the conclusion of *Così fan tutte* and of Cocteau's *Orphée* as a playful reference to a tradition, much repeated and sometimes abused.)[50] But at other times it is clearly an affirmation of faith, and the apotheosis of Apollo in Stravinsky's *Apollon musagète* (1928) and of the lyre in his *Orpheus* must be viewed in this perspective. The composer's concern with the continued existence of music is reflected, among others, in two later works, namely Carter's cantata of 1978 and Tippett's oratorio of 1984.

John Ashbery's 'Syringa', set to music by Carter, refers both to the perpetuity of music and the transfer to heaven:

---

[48] Cf. Jürgen Hunkemöller, 'Strawinsky rezipiert Monteverdi', in Finscher (ed.), *Monteverdi*, 237 47.

[49] Nicolas Nabokov, *Old Friends and New Music* (London, 1951), 153. In addition to Nabokov's recorded reminiscences, this discussion of Stravinsky's *Orpheus* is also based on several conversations with Stravinsky, Balanchine, Nabokov, and Lincoln Kirstein that the present writer had between 1944 and 1953; notably with Stravinsky in 1948 and 1953, after performances of *Orpheus* and *Rake's Progress*, conducted by the composer. Topics of discussion also included the nature and problem of the finale in Monteverdi's *Orfeo*, Mozart's *Don Giovanni*, and Stravinsky's *Rake's Progress*.

[50] Concerning Cocteau, cf. Edward Freeman (ed.), *Orphée: Jean Cocteau: The Play and the Film* (Blackwell's French Texts; Oxford, 1976), pp. xxxiii, 124.

> But it isn't enough
> To just go on singing. Orpheus realized this
> And didn't mind so much about his reward being in heaven
> After the Bacchantes had torn him apart . . .
> Some say it was for his treatment of Eurydice.
> But probably the music had more to do with it, and
> The way music passes, emblematic
> Of life . . .[51]

This concern with 'just going on singing' is powerfully expressed in Tippett's oratorio, whose last section, a wordless chorus, bears the title 'The singing will never be done', a quotation from a poem by Siegfried Sassoon (p. 564).[52] The work starts with a quotation from Yeats, 'All metaphor' (p. 7), and indeed the various bits and pieces from which the *Mask of Time* is constructed must be viewed in a metaphorical or allegorical manner. This applies particularly to Orpheus, whose power is invoked, plucking his lyre (p. 45; harp, pizzicato strings). In the opening Yeats quotation the artist had been exhorted to 'stalk on, stalk on' (p. 27) through life and history, and in the penultimate ninth section Orpheus reappears. A trio exhorts him, as he emerges from the underworld, to 'stalk on, stalk on' (p. 497; a verbal and musical quotation from p. 27) into the daylight, only to be torn to pieces by the Bacchic women, who throw his head into the river, where it floats, still singing. Two aspects of this 'Severed Head' section, based partly on Rilke's *Sonette an Orpheus*, are worth stressing. First, that only he who has suffered can truly 'sound the infinite praise' (p. 504; xylophone, harp). Secondly, that the Bacchic women hurl 'the head . . . into the stream of time; flowing, divining, singing' (p. 510; pizzicato strings). Once the 'singing god' has imposed order upon the chaos, the river miraculously bears 'the head and the lyre' (p. 526):

> tragend als Strömung das Haupt und die Leier.
>
> bearing on the river-race the head and the lyre

There is constant stress on continuity here. We are to stalk on and on, the praise is infinite, the severed head keeps divining and singing, head and lyre do not sink but are carried by the stream: the singing will never be done, and Orpheus is indeed a metaphor, a triumph of music, if not of artistic expression altogether.

We have come full circle. Stravinsky's apotheosis and Tippett's miracle of the head and the lyre are linked to Monteverdi's Apollo finale and to the

---

[51] Cf. David I. H. Harvey, *The Later Music of Elliott Carter* (Dissertations in Music from British Universities; New York, 1989). I am indebted to David Harvey for making the complete text of 'Syringa' from Ashbery's *Houseboat Days* available to me.

[52] All page-references are to the vocal score of Tippett, *Mask of Time* (1984). Cf. also the sleeve-notes, by Meirion Bowen, to the EMI recording, 1987.

allegorical interpretation of the Orpheus myth. This is not a question of influences, of deliberate imitation. Rather, it is a question of the historical continuity of certain themes and preoccupations in mythology, and the response of composers and poets to these themes. Certainly, the topic of the victory of the artist over time, the reaper, has occupied great minds, including that of Shakespeare, over the centuries. That the subject should loom large in Monteverdi's and Stravinsky's finale, and represent the creed with which the audience is dismissed, seems appropriate.

Of course, the *deus ex machina* who brings about the *lieto fine* is not always Apollo. The ubiquitous love duets of the seventeenth and eighteenth centuries, performed by so many couples besides Orpheus and Eurydice, hint at another kind of immortality, more readily grasped by audiences, and more frequently pursued by the human race. In countless operas Amor either intervenes directly or 'may at least be said to represent the preponderant force that propels the action. Perhaps Rinuccini's finale formula owed its widespread emulation not only to its suitability for courtly occasions, but also to the profound satisfaction that it afforded to the most elementary human aspirations. But whereas the Apollonian apotheosis may represent— in statistic terms—only a minority option, its artistic merits are such as to assure its inclusion in any account of opera. There are many mansions in the history of the finale.

6

The Lament

FUNCTION AND VOCABULARY OF THE SOLO LAMENT

The play of opposites looms large in the genre of opera: vocal versus instrumental sonorities, full-fledged music versus speech-song (aria versus recitative), melody versus accompaniment, and—last but not least—solo song versus ensemble. Here we have the classic contrast between expressive solo singing and the so-called 'choral' finale, whether performed by a small chamber chorus or an ensemble of soloists. The solo that acts as a foil for the ensemble finale need not be a lament, but it frequently is: in the *lieto fine* operas of the seventeenth and eighteenth centuries, such complaints add to the differences of texture and dynamics those of tempo and emotion (*affetto*). The plaint is slow, soft, and languorous, whereas the finale is brisk, sonorous, and optimistic (or hopeful, or assertive).

These are matters and procedures not necessarily restricted to Peri and Monteverdi: they are readily observed in succeeding centuries, for instance in the finales for Acts II and IV of *Le nozze di Figaro*. This is particularly true of the famous finale for Act II, a marvel of dramatic and musical construction,[1] where a concluding texture of seven vocal parts contrasts eloquently with the opening of the act, the countess's 'Porgi amor', in which Rosina poignantly laments her husband's inconstancy. Her solo, in larghetto tempo, and her melancholy act as counterpoints to the prestissimo, which, in stretta fashion, finishes the act, with brass fanfares and string flourishes. The countess speaks of 'duolo', 'sospiri', and 'O mi lascia almen morir' ('grief', 'sighs', 'oh let me at least die'), while the final seven-part ensemble stresses the confidence of the count and his party in having foiled Figaro's plans. No student of early opera can listen to the countess's 'O mi lascia almen morir' without being reminded of 'Lasciatemi morire', which looms so prominently in Rinuccini's and Monteverdi's lament of Ariadne (to be discussed later). One is not suggesting that Da Ponte copied or even knew Rinuccini's verse (though the latter is not impossible). Rather, it is true that the lament, from the dramas of ancient Greece to the operas of Verdi and Puccini, has a natural and fairly constant vocabulary in which certain words are encountered

---

[1] It is worth noting that the ottonari, so prominent in the finales of early opera, also open and finish Mozart's finale. Cf. Tim Carter, *Mozart: Nozze di Figaro* (Cambridge Opera Handbooks; Cambridge, 1987), 86 *et passim*. Carter's observations on verse and music are sensitive and sensible.

through the centuries: for instance, the terms for tears and weeping (*piangere,
pianto*; *lagrimare, lagrime*), for death and dying (*morire, morte*), sighing (*sospirare,
sospiro*), grief (*duolo, dolore, cordoglio*), bewailing (*lamentare, piangere*), etc. Frequently
the emotions expressed through these words are intensified through repetition,
straightforward or otherwise (echo, anaphora, palillogia, and so on). It is
characteristic that in the countess's short larghetto the phrase 'O mi lascia
almen morir' is stated four times in Mozart's music.

Among the typical vocabulary of the lament, farewells (*a Dio*; later usually
spelt *addio*) to the beloved, or to the unhappy character's home, or to heaven
and earth are prominent; and so are interjections and expletives expressing
pain or disappointment. Our 'alas' or 'alack' is often met as 'Ahimè' or
'Ohimè',[2] and these two words are frequently abbreviated to 'Ahi' or 'Ohi',
and sometimes to the single vowels 'a' and 'o'. A good example of repeated
'a Dio' and 'a' occurs in Ottavia's lament in the final act of Monteverdi's
Poppea. Here the librettist Busenello gives the composer a line of fourteen
syllables in which the farewell 'a Dio' appears three times. Monteverdi
expands this to twenty-three notes (or syllables) by inserting an expressive
and expletive 'a' six times and repeating the word 'a-mi-ci'. In the following
comparison of the opening line of the lament in Busenello[3] and Monteverdi
(see Ex. 6.1),[4] the syllables added by the composer are indicated by italics.

Busenello

A Dio Ro-ma, a Dio pa-tria, a-mi-ci a Di-o.

1 2   3   4   5 6   7   8   9 10 11 12 13 14

(Farewell Rome, farewell native land, friends farewell.)

Monteverdi

A A A A Dio Ro-ma, *a a* a Dio pa-tria, *a* a-mi-ci *a-mi-ci* a Di-o.

1 2 3 4 5   6   7   8 9 10 11   12 13   14 15 16   17 18 19 20 21   22 23

Together with the vowel 'a' in 'a Dio' and 'amici' supplying a syllable (and
a note), the expressive vowel appears in Monteverdi's vocal line eleven times,
supported by the unchanging harmony of A minor in the accompaniment
for the first twenty-one syllables. What with a static harmony, and the pitch *a'*
serving almost like a reciting-note, we can see that this lament, sung by the
famous soprano Anna Renzi, tended more in the direction of recitative or
arioso than in that of aria (it falls into sections but not into strophic stanzas).

As far as the intensification of the emotion of the lament through repeated
'a Dio' goes, Monteverdi had employed the same device decades earlier in

---

[2] Concerning the equivalents for some of these terms in classical Greek and Latin, see Ch. 7.

[3] Cf. Corte, *Drammi*, i. 505. Technically, Busenello's line is an 'endecasillabo piano', since syllables
4–5, 8–9, and 11–12 may be fused because of the adjacent vowels. (Such fusion is called 'sinalefe' in
Italian versification.) Monteverdi enlarges the time-span of Busenello's line in three ways: first by ignoring
the option of fusing syllables, secondly by repeating syllables and words, and thirdly by inserting rests.
Concerning the pathos of these rests, cf. Hans-Heinrich Unger, *Beziehungen zwischen Musik und Rhetorik*
(Würzburg, 1941; repr. Hildesheim, 1985), 127, s.v. 'suspiratio'.

[4] Cf. *Poppea*, ed. Malipiero (*Opere*, xiii), 229.

Ex. 6.1. Monteverdi, Ottavia's lament from *Poppea*, Act III

Orfeo. There the hero, learning of the loss of Eurydice, closes his lament (again not strophic, but more in the nature of an arioso) with three farewells,[5] each of them marked by an ascending or descending semitonal progression (see Ex. 6.2):

Ex. 6.2. Monteverdi, Orfeo's lament from *Orfeo*, Act II

> A Dio terra, a Dio cielo, e sole, a Dio.
> Farewell earth, farewell heaven, and sun, farewell

It may be noted parenthetically that this address to earth and heaven must have reminded some listeners of the Lord's Prayer. This may seem far-fetched, but whereas biblical and Christian references would be alien to the *Poppea* libretto, *Orfeo*—after all—concludes with a chorus obliquely alluding to the Psalms, an intimation more obscure than one of God's will 'in earth as it is in heaven',[6] to which the Christ *figura* of Orpheus refers (see Ch. 1).

---

5 Cf. Monteverdi, *Orfeo*, facs. of 1609 score, p. 40; libretto, l. 256. Some modern editors spell 'a Dio', others 'a dio', still others 'addio'. Capitalization of such nouns as 'Cielo' and 'Sole' is also a matter of discretion; cf. Solerti, *Albori*, iii. 256; Hanning, *Music's Power*, 313.

6 Striggio would, of course, have in mind the Latin or Italian text of the paternoster.

Finally, before leaving 'farewell' as part and parcel of the vocabulary of the lament, we may note two other examples. One is an English lyric by Thomas Wyatt from the earlier sixteenth century, 'Heaven and earth': the lover laments the treatment he suffers from his lady, concluding each stanza with two syllables that are repeated, including 'farewell, farewell'.[7] And it does not seem too fanciful to mention at this point the finale of Verdi's *Aida*, where Radamès and Aida bid 'farewell to earth, farewell to this valley of sorrow' ('Addio terra, addio valle di pianti'). We also note 'pianti', a key term in the vocabulary of the lament.

It is characteristic of the history of opera in the nineteenth century, touched upon in Chapter 3, that this 'Addio' is sung by Radamès and Aida at the tragic conclusion of the plot: the lament is not a foil for a *lieto fine*, it is the finale itself, and accepted as such in the age of high Romanticism. On the other hand, Ottavia's 'A Dio Roma' provides an effective contrast to the triumph of the god Amor, and of Nero's and Poppaea's passion, both of which are intertwined in an extensive concertato and *lieto fine* in the Neapolitan score of *Poppea*, as we have seen.

Having surveyed farewells from Verdi's *Aida* backwards to Monteverdi's *Orfeo*, it behoves us to look at the predecessors of the Mantuan *Orfeo*, notably the play of Poliziano, undoubtedly known to Rinuccini and Striggio. The passage where Monteverdi's Orpheus addresses earth, heaven, and sun is obviously reminiscent of Orpheus' lament in Poliziano's drama in the analogous situation, namely when the hero first hears of Eurydice's death (see the first of five passages in Table 6.1, in which the vowel 'o' occurs four times). That Striggio substitutes Apollo's sun for Neptune's sea is not surprising: Apollo plays a larger role in Monteverdi than in Poliziano, and the latter's 'sea' is obviously an echo of a Latin phrase by Terence (see Table 6.1, third passage). Poliziano wrote this quotation in the margin of his copy of Virgil (*Georgica*, iv. 504–5) where Orpheus vents his grief after the second loss of Eurydice. In fact, Poliziano himself, also upon the second loss, piles up again the expressive vowel 'o', introduced by the ubiquitous 'oimè' of the laments (Table 6.1, second passage); this time the 'o' appears five times. In both these laments of Poliziano fate (*sorte* or *fato*) is added to heaven as an object of address, and it is likely that a line from Petrarch (Table 6.1, fourth passage) may also have rung in the poet's ears when he attached fate and death to heaven and earth. The expression of Orpheus' grief after the first loss of Eurydice in Rinuccini's and Peri's *Euridice* will be scrutinized more closely later, but some lines must be quoted now (Table 6.1, fifth passage) to show that its sevenfold 'o' and general poetic diction are also likely to have been influenced by Poliziano's drama.

[7] Concerning the poetry and music of Wyatt's lyric, and its repetitions of 'I die' and 'farewell', cf. Sternfeld, 'Repetition and Echo in Renaissance Poetry and Music', in *English Renaissance Studies Presented to Dame Helen Gardner in Honour of her Seventieth Birthday* (Oxford, 1980), 39–40; cf. also John Ward, *Music for Elizabethan Lutes*, 2 vols. (Oxford, 1992), ii. 64 and 147.

TABLE 6.1. *Five laments*

---

1. Poliziano, *Orfeo*[a]

> O cielo, o terra, o mare! o sorte dira!
>
> O heaven, o earth, o sea! o dire fate!

2. Poliziano, *Orfeo*[b]

> Oimè, se' mi tu tolta,
> Euridice mie bella? O mie furore,
> o duro fato, o ciel nimico, o Morte!
> O troppo sventurato el nostro amore!
>
> Alas, thou hast been taken from me,
> my lovely Eurydice? O my fury,
> o hard fate, o hostile heaven, o death!
> O our too ill-fated love!

3. Terence, *Adelphi*, 790

> o caelum, o terra, o maria Neptuni . . .
>
> o heaven, o earth, o seas of Neptune . . .

4. Petrarch, *Canzoniere*, 298. 12

> O mia stella, o Fortuna, o Fato, o Morte,
>
> o my star, o fortune, o fate, o death,

5. Rinuccini, *Euridice*, ll. 227 - 36

> O mia cara Euridice . . .
> O mio core, o mia speme, o pace, o vita!
> Ohimè chi mi t'ha tolto . . .
> . . . o cara vita, o cara morte.
>
> O my dear Eurydice . . .
> O my heart, o my hope, o peace, o life!
> Alas, who has taken thee from me . . .
> . . . o dear life, o dear death.

---

[a] Tissoni Benvenuti, *Poliziano*, 150.
[b] Ibid. 160.

It will be seen from these few examples that if the vocabulary of the lament extends from 'a' and 'o' to 'addio' and 'ohimè', with 'cielo' and 'terra', and 'morte' and 'fato', and what not thrown in for good measure, the device that intensifies this expressive vocabulary is repetition in some form or other, and repetition carried out to a surprising degree: without fear of introducing the sensation of 'repetitiousness'. The operatic lament wallows in grief and scorns the danger of monotony.

POLIZIANO

Poliziano's *Orfeo* has been repeatedly referred to, and the three different versions in which this progenitor of the birth of opera survives have been discussed in Chapter 3, in conjunction with Tissoni Benvenuti's edition. These three texts differ in length: Text I comprises 342 lines, Text II 406, and Text III 450. We have already observed that a surprisingly large number of lines are sung, not spoken: in the case of Text II we may assume that about three-fifths involve the assistance of music (241 out of 406 lines). A large portion of these musical 'numbers' are strophic laments, and all of them are already encountered in the earliest version, namely Text I. There the strophic laments occupy 138 out of a total of 342 lines, or forty per cent. If we keep in mind that sung lyrics move much more slowly than recited lines, it is no exaggeration to say that more than half this fifteenth-century drama consists of laments, and musical laments at that. This is not surprising: the plot of Poliziano's play gives ample scope for lamenting, and Baccio Ugolini (who performed the role of Orpheus) possessed the necessary musical skills. As far as the plot goes, in the early part of the play there is the love plaint of Aristaeus; then there are the lyrical effusions of Orpheus after the first and second loss of Eurydice; and between these laments of Orpheus is his plea to the underworld. This last incantation ('O regnator di tutte quelle genti') is an important subdivision of the lament, combining eloquent pleading with poignant bewailing. The Italian term for such a plea or prayer, whether addressed by Orpheus to Pluto (as in Poliziano) or to Charon (as in Monteverdi), is 'preghiera' (literally 'prayer'); and in a letter of 9 December 1616 Monteverdi calls 'Possente spirto' from his *Orfeo* a 'preghiera'.[8] Such 'preghiere', then, which include references to the protagonist's chagrin or pains, will be treated as one of the several classes or branches of the genre of the 'lamento'.

Before proceeding to a more detailed consideration of the properties of one of Poliziano's laments, it will be useful to tabulate these four mournful lyrics, with the relevant references to Tissoni Benvenuti's edition (see Table 6.2).[9] It will be seen that these laments fall into various categories. Aristaeus' song is an amorous plaint, of which the collections of frottolas, madrigals, and monodies provide thousands of examples. Whether the melancholy expressed is playful or sincere, who can say? The poetic and musical vocabulary would not be affected. Orpheus' first and last lyrics could be described as dirges, for they are both occasioned by the loss of Eurydice. (As we have seen in Ch. 2, Milton's *Lycidas*, on the death of a friend, is called a 'monody'; and indeed 'monody' and 'lament' are frequently

---

[8] Monteverdi, *Lettere*, ed. Paoli, 87; extensive excerpts from this letter are quoted in Ch. 2.

[9] For a commentary on Poliziano's sources and analogues, Tissoni Benvenuti, *Poliziano*, is particularly valuable and up to date. The line-numbering in the editions of Pernicone and Sapegno differs from hers.

synonymous.) On the other hand, Orpheus' plea to Pluto ('O regnator') is a 'preghiera'. But the vagaries of terminology, whether in Italian ('lamento', 'pianto', 'lagrime', 'preghiera') or in English, do not matter; the melancholy note is common to elegies, threnodies, dirges, poignant pleas, 'funeral tears', and 'doleful dumps'. On the other hand, it is worth remembering that all four laments in Poliziano are strophic. This means that as in countless lute-songs (or in a later century, lyrics by Schubert) the musical setting usually fits the first stanza best, but accommodates in its general emotional climate and prosodic requirements subsequent stanzas as well. (It is for that very reason that the most famous madrigals are—as a rule—not strophic and that many of the early operatic laments are not organized by stanzas.)

TABLE 6.2.   *Four laments in Poliziano's* Orfeo

Protagonist	Incipit	Number of lines	Strophic structure
Aristeo	Udite, selve, mie dolce parole[a]	34	4 six-line stanzas, framed by 5 two-line refrains
Orfeo	Dunque piangiamo, o sconsolata lira[b]	32	4 eight-line stanzas; ottave rime
Orfeo	O regnator di tutte quelle genti[c]	40	5 eight-line stanzas; ottave rime
Orfeo	Qual sarà mai si miserabil canto[d]	32	4 eight-line stanzas; ottave rime

[a] Tissoni Benvenuti, *Poliziano*, 142, 171, 189.
[b] Ibid. 149, 176, 198.
[c] Ibid. 153, 178, 201.
[d] Ibid. 160, 181, 205.

A great deal could be said about the poetic devices employed by Poliziano in these strophic laments, and in the spoken dialogue connecting these musical numbers. We have already cited the fourfold 'o' in the first stanza of the second lament (Table 6.1, passage 1), and the fivefold 'o' in the dialogue preceding the last lament (Table 6.1, passage 2). The accumulation of such interjections to express intense emotion is, of course, one of the most elementary means of poetry and not restricted to threnodies: the spurned Bacchic women, eager for revenge, exclaim 'o' twelve times in the dialogue intervening between the last lament and the final chorus.[10] But at this point it will not be amiss to look at some musical settings of Poliziano's poetry.

Unfortunately, no contemporary composition of any lyric from his *Orfeo* is known to me, though Isaac's composition of the poet's Latin lament on

[10]   Tissoni Benvenuti, 163–4, ll. 294–301.

the death of Lorenzo de' Medici makes one suspect that poetic reiteration induced similar procedures in music.[11] But the last lament of Orpheus (Table 6.2, fourth lament) survives in several settings from the sixteenth century, among them those of Costanzo Festa, Verdelot, Rampollini, and Layolle. And the three-part madrigal by Festa, first printed in the 1540s, is worth examining in detail, both because of its artistic merit and its chronological proximity to the age of Poliziano. Whether the setting by Festa, or the other three composers mentioned, was ever used for a stage performance of *Orfeo* we cannot say with certainty. It seems more likely, on the whole, that Poliziano's play (like Guarini's *Pastor fido* later on) was used as a poetic miscellany into which composers dipped to find suitable excerpts for musical purposes. Such settings could easily be adapted for the theatre if and when needed. For instance, the two lower parts of Festa's madrigal are readily performed on a lute or keyboard instrument.[12]

The verbal text of the four ottave rime of the final lament has been discussed in Chapter 1, where we noted the explicit references to pederasty in the second and fourth ottava rima and the misogynistic note in the third. For that reason the lament was sometimes entirely omitted in several of the extant variants and *rifacimenti*, or at least the fourth stanza (with its references to Ganymede, Hyacinthus, and Hylas) excised. These mythological analogies have, of course, their poetic and dramatic justification, but they are of little consequence for the main emotion of the whole lyric, which may be summarized by such adjectives as 'miserabile' ('woeful', Festa's text, Ex. 6.3*a*) or 'lacrimabile' ('lachrymose', 'pathetic', Layolle's text, Ex. 6.3*b*). It is perhaps characteristic that in Verdelot's setting (Ex. 6.3*c*) 'miserabil pianto' has been substituted for 'miserabil canto', for the term 'pianto' functions occasionally as a synonym for 'lamento' and implies 'weeping', 'plaint', 'complaint'. Indeed, the categories of 'lamento' or 'pianto' are of paramount importance for this penultimate 'number' in Poliziano's drama. Festa's setting fits this general expression of grief and mourning perfectly. If and when the fourth stanza with its mythological references is omitted (as in *Orphei tragoedia*), the emotional outline of the drama is not affected.

Several factors combine to establish the elegiac note of the composition. One is a group of descending notes spanning the interval of a perfect fourth, the 'descending tetrachord'. This diatonic descent is common to the settings of Festa, Layolle, and Verdelot (see the square brackets in Exx. 6.3*a*, *b*, *c*) and used rather poignantly elsewhere in Festa (Ex. 6.4, bars 3–6, a concatenation of two overlapping tetrachords; bars 31–2, '[vi]ta mi terranno';

[11] See Ch. 7 for discussion of this work.

[12] A modern edn. is in Costanzo Festa, *Opera omnia*, vii, ed. Albert Seay (CMM 25; Stuttgart, 1977), no. 7. Cf. also the discussions by Wolfgang Osthoff, 'Zur musikalischen Tradition der tragischen Gattung im italienischen Theater', in Hans Heinrich Eggebrecht and Max Lütolf (eds.), *Studien zur Tradition: Kurt von Fischer zum 60. Geburtstag* (Munich, 1973), 121–43, 122, and by H. Musch, *Costanzo Festa als Madrigalkomponist* (Collection d'études musicologiques, 61; Baden-Baden, 1977), 76.

Ex. 6.3.   Settings of Orfeo's lament from Poliziano, *Orfeo*

(*a*) Festa

si   mi -   se - ra - bil   can   -   to

(*b*) Layolle

si   la - cri -ma - bil   can   -   to

(*c*) Verdelot

si   mi - se - ra - bil   pian   -   -   -   to

si   mi   -   se - ra - bil pian   -   to

bars 37–42, sequence on 'già mai non voglio amar'). It would be easy to write a whole book on the descending tetrachord as a constituent element of the lament, and articles have been written about it. Sometimes the interval of the fourth is filled diatonically, as in the present case, sometimes chromatically, as in some laments of Monteverdi and Cavalli. The chromatic variant is better known to the general public, what with famous examples from Purcell, Bach, Mozart's *Don Giovanni*, and Beethoven's 'Ninth'. Still, the impression of most music historians is that in the period before *c*.1650 the diatonic tetrachord is more frequently associated with the lament. A good example would be the *Lamento della ninfa* from Monteverdi's eighth madrigal book. (But again one must enter the caveat that the descent does not exclusively accompany laments: see the final love duet from Monteverdi's *Poppea*, whether by Monteverdi himself, or by Sacrati.[13]

The other factor that strongly characterizes Festa's composition as mournful is its expressive control over rhythmic movement. In most bars there are three or four notes, either in the melody or the accompaniment, but occasionally this natural flow deliberately is stopped to stress a phrase, for instance (at bars 22–4) 'Staromi [mesto e sconsolato in pianto]' ('I shall remain [sad and disconsolate in my lament]'), where the whole piece seems to come to a still, but eloquent climax.

---

[13]   Cf. also below and n. 31 on Monteverdi, Ferrari, or Sacrati as possible authors.

A third element contributing to the effect of this brief lyric, with its thin texture of three voices, is the striking recurrence of two alternating chords (A minor and E minor in modern parlance) in the two lower voices (Ex. 6.4, bars 6–7, 17–19, 42–3, 44–7).

In the setting of the final line, 'Già mai non voglio amar più donna alcuna' ('I do not wish ever again to love any woman'), these three compositional devices are all combined. For the sake of emphasis the first part of the line is sequenced a tone higher (bars 40–3), which means that we encounter the descending tetrachord twice. On the syllables 'già mai' (ever) the music slows down dramatically. And the sequence of alternating chords is also heard twice, and acts as an effective foil for the long-held note in the melody, which hardly leaves the pitch *e'* in the last five bars. But perhaps we had better quote chapter and verse rather than proceed to further verbal analysis of Festa's lament:

> Qual sarà mai si miserabil canto
> ch'apparegg'il dolor del mio gran danno?
> O come potrò mai lagrimar tanto,
> che sempre pianga il mio mortale affanno?
> Staromi mesto e sconsolato in pianto
> per fin ch'e cieli in vita mi terranno;
>   e poi che sì crudele è mia fortuna,
>   già mai non voglio amar più donna alcuna.

> How can ever such woeful song
> equal the pain of my great suffering?
> How can I ever find enough tears
> to bemoan constantly my mortal affliction?
> I shall remain sad and disconsolate in my lament
> as long as the heavens keep me in this life;
>   and since my fate is so cruel,
>   I do not wish ever again to love any woman.

The history of Western drama, from ancient Greece to the present, exceeds a time-span of two millennia, and it goes without saying that significant examples of lament loom large in this chronicle: several threnodies from Euripides to Gluck have been mentioned (Ch. 1). Many analogues to Festa's setting of Poliziano could be pursued, but this temptation must be resisted. On the other hand, I cannot forgo at this point mentioning apropos of the descending tetrachord in Festa (and other composers of the sixteenth century) its poignant employment by Stravinsky in his score of *Orpheus*. When the divine singer mourns the loss of Eurydice, the harp (miniature score, pp. 1–2) plays various diatonically descending tetrachords: sometimes disjunct, sometimes conjunct; sometimes rhythmically displaced; sometimes complicated by repetition of a note or by octave transposition (see the square brackets in Ex. 6.5*a*). The stage direction reads 'Orpheus weeps for Eurydice'. At

Ex. 6.4. Festa, 'Qual sarà mai'

the end of the ballet (miniature score, pp. 57 ff.) this harp 'accompaniment' is resurrected for the final apotheosis of Orpheus' lyre, extensively discussed and compared with Monteverdi earlier (Chs. 1 and 5). Again the set of four notes is subjected to various treatments as in the opening scene of mourning, to which another compositional device is added, namely inversion (see Exx. 6.5*b*, *c*). At the very end the tetrachord does not descend; it ascends, which 'raises his [i.e. Orpheus'] song heavenwards' and bestows upon it immortality, as we have seen: lament has turned into triumph (or transfiguration).

Ex. 6.5. Stravinsky, harp accompaniment to Orfeo's lament in *Orpheus*

(*a*) p. 1

(*b*) p. 57

(*c*) p. 59, lower half

PERI

When we move from consideration of laments by Poliziano (born 1454) and Festa (*c*.1490) to those by Rinuccini (born 1563) and Peri (1561) we make a leap of more than a century. During the intervening period many developments had taken place in the history of poetry, and drama, and music. Expressive devices to depict intense emotions in a short span of time had been explored in the genre of the madrigal, and a fondness for virtuoso singing reared its head in various court spectacles in the course of the sixteenth century. Certainly, the music contributed by singer-composers

such as Peri and Caccini to the Florentine intermedi of 1589 displays a florid
and melismatic style that requires a professional mastery of vocal resources.
A good example is offered by Arion's lament over his tragic predicament
before he is rescued by the dolphin. The text is anonymous, the music by
Peri. Peri's setting is scored for tenor voice with two vocal echoes ('due
risposte') plus an instrumental accompaniment in four parts.[14] In comparing
Peri's lament with Festa's one almost immediately becomes aware of several
differences, as one would expect, moving from the early prehistory of opera
to one of the principal composers of the first specimens of the genre. For
one thing, Peri's anonymous text is not strophic. True, strophic laments continued to be written by Peri, Monteverdi, Cavalli, and others: sometimes
the stanzas were eight lines long (ottave), sometimes only three lines (terzine);
sometimes we encounter strophic units between these two extremes. But
perhaps as the result of the flowering of the madrigal in the second half of
the sixteenth century, lyrics intended for music (including laments) tended
to fall into sections of irregular length, including important threnodies by
Peri and Monteverdi. In the present case the lament consists of eleven lines,
falling into two sections of six and five lines, both of them composed of
versi toscani, that is, of lines of seven and eleven syllables. The first section
(see Ex. 6.6) runs as follows (variant spellings are given in square brackets):

> Dunque fra torbide onde
> Gli ultimi miei sospir manderò fuore!
> Eco [or 'Ecco'] gentil con tuoi suavi accenti:
> Raddoppia i miei tormenti!
> Ahi [or 'Hai'] lacrime, ahi dolore,
> Ahi morte troppo acerba e troppo dura!

> Thus among the turbid waves
> Shall I breathe my last sighs!
> Gentle echo, with thy sweet accents,
> Redouble my torments!
> Ah tears, ah grief,
> Ah death, too bitter and too harsh!

Looking at the text of these six lines, we note, first of all, the typical vocabulary of the lament: last sighs, torments, tears, grief, harsh death. Several of
these suggestive terms are doubled and redoubled by echoes, for instance
'tormenti' in line 4 and 'morte dura' in line 6. But even more important for
creating the proper emotional atmosphere is the ubiquitous expletive 'ahi'
(ah, alas). It occurs three times in the lament (ll. 5–6) apostrophizing tears,
grief, and death; but in the music it occurs eleven times, thanks to double
echo and repetition. As is so often the case in stage music, verbal repetition
triggers an even larger amount of musical reiteration. But before

---

[14] Walker, *Musique des intermèdes*. Cf. pp. xxvi, 1, 98–106.

Ex. 6.6. Peri, 'Dunque fra torbid'onde', first section

considering the piling up of these pitiful exclamations, we had better say a word about Peri's intensifying echo. We have already mentioned the double echo in Vivaldi's *Giustino* as an analogue to the 1589 lament (the same doubling of key words is found in Handel's *Giustino*), and indeed Shakespeare uses the verb 'redouble' ('raddoppiare' in Peri's fourth line) when he describes the lament in *Venus and Adonis*:

> 'Ay me!' she cries, and twenty times, 'Woe, woe!'
> And twenty echoes twenty times cry so . . .[15]

Twenty echoes seems a lot, but the musical setting of Arion's lament accommodates a total of twenty-eight echoes in eleven lines, fourteen of them in the example just quoted (ll. 2–6). The lion's share of these fourteen reiterations is provided by the elevenfold 'ahi' (the equivalent of Shakespeare's 'ay'). Even the three 'ahi's in the text, amplified by echo and double echo in the music, would account for only nine expletives, but the composer repeats his woeful cry in the tenor solo both before 'lacrime' and 'dolore', as if the two echoes would not suffice. In fact, since several lines accommodate more than one double echo (e.g. 'ahi' and 'dura' in line 6) the echo device is more likely to linger in the memory of the listener than any individual melodic phrase.

[15] For fuller description of *Giustino* and *Venus and Adonis* see Ch. 1.

At the same time, two aspects of this tenor solo (sung by Peri himself) are obvious at a first hearing: its melismatic style and the occasional absence of movement in its supporting bass. The florid nature of the melodic line is apparent from the groups of semiquavers accompanying certain words, for instance in 'raddoppia i miei tormenti' (line 4) the syllable 'dop' has forty such rapid notes, and 'miei' thirty-two. (Similarly extensive melismas occur later in the piece, not included in Ex. 6.6.) This is clearly music written by a singer-composer who enjoys displaying his art to an appreciative audience. But it is not humanist word-setting, where poetry is the mistress and music the servant: in 'miei tormenti' (my torments) the noun 'tormenti' is more important than 'miei'. But in the development of virtuoso arias from Peri and Caccini to Mozart's Queen of the Night and to the present, the function of strikingly melismatic lines is to support overall characterization rather than to give emphasis to individual words and syllables. (The syllable 'men' in 'tormenti', bars 13–14, eight notes, has—after all—its expressive double echo.)

As to the supporting bass, Peri himself, in the preface to *Euridice*, stressed the fact that the pioneers of opera endeavoured to create a vocal melody that mirrored the affections without slavishly following the bass. Indeed, the dissonances (anticipations, suspensions, appoggiaturas, etc.) over a stationary bass are one of the distinguishing features of the 'stile recitativo' that Peri, Caccini, and Cavalieri created. And some of these we shall have occasion to observe in one of the laments from *Euridice* to be discussed presently. But one essential aspect of treatment of the bass may already be noted in the lament of 1589. We do not as yet encounter the dissonances and unexpected successions of chords familiar from the operas of Peri and Monteverdi. But we do perceive the contrast between stationary and moving basses. Ordinarily the bass moves in Ex. 6.6 (e.g. bars 1–5, or 8–13), but occasionally rhythmic motion, pitch, and harmony seem to be arrested. For instance *d* in the bass is once sustained for twenty crotchets (bars 5–7), another time for sixteen (bars 18–20). Usually these interruptions of harmonic flow are connected with echo passages, since these echoes usually require the bass to stay put for more than four crotchets. The first 'pedal' on *d* is achieved by continuing the bass for the first echo ('fuore') with that for the beginning of the next line ('Eco gentil . . .'); the second sustained *d* is obtained by continuing the bass of the sixth echo in Ex. 6.6 (on 'ahi') for the next word ('morte').

To interrupt the customary moving basses by stationary bass passages was one of the progressive features of Peri's lament of 1589. But important and impressive as this piece is, it still lacks the expressive poignancy of his later work, of which we may consider Orpheus' lament in the second scene of *Euridice*, 'Non piango e non sospiro'. Here unprepared dissonances with the bass, not 'dancing to its motion', are more frequent than in Festa's or the 1589 lament, in both of which they are really non-existent. And more importantly, the motion of the bass itself, the succession of harmonies, is more unconventional, expressive, and dramatic. Again, this lament, when Orpheus learns of the death of Eurydice, is not divided into stanzas and consists of eleven lines of *versi toscani*. The progression from despair to resolution in this piece does not lend itself to strophic subdivision, where the first and last stanza would have to be sung to the same music and harmonic changes. That Peri was capable of writing effective strophic laments is proved by the conclusion of this second scene, where 'Sospirate aure celesti' forms a melancholy choral finale in seven stanzas (see Ch. 5, Table 5.3), to which the preceding solo lament of Orpheus forms an effective foil (Ex. 6.7).

Non piango e non sospiro,	226
O mia cara Euridice,	
Che sospirar, che lacrimar non posso.	228
Cadavero infelice,	
O mio core, o mia speme, o pace, o vita!	230
Ohimè, chi mi t'ha tolto,	
Chi mi t'ha tolto, ohimè, dove sei gita?	232
Tosto vedrai ch'in vano	
Non chiamasti morendo il tuo consorte.	234
Non son, non son lontano:	
Io vengo, o cara vita, o cara morte.	236

I cry not, I sigh not,
O my dear Eurydice,
Because I cannot sigh or weep.
Unfortunate corpse,
My heart, my hope, my peace, my life!
Alas, who has taken thee from me,
Who has taken thee from me, alas, where hast thou gone?
Soon thou wilt see that in vain
Hast thou not called, dying, for thy spouse.
I am not, I am not far,
I come, o dear life, o dear death.[16]

After the examples cited earlier, it is hardly necessary to elaborate on the typical vocabulary of the lament: we start with weeping and sighing (l. 226, repeated 228) and end up by apostrophizing death. Equally typical is the repetitive rhetoric: the fourfold 'o' (230), followed by a twofold 'ohimè' (231–2), concluding with a twofold 'o' in the last line; this is very reminiscent of the repetitions of 'a' and 'ahi', already discussed. Repetition extends from single syllables ('non', 226; 'che', 228) to shorter and longer phrases ('non son', 235; 'chi mi t'ha tolto', 231–2).

Musically, we start with a stationary *A* in the bass (bars 1–5, twenty crotchets), but the last two lines express Orpheus' determination to 'harrow

---

[16] *Euridice*, ed. Brown, pp. xxii, 69–71; Hanning, *Music's Power*, 278; facs. of original score, p. 17; Solerti, *Albori*, ii. 123.

hell' with vigorous motion in the bass (bars 32–5). The vocal line does not follow the bass in consonant intervals: we encounter ninths (bar 3, second and third crotchets; bar 22, third and fourth crotchets; bar 23, fourth crotchet), and the realization of the basso continuo involves sevenths (bar 20, third crotchet). These passing notes, anticipations, and suspensions certainly

Ex. 6.7. Peri, Orpheus' lament from *Euridice*

do not 'follow the motion of the bass', and contribute to the expression of grief. But even more eloquent are the harmonic changes and juxtapositions.

The piece starts in A minor and seems to stay there for a long time (bars 1–17). With the dramatic repetition of the line 'chi mi t'ha tolto', reminiscent of Poliziano, we move to G minor (18–23) but seemingly return to A minor (23–6), only to land firmly in F major (27–35). Thus the progression from a stationary to a moving bass noted earlier is complemented by a switch from the minor to the major mode, and one can readily see how a strophic form would not have been suitable for the gradual change in the emotions of the protagonist who rises from despair to hope and action, anticipating the *lieto fine* of the opera.

Another detail worthy of mention in this brief lament is the dramatic juxtaposition of the chords of E major and G minor. That the dominant of A minor should unexpectedly be followed by G minor makes the listener take note, particularly because of the cross-relations between G♯ and G♮,

B♮ and B♭. Peri underlines three successive lines in this poignant fashion: the first 'Ohimè, chi mi t'ha tolto' (l. 231, bar 18), the second 'chi mi t'ha tolto' (l. 232, bar 21), and 'Tosto vedrai' (l. 233, bar 27). This sudden and pregnant switch from a major chord to an unexpected minor chord seems to be a hallmark of Peri: in the corresponding passages in Caccini it is absent.[17] On the other hand, it seems to have acted as an influence on Monteverdi, who has justly been praised for the surprising and effective manner in which he introduces the succession E major–G minor in the messenger scene of his *Orfeo*.[18] The first time it emphasizes the horror of Orpheus, the second time the sudden death of Eurydice.

MONTEVERDI

Laments are found frequently in the various kinds of works that Monteverdi produced in the course of his long life: operas, madrigals, sacred music. They were praised during his lifetime and have been admired ever since, and most critics agree that his threnodies constitute one of his more eminent achievements, as they also do in the case of his pupil Cavalli. Reference has already been made to Ottavia's farewell to Rome in *Poppea* and to Orpheus' threefold farewell to earth, heaven, and sun in *Orfeo*. Perhaps we should look next at another lament from the latter opera: the protagonist's plaint after the second loss of Eurydice, at the beginning of the last act.[19]

Again, the verbal text is not strophic, but neither is it lacking in formal organization. It falls into paragraphs of uneven length forming four large sections, held together by emotion (the dramatic content) and harmony (the behaviour of the bass). The opening seems to depict the utter desolation of Orpheus by a mostly stationary bass on G (thirty-six crotchets at the very beginning) and the sustained harmony of G minor (lines 563'–74'; facs., p. 89; *Opere*, xi. 138–9). In fact, the key of G holds this entire long lament together, which is concluded by an instrumental sinfonia in G minor. In the next section the bass is less stationary, but the chagrin of the divine singer is intensified and prolonged by the familiar echo technique (ll. 575'–94'; facs., pp. 89–91; *Opere*, xi. 139–42). In both sections the traditional vocabulary of the lament is obvious, and it is worth noting that the first and the last echoes adumbrate again the sound of 'ahi' in one spelling and meaning or another:

---

[17] For a detailed comparison of Peri's and Caccini's setting of the lament, see Theophil Antonicek, 'Die Musik als Dienerin der Poesie', in H. Krones (ed.), *Wort und Ton im europäischen Raum: Gedenkschrift für Robert Schollum* (Vienna, 1989), 53–67; Eitner's edn. of Caccini, *Euridice*, 59–60; facs. of 1600 score, pp. 15–16. For praise of the alternation of E major and G minor, see Donald J. Grout, *A Short History of Opera* (3rd edn., with H. W. Williams, New York, 1988), 63–4.

[18] Act II, ll. 217 and 226; facs. of 1609 score, p. 37, 2nd and 5th brace.

[19] Line 563'; facs., p. 89; Malipiero edn., xi. 138. References are to the facs. of the 1609 score of *Orfeo* (Augsburg, 1927), the libretto in the lineation of Solerti and Hanning, and *Opere*, ed. Malipiero.

[Orpheus] . . . ahi doglia, ahi pianto! [Echo] Hai pianto.

> ah, pain; ah, weeping!   Thou hast wept.
> (ll. 578' – 9'; facs., p. 90; *Opere*, xi. 140)

Here the sound of 'ahi' resonates three times, meaning either 'ah, alas' or 'thou hast'. And when Orpheus apostrophizes Echo in reply as 'Eco cortese' (courteous Echo), one cannot help but be reminded of the appeal to 'Eco gentil' (gentle Echo) in Peri's lament of 1589, following Peri's first echo (Ex. 6.6, bars 7–8). Monteverdi's last echo returns again to the 'ahi' sound which lurks behind 'guai' (woes), 'ahi' (ah), and 'hai' (hast):

> [Orpheus] . . . tanti guai. [Echo] Ahi.
> [Orpheus] S'hai del mio mal pietade . . .

> so many woes.   Alas.
> If thou hast pity for my plight . . .
> (ll. 588' – 9'; facs., p. 90; *Opere*, xi. 141)

Harmonically the music seems to move to A minor, eschewing stationary basses and pedal points. But with the words 'Ma tu anima mia' (l. 595'; facs., p. 91; *Opere*, xi. 142) we return to G minor, in which key Orpheus sings the praises of Eurydice, to whom he consecrates his lyre and his song. In the final section (ll. 607'–12'; facs., p. 92; *Opere*, xi. 143–4) the music switches to the major mode, and in G major, over a slightly more slowly moving bass, Orpheus expresses his determination to reject all other women. This brief section, cast metrically in sdruccioli, is, however, not quite the end of this lengthy lamentation: it returns to the key of G minor with the sinfonia we have heard in Act III, where it introduced 'Possente spirto' (to be discussed presently). In the final act it functions as a postlude to the lament and as a bridge to the Apollo finale. For much of the time, then, this lament remains anchored to the tonality of G, without neglecting to mirror the progression of emotions in the music. The fifty or so lines of the text show Orpheus first in stunned despair, then eulogizing Eurydice, and finally resolved to accept no other woman as a substitute for the beloved *sans pareil*. The behaviour of the bass, with its temporary digression to A minor, contributes to the musical characterization. One also suspects that with all the tone colours and timbres available in the orchestra of *Orfeo*, instrumentation did give Monteverdi's audience an indication of the 'affetti' involved. Unfortunately, the score has no specific remarks or rubrics for this rhapsodic monologue. We are, however, in a better position to assess the contribution of scoring to 'Possente spirto', the famous 'preghiera-lamento' that is placed at the precise centre of the opera, namely in the middle of Act III. Here the rubrics and the extra staves for obbligato instruments make clear the precise instrumentation for each of the six stanzas of the text.

With 'Possente spirto', then, we deal with a strophic lament, clearly organized by the librettist into stanzas of equal length. The form employed is called terza rima or terzina (plural terze rime, terzine) because the stanzas are composed of three lines each (the last stanza often extended by a fourth line to complete the rhyme scheme). This is, of course, the famous prosodic model bequeathed by Dante's *Divina Commedia*. As such it is likely to have been familiar to Italians from Monteverdi to Verdi, just as an Englishman would associate heroic blank verse with the 'mighty line' of Marlowe and Shakespeare, and a German 'Knittelverse' with Hans Sachs and Goethe's *Faust*. It is characteristic that when Verdi asks the librettist of *Aida* for some substitute lines, he demands 'il gran verso, il verso di Dante, ed anche la terzina' (the great verse, the verse of Dante, and even the terzina). Monteverdi quotes from the terzine of the *Divina Commedia* both in *Orfeo*, Act III, when he speaks of 'speranza' (hope), and in *Poppea*, Act II, when he speaks of 'amor'.[20] But more to the point at present are laments in early opera cast in the form of terza rima. We may mention here, in addition to Monteverdi's 'Possente spirto', the plaint of Tithonus at the beginning of Act II of Caccini's *Cefalo*.[21] Now in Caccini's lament the strophic form of Chiabrera's text is clearly reflected in the music. The same vocal line and bass are used for the first four stanzas, and even the fifth stanza is substantially unchanged, except that the music has been extended to accommodate an additional fourth line, rounding off the final terza rima.

The successive stanzas of 'Possente spirto', in contrast, are not clearly perceived as strophic by the general listener for a variety of reasons. The composer has set these six terze rime[22] in a manner to increase the urgency of the singer's pleading. The score gives the vocal line in two alternative versions: one is plain, not ornamented, and in comparatively slow notes; the other represents Monteverdi's model of ornamentation in a florid line fit for virtuoso singing. But performers are free to use the plain version as a point of departure for their own improvisatory or planned elaboration.[23] The first four stanzas increase the intensity with which the divine singer pleads for help and laments his misery by progressively more ornate melismas, which reach their climax in the fourth terzina where the two words 'Orfeo son' (I am Orpheus) receive sixty-four rapid notes: twenty-three on 'Orfeo' and forty-one on the single syllable 'son'. It is in such florid passages that the vocal melody does not 'dance to the motion of the bass'; over a sustained

[20] G. Cesari and A. Luzio, *I copialettere di Giuseppe Verdi* (Milan, 1913; repr. 1973), 665; *Opere*, ed. Malipiero, xi. 80 and xiii. 190; both these and other relevant references are noted in Wolfgang Osthoff, 'Dante beim späten Verdi', *Studi Verdiani*, 5 (1988–9), 35–64.

[21] Cf. *Nuove musiche*, ed. Hitchcock, 28 ff., 137–40. Cf. also Solerti, *Albori*, iii. 37, but Hitchcock's text is preferable.

[22] Lines 363–81; facs. pp. 52–65; *Opere*, xi. 84–100.

[23] Cf. John Whenham (ed.), *Claudio Monteverdi: Orfeo* (Cambridge Opera Handbooks; Cambridge, 1986), 62 and 192.

stationary *G* we encounter major sevenths, that is, accented F♯s (l. 372; facs., p. 62; *Opere*, xi. 96). Thus the ornamented vocal line continues the traditions both of virtuosity and of expressive dissonances, discussed earlier.

Throughout the entire incantation Orpheus flatters Charon as 'possente' (powerful, first stanza) or 'nobile' (noble, last stanza), but he supports his supplication by references to his grief (second stanza, ll. 366–8):

> Non vivo io nò, che poi di vita è priva
> Mia cara sposa il cor non è più meco,
> E senza cor com'esser può ch'io viva?

> I do not live, no, since of life is deprived
> My dear spouse, my heart is no longer with me,
> And without heart how can I be said to be alive?

Up to the fourth stanza Orpheus is accompanied by the plucked strings of the chitarrone and the wooden pipes of a little organ, but in addition successive stanzas have their own distinctive obbligato concertino: violins for the first and fourth stanzas, cornetts for the second, and double harp for the third. But at the end of the fourth stanza the memory of Eurydice's beautiful eyes so carries Orpheus away that the elaborate concertato between florid song and florid instrumental obbligato is dropped and the bard sings a vocal line, devoid of any traces of virtuosity, in plain 'stile recitativo', and without a distinctive obbligato. (We may note in passing that the thought of those beautiful eyes so excites Orpheus in the next act that he looks back and loses Eurydice a second time (l. 514), also interrupting a strophic song.) The fifth terzina, then, interrupts the florid concertato of the fourth, which loses thereby its instrumental postlude, but in spite of its simplicity the latter stanza (l. 377) finds a place, in the accompaniment of chitarrone and wood organ, for a chromatically descending tetrachord, a musical symbol to be discussed later:

> Ahi chi nega il conforto à le mie pene?

> Ah, who would deny relief for my afflictions?
> (l. 377; facs., p. 64; *Opere*, xi. 99)

We note again that the exclamation 'ahi' introduces a typical line of lamentation.

For the sixth and final stanza the florid style of singing does not return; the lament concludes with a plain vocal line, accompanied by a string ensemble, notated on four staves and playing 'pian piano' (very softly).

To summarize, the opening stanzas display a highly ornamented style, both in the voice and the instrumental obbligatos, whereas the final two stanzas are of almost syllabic simplicity in the vocal line, and fairly plain and slowly moving in the accompaniment. In fact, the very term 'accompaniment' refers to another distinguishing element. In the first four stanzas voice and obbligato instruments vie for the listener's attention, but these interludes and postludes are absent from the last two stanzas. Both these procedures tend to obscure the strophic form.

Another factor is the treatment of the bass, which we must now consider. Five of the six stanzas are variations over a slowly moving bass. Such ostinato basses were frequently used by Monteverdi's predecessors and contemporaries, either as the basis of instrumental or vocal variations, or as a skeleton upon which to improvise the recitation of stanzas from the favourite verse epics of Ariosto, Tasso, and others. Sometimes the bass formula was short and pregnant (as in the case of the diatonic or chromatic tetrachord), at other times the repeated formula was more extended.[24]

Variations over a repeated bass are frequently met in the works of Monteverdi, also in those of Caccini, but more rarely in those of Peri. Monteverdi seems to have preferred to control details of expression in successive stanzas or sections, rather than to provide the first stanza of a strophic lyric with a piece of music, giving the text of subsequent stanzas below, to be sung to the same music. (Needless to say, such straightforward strophic songs are also occasionally encountered in Monteverdi's operas.) The strophic method is employed by both Peri and Caccini in their respective prologues to *Euridice*, whereas in Monteverdi's *Orfeo* score each stanza of the prologue is separately printed with its music, and these successive instalments are variations over a repeated bass (or harmonic framework). However that may be, the bass that supports 'Possente spirto' consists of two strains, usually followed by a codetta or postlude that cadentially confirms the key of G minor. The first strain starts on the tonic, tarries on the flattened leading-note, and cadences on the dominant; it usually accommodates the first two lines of a terza rima. The second strain starts on the mediant, and cadences on the tonic; it usually accommodates the third line of the terzina. The codetta supports the final full cadence; it also provides the bass for the obbligato postlude in the first three stanzas, is omitted in stanzas 4–5, and reappears, slightly varied, accommodating the extra fourth line in the sixth stanza. Ex. 6.8 gives the schematic outline of the bass that forms the basis of the variations of 'Possente spirto'. It is not possible to indicate more than an outline, since the duration of the individual notes varies from stanza to stanza. For instance, the opening G may last eight crotchets (second stanza), or twelve (sixth), or sixteen (first and third), or twenty-four (fourth stanza, 'Orfeo son', just discussed). Similarly the note d, which concludes the first strain, may last four or eight or twelve crotchets.

---

[24] The literature on this vast subject is widely scattered, and the precise differences between such terms as 'ostinato', 'passacaglia', 'chaconne', etc. are far from clear. Cf. standard dictionaries s.v. Chaconne, Ground, Ostinato, Passacaglia. Concerning specifically named repeated basses, to be compared with that of 'Possente spirto', cf. articles s.v. Folia, Passamezzo, Romanesca, Ruggiero. Further material will be found in articles on Figures (German 'Figuren'), Lament, and Rhetoric. Additional bibliography on the tetrachord will be cited later. The first two phrases of the Ruggiero bass will be found in Peri's setting of Arion's lament 'Dunque fra torbide onde' (Ex. 6.6, discussed earlier).

As has been stated, the fifth stanza is freely composed and does not make use of the repeated bass.

Ex. 6.8. Schematic outline of bass of 'Possente spirto'

Strain 1   Strain 2

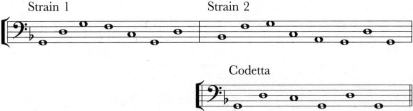

Codetta

Among the basses supporting variations, particularly popular in the sixteenth and seventeenth centuries, are three that display similarities with Ex. 6.8: the folia, the romanesca, and the passamezzo antico. These three standard basses have several features in common, among them the minor mode and the prominence given, in addition to tonic and dominant, to the

Ex. 6.9*a*. Comparison of bass of 'Possente spirto' with ostinato basses

Possente

Romanesca

Folia

Passamezzo antico

Passamezzo antico

Possente

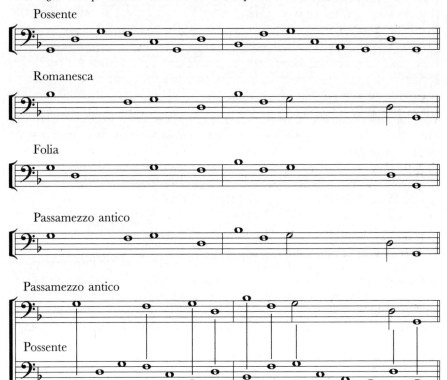

Ex. 6.9*b*. Framework of 'Possente spirto'

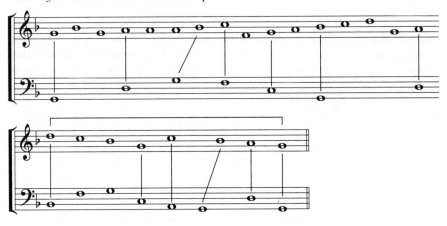

Ex. 6.9*c*. Passamezzo antico harmonized

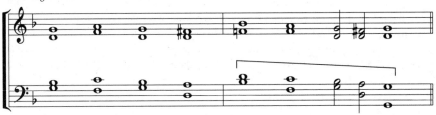

seventh and third degree of the scale. Since these three formulas were frequently used in ornamented versions, one could view the bass of 'Possente spirto' as a variant of this family, particularly of the passamezzo antico. Whether the similarity was deliberate or unconscious on Monteverdi's part is a moot question. In Ex. 6.9*a* the three popular basses and the two strains of the 'Possente spirto' bass (without the cadential codetta) are easily surveyed and compared. The additional notes in Monteverdi are far from being more numerous than in the ornamentations of the standard formulas encountered in many compositions of the early seventeenth century.[25]

There are other reasons why the strophic variations of 'Possente spirto' are not easily recognized. For one thing, the average listener is more likely to notice the vocal line than the instrumental bass. Now the plain version of the tenor part shows certain similarities in five of the six stanzas. But in the ornamented vocal line (almost invariably performed in revivals for stage,

---

[25] For a more ample discussion of the passamezzo, see Ward's article in *MGG*, with bibliographical references to the valuable spadework done by Gombosi. Ward's examples are given in four-part harmony, and it is interesting to compare the tenor part of the passamezzo antico with Monteverdi's vocal line.

concert hall, or sound recordings), the underlying similarity is not easily perceived. If, on the other hand, one studies the plain version, searching for a common denominator to the five relevant stanzas, some basic framework (such as Ex. 6.9*b*) may be observed in the vocal line as well as in the bass. Certainly, the scheme for the melody accompanying the second strain of the bass is rather reminiscent of the tenor of the conclusion of the passamezzo antico (see square brackets in Ex. 6.9*b* and *c*).

But whatever the derivation or affiliation of Monteverdi's bass may be, the overall impression on the listener, lay or learned, is—as already stated— one of increasing virtuosity up to the point (l. 374; facs., p. 64; *Opere*, xi. 98) where the fourth stanza is interrupted, deprived of its florid instrumental postlude, and the variations over the repeated bass temporarily stop. The fifth stanza, with its plain vocal line, and the absence of obbligato instruments, comes as a dramatic and exciting surprise. Orpheus is not trying to elicit Charon's pity and support through the charms of music, but speaks his own mind. This journey through successive stages of the protagonist's mind is accomplished without deserting the tonality of G minor, which is solidly maintained from the opening sinfonia to the last line of the lament. But after the climax of expressive ornamentation, the two final stanzas are not only more simple, they become also more pregnant: the fifth and sixth terze rime occupy shorter spans of time. The sixth and last stanza, where the bass returns, is still characterized by the lack of floridity, but here the plain vocal line is surrounded by the halo of an obbligato string ensemble; its simplicity is conspicuous but no less eloquent for the ... reminds some listeners of the magic effect of some Bach cantatas, where ... unadorned chorale acts as a finale, after it has undergone elaborate variations and developments in the previous movements. Thus the six stanzas of Monteverdi's strophic lament may be summarized as falling into three sections: a plea employing the power and artifices of music (stanzas 1–4); a plain recitation that reflects the mind of the singer (stanza 5); and the peroration of the final stanza which brings the opening plea to a simplified and transfigured conclusion.

The *Lamento della ninfa*[26] is another lament of Monteverdi's where the strophic articulation of the literary text is hardly noticed because the composer transforms the lyric into a tripartite drama. Rinuccini's text is divided into ten stanzas, each one consisting of six lines, namely four settenari narrating the plight of the deserted nymph, followed by a commiserating refrain of two further settenari. Monteverdi's setting uses the refrain only in the central lament (stanzas 4–9), which unfolds over a descending tetrachord, diatonic and in the minor mode,[27] repeated thirty-two times. In this lament proper

[26] *Opere*, viii. 286 94.

[27] Concerning laments and tetrachords (minor or major mode, descending or ascending, diatonic or chromatic) see, in addition to the dictionary articles and their bibliographies cited in n. 24, particularly Lorenzo Bianconi, *Il Seicento* (Turin, 1982), 209 18; Ellen Rosand, 'The Descending Tetrachord: An

the complete refrain appears only three times; in other stanzas it is reduced
to a single word, as we shall see. And to complicate matters further, the
central threnody is framed by a prologue (stanzas 1–3) and an epilogue
(stanza 10). This framing structure of four stanzas is performed by a male
trio of two tenors and a bass. The same trio also adds its sonority and texture to the lament proper, in which the 'ninfa' (a soprano) gives vent to her
grief, which is observed and commented upon by tenors and bass. Obviously,
this is a dramatic scene, involving all kinds of contrasts: vocal treble versus
instrumental bass, soprano solo versus male trio, narration versus direct
speech, and stanzas without refrain versus those with full (or overlapping
or abbreviated) refrain. But the overall impression is of a division into three,
not ten sections, namely the opening and closing narration and comment, and
the central soprano section. This latter, with its expressive dissonances, does
not at all 'dance to the motion of the bass', as numerous sevenths (e.g. bars
11, 12, 15, 27, 31, 42, 53, 60) and tritones (e.g. bars 22, 36, 40, 58, 62, 64)
testify. The effect is 'dramatic', a fact which Monteverdi emphasizes when
he calls the piece 'rappresentativo', an adjective with which he also labels
the 'Combattimento di Tancredi e Clorinda' and the 'Ballo dell'ingrate', published in the same madrigal book, which advertises in its title 'Madrigals of
war and love, with some pieces in dramatic style [in genere rappresentativo]'.

   A word should be said about the 'Phrygian' aspects of the nymph's
lament, which add a special note of eloquence to this composition, and
connect it with other threnodies already discussed, namely Festa's 'Qual
sarà mai' and Peri's 'Non   '. What distinguishes Phrygian laments
from other dirges in the minor mode are the notes surrounding the 'tonic'
(or 'finalis' in medieval terms). From above it is approached by a semitone,
from below by a whole tone (F–E, and D–E; transposed B♭–A and G–A).
It is usually the descending semitone that strikes the modern listener with its
distinctive flavour. In the case of Monteverdi, its prominence in the soprano
line (bars 11–12) is supported and enhanced by the constantly recurring F–E
in the four-note ostinato bass. But the ascending whole tone (bar 38) also
makes its appearance at a cadential climax, preceded by the semitone in
the same soprano line, and counterpointed against it in the bass. In Festa's
setting of Poliziano's plaint the descending semitone, F–E, is also prominent
at cadential points in treble (Ex. 6.4, bars 5–6, 17–18, 42–3) and bass (bars
9–10, 32, 44, 46–7). The whole tone below E is also duly stressed (bars
9–10 and 32, tenor; 43–7, soprano; in all three instances counterpointed

Emblem of Lament', *MQ* 65 (1979), 346 59; Whenham, *Duet and Dialogue*, i. 175, 191; ii. 189, 331 *et passim*.
Cf. also Haas, *Musik des Barocks*, s.v. 'Chromatik', 'Ciaconna', 'Ostinato', 'Quartfall'; id., *Mozart* (Potsdam,
1933), s.v. 'Quartgang'; Unger, *Musik und Rhetorik*, s.v. 'passus duriusculus', 'pathopoiia', 'suspiratio' (pp. 66,
86, 93, 153, *et passim*); Peter F. Williams, 'Figurenlehre from Monteverdi to Wagner', *Musical Times*, 120
(1979), 476 9, 571 3, 648 50, 816 8; id., 'Encounters with the Chromatic Fourth; . . . or More on
Figurenlehre', ibid, 126 (1985), 276 8, 339 43.

against the semitone in the bass). In Peri's 'Non piango' the expressive vocal line for tenor, unfolding over stationary notes in the bass, curiously wavers between A minor ('Aeolian') and transposed 'Phrygian', with the semitone B♭ above A: this switch from B♮ to B♭ (Ex. 6.7, bars 1–5 and 6–9) seems related to the examples cited earlier. But, needless to say, chromaticism and poignancy are not restricted to Phrygian melodies or harmonies, and also occur in other minor-mode laments.

Several aspects of Monteverdi's setting of the nymph's lament merit inspection: its treatment of strophic form and of refrain, as well as its use of a descending tetrachord in the minor mode as a repeated bass. As far as we can deduce from other settings of the same poem, Monteverdi differs from his fellow composers by obscuring the strophic form. Brunelli (1614), Kapsberger (1619), and Piazza (1633) adhere to it more closely than the 'rappresentativo' piece in Monteverdi's eighth book of 1638 (though the lyric may have been composed before it was included in that printed collection). Perhaps a comparison with Kapsberger's setting, readily available in a modern reprint, will clarify this.[28] Kapsberger uses identical music for all stanzas: the prologue, the nymph's lament, and the epilogue; the two-line refrain is heard at the end of each stanza. To put it differently, Kapsberger does not break up the lyrical integrity of the poem in order to arrive at three blocks (or sections) of irregular length, corresponding to the 'affetti' of the lament, as Monteverdi perceives it. It is perhaps worth observing Monteverdi's treatment of the refrain in some detail, since it illuminates the sovereign freedom with which he subjugates the strophic form to his dramatic purposes. The keynote of the refrain is its first word 'miserella' (poor thing, poor girl, unfortunate one, wretched one): it denotes a gullible woman, tricked and betrayed by a man. (The term 'poverina', used by Leporello and Don Giovanni as they comment on the lamenting Elvira in the first act of Mozart's opera, offers a suitable analogue.) The frequency with which Monteverdi employs 'miserella' as the summing up of the predominant emotion of the entire lyric shows the economy of the born dramatist. Since the refrain is omitted in the prologue (stanzas 1–3) and the epilogue (stanza 10) we are left with the six stanzas of the central section. This differs from the framing sections not only by virtue of its slowly moving ostinato bass and the range and timbre of its soprano line, but also by the extension that the refrain provides for the four-line stanzas. It would have been easy for the composer to attach this two-line refrain on to stanzas 4–9, having the three male voices fully commiserating six times with the 'miserella', for whose lament they provide the foil. Instead, Monteverdi uses the refrain

---

[28] *Nuovo Vogel*, nos. 434 (Brunelli), 1362 (Kapsberger), 1941 (Monteverdi), and 2217 (Piazza). For Kapsberger (music, text, translation) cf. Whenham, *Duet and Dialogue*, ii. 189, 332. For comments on strophic form cf. Rosand, 'Descending Tetrachord', 350; Leopold, *Monteverdi* (1982 edn.), 177; Gary A. Tomlinson, *Monteverdi and the End of the Renaissance* (Oxford, 1987), 213.

completely only three times, as already stated, but the keyword 'miserella' runs through the entire central section: it is stated only once on one occasion (bar 12), but repeated as many as ten times on another (bars 27–46).[29] Sometimes the composer reduces the refrain to the single word 'miserella' (stanza 1, bar 12; stanza 9, bars 60–6), but at other times he expands the time-dimension and poignancy of the refrain not only by repetition but also by adding the expletive 'ah'. (What would laments be without the repeated sighs and sobs of 'ah' and 'oh'?) Thus, overlapping with the soprano's recitation of the sixth and seventh stanzas (bars 25–33, 35–46), we have the tenfold repetition of 'miserella', occasionally intensified by 'ah miserella' (bars 27, 29, 31, 42) and 'miserella ah' (bars 33, 39, 45).

In the following excerpts, giving the text of three of Monteverdi's stanzas (1, 4, 5), square brackets indicate the partial or total omission of Rinuccini's two-line refrain.[30]

first stanza:

Non havea Febo ancora	Phoebus had not yet
recato al mondo il dì,	brought to the earth the day,
ch'una donzella fuora	when a maiden came forth
del proprio albergo uscì.	from her home.
[Miserella, ah, più no, no,	Wretched one, ah, no more, no,
tanto gel soffrir non può.]	such icy scorn she cannot suffer.

fourth stanza:

'Amor', diceva, il piè,	'Love', she said, and her foot
mirando il ciel, fermò,	stopped as she gazed at the sky,
'dove, dov'è la fè	'where, where is the faith
che 'l traditor giurò?'	that the traitor swore?'
Miserella [ah, più no, no,	Wretched one . . .
tanto gel soffrir non può].	

fifth stanza:

'Fa che ritorni il mio	'Bring about that my love
amor, com'ei pur fu,	returns to me, as he was,
o tu m'ancidi ch'io	or kill me so that I
non mi tormenti più.'	no longer torture myself.'
Miserella, ah, più no, no,	Wretched one . . .
tanto gel soffrir non può.	

The *Lamento della ninfa* is much discussed in the literature on Monteverdi and on the lament, and the extensive description of its features may give the erroneous impression that it is altogether typical. True, some of its traits are fairly characteristic of several laments of the first half of the seventeenth

[29] All references to bar-numbers in Monteverdi are based on Malipiero's edn., whose eighth volume was reprinted in 1967 with bar-numbers (pp. 288–93).

[30] The interpunctuation has been modernized, but the spelling follows the refrain as it appears in Monteverdi: 'gel' instead of 'giel' (chill, icy disdain), and the expletive 'ah' instead of 'ahi'. (The same variants appear in Kapsberger's setting.)

century: its irregular proportions, the use of the tetrachord, and the minor mode. But none of these features could be codified as 'rules', because different procedures are readily found. Also, the tetrachord need not partner a lament: in the final love duet from *Poppea* a passionate, if not lascivious, interchange between Nero and Poppaea is accompanied by a descending ostinato tetrachord in the major mode.[31] The dramatic and emotional context of these two passages may readily account, at least to modern sensibilities, for the employment of the major mode. But the 'Lamento di Madama Lucia', published in 1628 with the ascription to 'Il Fasolo', presents more of a puzzle, and warns us not to generalize too hastily. The lament is accompanied by a descending ostinato tetrachord, in the minor mode. The same text was set to music by Manelli in a collection of 1636, with different music, and a descending tetrachord ostinato, but in the major mode. And to complicate matters further, several students of the subject have suggested that 'Fasolo' was a pseudonym for Manelli. If we accept this hypothesis, the composer would have improved his own lament in various ways, including the substitution of the major for the minor mode.[32]

The question of the chronological priority of the *Lamento della ninfa* (published in 1638, but perhaps composed in the 1620s) compared with the 'Lamento' by 'Fasolo' is difficult to establish; and the problem of the frequency with which the minor or the major modes were employed in laments is similarly hard to solve. In addition to printed sources, it is also necessary to consider extant manuscript scores of operas and manuscript collections of poetry. Also, the association of the minor mode with sorrow and suffering, in western music, was less strong in the earlier seventeenth century than it is now, although examination of secular and, more surprisingly, even of sacred music suggests that it existed. Surveying, then, the material referred to in the relevant literature and discussed in this chapter, one may summarize the following conclusions. Whether a composition is called a 'lament' (or 'tombeau' or 'dump' or 'passacaglia'), whether it is a madrigal or an instrumental piece or an operatic excerpt, sad and sorrowful works are frequently, though not invariably, in the minor mode. That certainly would apply to compositions based on standard basses, such as the passamezzo antico and the romanesca, discussed in conjunction with 'Possente spirto'. As far as tetrachords are concerned, we have so far surveyed only the diatonically descending fourth. When one also considers the

---

[31] The controversy about the authorship of this duet has already been discussed. Suffice it to say here that some scholars ascribe it to Monteverdi, others to Ferrari, still others to Sacrati. No general consensus has as yet emerged.

[32] Cf. Rosand, 'Descending Tetrachord', 353; Whenham, *Duet and Dialogue*, i. 175, 191. I am grateful to Dr Whenham for having provided me with copies of the compositions of 1628 and 1636. Cf. also *Nuovo Vogel*, nos. 911 and 1568. The largest number of examples of tetrachord passages, employing both minor and major modes, is given by Rosand, who also returns to the Fasolo–Manelli question in *New Grove*, s.v. 'Lament'.

many pieces, from the sixteenth century onwards, based on chromatically descending (or ascending) tetrachords, the preference for the minor mode becomes even more apparent. Descending motion is encountered more frequently, but inversion (i.e. ascent) accompanies the tetrachord from its inception onwards (say from Rore to Stravinsky).[33] Sometimes the figure repeated in the bass is short and restricted to the interval of a fourth; at other times it is extended, for instance by a cadential formula, and occupies a larger span of time.

Laments are important in the three extant operas of Monteverdi (*Orfeo*, *Ulisse*, *Poppea*), but they fulfil an even more integral role in the works of his pupil and successor Cavalli. All Cavalli's operas include at least one lament, and some of them several. Moreover, these threnodies fulfil their task admirably: they 'purge' the passions in the Aristotelian sense; being placed near the finale they act as an effective foil for the *lieto fine*—and they provide opportunities for good solo singing and for good music to boot. Since twenty-seven operatic scores of Cavalli survive, it is of course much easier to generalize about him than about Peri or Monteverdi. Of his laments, based on a diatonically descending tetrachord, we may select as an example one from his *Ormindo* (libretto by Faustini; Venice, 1644). In this lament Queen Erisbe, erroneously believing that she and her lover Ormindo are condemned to death, eloquently complains that the promised wedding and happiness with Ormindo are now eluding her. Everything about this piece is fairly formulaic: the descending tetrachord in the minor mode; the cadential extension; intensification by the repetition of words ('ah', 'questo', 'himeneo'; and others appearing later than the excerpt shown in Ex. 6.10);

Ex. 6.10. Cavalli, Erisbe's lament from *Ormindo*

the complaint of the disappointed woman who joins the ranks of such 'miserelle' as Ariadne and Dido. (As in *Tristan*, the potion is only believed to be lethal; the lovers survive, and a *lieto fine* is shortly arrived at. The curious manner in which the triangle of old king, queen, and young lover anticipates the plots of *Tristan* and *Pelléas* has been commented upon before.

---

[33] The use of the tetrachord is, of course, not restricted to the bass, as we have seen in the case of Festa (Ex. 6.4). But in the extensive literature on the subject, and in the examples cited in the remainder of this chapter, the fourth (whether descending or ascending) occurs mostly in the bass, or pervades all voices, including the bass.

Certainly, in the seventeenth and eighteenth centuries, love and youth are bound to emerge triumphant.)

Ah, ah, questo, questo	Ah, ah, is this, this
è l'himeneo, l'himeneo . . .	the wedding celebration [promised] . . .[34]

LAMENTO D'ARIANNA

No lament of Monteverdi's, or indeed of the seventeenth century, has been praised more warmly or more frequently than the lament of the heroine towards the end of *Arianna*.[35] From the first performance of the opera in 1608 until our century court chroniclers, ambassadors, composers, and students of opera have not ceased to single out the 'pianto' of the deserted Ariadne for its emotional, dramatic, and musical appeal. In 1608 Follino wrote that

every part succeeded well, most especially . . . the lament which Ariadne sings on the rock . . . which was acted with so much emotion (*con tanto affetto*) and in so piteous a way that no one hearing it was left unmoved, nor was there among the ladies one who did not shed tears (*qualche lagrimetta*) at her plaint (*pianto*).[36]

In the 1630s Doni judged the piece to be 'perhaps the most beautiful composition of this kind (*in questo genere*) which our times have produced', to quote Burney's translation. And as late as 1783 Arteaga compared the success of the plaint with that of Pergolesi's *Serva padrona* in his time.[37] Around the turn of the nineteenth and twentieth centuries the complete musical text of the solo portions of Monteverdi's lament became available in the publications of Vogel (1887) and Solerti (1904), and further investigation and assessment have continued right up to the present.[38] The text of the lament (as indeed the entire libretto) is by Rinuccini, and it must be owned that at least part of its success is to be attributed to the poet, whose methods of repetition and variation, of inserting his 'ah' and his 'oh' at the right place and the right time, greatly aided the composer. Monteverdi does not use the tetrachord formula, nor does he employ an ostinato bass.

[34] Cf. MS score in Contarini Collection, Biblioteca Marciana, Venice, fo. 166ᵛ. Cf. also vocal score, ed. R. Leppard (London: Faber, 1969), 176, where the passage is transposed from C minor to B minor.

[35] Solerti, *Albori*, ii. 175 9 (ll. 782 905); the entire libretto is reprinted pp. 143 88. All references to line numbers of the 'Lamento' in this chapter refer to Solerti's lineation.

[36] Quoted in Solerti, *Albori*, ii. 145; see also i. 99.

[37] Charles Burney, *A General History of Music*, 4 vols. (London, 1776 89; repr. in 2 vols., ed. F. Mercer, 1935; repr. 1957), iv. 24. Fortune in Arnold and Fortune, *New Monteverdi Companion*, 193 4 gives a judicious selection from the chorus of praise through the ages, and mentions various composers of the 17th c. who imitated Monteverdi's successful formula.

[38] For details see Whenham's articles on 'Arianna' and 'Monteverdi' in the forthcoming *New Grove Dictionary of Opera*. The 'Monteverdi' article contains a comprehensive bibliography on the *Lamento d'Arianna*. Cf. particularly the contributions by Vogel, 1887; Solerti, 1904; Epstein, 1927/8; Westrup, 1940; Gallico, 1947; Anfuso and Gianuario, 1969; Galleni Luisi, 1969; Michels, 1984.

But building on the proportions of Rinuccini's non-strophic text, employing chromaticism eloquently but not excessively, and maintaining the tension between melody and bass that is so essential for the 'stile recitativo' he has created a piece of singular passion and intensity, which—being placed near the *lieto fine*—became the *pièce de résistance* of the opera and is the only surviving portion of it today.

The only source that transmits the entire lament is Rinuccini's libretto, printed in various editions in 1608; notably, it is included in the account of the festivities of 1608 by the court chronicler Federico Follino, published at Mantua in 1608 and reprinted by Solerti.[39] In the libretto we have not only the lines allotted to the soloist, Ariadne, but also the interspersions, made by the chorus and the confidante Dorilla, with which the heroine's lament is punctuated. Of course, Ariadne's portion constitutes the lion's share (84 out of 124 lines), consisting of nine sections of very unequal length (varying between 3 and 24 lines). But the punctuations (ranging from 3 to 12 lines) increase in length as the lament proceeds. The musical sources, discussed below, do not provide any setting for the interspersions of the chorus and Dorilla.

All nine sections of the soloist survive in a musical setting, transmitted in two manuscripts, one in Florence, the other in London.[40] This version of Monteverdi's music is only rarely heard, because it fits the dramatic context of an operatic performance better than the requirements of the concert hall. Sections six through nine allot little space to the main protagonist (3, 3, 4, and 5 lines respectively) and more to the punctuations of Dorilla (12, 4, and 7 lines). As a result, the concluding portion of the lament offers fewer opportunities to the composer and is of less interest to a public eager for expressive singing by an accomplished soloist.

The version most frequently encountered today is an arrangement of the first five sections, published twice in 1623, and also surviving in two manuscripts, in Venice and Modena. This setting is for solo voice and bass, consisting of two staves, and has been frequently reprinted, notably in Malipiero's edition of Monteverdi's works.[41] In Rinuccini's libretto the opening five sections occupy a total of eighty-six lines. If one detaches the 'punctuations', as composers of monodies not intended for operatic performance usually did, this leaves Monteverdi with a substantial number of lines allotted to

---

[39] Solerti, *Albori*, ii, pp. vii–ix, lists seven edns., printed between 1608 and 1640.

[40] Florence, Biblioteca Nazionale; London, British Library. Both MSS are discussed and described in Jack Westrup, 'Monteverdi's *Lamento d'Arianna*', *MR* 1 (1940), 144 54; and by Whenham (cf. n. 38). The music is reprinted in Emil Vogel, 'Claudio Monteverdi', *Vierteljahrsschrift für Musikwissenschaft*, 3 (1887), 443 50; Solerti, *Albori*, i (16 pp. inserted between pp. 96 and 97); N. Anfuso and A. Gianuario, *Monteverdi: Lamento d'Arianna; studio e interpretazione* (Florence, 1969), 37 48.

[41] *Opere*, xi. 161 7. All musical references to the *Lamento* in this chapter refer to this edn. The printed edns. are those published at Venice in 1623 (title-page reproduced in Malipiero); and another appearing in an anthology published at Orvieto, also in 1623. The extant MSS at Venice and Modena are described in Whenham (cf. n. 38).

Ariadne (69 lines, or 80%). Before examining this important and influential variant, first published in 1623, we must briefly survey two other versions that appeared in print before Monteverdi's death, in 1614 and 1641.

One is a sacred contrafactum ('parody'), entitled 'Pianto della Madonna', where the plaint of Ariadne becomes that of the Blessed Virgin. The 'Pianto' is scored for voice and bass (like the 'Lamento' of 1623), uses only the first four (not five) sections of the plaint, and substitutes Latin words for the original Italian text. This spiritual parody was published in 1640/1 (preface dated 1641), together with many other sacred works of Monteverdi, in the composer's *Selva morale*, and has been reprinted by Malipiero (xv. 757–62). In the 'Pianto' some of the more frequent textual changes result in the many appeals to the Madonna's son. For instance, at the start of the first section 'Lasciatemi morire' becomes 'Jam moriar, mi Fili', retaining the wish 'to die', but inserting the address to 'my Son' (xv. 757). Similarly, at the beginning of the second section the appeal to Theseus 'O Teseo, o Teseo mio' becomes 'Mi Jesu, o Jesu mi sponse' (xv. 757). Musically this is still an attractive arrangement for solo voice. The first four sections, with punctuations, occupy seventy lines in Rinuccini, of which fifty-eight (or 83%) remain for the soloist. The sacred words fit the vocal line surprisingly well, but the general preference for the original Italian text, in our increasingly secular musical culture and age, is understandable.

Still, the first four sections include the musical plums of the lament, and in 1614 Monteverdi published an arrangement of them, not for solo voice, but for five vocal parts, and placed it as the opening number of his sixth book of madrigals, utilizing the original Italian text. This sixth book was reprinted in 1615, 1620, and 1639.[42] When we add the four editions of the madrigal to the other arrangements discussed so far, we arrive at a total of eleven musical sources, seven in print and four in manuscript, transmitting to us Monteverdi's setting of the lament in various guises and with differing degrees of completeness. Let us now consider the *Lamento d'Arianna* as it was published in 1623, a variant that strikes many of the composer's admirers as the most exquisite fashioning of the lyric.

This is the version that comprises the first five sections, all of which clearly cadence in D minor, and even without the punctuation of the interspersed choruses the irregularity of their length is readily recognized. The first thing that occurs to the observer is how perfectly the poet has caught the 'affetto', the pathos of the lament, in his verbal music. He has provided 'poesia per musica' to such a degree that Monteverdi had to add very little to the text by way of repeating individual words or phrases, or lines. As we have seen, this monodic variant is made up of sixty-nine lines, to which the composer has added only two: one at the end of the first section (l. 787', after

[42] Cf. *Nuovo Vogel*, nos. 1932 5. For a transcription see *Opere*, vi. 1 21.

Rinuccini's l. 787) and one near the beginning of the fifth section (l. 836', after l. 836). Otherwise, Monteverdi's setting dispenses with any expansion of Rinuccini's structure.

Perhaps we may clarify this by looking at the first section, famous for its chromatic intensity, and also for many decades better known than the remainder because it was the only excerpt quoted in histories and anthologies of music (for instance, Winterfeld's *Gabrieli und sein Zeitalter* of 1834). Rinuccini's text runs to six lines (782–7), in which repetition plays a large part to express the depth of Ariadne's grief. The opening line is stated three

Ex. 6.11. Monteverdi, *Lamento d'Arianna*, opening section

times (782, 783, 787); when we add to that the anaphora on 'In così' before the end (785–6) it is understandable that Monteverdi hardly saw any need to repeat individual words, as he does so often in his madrigals (and as Beethoven does with the word 'dahin' in his setting of 'Mignon', much to Goethe's chagrin). On the other hand, the composer did repeat the last line (787') in order to accommodate the chromaticism of his melody. Thus the words 'Lasciatemi morire' are heard four times, but the same music only twice: the setting of ll. 782–3 is repeated for ll. 787–7', as will be seen in Ex. 6.11. To put it differently: in the monody of 1623 the repetition of Rinuccini's line merely spells out the implications of the poet's structure.

When we look at the madrigalian setting of 1614 we encounter more radical changes wrought on the poetic architecture by the insertion of repeated lines. (The madrigal is not a mere transcription for five vocal parts; it represents a reconsideration and rearrangement.) There an additional statement of l. 782 is inserted after ll. 784–6 (*Opere*, vi. 2), and this is followed by an extra setting of ll. 784–6 (vi. 2–3), after which the madrigal, like the monody, concludes with the chromatic setting of ll. 787–7'. Similarly, in the madrigalian setting of the third section, Rinuccini's structure is altered by inserting repetitions of ll. 826–7 and 829–32 (*Opere*, vi. 13–14 and 15). Such and other repetitions of lines change, of course, the time-dimension and symmetry of Rinuccini's verse, and are wholly absent from the monody. Nor, may we add, has Monteverdi omitted any of the poet's lines, as he did in the case of the *Lamento della ninfa*. In the monodic setting of 'Lasciatemi morire' the fit of text and music is perfect (see Ex. 6.11).

782	Lasciatemi morire,	Let me die,
783	Lasciatemi morire;	Let me die.

784	E che volete voi che
	    mi conforte
		And what is your wish that should
		    comfort me

785	In così dura sorte,	In so dire a fate,
786	In così gran martire?	In so great an affliction?
787	Lasciatemi morire,	Let me die,
787'	Lasciatemi morire.	Let me die.

Before discussing Ex. 6.11, I must admit that, following Westrup and many others, I have emended the positioning of the sharp of bars 4 and 17 in the 1623 print and in Malipiero's transcription.[43] In Malipiero the voice ascends a whole tone from b' to $c\sharp''$ whereas the madrigal version (*Opere*, vi. 1, 3), the 'Pianto della Madonna' (*Opere*, xv. 757), and the manuscript versions of Florence and London all ascend chromatically from b' to c'' to $c\sharp''$ (see

[43] Cf. *Opere*, 161, with bars 4 and 17 of Ex. 6.11. The present transcription differs from Malipiero's in the following respects: (*a*) by supplying bar-numbers; (*b*) by shifting the sharp in bars 4 and 17; (*c*) by supplying a flat below the second minim in the bass in bar 18, by analogy with bar 5, and in agreement with the Florence MS. Concerning the position of the sharp, cf. Westrup, 'Monteverdi's *Lamento*', 149; Arnold, *Monteverdi* (2nd edn., 1975), 114; (3rd edn., 1990), 105.

Ex. 6.12. Variant versions of melody to 'lasciatemi'

Florence MS   Malipiero

Ex. 6.12). The congruence of these other sources suggests that the printer of the 1623 publication misplaced the sharp, and that the progression should be a semitonal one.

The crucial ingredient of this opening section is the chroma A–B♭: horizontally it initiates the melodic line with the ascending semitone, doubly conspicuous since it is followed by a descending leap. Vertically, the same chroma creates the striking and expressive dissonance of A in the bass against B♭ in the voice. No such dissonance occurs in the repeated statement (bars 4–6), but the ascending chromaticism of the melody is raised in pitch and extended, and the size of the descending leap increased. The return of all this material (bars 14–20) is eloquent, but to insert yet another statement of 'Lasciatemi morire', with its chromaticism, in the middle of the section, as the madrigalian setting of the same text does, seems to show less control of the means of expression. In both the monodic and the madrigalian versions the chroma A–B♭ reappears several times, for instance at the conclusion of the second section (p. 164; ll. 813–14) and near the conclusion of the third section (p. 165; l. 830). In both these cases the semitonal progression is extended upwards, and followed by a large descending leap, as in the first section.

The various addresses to Theseus, usually intensified by the addition of 'oh' or 'ah', involve verbal repetition, reflected musically by sequences (or modified sequences), rising in pitch. Note the appeal that begins the second section and is heard three times: 'O Teseo, o Teseo mio' (O Theseus, o my Theseus; ll. 791, 801, 844; pp. 162, 166); or 'Ah Teseo, ah Teseo mio' (l. 828; p. 165); or 'Volgiti, Teseo mio, volgiti, Teseo' (Turn back, my Theseus, turn back, Theseus; l. 794; p. 162). Obviously, 'Lasciatemi' and 'O Teseo' (and its variants) are of thematic importance for the articulation of Ariadne's lament. By positioning these two germinating cells at the start of the opening two sections Rinuccini and Monteverdi have deliberately stressed their prominence. As the result of the happy teamwork between poet and composer, the occasions where verbal repetition of one sort or another begets analogous musical procedures are so frequent that a complete catalogue would be lengthy and tiresome. But we may observe the anguished cry 'O Dio' (Oh God; ll. 795 and 802; pp. 162 and 163), twice giving rise to the leap of a diminished fifth, d''–$g\sharp'$. The second of these diminished fifths leads us to one of the many instances of Rinuccini's anaphoras that Monteverdi found so congenial: 'Se tu sapessi' (If you but knew; ll. 802–3; p. 163), where both the rising sequence and the enlarged descending leap, d''–$f\sharp'$, give poignancy to the feelings of the 'povera Arianna' (l. 804; p. 163), the 'misera Arianna' (l. 831; p. 165). Between these two passages is another of the libretto's repetitions, mirrored in a rising sequence in the music: 'In van piangendo, in van gridando' (In vain weeping, in vain calling; l. 830; p. 165). But not all repetition begets rising sequences; sometimes Monteverdi finds that repetition on the same pitch serves his purpose. Note, for instance, his setting of '. . . queste le corone . . . questi gli scettri . . . queste le gemme . . .' (Are these the crowns . . . these the sceptres . . . these the gems; ll. 822–5; p. 164). On the other hand, the only time the composer inserts a new line into Rinuccini's near-perfect text, he manages to get an extra 'Ahi' in, and to accommodate another rising sequence: 'Ahi, che non pur risponde, Ahi, che più . . . è sordo' (Alas he does not answer, Alas he is more . . . deaf; ll. 836–6'; p. 165).

The 'misera Arianna' reminds us in many ways of the 'miserella' of the *Lamento della ninfa*, after all also written by Rinuccini. There are many verbal echoes, such as 'Dove, dove è la fede, Che tanto mi giuravi' (Where, where is the faith that you have so much sworn to me; ll. 818–19; p. 164) and 'dove, dov'è la fè che 'l traditor giurò' (where, where is the faith that the traitor swore; fourth stanza of 'Ninfa', quoted earlier in this chapter; *Opere*, viii. 288–9), where we meet in both lyrics the same repetition of 'dove' and the same complaints about broken oaths encountered in the threnodies of deserted women from classical antiquity (such as those in Ovid's *Heroides*) to Hofmannsthal's *Ariadne*. The *Lamento d'Arianna* employs, needless to say, expressive dissonances between vocal melody and bass besides the chroma of B♭ over A, already mentioned. Note for instance E over F♯ (l. 796; p. 162) and C over C♯ (l. 826; p. 164). But tempting as it would be to explore the many marvels of Ariadne's plaint,[44] we must proceed to considerations of laments over chromatic tetrachords, which perhaps exercised influence over an even longer period of time.

THE CHROMATIC TETRACHORD

Here we deal with a formula whose popularity from the sixteenth to the eighteenth century, and beyond, is well documented outside the realm of opera: in madrigals, motets, and masses, as well as in instrumental compositions. Even the ordinary music-lover, as distinct from the student of opera, is familiar with such passages as Dido's lament from Purcell's *Dido and Aeneas*,

---

[44] For the emulation of Rinuccini's verse and vocabulary, cf. Paolo Fabbri, *Il secolo cantante: per una storia del libretto d'opera nel Seicento* (Bologna, 1990), 25–30. For musical settings of the same text by other composers (Antonelli, Bonini, Costa, Il Verso, Pari) cf. n. 37; also *Nuovo Vogel*, nos. 390, 639, 1334, and 2141.

the Crucifixus from Bach's B minor Mass, or the Coda of the first movement from Beethoven's Ninth. And with the Ninth we enter the realm of
instrumental music, extending from the rarefied category of chamber music
(Mozart's String Quartet in D minor, K. 421, discussed below) to the more
popular repertory of symphony concerts (Tchaikovsky's 'Pathétique'). To
account for this ubiquity is more difficult than merely to record it. The
expressive qualities of chromaticism have something to do with it, but the
poignancy of semitonal progressions in a primarily diatonic idiom need not
be harnessed to the interval of the fourth; it could encompass a larger or
smaller segment of the available range, as demonstrated in Marenzio's
madrigal 'Solo e pensoso'[45] or Wagner's *Tristan*. Perhaps the polarity between
tonic and dominant in our harmonic system favours a descent from the former to the latter, requiring a perfect fourth. Also, the fourth has cadential
implications and endows the bass line with a structural robustness, particularly when it occurs in ostinato fashion. Thus it helps to create the
tension between treble and bass, when the cadences of the melody do not
coincide with those of the tetrachord. In the great operatic laments from
Monteverdi to Purcell different phrase-lengths in melody and bass significantly add to that proverbial tension. And the ostinato return of the bass
formula bestows on the entire lament a sense of inexorable tragedy, of static
immutability. For that reason such ostinatos are more likely to be encountered
in Baroque operas than in symphonies of later centuries. The descending
fourth in the 'Ninth' is the exception rather than the rule.[46]

Repetition, if not straightforward, is sometimes achieved through successive
imitative entries, pervading a polyphonic texture. That is the procedure
frequently encountered in madrigals, secular motets, and sacred music. On
the other hand, we also meet the formula without any reiteration (straightforward, sequential, or polyphonic): after 1600 its expressive connotations
are well enough understood to be apprehended by the listener. Such pregnant statements, dispensing with ostinato or imitation, are encountered in
Monteverdi's Orfeo, as we have seen in 'Possente spirto'; after the death of
the Commendatore in Mozart's *Don Giovanni*; and preceding and succeeding
Tom Rakewell's final lament in Stravinsky's *Rake's Progress*.[47] That Stravinsky

---

[45] This Petrarchan lament was also set to music by other Italian madrigal composers, cf. *Nuovo Vogel*, iii.
541 2. In the 19th c., the chromaticism of Schubert's setting of the same poem, in Schlegel's German
translation, is remarkable. Maria Antonella Balsano has made a detailed and sensitive comparison of the
settings of Marenzio (1599), Haydn (1798), and Schubert (1818) in a paper for the 14th Congress of the
Associazione per gli Studi di Lingua e Letteratura Italiana (Odense, 1991), to be published in the
Proceedings of the Congress. She is also preparing a complementary paper on settings of 'Solo e
pensoso' by composers of the Renaissance.

[46] Cf. Wolfgang Osthoff, 'Symphonien beim Ende des Zweiten Weltkriegs', *AcM* 60 (1988), 97 ff.,
with references to ostinato technique in Mozart, Beethoven, Stravinsky, and Shostakovich.

[47] The fifth terzina of 'Possente spirto' has been discussed earlier in this chapter, cf. *Opere*, xi. 99, l.
377. In *Don Giovanni* the overture and the D minor section of the second finale employ the tetrachord
more prominently, but the orchestral postlude after the death of Donna Anna's father is eloquent and

was aware of the precedent of Monteverdi and Mozart cannot be doubted. But this lament of the twentieth century also stresses the Ovidian connection. It was Ovid who had intertwined the story of Orpheus and Eurydice with that of Venus and Adonis (see Ch. 1). When Tom Rakewell believes himself to be Adonis and precedes his threnody, 'Weep for Adonis', with such phrases as 'I feel the chill of death's approaching wing' and 'Orpheus, strike from thy lyre a swan-like music' (vocal score, pp. 228–9), we are deliberately reminded of such symbols or *figurae* as Orpheus and Adonis, and of the precedent of classical antiquity, where the genre of the lament is so prominent in dramatic as well as in narrative poetry, for instance in Euripides and Ovid.

In the operas of Monteverdi's successor Cavalli the chromatic fourth looms so large that one is bound to ask how the formula, in one shape or another, was established in the century preceding Cavalli. One of the first instances that spring to mind is Rore's 'Calami sonum ferentes', a remarkable secular motet, published in 1555, and singled out for its extreme chromaticism by Burney in the 1780s, and by Kroyer and Lowinsky in our own century.[48] The piece laments the absence of Alfonso d'Este, heir to the throne, from Ferrara in the 1550s, and expresses its grief by having the chromatic fourth enter successively into the polyphonic texture of all four voices.[49] The work is exceptional in several respects: its date is surprisingly early; the text is Latin and not vernacular; and the direction of the chromatic fourth is ascending instead of descending, as in the majority of well-known examples. Let us therefore consider for a moment two madrigals, published before 1600, with Italian texts, and with descending tetrachords. The first is Caimo's 'Piangete valli abbandonate', a lament from Sannazaro's *Arcadia*, of which the first extant printed source dates from 1564, nine years later than the first known publication of Rore. Again the descending chromatic tetrachord appears in all four voices.[50] Monteverdi's 'Là tra 'l sangu'e le morti'

of dramatic importance; cf. Haas, *Mozart*, 144 n. 22. Concerning the *Rake's Progress* cf. the instrumental postlude to the duettino that precedes Tom's lament (vocal score, 1951, p. 226), where the bass descends a perfect fourth from C to G; and Tom's last words, preceding the mourning chorus (vocal score, p. 229), where the bass descends a diminished fourth, A♭ to E; and the overlapping descents (G to D, and E to B) at the conclusion of the mourning chorus (vocal score, p. 230); cf. also Jean-Michel Vaccaro, *The Rake's Progress . . . Études de J. Jacquot, J.-M. Vaccaro, et M. Chimènes* (Paris, 1990), 75 and 126–7.

[48] Cf. Cipriano de Rore, *Opera omnia*, ed. Bernhard Meier, 8 vols. (CMM 14; Rome and Stuttgart, 1959–77), vi, pp. xi–xii, 108 ff. Meier's commentary gives bibliographical references for Burney (1789), Ambros (1891), Kroyer (1902), Riemann (1920), Lowinsky (1962).

[49] Only the entry in the bass (bar 10 in Meier's edition) modifies the chromaticism slightly, but not significantly, for harmonic reasons. After the completion of this chapter my attention was drawn to E. E. Lowinsky, '*Calami sonum ferentes*: A New Interpretation', in his posthumous *Music in the Culture of the Renaissance and Other Essays*, ed. B. J. Blackburn, 2 vols. (Chicago, 1989), ii. 595–626. Lowinsky throws new light on music and text of this famous but elusive piece, on various kinds of chromaticism espoused in the 16th c. (Vicentino, Rore), and on the reception of *Calami* from Zacconi to Meier. Meier's commentary of 1975 must be revised in view of this essay of 1989.

[50] Alfred Einstein, *The Italian Madrigal*, 3 vols. (Princeton, NJ, 1949; repr. 1971), iii. 216; *Nuovo Vogel*, no. 459; Leopold, 'Madrigali', 113.

was first published in his third book of madrigals of 1592, and frequently reprinted. It is a setting of a stanza (ottava rima) from Tasso's *Gerusalemme liberata*. Strictly speaking, it is not a lament, but a curse and vow of vengeance in which the sorceress Armida expresses her intention that Rinaldo

> There lying wounded 'mongst the hurt and slain,
> Of these my wrongs thou shalt the vengeance bear . . .

to quote the Fairfax translation of Tasso.[51] But it is not possible to omit this important composition from a history of the lament. Its chromaticism is not only an expression of compassion for the 'bleeding and dead' on the battle-field, but also of the grief of a woman who has lost her lover and as a result

> Hor qui mancò lo spirto a la dolente . . .
>
> Here fainted she with sorrow, grief, and pain . . .

On these very words (the fifth line of the ottava rima) the top voice enters the five-part texture with a chromatically descending fourth whose semi-tonal progression (bar 25) sharply contrasts with its continuation, an ascending octave leap. The chromatic descent, however, is faithfully imitated in the quinto (bar 26), basso (bar 28), tenore (bar 32) and alto (bar 40) parts. In fact, the tetrachord pervades the entire polyphonic structure: an instance is the additional entry in the canto part after the octave leap (bar 29). A similarly imitative procedure may be observed in a 'Crucifixus' for four voices by Monteverdi, published almost half a century later than the third book of madrigals.[52] Again the descending fourth is first stated in one voice but permeates the entire polyphonic texture by way of subsequent entries in the other voices.

The transfer of these contrapuntally treated tetrachords to the homophony of the monodic style was above all due to Cavalli, whose operatic laments in general, and chromatic ostinatos in particular, created a veritable European vogue. It was the reiteration of the chromatic fourth in the bass (analogous to the diatonic fourth in Monteverdi's *Lamento della ninfa*) that created the harmonic tension appropriate to the 'stile recitativo', and capable of infusing the monodic threnody with the intensity and poignancy germane to the genre. By 1640 or thereabouts the progression had been used widely enough to be recognized as an 'emblem' of the lament, as Rosand has called it, and Cavalli employs it frequently, either in a few isolated statements or in exten-sive ostinato repetition. In his *Ormindo* of 1644, for instance, we encounter several pregnant occurrences of the formula that remind us of the examples

    51 Cf. *Opere*, iii.52–5; *Nuovo Vogel*, nos. 1906–13.
    52 In the *Selva morale* of 1640/1, which also contains the 'Pianto della Madonna', mentioned earlier. Cf. *Opere*, xv. 178. This 'Crucifixus' is also quoted as an example of the chromatic tetrachord by Haas, *Musik des Barocks*, 81, who also reprints a comparable passage from Cavalli's *Requiem*. Cf. also Leopold, *Monteverdi*, 170–1.

from Monteverdi to Stravinsky mentioned earlier. In *Ormindo* the 'emblem' is frequently found in one of those 'ombra' scenes, characteristic of early opera, where shades or ghosts of the departed make their appearance. Prince Amida thinks he is confronted by the ghost of his former beloved, the Princess Sicle, and his old ardour is revived. Actually the ghost ('ombra') is enacted by the real Sicle, who is still alive, and the two lovers are united in a *lieto fine* at the end of the opera. But in the conjuring scene, here discussed, the nether world of shades of the dead, Sicle's lament and Amida's compassion for the supposedly lost Sicle are expressed by the ubiquitous formula in several fleeting appearances. When Sicle bemoans that Amida has betrayed her, the tetrachord descends twice in the bass: once incomplete in five notes, the second time with all six semitones present (Ex. 6.13*a*). When Amida responds with chagrin and compassion, his feelings are expressed by two overlapping ascending fourths in the bass and a single tetrachord, also ascending, in the voice (Ex. 6.13*b*). And when Amida's conversion is completed he asks the 'ombra' to depart in peace (Ex. 6.13*c*, *d*).[53]

Così, così tradirmi?	Thus, thus to betray me?
Così per una adultera lasciarmi?	Thus for an adulteress to leave me?

. . . . . .

A poco, a poco il petto mio	Gradually my heart filled again
si riempì [di foco]	[with fire]

. . . . . .

Va in pace, ombra vezzosa	Go in peace, lovely shadow

Cavalli's ostinato (or quasi-ostinato) laments are usually longer than these passing passages, and involve more frequent repetition of the tetrachord. They are usually, though not invariably, distinguished from the preceding recitative by triple time, strophic form, and accompaniment by strings (rather than merely by continuo instruments). The repeated tetrachord is usually extended, often by a cadential formula. Such extensions increase the length of the phrase, treated in ostinato, and consequently the number of repetitions is smaller than in the *Lamento della ninfa*, but still sizeable enough to be recognized as an ostinato: ten to twenty reiterations are quite common. Finally, we must distinguish between a strict ostinato treatment and more flexible procedures. In the former, one bass statement succeeds the other without interruption and without change of pitch; in the latter, entries in the bass differ in pitch, and are at times interspersed with other material. It is the first kind that has exercised such a striking influence on later composers. The discipline of strict repetition and adherence to a single

[53] Cf. n. 34 concerning the MS score of *Ormindo* at Venice and Leppard's score of 1969. In Ex. 6.13*a* the bass descends from *a* to *e* (fo. 141ʳ), in Leppard (p. 143), transposed, from *f* to *c*. In Ex. 6.13*b* the bass ascends from *F* to *B♭* and from *A* to *d* (fo. 141ᵛ), in Leppard (p. 145), transposed, from *E♭* to *A♭* and *G* to *c*. In Exx. 6.13*c* and *d* the bass descends both times from *d* to *A* (fo. 144ᵛ), in Leppard (pp. 148–9), transposed, from *c* to *G*.

Ex. 6.13. Descending tetrachords in Cavalli, *Ormindo*

(d)

Va in pa - ce, va in pa - ce, om - bra vez - zo - sa

pitch and tonality seems to have acted as a challenge to such diverse person-
alities as Purcell, Bach, and Beethoven. (With the exception of Purcell they
are unlikely ever to have heard of Cavalli, but strict ostinato technique was
widely practised both in and outside Italy.)

Good examples of chromatic tetrachords with cadential extensions, treated
in strict ostinato fashion, are provided by two operatic laments by Cavalli,
often quoted in conjunction with Purcell's 'When I am laid in earth', namely
that of Climene in *Egisto* (Venice, 1643) and that of Hecuba in *Didone*
(Venice, 1641).[54]

Hecuba's lament from Cavalli's Didone, *Ex. 6.14a*

Tremulo spirito	Tremulous spirit,
Flebile, e languido	Woeful and languishing,
Escimi subito . . .	Leave me forthwith . . .

Climene's lament from Cavalli's Egisto, *Ex. 6.14b*

Piangete occhi dolenti . . .	Weep, doleful eyes . . .

Dido's lament from Purcell's Dido, *Ex. 6.14c*

When I am laid in earth . . .

The inexorable pattern of repetition is broken in those instances where
Cavalli has the entries of the chromatic tetrachord wander in pitch. In
Ex. 6.15a, from *Didone*, Cassandra laments the impending fall of Troy.
Each of the four stanzas of her strophic threnody contains five entries of
the chromatic fourth: two starting on D, two on G, and one on A. This
last entry differs not only in pitch, but also in length: it moves in minims,
not in crotchets. Moreover, Cavalli breaks the continuity of the ostinato
pattern by inserting between the fourth and fifth bass entry a long-held
note in the bass (bars 9–10), accommodating nine or more syllables, with a
freedom more characteristic of recitative than of a lyric where melody and

---

[54] Cf. Jack Westrup, *Purcell* (8th rev. edn., London, 1980), 121 ff.; Robert Klakowich, '*Scocca pur:*
Genesis of an English Ground', *JRMA* 116 (1991), 63–77 at 72; Nino Pirrotta, *Storia dell'opera, anno
academico 1972–73* (Rome, n.d. [?1973]), 66, 84; *Egisto*, vocal score, ed. Leppard (London: Faber, 1977),
93–6. Concerning the lament from *Egisto*, Westrup gives the music for three entries of the bass, Pirrotta
for ten, Leppard for nineteen.

Ex. 6.14*a*. Cavalli, Hecuba's lament from *Didone*

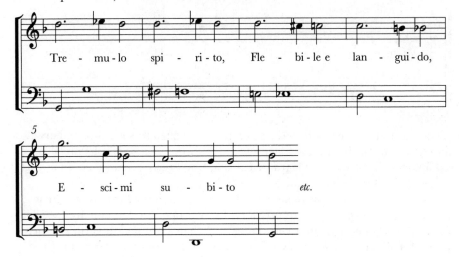

Tre - mu - lo   spi - ri - to,   Fle - bi - le e   lan - gui - do,

E - sci - mi   su - bi - to   *etc.*

Ex. 6.14*b*. Cavalli, Climene's lament from *Egisto*

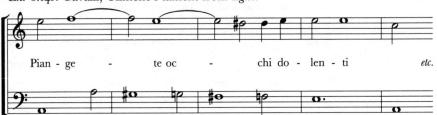

Pian - ge — te oc — chi do - len - ti   *etc.*

Ex. 6.14*c*. Purcell, Dido's lament from *Dido and Aeneas*

When   I   am   laid,   am   laid   in

earth,   May   my   wrongs   cre - ate

Ex. 6.15. Cavalli, Cassandra's lament from *Didone*

(*a*) third stanza

(*b*) comparison of third and fourth stanzas, bars 9–11

bass move at comparable speeds. In fact, throughout this lament one admires the flexibility with which the vocal line follows the declamation of the text, although the strophic form requires the voice to partner twenty appearances of the tetrachord in the bass. Cavalli achieves this by repeating the bass for each stanza strictly but varying the melody slightly from stanza to stanza. The entire third stanza, a masterly expression of grief, is quoted in Ex. 6.15*a*, and a comparison of the third and fourth stanzas in regard to the vocal line over the long-held note in the bass in Ex. 6.15*b*.[55]

Cassandra, e che di te	Cassandra, and what shall
Questa notte sarà?	become of you this night?
S'aita più non c'è	If there is no help
La tua vita cadrà.	your life will fall.
O della patria mia stragi fatali,	O, my fatherland's fatal massacre,
O in van da me profetizzati mali!	O, ills in vain by me prophesied!

O della patria mia stragi fatali . . .	
E s'all'altar morrò, vi prego,	And if I am to die at the altar,
O dei . . .	I beg you, o gods . . .

This sketchy and selective survey of the chromatic tetrachord has under-standably concentrated upon Italy, but it goes without saying that the formula is encountered in all regions, including France, the Low Countries, and Germany. Students of English music are not likely to forget the many examples of chromaticism found in Elizabethan and Jacobean works. In fact, we may safely say that Purcell, in addition to responding to Italian influences that may have reached him directly or indirectly, was also heir to a native tradition, where the tetrachord makes its appearance in instrumental as well as vocal music. In the former it is usually the title that indicates the connotations of lamentation and serious concern, such as Dowland's 'Forlorn Hope Fancy' (descending fourth) or Peter Phillips's 'Pavana Dolorosa' (ascending). In the case of madrigals and lute-songs the verbal text usually accounts for the presence of the tetrachord, for instance Weelkes's 'Cease, sorrows, now' (ascending), Farnaby's 'Construe my meaning' (descending), and Campion's 'Follow thy fair sun, unhappy shadow' (ascending).[56] And many other English examples, from Gibbons to Blow, could be added. Nor

---

[55] For the complete text of all four stanzas cf. Pirrotta, *Storia dell'opera*, 66, 82 3. Cf. also Leppard's transcription (London: Faber, 1966), where performance marks are added, such as 'recitativo', 'liberamente', 'misurato', etc.

[56] Cf. E. J. Fellowes, D. Greer, and F. W. Sternfeld (eds.), *English Madrigal Verse* (3rd rev. edn., Oxford, 1967), 281 (Weelkes, *Madrigals*, 1597); 109 (Farnaby, *Canzonets*, 1598); 655 (Campion–Rosseter, *Ayres*, 1601). Since two of the vocal examples (Weelkes and Campion) are ascending, it is worth remembering that the ascending chromatic tetrachord is also employed by Monteverdi in the vocal trio of the members of Seneca's household ('famigliari') in *Poppea*, Act II, scene iii, on the words 'Non morir, non morir, Seneca' (Do not die, do not die, Seneca; *Opere*, xiii. 128, 133; ed. Curtis, 122, 128; Leopold, *Monteverdi*, 212 13).

is there any reason to neglect other countries, for instance the works of Sweelinck or Schütz, to name but two composers.

It is curious that no monograph about the chromatic tetrachord has ever appeared. In fact, one is unaware of even dictionary articles, with comprehensive bibliographies on the subject.[57] Perhaps the ubiquity of the formula has deterred historians from attempts to treat the subject fully, if not exhaustively. It is interesting, though, that few scholars omit to mention Mozart's String Quartet in D minor (K. 421), although it is a purely instrumental work and lacks any of the indications of its meaning, such as titles or rubrics, let alone a verbal text. It is therefore significant, as Bianconi and Rosand have pointed out, that at the beginning of the nineteenth century Momigny, in his *Cours complet d'harmonie et de composition* (Paris, 1803–6), applied to the first violin part of the first movement the text of a lament of Dido. Such explications, interpretations, and analyses became increasingly important in the course of the nineteenth and twentieth centuries when the established formulae of previous ages seemed more remote, and the size of the general public increased considerably. In fact, the descending tetrachord, diatonic and chromatic, looms so large in the D minor Quartet, and not only in the bass, that one would have to annotate other parts in addition to the first violin for modern audiences, and exegesis would have to extend also to the third and fourth movements. Still, in spite of the abundance of non-vocal examples, there can be no doubt that it was the operatic lament that established the chromatic fourth, or 'Schmerzensbaß' as some German scholars have called it, as one of the more prominent means of expression for grief, sorrow, and forlorn hopes.

LAMENT AS 'NUMBER'

These reflections on laments from Poliziano to Stravinsky reveal their considerable variety. Some of these pieces are short and pregnant, others long and extensive; they may be divided into irregular blocks of verse or be organized into stanzas; refrains may be frequently or sparingly employed, or spurned altogether. Clichés and formulas may be present or absent, but somehow or other the lament always seems distinct from its surroundings by an intensity of verbal and musical rhetoric, no matter how it is achieved: one is inclined to regard it as a 'number', although—strictly speaking—the fluidity of the 'stile recitativo' in early opera usually impels historians to reserve the term 'number opera' for the eighteenth century, for 'Italian-Mozartian opera', as Stravinsky has called it, or 'Metastasian opera', a label often employed by students of operatic structure.

---

[57] But see notes 27, 32, 47 9, and 54. Unfortunately, some works (e.g. Einstein's *Madrigal*) are not furnished with an index of subject-matters, which would facilitate locating discussions of 'chromaticism' or 'lament' or 'tetrachord'.

Certainly, as early as 1600, the second scene of Peri's *Euridice*, in spite of its fluid transitions, contains two set-pieces that function as expressions of grief, as we have seen. One is the solo lament of Orpheus, 'Non piango e non sospiro', which in its poignant way says everything in the shortest space. This is complemented by the ensemble threnody that concludes the scene, an extensive piece whose parts are held together by the refrain 'Sospirate aure celesti'. To deny these two laments the label 'number' because they are not set off in the score by title, rubric, double bar, or any other notational sign would be doctrinaire. Similarly, Orpheus' echo lament in Monteverdi's opera of 1607, although not an aria, is a number that functions as a lyrical unit, in which the main soloist expresses his feelings and during which no action propels the drama, until divine intervention turns grief into joy. The same characteristics apply to the echo lament in the second half of Act I of Gluck's *Orfeo* in the eighteenth century: the essence of the 'affetto' is distilled into the vocal line of the protagonist, pitted against a bass; and the lyrical effusion is not disturbed by new developments in the plot. Such a working definition of an operatic number applies equally well to the laments of Peri or Purcell or Hasse, and—in some cases—even later instances, such as those in Verdi's *Otello* or Stravinsky's *Rake*. Both Desdemona's 'Willow Song' in the last act of Verdi's opera[58] and 'Weep for Adonis' in the final act of Stravinsky are swan-songs preceding the death of the soloist, both are laments about the inevitably tragic conclusion of the action, and neither of them functions as a contrast for a *lieto fine* in the strict sense of the term, since Desdemona and Othello, Tom Rakewell and Anne Truelove are not happily united at the end of these operas. Yet both are lyrical numbers, preceding a finale with a different 'affetto', for which they act as a foil. The notion of the dying swan, since classical antiquity associated with Orpheus and music, is common to both of them. In Shakespeare's *Othello* the dying Emilia says to Desdemona

> What did thy song bode, lady?
> Hark, can'st thou hear me? I will play the swan
> And die in music. [*sings*] 'Willow, willow, willow'.

In Verdi's opera the importance of the Willow Song is further magnified by the prelude to the final act, where the main musical material of the song is announced in the cor anglais. In fact, it could be said that the sombre tone colour of the unaccompanied cor anglais in this prelude, scored for winds only, has much in common with the 'sad tune' pronounced by the same instrument at the beginning of the final act of *Tristan*. The 'sad tune' is also a lament about impending death and doom. And in *Otello* as well as *Tristan* these laments function as contrasts to the finale, which in both cases is a

---

[58] Concerning Verdi's use of the chromatic fourth in the 'Dies irae' of his *Requiem*, cf. Williams, 'Chromatic Fourth', 343.

transfiguration of a love duet, a recollection of past happiness. (Such 'recollections of tranquillity' must substitute for the *lieto fine* of past centuries, which
would not be acceptable to Romanticist sensibilities.) There is no doubt that
whereas much of Verdi's *Otello* is continuous music, with more fluid transitions than in his earlier operas, the Willow Song is a 'number', a lament
that acts as a foil for the finale, with its evocation of the 'bacio' duet.

Tom Rakewell's final lament is a similar 'swan-like music', to quote
Stravinsky's librettist, Auden. And again it contrasts sharply with the finale
of the opera, the Epilogue, in which the singers 'point' the moral for the
audience, in a manner reminiscent of the finales of *Don Giovanni* and *Falstaff*.
But, then, the *Rake* is deliberately shaped as a number-opera and con-
sciously revives such clichés of the eighteenth century as the lamenting solo
and the ensemble finale. Perhaps we may quote Stravinsky himself, in his
inimitable Russian-French English, when he 'points' the difference between
(hyphenated) 'musical-dramatists' who endeavour to write 'music-dramas',
and neoclassical composers who emulate Mozartian number-operas with
their poignant laments.

When it was announced that I was at work on an opera, I read speculations in the
press . . . These were invariably based on my two earlier 'operas'—*The Nightingale*
and *Mavra*. *The Nightingale* seems more remote to me now than the English operas
of three centuries ago or than the Italian-Mozartian opera which has been so
neglected and misunderstood by the world of the musical-dramatists. In so far as
Mavra suggests any comparisons to my present work, it is in my conception of opera.
I believe 'music-drama' and opera to be two very, very different things. My life work
is devoted to the latter.
The Rake's Progress is, emphatically, an opera—an opera of arias and recitatives,
choruses and ensembles. Its musical structure, the conception of the use of these
forms, even to the relation of tonalities, is in the line of the classical tradition.

[signed: Igor Stravinsky][59]

The contrast between continuous music-dramas and operas containing
arias, ensembles, and other numbers brings to mind the first of Gluck's
reform operas, *Orfeo*, and its final lament, 'Che farò senza Euridice', whose
qualities as a plaint have been the subject of heated controversy for over
two centuries. Whether it is right and proper to claim *Orfeo* of 1762 as a
predecessor of Wagnerian music-drama has also been a topic for debate.[60]
There can be no doubt, however, that at times Gluck was singularly
successful in eschewing the short Metastasian number, and welding several
such units into larger structures, notably in the scene between Orpheus and
the furies in Act II. But the famous 'Che farò' is, for better or worse, an

[59] The quotation is taken from the printed programme book for the performance of the *Rake*,
conducted by the composer, directed by Sarah Caldwell, Boston, 18 May 1953.

[60] Cf. Hortschansky (ed.), *Gluck*, 390 ff., about the assessment of Gluck by E. T. A. Hoffmann,
Wagner, Debussy, and others.

aria or number, which has been praised for its expressiveness by Rousseau, but castigated by Boyé. The latter felt that the 'affetto' of chagrin was not clearly established, and that the vocal line accommodating the words 'J'ai perdu mon Eurydice' (the incipit of the French version) is too readily fitted to its emotional opposite, 'J'ai trouvé mon Eurydice'. Gluck defended himself against these and other criticisms by claiming that only an adequately rehearsed performance, with punctiliously observed nuances of dynamics and tempo, supervised by the composer, could prevent the famous lament from becoming 'un saltarello di burattini' (a dance of puppets).[61] This opinion was endorsed by Berlioz, who praised Pauline Viardot-Garcia's singing of this plaint as making of it 'what it is, one of those marvels of expression, which are well-nigh incomprehensible to vulgar singers—and which are, alas, too often profaned'.[62]

In fact, the tragic aspects of Gluck's laments, both in *Orfeo* and *Alceste*, are—if anything—reinforced by the sudden emotional contrast of the *lieto fine*. In terms of the aesthetics of the period, one could regard the happy conclusion as a foil for the tragic grandeur of the plaint. This complementary reciprocity between 'lamento' and *lieto fine* is still a creative concept for the late eighteenth century.[63]

Taking an overall view of the history of opera after the Congress of Vienna, and deeming the collaborations of Strauss and Hofmannsthal, of Stravinsky and Auden as exceptions confirming the rule, one can say that the lament proved to be a more permanent staple of the operatic diet than the *lieto fine*. This is not surprising, because as a vehicle for expressive (and at times impressive) solo singing, the lament continued to function, after Gluck and Mozart, as a challenge for librettists, composers, and performers. It seemed to fulfil a craving of audiences for emotional, dramatic, and musical satisfaction. Lamenting the human condition seems as apposite for *Boris*, *Pelléas*, and *Wozzeck* as it is for the dramas of Ibsen, Strindberg, and Beckett. Whether we call the plaint a 'building-block', an 'ingredient', or a 'number' of musical drama, reports of the demise of the lament, after the decline of Metastasian opera, must be judged as greatly exaggerated. Its hold on the artistic imagination extends from biblical and ancient literature to modern times.

---

[61] Cf. ibid. 136 ff., 184 ff., 399 ff.

[62] *A travers chants* (Paris, 1862), 120.

[63] Cf. the discussions of Gluck's and Calzabigi's treatment of the Orpheus and Alcestis plots in earlier chapters; also Hortschansky, *Gluck*, 414.

7

Repetition and Echo in Poetry and Music

The rise of the echo technique in opera and stage music presupposes the existence of echo poetry and its antecedent, the rhetorical use of repetition of various kinds. Here we have a vast repertory extending from classical antiquity to our own century, from Greek works of Euripides, Aristophanes, and Callimachus to the poetry of Thomas Hardy and T. S. Eliot. Between these two chronological extremes we encounter the literature of ancient Rome, the neo-Latin works of the Middle Ages and Renaissance, and—last but not least—vernacular poetry in various countries, including England, France, and Italy. Among the many English examples we may instance Shakespeare's reference to 'twenty echoes' in *Venus and Adonis* and the famous echo scene from Webster's *Duchess of Malfi*. French examples are discussed in this chapter. But our main concern is, of course, with Italian verse between Poliziano and Rinuccini. Here that favourite pastoral, the *Pastor fido*, seems to have been particularly influential. It boasted an echo scene (Act IV, ll. 1030 ff.),[1] a pastoral lyric ('Care selve beate', Act II, l. 600) that was turned into another echo scene in Agazzari's opera *Eumelio*;[2] and in the 1598 performance of Guarini's play (discussed in Ch. 4), the third intermedio (after Act II) employed a double echo lyric ('con una doppia voce echo').

In temporal arts such as poetry and music, repetition fills a great number of functions: it extends the dimensions of the basic elements such as the line of verse or the musical phrase; it creates coherence between the elements; it contributes to emphasis and intensification. Thus, in poetry and in music, where the temporal dimension is of central importance, the principle of repetition can be considered one of the fundamental tools. From antiquity to the Renaissance (and even later) rhetoricians designated the procedures of repetition by various technical terms: echo, repetitio, anadiplosis, anaphora, palillogia, and paronomasia.[3] Whether or not one uses such terms, it must be remembered that echo is only a special type of repetition. In the majority

---

[1] Excerpts from this scene, starting at l. 1033, were set as an echo madrigal for eight voices ('uno Echo a otto') by Monte. See Table 7.1 under 1599. I am indebted to James Chater for letting me see his unpublished ' "Il pastor fido" and Music: A Bibliography', an attempt to list all musical compositions whose verbal text is based on or inspired by passages from the play.

[2] Agazzari's librettists, De Cupis and Tirletti, produced a *rifacimento* of Guarini's scene, adding the echo device. Cf. the 1606 score of *Eumelio*, pp. 3 5.

[3] These terms and others, such as analepsis and reduplicatio, have been studied by Heinrich Lausberg in *Handbuch der literarischen Rhetorik*, 2 vols. (Munich, 1960); see also *Riemann Musik-Lexikon*, ed. H. H. Eggebrecht, Sachteil (Mainz, 1967).

of poetic examples mentioned below, the echo occurs either at the end of a line or from the end of one line to the beginning of the next. Sometimes the repetition uses the same word; often the sense is different, but the sonority the same (a procedure usually called paronomasia). Finally, frequently one line poses a question to which the echo furnishes the answer.

In music, repetition can be literal (echo), it can be transposed (sequence), and it can form part of a polyphonic complex (imitation). Moreover, repetition can involve a single part or two groups can respond to each other (*cori spezzati*).

An echo in a poetic text often prompts the composer to use one of the types of repetition. In this sense, it could be said that the poetic echo functions as a libretto for the musical echo. Frequently the emphasis on repetition is greater in music than it is in poetry. A striking example of this is found in Monteverdi's setting of Petrarch's 'Ohimè il bel viso' in his sixth book of madrigals. In Petrarch's text the word 'ohimè' comes back four times in the course of the first five lines, whereas in Monteverdi's setting the two upper voices (canto and quinto) repeat 'ohimè' sixteen times, creating a sort of pedal under which the lower voices declaim the six initial lines of the sonnet.

The age-old device of repetition is first referred to in Aristotle's *Rhetoric*. Aristotle points out that when Homer thrice names Nireus at the beginning of three successive lines 'he has increased the reputation of Nireus and has perpetuated his memory'.[4] In the *Andromeda* of Euripides, parodied in the *Thesmophoriazusae* of Aristophanes, the heroine, bound to a rock, laments her fate, answered by echo, that is, by anadiplosis at the end of the line. Similarly, in Aristophanes, Mnesilochus, bound to a plank, laments his fate, punctuated by anadiplosis. Naturally, in these laments of ancient Greece, as in those of Rinuccini and Striggio in the cinquecento and seicento, certain key words such as 'woe', 'bewail', and 'alas' are intensified by repetition.[5] The only extant musical fragment from an ancient Greek drama is the papyrus recording music for a choral passage from the *Orestes* of Euripides (409 BC). The opening word, significantly, is κατολοφύρομαι (I bewail) and that word, as well as the word δάκρυα (tears)—not present in the fragment— is subjected to anadiplosis.

The traditions of straight repetition (anadiplosis), which we have seen in Euripides and Aristophanes (sometimes with differing syntactical functions), and of repetition at the beginning of a clause but interrupted by the intervention of different words in between (anaphora), which we have seen in Homer, extend through later antiquity (Callimachus, Greek Anthology) and the Byzantine Middle Ages (Tzetzes, Prodromos, Stilbes) to the Florentine Renaissance of the quattrocento.[6] An edition of the Greek Anthology, edited

---

[4] Aristotle, *Rhetorica* 1414ᵃ; ed. and tr. J. H. Freese (London, 1926), 421.

[5] Aristophanes, *Thesmophoriazusae* 1019 ff.; cf. K. Dover, *Aristophanic Comedy* (London, 1972), 75–6.

[6] See the articles on Echo in Georg Wissowa (ed.), *Pauly's Real-Encyclopädie der classischen Altertumswissenschaft*, v (1905), 1926–30, and Konrat Ziegler (ed.), *Der Kleine Pauly*, ii (1967), 195–6. See also Karl

by Lascaris, was printed at Florence in 1494. The Biblioteca Nazionale in Florence possesses a copy bearing a special dedication to Piero de' Medici and illuminated by hand. Angelo Poliziano refers to one of the poems by Gauradas in the Greek Anthology as his model for the first Italian echo poem.[7] In his *Miscellanea* of 1489 he printed this poem both in Greek and in Latin translation:[8]

> Echo chara mihi assona aliquid. —Quid?
> Amo puellam, illa vero me non amat. —Amat.
>
> Dear Echo, make me a rhyme. —What?
> I love a girl, but she does not love me. —She loves.

The poem consists of six lines, each one echoing the last syllable, or the two last (*amat* in l. 2 and *amo* in l. 4).

Poliziano indicates that he had offered his own echo poem to the humanist Pietro Contarino ten years earlier and that it was set to music by Henricus (Isaac). We may therefore date the poem as of 1479, or even earlier:

> Che fai tu, Ecco, mentr'io ti chiamo? —Amo.
> Ami tu dua o pur un solo? —Un solo.
> E io te sola e non altri amo. —Altri amo.
> Dunque non ami tu un solo? —Un solo.
> Questo è un dirmi: io non t'amo. —Io non t'amo.
> Quel que tu ami amil tu solo? —Solo.
> Chi t'ha levata dal mio amore? —Amore.
> Che fa quello a chi porti amore? —Ah more!
>
> What do you do, Echo, when I call you? —I love.
> Do you love two or only one alone? —One alone.
> And I love you alone and none other. —I love another.
> Then you do not love one alone? —One alone.
> This amounts to saying: I do not love you. —I do not love you.
> The one whom you love: do you love him alone? —Alone.
> Who has taken you from my love? —Love.
> What does he do, whom you love? —Ah, he dies.

This is a model work in several respects. By focusing the repetition at the end of the line, it created a genre very appropriate to the vernacular, where the conclusion of the line is much more important than in ancient poetry.

Krumbacher, *Geschichte der byzantinischen Literatur* (Handbuch der klassischen Altertumswissenschaft, ix/2; 2nd edn., Munich, 1897), s.v. Tzetzes, Prodromos, Stilbes.

[7] The version of the Greek Anthology known in Florence and Italy in the last quarter of the 15th c. was the work entitled *Anthologia Planudea*, which included the poem by Gauradas. There is no proof that Poliziano knew the other version, the *Anthologia Palatina* (today preserved partly at Heidelberg and partly at Paris), which contained echo poems by Callimachus.

[8] *Miscellaneorum centuria* (Florence, 1489), sig. e3^{r-v}. The Italian poem was printed for the first time in *Cose vulgare* (Bologna, 1494), sig. F3^r; both the Latin and the Greek text are quoted in Ida Maier, *Ange Politien* (THR 81; Geneva, 1966), 244. Cf. also Daniela Delcorno Branca, 'Da Poliziano a Serafino', in *Miscellanea di studi in onore di Vittore Branca*, 5 vols. (Biblioteca dell'Archivum Romanicum, 78–82; Florence, 1983), iii. 423–50. She comments on this poem and other echo poetry by Poliziano and Serafino.

By concentrating on the verb *amare* (which Poliziano used twice in the Latin translation of the poem by Gauradas), the amorous complaint, it established the model for this literary genre from Serafino to Guarini. Of the eight lines of the ottava rima by Poliziano, five end in *amo* or *amore*, and, by a deft instance of paronomasia, the eighth and last is a variation of the preceding echo rhyme. The word *Amore* answers the first question; in the last line the same sonority, but this time derived from the word *morire*, introduces a felicitous change of meaning and, at the same time, an appropriate note of sadness, real or feigned: '. . . amore? —Ah, more'. Although the echo rhymes derived from *amare* and *morire* do not suffice to delimit the characteristic vocabulary of the genre, they nevertheless will continue to play a major role during more than a century.

Unfortunately, the musical setting by Isaac of Poliziano's Italian poem has not been preserved. The earliest compositions on Italian echo poems that have come down to us are 'La pastorella se leva per tempo' and several pieces on texts by Serafino. The text of 'La pastorella' (sometimes attributed to Poliziano) printed below derives from the 1568 edition, *Canzone a ballo composte dal Magnifico Lorenzo et da M. Agnolo Poliziano* (Florence, no printer), Canzone 144.[9] Each stanza begins with two lines of endecasillabi, which are followed by four lines of the more popular quinari, concluding with a final endecasillabo. In order to save space, the printer has combined each pair of quinari into a single line, but in the first stanza the metrical intention is made clear by the space that separates the first two quinari and by the capital letter in the article 'La' that follows that space. It is interesting that each time the echo intervenes it is set off by the metrical change from endecasillabi to quinari. The first two stanzas, with proper line-divisions, run as follows:

> La pastorella si leva per tempo
> Menando le caprette a pascer fora
> Di fora, fora,
> La traditora
> Coi suoi bei occhi
> La m'innamora,
> Et fa di mezza notte apparir giorno.
>
> Poi se ne giva a spasso alla fontana
> Calpestando l'herbette, ò tenerelle,
> O tenerelle,
> Galante, e belle,
> Sermolin fresco,
> Fresche mortelle,
> E il grembo ha pieno di rose, & viole.

---

9 In the 16th c. the lyric was attributed to Poliziano; later editors grouped it under Poliziano's doubtful poems. See *Le Stanze*, ed. Carducci, 340, and Ida Maier, *Les manuscrits d'Ange Politien* (Geneva, 1965), 254. Sapegno excludes the poem in his edn. of the *Rime*, as does Daniela Delcorno Branca in the most recent edn. of Poliziano's *Rime* (Venice, 1990).

> The shepherdess arises early,
> Leading the goats to graze outside
> From outside, outside
> The traitress
> With her beautiful eyes
> Makes me fall in love with her,
> And midnight appears full day.
>
> Then she trips down to the fountain
> Treading on the fresh grass, so tender,
> So tender,
> Careless and lovely,
> Fresh thyme,
> Fresh myrtle,
> And her lap full of roses and violets.

Printed in this way, the four lines of quinari accompany perfectly the musical phrase, which is sung four times. The word 'fora' is taken over from line 2 and repeated at the end of line 3. In the music (see Ex. 7.1),[10] the first 'fora' is accompanied by a short phrase descending a minor third and then returning. A modification of this phrase in ternary metre accompanies the repetitions of line 3, but the musical phrase itself is heard four times. In other words, three verbal statements engender five musical statements.

The same anthology contains, in addition to lyrics of Lorenzo de' Medici and Luigi Pulci, several poems securely attributed to Poliziano, among them his 'Ben venga maggio' and 'Canti ogn'un ch'io canterò', both of them of a distinctly popular stamp. The second of these is relevant here, since it employs repetition prominently in the opening ten lines. This game of words, *ludus verborum*, is supported by another popular device, the pseudo-rustic sdrucciolo (rhyme with accent on the third syllable from the end). In the first stanza the rhyme in question is 'sdrúcciola–lúcciola', and Poliziano stresses the metrical surprise of the sdrucciolo by employing the very term, as he does also in his *Favola d'Orfeo*, where the shepherd Mopso concludes his stanza with the rhyme 'cúcciola–sdrúcciola'. The first stanza is reprinted below with the repetitive effects indicated by italics:[11]

---

[10] The music is taken from Florence, Biblioteca Nazionale Centrale, MS Magl. XIX. 108, no. 13. A complete transcription is in Osthoff, *Theatergesang*, ii. 174.

[11] The poem is found in the *Canzone a ballo of 1568*, fo. 18ʳ, and also in standard edns. of Poliziano, e.g. Carducci's edn. of 1912, p. 667. Carducci's footnotes are useful with their references to children's games, such as 'lucciola–lucciola'. The ubiquitous 'cu-cu' call in the third stanza (with its consequent 'cuccuvegia' three lines later) is another repetition associated with popular lyrics and word games through the ages. The 'cucciola–sdrucciola' rhyme in the *Favola d'Orfeo* will be found in Tissoni Benvenuti, *Poliziano*, 145 (also 172, 191). Concerning versi sdruccioli in general, cf. the subsection 'Poliziano: the prosody' in Ch. 3, with its ample bibliographical notes, referring, *inter alia*, to Leopold, 'Madrigali' and Osthoff, 'Musica'.

Ex. 7.1. Anon., 'La pastorella'

La pas-to-rel-la si le-va per tem-po, -po, Me-
-nan-do le ca-pret - te a pas-cer fo - ra,
Di for' in fo - ra la tra-di - to - ra coi suoi begl' oc-chi La m'in-na-
mo-ra, E fa di mez-za not - te ap-pa-rir gior - no, E
fa di mez-za not - te ap-pa-rir gior - no.

Canti ogn'un ch'io canterò,
  Dondol dondol dondolò.
Di promesse io son già stucco,
Fa' ch'omai la botte spilli.
Tu mi tieni a badalucco
Con le man piene di grilli.
Dopo tanti *billi billi*
Quest'anguilla pur poi sdrucciola,
Per dir pur—*lucciola, lucciola.*
Vieni *a me,—a me* che pro?

Let everyone sing for I shall sing,
  Dondol dondol dondolò.
Of promises I've had enough.
See that you broach the cask.
You trifle with me
With hands full of crickets.
After so many cluck clucks
This eel slithers away,
To say just—firefly, firefly.
Come to me—what's in it for me?

In the works of Serafino the device of echo occurs more frequently than in the lyrics that are rightly or wrongly ascribed to Poliziano. Obviously, Serafino enjoyed the game of words and sounds, which is one of the reasons why he was so frequently set to music. One instance is the poem

Soffrir i' son disposto ogni tormento,
Tormento dove sia fin' e riposo . . .[12]

I am disposed to suffer every torment,
Torment where there's end and repose . . .

The effect of palillogia is maintained throughout the eight lines of the poem, that is to say, it occurs seven times on the words 'tormento', 'riposo', 'contento', 'ascoso', 'sento', 'doglioso', and 'consento'. The extant musical setting accommodates the opening two lines and is expected to be repeated for the remaining six lines (see Ex. 7.2).[13] Again, the second 'tormento' of the text is musically set to a modified repetition of the first phrase. In the case of 'La pastorella' the modification is metrical, as is shown above; here it involves pitch by way of sequence (see bars 1–17).

---

[12] For the text see Bauer-Formiconi, *Strambotti des Serafino Aquilano*, no. 198. Giuseppina La Face Bianconi and Antonio Rossi have recently cast doubt on the authorship of the poem, which does not appear in the *editio princeps* of Serafino's works: see '*Soffrir non son disposto ogni tormento*': Serafino Aquilano: figura letteraria, fantasma musicologico', in *Atti del XIV Congresso della Società Internazionale di Musicologia: Trasmissione e recezione delle forme di cultura musicale*, 3 vols. (Turin, 1990), ii. 240–54.

[13] The music is taken from Florence, Biblioteca Nazionale Centrale, Magl. XIX. 121, fo. 18ᵛ.

Ex. 7.2. Anon., 'Soffrir i' son disposto'

* Orig.: C

'Gridan vostri occhi' is another example of an echo poem by Serafino:[14]

> Gridan vostri occhi al cor mio fora fora
> C'ha le difese sue si corte corte
> Su suso a sacho a sacho mora mora . . .

> Your eyes cry out to my heart 'come out, come out!'
> Whose defences are so short, short
> Up, upwards, to be sacked, sacked, let it die, die . . .

At the end of the first line one finds the 'fora–fora' already present in 'La pastorella'. 'Fora' or 'fuori' hark back to pastoral poetry and the summits of the hills and mountains that facilitate the echo effect; it is not surprising to find these same words in more than one aria up to Peri's in the Florentine intermedi of 1589. The third line of Serafino's ottava rima (sung to the same music as the first; see Ex. 7.3) ends in 'mora–mora', in the same tradition of Poliziano's 'Ah – more' mentioned earlier.

An attentive reading of Serafino's text reveals an excessive accumulation of verbal repetitions. In addition to the repetitions at the ends of lines, that is, echo in its narrowest sense, one finds words repeated internally, for example in l. 5: 'Io pian pian dico dico alhora alhora'.

Some editors have censured Serafino for such childishness and his gratuitous play with words (*Spiel* and *Wortspielerei* are the terms used in editions of Italian echo poetry and also Byzantine poetry of the same type). Nevertheless, one should recall that this pleasure in sonority for its own sake unites the poet and musician, and that artists can occasionally experiment with a new device (even to excess) with a view to a more judicious application in the future. In the vernacular literature of the Middle Ages and Renaissance, rhyme receives—thanks to the echo repetition—an additional sonorous quality, and the repeated word gains in meaning. Serafino is a poet of lesser rank than Poliziano, but, in view of his authorship or supposed authorship of texts set to music that have survived (one might even say as librettist), he should not be ignored. Sometimes his charming repetitions of words are associated with varied musical repetitions (as in Ex. 7.2); elsewhere the musician limits himself to a simple musical setting in which the verbal and literary play is readily perceived (as in Ex. 7.3).

Tempting as it would be to quote additional instances of anadiplosis and anaphora from antiquity and the Middle Ages, I shall return to the fountain-head of the history of the opera. In Chapters 1 and 3 I discussed some aspects of Poliziano's *Orfeo*. Here I shall examine the funeral dirge written for Lorenzo de' Medici's death in April 1492 by Poliziano and set to music by Isaac.

Poliziano's Latin poem is entitled 'Monodia in Laurentium Medicem , intonata per Arrighum Isac' (*sic*). This dirge, here called 'monodia', naturally

---

[14] For the poetry see Bauer-Formiconi, *Strambotti*, no. 186. For the music, see Milan, Biblioteca Trivulziana, MS 55, fos. 1ᵛ and 3ʳ. A modern transcription is in Jeppesen, *La frottola*, iii. 181.

Ex. 7.3. Anon., 'Gridan vostri occhi'

employs a variety of rhetorical repetitions for emphasis, notably anaphora at the beginning of clauses: 'Quis dabit capiti meo . . . Quis oculis meis/Ut nocte fleam, Ut luce fleam/Sic turtur . . . Sic cygnus . . . Sic luscinia' (Who will give to my head . . . Who to my eyes/That I weep by night, that I weep by day/Thus the turtledove . . . Thus the swan . . . Thus the nightingale), and last, but not least, referring to the laurel tree, as well as to Lorenzo de' Medici by the term 'laurus': 'Laurus impetu fulminis . . . Laurus omnium celebris musarum' (The laurel, by the force of lightning . . . the laurel, celebrated by the dancing chorus of all the muses).

At the same time, plain repetition (anadiplosis) is not disdained for emphasis: when we hear that the laurel tree is suddenly felled by lightning and lies right here, the repeated word supplies emphasis: 'illa illa iacet subito'. Equally, misery and chagrin are also stressed by anadiplosis: 'Heu miser miser, O dolor dolor'. These verbal repetitions are metrically and poetically indispensable and are faithfully reflected in the music (see Ex. 7.4). Note, for instance, how in Ex. 7.4a the verbal repetition of 'illa' begets musical repetition. Note, also, how that musical repetition is analogous to the opening bars ('Quis dabit capiti') in that the first three repeated notes are on the same chord, whereas the fourth note—still on the same pitch—is supported by a different chord (see Example 7.4b). We shall have more to say about this motif of three repeated notes, accompanied by the same chord.

Ex. 7.4. Isaac, 'Quis dabit capiti meo'

(a) DTO, p. 47, bars 8–9   (b) DTO, p. 45, bars 1–3

There is no doubt that Poliziano's idea of starting a Medici threnody with the words 'Quis dabit', emphasizing the chagrin by repetition, created a veritable school of laments throughout the sixteenth century, particularly after Petrucci printed Isaac's setting in 1503. Probably the original inspiration represents a combination of auditory memories, one from the Bible:

Quis dabit capiti meo aquam, et oculis meis fontem lacrimarum? . . .
Quis dabit me in solitudine diversorium viatorum?

(Jer. 9: 1)

Who will give water to my head, and a fountain of tears to my eyes?
Who will give me in the wilderness a lodging place of wayfaring men?

(Incidentally, Poliziano increases the amount of anaphora by changing Jeremiah's 'et oculis meis' to 'quis oculis meis').

The other likely reminiscence is from the chorus of a Latin tragedy, the *Hercules Oetaeus* attributed to Seneca, 'Quis dabit pacem populo timenti'.[15] And since anaphora, anadiplosis, and parallelismus membrorum are common to the Bible and to the ancients (and since both are quoted in Renaissance primers on rhetoric), both the incipit and the poetic technique would suggest themselves naturally to a Christian humanist at the court of Lorenzo de' Medici.

In the influential *editio princeps* of Poliziano's Greek and Latin poems, published by Aldus Manutius at Venice in 1498, the poem 'Quis dabit capiti meo' appears twice,[16] first in its expected place among the shorter Latin poems (*Liber Epigrammatum*, signature ii.vi), and again on the last page of the volume (signature kk.x), where its thirty lines take up the space left after the final lines of the Registrum. Rather elegantly for our discussion of anadiplosis, the entire poem is thus repeated within the final eleven leaves, and the last printed line employs rhetorical emphasis: 'o dolor, dolor!' Of the many imitations of Poliziano's poem between the 1490s and the middle of the seventeenth century, this line provides a convenient fingerprint, as it were, with which to spot Poliziano's influence.

The repetition of 'dolor' is, of course, already fairly prominent in the model. Not only does it provide the final line of the poem (l. 30), but since the entire first ten lines are repeated as lines 21–30 it has been heard before (l. 10). However that may be, a year or two after Lorenzo's death in 1492 Pamfilo Sassi wrote several lamentations on the turmoil in which Italy found itself; one of these contains the line 'Nos cogit dolor, nos stringit dolor'. When Poliziano himself died in 1494, Pietro Bembo's dirge on the passing of his fellow poet contained two lines ending with 'dolorem' and 'dolor':

> miscebat precibus lacrimas, lacrimisque dolorem;
> verba ministrabat liberiora dolor

Bembo's poem, with its repetition of the terms for tears and chagrin, is reminiscent of the anadiplosis employed in the passage from Euripides'

---

[15] Lines 1541 ff.; ed. and tr. F. J. Miller (London, 1917; rev. 1929), 308. One imagines it was on humanist advice, probably that of Poliziano, that Isaac composed another dirge for the death of Lorenzo, based on this same chorus. See Albert Dunning, *Die Staatsmotette* (Utrecht, 1970), 22–3. Pierre de La Rue set the same text (ibid. 24–6).

[16] For the present discussion Poliziano's text has been checked against a copy of the *editio princeps* now in the Bodleian Library at Oxford, originally donated by Aldus Manutius to the monastery of San Marco at Florence, shelf-mark Auct. 2.R.2.18. Inscription on title-page, partly deleted: 'C[onventu Sancti Marci de Florentia ordinis predicatorum] ex liberalitate Aldi Manucii Romani pro quo tenemus orare.' A similar inscription appears in the second part. The original ownership of this copy has been investigated by A. de la Mare following a suggestion by Sir Roger Mynors. The text has been edited by John Sparrow in 'Latin Verse of the High Renaissance', in E. F. Jacob (ed.), *Italian Renaissance Studies* (London, 1960; repr. 1966), 354–409; and also by Alessandro Perosa and John Sparrow (eds.), in *Renaissance Latin Verse* (London, 1979), 140 and 171. See also Poliziano, *Opera omnia*, ed. Ida Maier, 3 vols. (Turin, 1970–1), i. 621; ii. 274 for facsimiles of other edns.

Orestes referred to earlier. It also engages in considerable poetic licence in feigning that Poliziano died while singing his funeral ode for Lorenzo, 'Quis dabit capiti meo', since the deaths of the two men are two years apart. Finally, it notes, perhaps critically, the irregular metre of Poliziano's verse ('liberiora verba'), which Bembo nevertheless echoes in ways more than one.[17]

It was probably in 1500, for the death of the poet Marullo, that Andrea Dazzi wrote an elegy containing these lines:

> Quis dabit, quis, meo pares
> dolori lachrymas?
> Miser, vae, miser!
> Dolor, heu, dolor!

The death of Anne of Brittany, wife of Louis XII, in 1514 generated a number of funeral odes.[18] The dirge by Quintianus Stoa contains the line 'proh dolor, dolor!' The continuing influence of Poliziano on neo-Latin lamentations may be observed in two publications of the seventeenth century. Francesco Roggeri (Milan, 1627) has

> O miser, miser,
> O dolor, dolor.

Vincenzo Guiniggi (Venice, 1654):

> Ah, furor, furor,
> O dolor, dolor!

Of particular interest in Isaac's setting of Poliziano's lament is the prominent conclusion, which sets off the words 'Requiescat in pace' as a coda. Three repeated notes occur six times in the bass on the syllables 'Et re-qui[-e-sca-mus in pa-ce]' (see Ex. 7.5a). This repetition is characteristic of the Gregorian cantus firmus that was Isaac's model. In fact, Isaac's melodic curve for the liturgical words is a quotation from the concluding phrase of the chant *Salva nos*. It will be seen, then, that the three repeated notes of the Gregorian chant phrase have influenced Isaac's homophonic incipit

---

[17] There are many other phrases echoed by Poliziano's imitators. For instance, in 1492 lightning struck the lantern of Florence Cathedral, an event popularly connected with Lorenzo's subsequent death on 9 Apr. 1492. Poliziano's line 11, 'Laurus impetu fulminis', obviously refers to this belief, which was widely held at the time. It has influenced Sassi's 'barbarici fulminis impetu'. Similarly, Poliziano's repetition of 'laurus' in lines 11 and 13 is echoed in Bembo's 'Laurente' and 'Laurentem' in the latter's lyric. Further details of Poliziano's imitators can be found in Sparrow's article cited in the previous note. I am indebted to A. de la Mare, N. Rubinstein, and the late J. Sparrow for several helpful suggestions.

[18] In my article 'Poliziano, Isaac, Festa: Rhetorical Repetition', in Garfagnani (ed.), *Firenze e la Toscana dei Medici*, ii. 549–64, I discussed the settings of 'Quis dabit oculis nostris fontem lacrimarum' by Mouton and Festa and two later settings, for the death of Emperor Ferdinand in 1564, by Jean de Chainée and Michael Deiss. Poliziano's text was also set by Nicholas Payen; it was published in 1547 but it is not known for whom it was written. On all these settings, see Dunning, *Staatsmotette*, who has also edited the works by Deiss and de Chainée in *Pietro Giovanelli, Novus Thesaurus Musicus (1568)*, Book V (CMM 64; Rome, 1974).

Ex. 7.5, Isaac, 'Quis dabit capiti meo'

(*a*) DTO, p. 47, bars 2–6

et   re - qui - e - sca - mus   in pa - ce

(*b*) DTO, p. 45, bars 1–8

Quis   da - bit   ca - pi - ti   me - o   a - - - quam

(cf. Exx. 7.4*b* and 7.5*b*). Moreover, these repeated notes, sustained by the same chord in several prominent places,[19] pervade the entire texture of Isaac's motet. The recurrence of such opening motifs is not rare. What makes Isaac's motet remarkable is the amount of repetition, which seems generated by the rhetorical procedure of Isaac's poet and Florentine contemporary, Poliziano.

The unifying function of this musical motif has already been discussed in a variety of publications between 1963 and 1977, notably by Just, Osthoff, Dunning, Atlas, and Staehelin.[20] It was Staehelin who identified sections of the motet as being closely related to Isaac's *Missa Salva nos* and the crucial motif as the concluding section of the chant *Salva nos*. The question as to whether the mass preceded the motet or vice versa need not concern us here; suffice it to say that the sections of the motet discussed above do not occur in the mass and represent original (not parody) material, namely, the homophonic beginning of the *prima pars* ('Quis dabit capiti') and the entire *tertia pars* ('Laurus impetu' with 'et requiescamus' in the bass).

We have already commented on the amount of repetition Isaac employs in the *tertia pars*. But the musical emphasis is not merely the result of accumulation. The repetition occurs in the same voice and represents a kind of rhetoric, intelligible to any listener, whereas awareness of polyphonic imitation in a contrapuntal web requires more professional perception. It is the former

---

[19] For all musical references see Isaac, *Weltliche Werke*, ed. J. Wolf (Denkmäler der Tonkunst in Österreich, 14/i; Vienna, 1907), 45–8. Isaac's motet falls into four parts, each of which is a setting of five of Poliziano's lines (but ignoring Poliziano's repetition of ll. 1–10 as ll. 21–30). The repeated notes, sustained by the same chord, are encountered at the beginning of each section: p. 45: 'Quis dabit', bars 1–2; 'Quis oculis', bar 9; p. 46: 'Sic turtur', bar 33; 'Sic luscinia', bar 47; p. 47: 'Et requiescamus', bars 2–3; 'illa illa', bars 8–9; p. 48: 'Sub cuius', bars 1–2; 'Et Phebi', bars 9–10. For a catalogue of musical settings of texts by Poliziano, Latin or Italian, cf. Giulio Cattin, 'Le rime del Poliziano nelle fonti musicali', in *Miscellanea di studi in onore di Vittore Branca*, 5 vols. (Biblioteca dell'Archivum Romanicum, 78–82; Florence, 1983), iii. 379–95. Cattin mentions both 'Quis dabit' and 'Che fai tu, Echo', discussed earlier.

[20] The earlier literature is summarized by Atlas and Staehelin. See *The Cappella Giulia Chansonnier*, ed. Alan Atlas, 2 vols. (Brooklyn, 1975–6), i. 155–60 (no. 60); Isaac, *Messen*, ed. H. Birtner and M. Staehelin, 2 vols. (Musikalische Denkmäler, 7–8; Mainz, 1970–3), ii. 45 ff. and 149 ff.; M. Staehelin, *Die Messen Heinrich Isaacs*, 3 vols. (Publikationen der Schweizerischen Musikforschenden Gesellschaft, ser. 2, 28; Berne, 1977), i. 8 n. 61, 83, 87, 95, 98; ii. 36–8, 202–3.

kind of rhetoric, corresponding to anaphora and anadiplosis in Poliziano's text, and inspired by it, that demands our attention. Another aspect to be considered is the position of the voice that carries the burden of repetition. When Isaac or Josquin wish to emphasize a point rhetorically, they usually reiterate that point in an outer voice, treble or bass. Good examples (belonging to the generation of Josquin, Isaac, and Obrecht) are the several settings of the motet text 'Virgo prudentissima'. In Josquin's setting the biblical quotation from the Song of Songs ('ut luna, ut sol'), with its *parallelismus membrorum*, or, to put it more in terms of Renaissance rhetoric, its anaphora, begets a musical *ut–sol* motif four times in the bass.[21] When, however, Isaac or Josquin do not aim at such conspicuous emphasis, they proceed differently. In his dirge on the death of Ockeghem (1497, five years after the death of Lorenzo) Josquin also weaves a sacred voice into the polyphonic texture. While the other voices sing in French, one voice sings in Latin 'Requiem aeternam dona eis'. But this text is allotted to the tenor, not to the bass, and the music is not repeated.

Returning now to the *tertia pars* of Isaac's 'Quis dabit capiti meo', we note not only the amount of anadiplosis and its positioning in an outer voice, but also the thinning out of texture that makes all musical procedures more transparent. Whereas the preceding and the succeeding *pars* of the motet are scored for four voices, the *tertia pars* bears the rubric 'Tenor Laurus tacet'. Apart from the obvious meaning that Lorenzo (*Laurus*) lives no longer, the result is that the reiterated words 'Et requiescamus in pace' in the bass are more conspicuous against the declamation of 'Laurus impetu fulminis' in the upper two voices.

The *locus classicus* of the technique of echo is of course Ovid's account of Narcissus and the nymph Echo in the *Metamorphoses*. I have sketched the importance of the *Metamorphoses* for music in Chapter 1. They have been called the 'Bible of Renaissance painters' because of the popularity of their subjects in the visual arts, but, from Poliziano to Rinuccini, they can just as well be called the 'Bible of librettists and dramatic authors of the Renaissance'.[22] Moreover, the technique of verbal repetition employed by Ovid in the telling of this story was no doubt one of the most powerful influences on echo lyrics from Poliziano and Serafino to Tasso and Guarini.

In addition to numerous and remarkable repetitions of words in the *Metamorphoses*, the same rhetorical procedures are found in the *Heroides*, for example in number 15, the story of Sappho, where Ovid (if the poem is his) insistently repeats (with different syntactical function) a whole clause: 'nulla futura tua est, nulla futura tua est'. Erasmus' *Colloquia*—probably the

---

[21] For a late descendant of the ascending fifth for *ut–sol*, see 'Audi coelum' from Monteverdi's Vespers, where the two ascending fifths in the bass are sandwiched in between echo treatments (anadiplosis) of the words 'Benedicam' and 'Maria'; *Opere*, ed. Malipiero, xiv. 228.

[22] See H. C. Wolff, 'Ovids Metamorphosen und die frühe Oper', *Quadrivium*, 12/2 (1971), 89–107.

most popular source of neo-Latin literature—contains a charming and elegant word-play on 'Echo', published for the first time in 1526 and frequently reprinted during the course of the century.[23] Other neo-Latin works whose authors probably knew both Ovid and Erasmus include the *Silvae* of Joannes Secundus of the 1530s (with their echo rhyme *amori–mori*) and the *Elegiae* of Thomas Campion, published in 1619, which presents not only the repetitions attributed to Echo

> Ver Anni Lunaeque fuit. . .
> . . . tu dea *Veris eris*
> Et vocalis, *eris*, blanditaque reddidit Echo
>
> It was the spring of the year and the Moon . . .
> . . . thou shalt be the goddess of Spring
> and, taking voice and in flattery, 'thou shalt be' Echo replied

but also repeats the initial word 'Ver' eight times in twenty lines.[24]

The achievement of Poliziano—who was an assiduous reader of and commentator on Ovid—consisted in uniting the traditions of writing about echo in Greek and Latin literature. In this respect we possess two important sources. One is a copy of Ovid's works, printed at Parma in 1477, which had belonged to Poliziano and preserves his marginal annotations. This copy is now in the Bodleian Library. The other source grew out of a series of lectures that Poliziano gave on Ovid: a manuscript of his notes.[25] These two sources show that he was particularly interested in repetitive figures of speech. These hobby-horses, well known to professors of rhetoric, were supposed (to cite Poliziano) to add aural beauty to speech ('auditui suavitatem'). This notion of beauty or *suavitas* is important, because the pleasure that the artist takes in it leads him copiously to annotate certain passages in Ovid. For example, the repetition of the phrase 'Nulla futura tua est', mentioned above, is the object of an extended commentary, both in the copy of the works printed at Parma and in his lecture notes. In both cases he uses the term anadiplosis.

While repetition for rhetorical effect occurs in a number of compositions, very little music utilizing the echo effect is known before the middle of the sixteenth century. Engel's article in *Die Musik in Geschichte und Gegenwart* (based on an earlier article by Kroyer) refers to a madrigal by Sperindio, published in 1561.[26] In the later sixteenth century 'echoes' or 'dialogues', so named, frequently constitute the last or penultimate piece. Not infrequently the 'dialogue' employs not only the question-and-answer technique, but the

[23] See *The Colloquia of Erasmus*, tr. C. R. Thompson (Chicago, 1965), 373–7; *Opera omnia Desiderii Erasmi*, tomus 1–3 (Amsterdam, 1972), 555–8. The first edn. was brought out by Froben in Basle in 1526.

[24] See D. Crane, *Joannes Secundus* (Leipzig, 1931), 33–5, 91–2, for the probability of influences of Callimachus, Gauradas, and Erasmus; see also *Campion's Works*, ed. O. Vivian (Oxford, 1909), 315.

[25] Edited by Elisabetta Lazzeri: *Poliziano: Commento inedito all'epistola ovidiana di Saffo a Faone* (Istituto Nazionale di Studi sul Rinascimento, Studi e Testi, 11; Florence, 1971).

[26] 'Son io, son altri. Echo'; see *Nuovo Vogel*, no. 2632.

echo device as well, so that the two categories coincide. Examples are to be found in the works of such well-known masters as Verdelot, Willaert, Rore, Wert, Hans Leo Hassler,[27] Andrea Gabrieli, Monteverdi (and, as we shall see, Le Jeune). Among the many minor masters who so conclude some of their collections are Sperindio,[28] Agostini, Cambio, Donato, as well as Vecchi and Anerio at the end of the century. The echo repetition usually takes place at the end of the poetic line. Sometimes the relevant word (or syllables) is restated at the end of the line; at other times it is carried from the end of one to the beginning of the next line (palillogia).

In 1977 Alexander Silbiger made known 'An Unknown Partbook of Early Sixteenth-Century Polyphony', namely MS Vat. mus. 571 of the Biblioteca Vaticana.[29] No. 17 of the manuscript makes an important contribution to the history of echo music in revealing a musical setting, presumably from the 1520s, of the neo-Latin poem 'Quae celebrat Thermas Echo'. As in the case of Serafino the anonymous author employs echo technique across the line ('An Echo—Echo'), at the end of the line ('amore—morae'), and throughout the line ('clamor–amor', 'furor–uror'). At times the sonorous effect of repetition is almost lost on the modern reader ('Narc*issum*—ipsum'):

> 1 Quae celebrat Thermas Echo et stagna alta Neronis . . .
> 2 Quisnam clamor? Amor. Quisnam furor? Uror. An Echo?
> 6 Echo. Quae maior poena in amore? Morae.
> 7 Expectas Narcissum? Ipsum . . .
>
> What Echo makes famous the baths and deep pools of Nero?
> What cry? Love. What madness? I burn. Or Echo?
> Echo. What is the greatest torment in love? Delays.
> Are you waiting for Narcissus? For him . . .

Here the reference to Narcissus in line 7 is important, because it refers to Ovid's account of Narcissus and the nymph Echo in the *Metamorphoses*. Another setting of 'Quae celebrat' was published in Claude Le Jeune's *Livre de melanges* by Plantin at Antwerp in 1585 and reprinted at Paris in 1586 and 1587.[30] This is obviously one of several compositions of Le Jeune influenced by Italian models, and he uses his 'Echo' as the crowning piece to conclude the collection. It is scored for ten voices, and has not been included in modern reprints of Le Jeune by Expert and other scholars,

---

[27] Ibid., no. 1309. The music is reprinted in Denkmäler der Tonkunst in Bayern, 20 (1962), 151. This madrigal, composed for an Italian wedding, employs the same echo 'amore'—'ah, more' as in Poliziano's 'Che fai tu, Eco'.

[28] See n. 26. No. 2633 also concludes with a dialogue.

[29] *SM* 6 (1977), 43–67.

[30] See *Nuovo Vogel*, no. 1495 for the first edn. by Plantin, and F. Lesure and G. Thibault, *Bibliographie des éditions d'Adrien Le Roy et Robert Ballard* (Paris, 1955), nos. 280 and 292 for the Paris reprints. See also K. Levy, 'Le Jeune', in *MGG*, viii, cols. 589–94, more particularly 592 on dialogue and echo in Le Jeune. Levy believes that the date of composition of 'Quae celebrat' belongs to the period of 1565–75, i.e. considerably before the first publication.

Ex. 7.6. Claude Le Jeune, 'Quae celebrat Thermas Echo', bars 25–35

which have tended to concentrate on Le Jeune's French rather than Latin texts. A few bars of this later 'Quae celebrat', scored from a copy of the 1586 edition in the British Library,[31] may be of interest (Ex. 7.6).

The humanist Luigi Groto (1541–85) was one of the most remarkable poets of the genre towards the end of the sixteenth century. His *Rime* were published six times between 1577 and 1610. One of these poems, 'S'io am'altra che voi', repeats the incipit twelve times at the beginning of the line (anaphora) in the course of the first four stanzas. Groto adds an explanatory note to many of his texts at the end of the book. Regarding 'S'io am'altra che voi' he says: 'questa canzon fu fatto a imitatio [*sic*] di quella di Petrarca'.[32] He does not specify which poem of Petrarch he refers to; however, one thinks immediately of 'S'i' 'l dissi mai', formed, as is that of Groto, of nine-line stanzas, repeating the incipit three times in each of the first four stanzas, at the beginning of the first, third, and fifth lines. The numbers of these lines, after the duplication of the initial phrase, consequently are identical in Petrarch and Groto (i.e. 1, 3, 5; 10, 12, 14; 19, 21, 23; 28, 30, 32). This striking similarity should remind us of the considerable debt to Petrarch of certain authors such as Serafino, Bembo, Groto, and Guarini. This influence concerns not only attitudes, amorous and otherwise, but also the art of arranging the words (including anaphora and other types of repetition). Several musical settings of this model song by Petrarch (no. 206) have come down to us: by Tromboncino (1507), Pisano (1520), Boyleau (1546), Ruffo (1554), Palestrina (1551), and Cossa (1569).[33] Among these, it is worth while examining Tromboncino's frottola, which belongs to the same period as the compositions by Serafino discussed earlier. Once again the triple verbal repetition of the first stanza is associated with multiple musical duplications. The incipit appearing at ll. 1, 3, and 5 is sung to a motif of five repeated notes. This motif is used four times (not three) in the course of the stanza (Ex. 7.7a). But Petrarch's repetition scheme of only three syllables is considerably developed in Tromboncino's setting, where whole lines of eleven syllables are sung to the same melody (lines 1 and 5, 2 and 3) (see Exx. 7.7b and c).

> S'i' 'l dissi mai, ch'i' venga in odio a quella
> Del cui amor vivo e senza 'l qual morrei:
> S'i' 'l dissi, ch'i miei dì sian pochi e rei,
> E di vil signoria l'anima ancella:
> S'i' 'l dissi, contra me s'arme ogni stella . . .

---

[31] I am indebted to Miss Margaret Gilmore, St Hugh's College, Oxford, for making this transcription available. Bars 1–35 were included in my article 'Aspects of Echo Music in the Renaissance', *SM* 9 (1980), 45–57.

[32] See Luigi Groto, *Delle rime* (Venice: Zoppini, 1598), 68–70 and 187. The pagination is identical in the edn. of 1601.

[33] On Tromboncino's setting see Einstein, *Italian Madrigal*, iii. 12; see also W. Rubsamen, *Literary Sources of Secular Music in Italy ca. 1500* (Berkeley, Calif., 1943; repr. New York, 1972), 60; for the later versions see *Nuovo Vogel*.

Ex. 7.7. Tromboncino, 'S'i'l dissi mai'

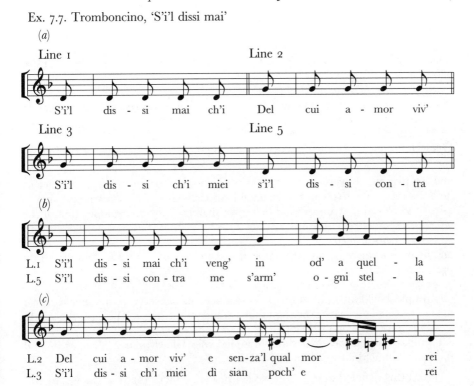

If I ever said that I am in her displeasure
Of whose love I live and without should die:
If I ever said that my days were few and cruel,
And my soul vassal to unworthy rule,
If I ever said it, let every star take up arms against me . . .

Verbal repetition was very popular in sixteenth-century plays. I shall limit myself here to two early examples for which music has been preserved, examples preceding the Florentine intermedi of 1589. The first concerns a series of intermedi performed in Florence about 1525 during a sacra rappresentazione, *Santa Uliva*. As was customary, the spoken text was interspersed with musical episodes. In fact, *Santa Uliva* has no fewer than fourteen of these interludes. The second concerns the story of Echo and Narcissus from the third book of the *Metamorphoses*. Narcissus' lament utilizes repetition:[34]

e la ninfa a ogni fermata di parole replichi nel medesimo modo che egli ha fatto le ultime parole da lui dette, e massime certe come sarebbe *ahimè* e simili. E perchè

---

[34] For the second interlude of *Santa Uliva* see D'Ancona, *Sacre rappresentazioni*, iii. 235–315 (esp. 268–9); M. Bonfantini, *Le sacre rappresentazioni italiane* (Milan, 1942), 656–728 (esp. 684 and n. on p. 728); Becherini, 'La musica nelle sacre rappresentazioni', esp. 215; ead., 'Rappresentazione sacra', *MGG*, x, cols. 1928–30. Further information on plot and two finales of *S. Uliva* has been given in Ch. 4.

meglio intendiate vi daremo l'esempio: e diremo: s'el detto giovane dicesse questo verso:

    Sa quest'altier ch'io l'amo,

e facessi fermata dove dice *ch'io l'amo*; la ninfa dica: *ch'io l'amo*. Se dicesse tutto il verso, cioè:

    Sa quest'altier ch'io l'amo e ch'io l'adoro

la ninfa dica solamente con la medesima voce: *l'adoro*; e cosi replichi l'ultime parole del verso, secondo il modo di chi lo canta. Questi sono i versi:

    Misero a me, che bramo e che desio

Questi finiti, dica tre volte ad alta voce e adagio: *Ahimè, ahimè, ahimè*; e la ninfa gli risponda . . .

and the nymph, at every pause in the words, should reply in the same manner as he had used for the last words he said, and especially those such as *ahimè* and similar ones. And so you may understand better we shall give you an example, thus: if the young man should say this line:

    Sa quest'altier ch'io l'amo,

and he pauses where he says *ch'io l'amo*; the nymph should say: *ch'io l'amo*. If he says the whole line, that is:

    Sa quest'altier ch'io l'amo e ch'io l'adoro

the nymph should say only, in the same manner, *l'adoro*. And thus she should repeat the last words of the line, according to the manner of the singer. These are the words:

    Misero a me, che bramo e che desio

After this, he should say three times in a loud voice, slowly: *Ahimè, ahimè, ahimè*; and the nymph should answer him . . .

From this detailed description we learn several facts: that Narcissus' lament, consisting of four stanzas (ottave rime), was performed with an echo effect at the end of the line or at the end of the hemistich, according to the manner in which it was sung ('secondo il modo di chi lo canta'). As a model to add to Narcissus' lament, the author gives the ottave rime of Bradamante's lament for Ruggiero from Ariosto's *Orlando furioso*.[35] Notable in Narcissus' lament are certain rhyme words such as 'morte' (l. 8), 'cordoglio' (l. 22), and 'ahimè' (end of the first hemistich of l. 25). All these words recur frequently in echo poetry and songs of the sixteenth century. No musical setting of Narcissus' lament has yet been found, though a few musical settings of the first half of the century of the passage from Ariosto that served as model have come down to us.[36] A later one by Antonio Cifra entitled 'Aria di Ruggiero' uses the famous bass Ruggiero, which seems most apt for a lament. However that may be, it employs echoes not only at the hemistich ('ch'io l'amo') and at the end of the line ('ch'io l'adoro'), but also in the four initial syllables ('Sa quest'altier') ('This haughty man knows that I love him and adore him'). It is too good an example of the use of

---

[35] Canto XXXII, stanza 19 of the final version of *Orlando furioso* published in 1532. The stanza appeared for the first time in an earlier version of 1516. See the modern edns. by S. Benedetti and C. Segre (Bologna, 1960), 1094, and by C. Segre (Milan, 1976), 826.

[36] By Lupacchino, Bifetto, Hoste da Reggio, and Martoretta. See Balsano, *L'Ariosto*.

echo not to cite; it proves that the same repetitive procedures were applied to the same ottave rime for several decades (see Ex. 7.8).[37]

Ex. 7.8. Antonio Cifra, 'Sa quest'altier'

The second example of dramatic music using verbal and musical repetition comes from the Florentine intermedio of 1565, where the story of Cupid and Psyche, arranged by G. B. Cini in six episodes, punctuated the play by Ambra, *La cofanaria*. In the fifth intermedio Psyche expresses her sadness, intensified by the repetition of the word *fuggi*:

> *Fuggi* speme mia *fuggi*
> E *fuggi* per non far più mai ritorno
> Flee, my hope,
> Flee and flee, no more to return.

The presence of *fuggi* at the beginning of the two lines (anaphora) is accompanied by a cross-link from the end of line 1 to the beginning of line 2

---

[37] Florence, Biblioteca Nazionale Centrale, MS II. I. 296 (*olim* Magl. XIX. 186).

(palillogia). Musically, the second and third *fuggi* are exact repetitions of the first, both melodically (descending semitone) and harmonically (alternation of tonic and dominant) (see Ex. 7.9).[38]

Ex. 7.9. Striggio, 'Fuggi speme mia'

Rinuccini's echo scene in *Dafne*, as set to music by Gagliano in 1608, seems to be his third effort to present the battle between Apollo and the Python. In the Florentine intermedi of 1589 the third intermedio deals with that battle; a fragment of four lines has been preserved,[39] the first two of which are identical with the opening couplet of the texts set by Peri and Gagliano, except that it omits the echo 'Era' at the end of the second line:

> Ebra di sangue in questo oscuro bosco
> Giacea pur dianzi la terribil fera. —Era.
>
> Inebriated with blood in these dark woods
> just now the terrible beast did lie. —It did.

The echo 'Era', however, is present in the libretto of 1598 (Peri's music is not extant) and in Gagliano's score of 1608.[40] It is therefore a fair surmise

---

[38] See O. G. Sonneck, 'A Description of A. Striggio's and F. Corteccia's Intermedi "Psyche and Amor", 1565', in *Miscellaneous Studies in the History of Music* (New York, 1921; repr. 1968), 269–86; Pirrotta, *Music and Theatre*, 181; H. M. Brown, 'Psyche's Lament: Some Music for the Medici Wedding in 1565', in L. Berman (ed.), *Words and Music: The Scholar's View. A Medley of Problems and Solutions Compiled in Honor of A. Tillman Merritt* (Cambridge, Mass., 1972), 1–27 (esp. 17–19); id., *Sixteenth-Century Instrumentation*, 100. The music is in the 2nd edn. of V. Galileo, *Fronimo* (Venice; RISM 1584[15]). For another setting of 'Fuggi speme mia', see Marenzio, *Secondo libro de madrigali a sei* (Venice, 1584).

[39] Rossi's account, summarized in Walker, *Musique des intermèdes*, p. xliii; Marenzio's music is not extant.

[40] A facs. of this page of the libretto is given in my article 'The First Printed Opera Libretto', 127. Interestingly, while the printed libretto has a text of twelve lines with the conventional echo, in

that Rinuccini intended the composer of 1589, Marenzio, to employ the same device. Obviously the task of giving his musical collaborators opportunities for echo scenes intrigued Rinuccini, and in his libretto of *Narciso* (written probably about 1608), the technique appears twice: once in a scene involving Lydia, Narcissus, and an ensemble of nymphs (Act IV, scene iii) and once in the finale.[41] In the former we seem to hear reminiscences of the vocabulary familiar from Poliziano's lyric 'Che fai tu Eco':

> . . . Eco, che fai? —Ahi.
> . . . dov'io ti chiamo? —Amo.
>
> Echo, what dost thou? —Alas.
> where do I call thee? —I love.

In Rinuccini's finale the phrases are shuttled back and forth between chorus and messenger, sometimes in straightforward repetition, sometimes in inverted order (a procedure rhetoricians call 'chiasmus'):

| [Coro] | . . . al fin nud'ombra e suono. |
| [Nunzio] | Dunque nud'ombra e suono . . . |

| [Nunzio] | La bella imago ch'ei mirò ne l'acque. |
| [Coro] | Qual ne l'acque mirò sì bella imago? |

| . . . | Finally a mere shadow and sound. |
| | Thus a mere shadow and sound . . . |

> The beautiful image that he admired in the water.
> In the water he admired what beautiful image?

All our examples so far, with the possible exception of Le Jeune, have been taken from the tradition of the Italian Renaissance, and not without justice, since the poetry of Petrarch, Poliziano, Serafino, Sannazaro, and Ariosto exercised its influence not only on their Italian successors but also on the rest of Europe. And, even though the models of antiquity could have been studied directly by the humanists in countries such as France, the Netherlands, and England, in fact the Italian humanists often played the role of intermediary or, at least, transmitted complementary influences. Nevertheless, a rapid incursion in other regions should not be omitted. We have already evoked the Netherlands with Erasmus and Joannes Secundus, and England with Thomas Campion. What about echo poetry in France? It is generally admitted that the 'Dialogue d'un Amoureux et d'Echo' of Du Bellay (1549) is the first French text in the genre, a text inaugurating a tradition that extends to Victor Hugo's 'La chasse du Burgrave' (1828). No one will contest the role of Italian influence in Du Bellay, but the analysis of poetic traits of

Gagliano's setting ten more lines have been added, which he sets antiphonally. These choral echoes, within a five-part texture, are more reminiscent of *cori spezzati* than of Peri's echo aria from the intermedi of 1589 or the echo aria in the fifth act of Monteverdi's *Orfeo*.

[41] Solerti, *Albori*, ii. 226–7 and 235.

the fifteenth and sixteenth centuries shows that he had predecessors whose verbal skill comprised a great variety of repetitive techniques.

The essential works to consider lie between the Rhétoriqueurs (including Molinet, born *c.*1430) and the *Deffense . . . de la langue françoyse* of Du Bellay (1549). Du Bellay was born *c.*1520, and thus the period comprises more than a century. The principal treatises to examine are those of Fabri (1521), Du Pont (1539), and Sebillet (1548).[42]

In his treatise, Sebillet speaks of three categories of rhymes where the sonorities of the last syllables are repeated at the end of the line. He calls these categories 'rime couronnée', 'empérière', and 'rime en écho'. He gives as example of 'rime couronnée' the second stanza of Clément Marot's third chanson, beginning with 'Dieu gard ma Maistresse et Regente'. Marot wrote this chanson before 1531: it was published for the first time in a musical setting by Claudin de Sermisy in *Vingt et huit chansons* (Attaingnant, 1531[1]).[43] The second stanza uses repetition of sonorities at the end of each line, changing the sense (paronomasia):

> La blanche colom*belle belle,*
> Souvent je voys p*riant criant.*
> Mais dessoubz la cor*delle d'elle*
> Me jecte ung œil *friant, riant,*
> En me con*sommant* et *sommant*
> A douleur qui ma *face efface.*
> Dont suis le recl*amant amant,*
> Qui pour l'oul*trepasse trespasse.*

> The white dove beautiful
> often I see pleading, crying;
> But beneath her sash
> She casts at me a glance fond and smiling.
> This eats me up and enjoins
> To pain which hides my face.
> Of this I am the claimant lover
> Who to reach the limit dies.

[42] See H. Zschalig, *Die Verslehren von Fabri, Du Pont und Sibillet* [Sebillet] (Leipzig, 1884); E. Langlois (ed.), *Recueil d'arts de seconde rhétorique* (Paris, 1902); Thomas Sebillet, *Art poétique Françoys*, ed. F. Gaiffe (Paris, 1910; repr. 1932); E. Lüken, *Du Bellays 'Deffence . . .' in ihrem Verhältnis zu Sebillets 'Art . . .'* (Oldenburg, 1913); W. T. Elwert, *Traité de versification française des origines à nos jours* (Paris, 1965). I should like to thank Prof. John McClelland of the University of Toronto for having drawn my attention to Gaiffe's edn. of Sebillet and its importance with regard to the question of the existence of French echo poetry before Du Bellay.

[43] See Langlois, *Recueil*, 225 (Guerre la pu*lente lente*, / qui tout en sa *tasse tasse*, / . . .); Sebillet, *Art poétique*, ed. Gaiffe, 199–205 (with references to the treatises of Fabri and Du Pont); Elwert, *Traité*, 110–11; Clément Marot, *Œuvres lyriques*, ed. C. A. Mayer (London, 1964), 176; F. Lesure, 'Autour de Clément Marot', *Revue de musicologie*, 33 (1951), 109–19 (esp. p. 116, 'Dieu des amans'); D. Heartz, *Pierre Attaingnant: Royal Printer of Music* (Berkeley, Calif., 1969), 244; F. Dobbins, 'Moderne's *Parangon des Chansons*', *RMA Research Chronicle*, 12 (1974), 1–90 (esp. p. 30); Claudin de Sermisy, *Opera omnia*, iii, ed I. Cazeaux (CMM 52; Rome, 1974), pp. xviii, 64–6 (no. 41).

There are two remarkable aspects of the technique of echo in Marot's poem. First, the technique is used only in the second stanza; it appears neither in the first nor in the third. Secondly, Claudin's music, which was printed only with the first stanza, but surely served for the two following stanzas, does not use an echo formula; it constitutes an undifferentiated support for the echo poem, like the setting of Serafino's 'Gridan vostri occhi' discussed above. Unfortunately, nothing can be said about Janequin's setting of Du Bellay's echo poem of 1549. Only the bass part of the *Premier livre de chansons* of 1557, published by Du Chemin, has been preserved.[44]

It is impossible to retrace here in detail the development of the technique of echo in Italian poetry and music at the end of the sixteenth and beginning of the seventeenth century. As far as themes are concerned, it is clear that certain subjects predominate: laments of lovers or other protagonists, funeral scenes, sad or melancholy situations. Rinuccini's echo aria 'Ebra di sangue', as set to music in Gagliano's *Dafne*, undoubtedly belongs to this category, at least for its first seven lines, before Apollo reveals his intention to destroy the monster. However, there are several examples where repetition expresses joy. This is the case in Orfeo's 'Gioite al canto mio' in Peri's *Euridice*, where Rinuccini's line 'Eco ribombi delle valle ascose' suggests to the musician a repetition of the musical phrase and even a triple exposition at the parallel passage in the second stanza.

On the level of poetic technique, the persistence of the vocabulary should not surprise us. The pastoral style privileges the hills, the valleys, the woods, and open air ('colli, valli, selve, fuori'), and certain Italian words are used because of their suggestive character, because they lend themselves to rhyme, or because they are easily divisible to form echoes. Frequently the syntax is modified to adapt to metres and rhymes, but entire families of words form the common fund of the poetic vocabulary of echo: *ribombo, ribombi, ribombano; ascondere, ascose; rispondere, risponde; moro, morire, morto, morte; amare, amore*, etc. The continuous tradition observable, from Poliziano to the texts of madrigals by Marenzio, from the librettos of the first operas to Calzabigi's text for Gluck, is truly striking. Among all the techniques of repetition catalogued by the rhetoricians, it seems that the echo held a more important place than anaphora or palillogia in the field of opera. The reason is perhaps that the end of the musical phrase, corresponding to the end of a line, is the most propitious place for harmonic confirmation.[45]

---

[44] See H. Chamard, *J. du Bellay* (Lille, 1900), 64, 232–3 (commentaries on the influence of Poliziano, Sannazaro, Bembo, and Joannes Secundus); Du Bellay, *Poems*, ed. H. W. Lawton (Oxford, 1961), 15 and 139 (reference to Pasquier's opinion, according to which this work by Du Bellay is the first French echo poem); Clément Janequin, *Chansons polyphoniques*, ed. A. T. Merritt and F. Lesure, 6 vols. (Monaco, 1965–71), vi. 180, no. 249.

[45] Echo effects can also be found in instrumental music; for two instances, see my 'Écho et répétition dans la poésie et la musique' in Vaccaro (ed.), *Chanson à la Renaissance*, 242–53 at 253.

The history of echo music, embracing all genres, is so vast that to do it justice would require a separate monograph. But from what has been said it is evident that towards the end of the sixteenth century the application to stage music of a device explored in the repertoire of frottolas and madrigals[46] becomes widespread and more frequent. Even in the field of opera alone, instances are far more numerous than suggested in the present volume. What with the paucity of extant scores our knowledge is largely based on librettos, and literary texts do not always indicate echo technique, as we have seen in the case of Ariosto's 'Sa quest'altier' and the earliest version of Rinuccini's 'Ebra di sangue'. It is a fair guess that many other lyrics in printed librettos employed the ubiquitous device, particularly when they made use of the vocabulary typical of echo poetry. However that may be, from some hundred examples of echoes in stage music we list in Table 7.1 about a third of the more famous instances. In each case echo technique is indicated either in libretto or score, sometimes in both. The texts are almost invariably Italian, except for Walliser's choruses for a Latin school drama (1612) and a Latin oratorio by Carissimi. Walliser's *Andromeda* reminds us of the importance of music in schools (whether Jesuit or Protestant), and its subject-matter harks back to the archetypal lament of Euripides. The echo aria in Carissimi's *Jephte*, with its use of such verbs as *ululare* and *lacrimare* (wail, weep), reminds us of the fact that it would be easy to compile a similar list from Latin motets, 'concerti ecclesiastici', and other non-secular works.[47] We have also refrained from including works of the English Restoration: plays with incidental music, semi-operas, operas; echo scenes by Banister, Locke, and Purcell come to mind. Similarly, German opera has not been surveyed, except for three works: Schütz's *Dafne*, based on Opitz's translation of Rinuccini's *Dafne*; Staden's *Seelewig*, the first extant German opera 'in genere recitativo'; and *Ariadne* by Strauss and Hofmannsthal, where the nymph 'Echo' is only one of the fingerprints of many Italianate traits.[48]

[46] Even Palestrina wrote an echo madrigal, 'Dido, chi giace', on the death of Dido, published in 1586 (RISM 1586⁹); mod. edn. in *Werke*, ed. Haberl, vol. xxviii, and *Opere*, ed. Casimiri, vol. xxxi. Cf. also R. Schwartz, 'H. L. Hassler unter dem Einfluß der italienischen Madrigalisten', *VfMw* 9 (1893), 1–61, esp. 33.

[47] Concerning Walliser see A. G. Ritter, 'Die musikalischen Chöre des Chr. T. Walliser zur Tragödie "Andromeda"', *Monatshefte für Musikgeschichte*, 1 (1869), 134–41; particularly the echo 'eheu–heu' (p. 138). Concerning Carissimi's 'Plorate, plorate colles' from *Jephte*, see the edn. by J. Beat (London: Novello, 1974), pp. 25–9; also the discussion of this lament in histories of the oratorio (Schering, Smither).

[48] For a facs. of the libretto of Schütz's *Dafne* cf. Martin Opitz, *Weltliche Poemata, 1644, Erster Teil*, ed. E. Trunz (Deutsche Neudrucke, Reihe: Barock, 2; Tübingen, 1967), 110–11, which shows the echo rhyme 'sich–ich', derived from Rinuccini's 'rio–io'. Staden's *Seelewig*, mentioned in Ch. 2, has been reprinted by R. Eitner in *Monatshefte für Musikgeschichte*, 13 (1881), 53–147; the two echo scenes occur in Acts II and III (pp. 103 ff., 117 ff.). Concerning other, non-operatic, echo passages in Schütz, cf. Silke Leopold, 'Echotechniken bei H. Schütz und seinen italienischen Zeitgenossen', in *Kongreß-Bericht Stuttgart 1985* [Gesellschaft für Musikforschung, *Alte Musik als ästhetische Gegenwart: Bach, Händel, Schütz*], 2 vols. (Kassel, 1987), i. 86–94. Hofmannsthal's 'Echo' probably derives from the lyric 'Sweet Echo, sweetest nymph' from Milton's *Comus* (1634), as Karen Forsyth suggests, *Ariadne auf Naxos by Hugo von Hofmannsthal and Richard Strauss: Its Genesis and Meaning* (Oxford Modern Languages and Literature Monographs; Oxford, 1982), 83. Concerning repetition and echo in that opera, see the vocal score of the opera, ed. Otto Singer (Berlin, 1912), 68, 74, 77, 87–9, 180, 182, 193, 198, 208, 239.

Table 7.1. *Selective list of echo passages in Italian stage music*

Date	Composer	Title/incipit	Remarks
c.1525	?	*S. Uliva*	See Ch. 7.
1565	Striggio	'Fuggi speme mia'	5th intermedio; see Ch. 7.
1589	Marenzio	'Ebra di sangue'	Rinuccini; see Ch. 7.
1589	Peri	'Dunque fra torbide'	5th intermedio; see Ch. 6.
1598	Peri	'Ebra di sangue'	*Dafne*; see Ch. 7.
1598	?	*Pastor fido*	Third intermedio; double echo; see Ch. 7.
1599	Monte	'Chi se' tu che rispondi?'	From *Pastor fido*, 1589; Act IV, l. 1033 (*Nuovo Vogel*, no. 734, last item); see Ch. 7.
1599	?	*Armenia*	Schiaffinati, 1st intermedio; see Ch. 1.
1600	Cavalieri	*Anima e corpo*	Nos. 28, 54, 90 of 1600 score.
1606	Agazzari	*Eumelio*	'Care selve beate', pp. 3–5 of 1606 score; cf. *Pastor fido*, Act II, l. 600; see Ch. 7.
1607	Monteverdi	*Orfeo*	Act II, 'Questi i campi'; see Ch. 6.
1608	Gagliano	*Dafne*	'Ebra di sangue'; see Ch. 7.
c.1608	?	*Narciso*	Rinuccini's libretto; see Ch. 7.
1612	Walliser	*Andromeda*	Choruses for Latin school drama; see Ch. 7.
1619	Landi	*Morte d'Orfeo*	Solerti, *Albori*, iii. 313.
1626	D. Mazzocchi	*Catena d'Adone*	Goldschmidt, *Studien*, i. 158–9.
1627	Schütz	*Dafne*	See Ch. 7.
1633	M. Rossi	*Erminia*	Act I finale; Goldschmidt, *Studien*, i. 67.
1639	Vittori	*Galatea*	Goldschmidt, *Studien*, i. 279–81.
1639	Marazzoli and V. Mazzocchi	*Chi soffre speri*	Act II, sc. vi; echo in libretto, not in score.
1640	Ferrari	*Pastor regio*	Corte, *Drammi*, i. 305.
1640	Cavalli	*Amori d'Apollo*	Act I, sc. iv.
1640–9	Carissimi	*Jephte*	See Ch. 7.
1641	V. Mazzocchi	*Innocenza difesa*	Act V, sc. v (alternative title: *Genoinda*).
1642	L. Rossi	*Palazzo incantato*	Facs. of score, ed. Brown, pp. 39–40.
1644	Staden	*Seelewig*	See Ch. 7.
1656	Cavalli	*Artemisia*	Act II, sc. vi.
1656	Marazzoli	*Vita humana*	Act I, sc. iii.
1683	Legrenzi	*Giustino*	Wolff, *Venezianische Oper*, 90.
1702	F. Gasparini	*Tiberio*	Paris, MS Vm7 4854, fos. 92^r–95^v.
1724	Vivaldi	*Giustino*	See Ch. 1.
1737	Handel	*Giustino*	See Ch. 6.
1762	Gluck	*Orfeo*	Act I; see Ch. 1.
1779	Gluck	*Echo et Narcisse*	Score of 1780, Act II (p. 166), Act III (pp. 216–18).
1887	Verdi	*Otello*	Rubric 'come un eco'; see Chs. 1, 6.
1912	Strauss	*Ariadne*	See Ch. 7.

We have noted earlier how Doni chided Cavalieri for his many artifices 'such as repetitions, echo effects, and similar devices, which have nothing to do with good and true theatrical music'. But a study of stage music shows that repetition and echo are far from being old-fashioned tricks for Cavalieri, Peri, Monteverdi, and their successors. Rather, throughout the history of opera in the seventeenth and eighteenth centuries, they function as most eloquent devices to partner question-and-answer games, amorous dalliance, pastoral happiness, and—last but not least—the grief of the protagonists. From Arion to Orpheus, from Andromeda to Dido and Desdemona, heroes and heroines have expressed their emotions, intensified by repetition and echo. These rhetorical tools, proved and tried through centuries, and even millennia, find their most convincing application in the solo lament, which persists as an operatic staple even beyond the age of Gluck and Mozart.

Bibliography

The Bibliography includes a wide selection of literature not specifically referred to in the text. *Festschriften*, congress reports, and similar works are listed under the editor, but in a few exceptional cases cross-references under the title have been added. When several articles are cited from another work, that work is listed separately with a complete reference (e.g. Hortschansky (ed.), *Gluck*).

ABERT, ANNA AMALIE, 'Der Geschmackswandel auf der Opernbühne, am "Alkestis"-Stoff dargestellt', *Mf* 6 (1953), 214–35 (repr. in Hortschansky (ed.), *Gluck*, 50–82).
—— *Monteverdi und das musikalische Drama* (Lippstadt, 1954).
—— 'Tasso, Guarini e l'opera', *NRMI* 5 (1970), 827–40.
ADEMOLLO, A., *I teatri di Roma* (Rome, 1888; repr. Bologna, 1969).
ALBERTI, LEON BATTISTA, *Ten Books of Architecture, translated into Italian by Cosimo Bartoli and into English by James Leoni*, ed. J. Rykwert (London, 1965).
ALDRICH, PUTNAM, *Rhythm in 17th-Century Italian Monody* (New York, 1966).
ALGAROTTI, FRANCESCO, *Saggio sopra l'opera in musica* (Livorno, 1755; 2nd edn., 1762).
ALLACCI, LIONE, *Apes urbanae* (Rome, 1633).
—— *Drammaturgia* (rev. edn., Venice, 1755; repr. Turin, 1961).
ANFUSO, N., and GIANUARIO, A., *Monteverdi: Lamento d'Arianna; studio e interpretazione* (Florence, 1969).
ANTONICEK, THEOPHIL, 'Die Musik als Dienerin der Poesie', in H. Krones (ed.), *Wort und Ton im europäischen Raum: Gedenkschrift für Robert Schollum* (Vienna, 1989), 53–67.
APOLLONIO, MARIO, *Storia del teatro italiano* (2nd edn., 4 vols.; Florence, 1940–50; new edn., 2 vols.; Florence, 1981).
Archivio di Stato, Florence, *Archivio Mediceo avanti il Principato: Inventario*, 4 vols. (Rome, 1955–66).
—— *Archivio Mediceo del Principato: Inventario sommario* (Rome, 1966).
ARIANI, MARCO, *Tra classicismo e manierismo: Il teatro tragico del Cinquecento* (Florence, 1974).
ARNOLD, DENIS, *Monteverdi* (London, 1963; 2nd edn., 1975; 3rd edn., rev. T. Carter, 1990).
—— and FORTUNE, NIGEL (eds.), *The New Monteverdi Companion* (London, 1985) (rev. edn. of *Monteverdi Companion*, 1968).
ARTEAGA, ESTEBAN DE, *Le rivoluzioni del teatro musicale italiano*, 2 vols. (Bologna and Venice, 1783–5).
ATLAS, ALAN (ed.), *The Cappella Giulia Chansonnier*, 2 vols. (Brooklyn, 1975–6).
AUERBACH, ERICH, 'Figura', *Archivum Romanicum*, 22 (1938), 436–89. Repr. in Auerbach's *Scenes from the Drama of European Literature* (New York, 1959; repr. Gloucester, Mass., 1973), 9–76.
—— *Mimesis: The Representation of Reality in Western Literature*, trans. W. Trask (Princeton, NJ, 1953; paperback edn., 1968).
Autori italiani del Seicento: Catalogo bibliografico, iv: *Il teatro, la musica, l'arte, la religione* (Milan, 1951).

BALSANO, MARIA ANTONELLA (ed.), *L'Ariosto: la musica, i musicisti: quattro studi e sette madrigali ariosteschi* (Quaderni della Rivista italiana di musicologia, 5; Florence, 1981).

BANFI, LUIGI (ed.), *Sacre rappresentazioni del Quattrocento* (Turin, 1963).

BARBLAN, GUGLIELMO, 'Contributo a una biografia critica di Agostino Agazzari', *CHM* 2 (1957), 33–63.

BARGAGLI, G., *La Pellegrina*, ed. F. Cerreta (Biblioteca dell'Archivum Romanicum, ser. 1, vol. 3; Florence, 1971).

BARKAN, LEONARD, *The Gods Made Flesh: Metamorphosis and the Pursuit of Flesh* (New Haven, Conn., and London, 1986) [Ch. II on Ovid, IV on Dante, VI on Shakespeare].

BARON, JOHN H., 'Monody: A Study in Terminology', *MQ* 54 (1968), 462–74.

BARTEL, DIETRICH, *Handbuch der musikalischen Figurenlehre* (Laaber, 1985).

BATINES, COLOMB DE, *Bibliografia delle antiche rappresentazioni italiane sacre e profane* (Florence, 1852).

BAUER-FORMICONI, BARBARA, *Die Strambotti des Serafino dall'Aquila* (Munich, 1967).

BEARE, W., *The Roman Stage* (3rd rev. edn., London, 1964 [orig. publ. 1950]).

BECHERINI, BIANCA, 'La musica nelle "Sacre rappresentazioni" fiorentine', *RMI* 53 (1951), 193–241.

BECKER, HEINZ, 'Opernforschung', *Mf* 27 (1974), 153–65.

—— OSTHOFF, W., SCHNEIDER, H., and WOLFF, H. C. (eds.), *Quellentexte zur Konzeption der europäischen Oper im 17. Jahrhundert* (Musikwissenschaftliche Arbeiten, 27; Kassel, 1981).

BELLONI, ANNALISA, *Il Seicento* (Storia letteraria d'Italia; 4th edn., Milan, 1955).

BERNSTEIN, LAWRENCE F., 'The "Parisian" Chanson: Problems of Style and Terminology', *JAMS* 31 (1978), 193–240.

BERTOLOTTI, ANTONIO, *Musici alla corte dei Gonzaga in Mantova dal secolo XV al XVIII* (Milan, 1890; repr. Bologna, 1969; Geneva, 1978).

BIANCONI, LORENZO, 'L'"Ercole in Rialto"', in Muraro (ed.), *Venezia e il melodramma nel Seicento*, 259–68.

—— 'Funktionen des Operntheaters in Neapel bis 1700 und die Rolle Alessandro Scarlattis', in *Colloquium Alessandro Scarlatti, Würzburg, 1975* (Tutzing, 1979), 41 ff.

—— 'Giulio Caccini e il manierismo musicale', *Chigiana*, 25 (NS 5) (1968), 21–38.

—— *Il Seicento* (Turin, 1982); Eng. trans. by David Bryant, *Music in the Seventeenth Century* (Cambridge, 1987).

—— (ed.), *La drammaturgia musicale* (Bologna, 1986).

—— and WALKER, T., 'Dalla *Finta pazza* alla *Veremonda*: storie di Febiarmonici', *RIM* 10 (1975), 379–454.

———— , 'Production, Consumption and Political Function of 17th-Century Italian Opera', *EMH* 4 (1984), 209–96.

BOER, CORNELIUS DE (ed.), *Ovide moralisé, poème du commencement du quatorzième siècle*, 5 vols. (Verhandelingen der K. Akademie van Wetenschappen te Amsterdam, Afdeeling Letterkunde, NS, 15, 21, 30, 37, 43; Amsterdam, 1915–38).

BOETTICHER, WOLFGANG, *Lasso und seine Zeit* (Kassel, 1958).

BOLTE, JOHANNES, 'Das Echo in Volksglaube und Dichtung', *Sitzungsberichte der Preußischen Akademie der Wissenschaften, philosophisch-historische Klasse* (1935), 262–88; 852–62.

BÖMER, FRANZ, *Ovidius, Metamorphosen: Kommentar* (Heidelberg, 1969–).

BOMPIANI, VALENTINO, *Dizionario letterario Bompiani delle opere e dei personaggi*, 11 vols. (Milan, 1947–66). [For French version see Laffont, R.]

BONFANTINI, MARIO, *Le sacre rappresentazioni italiane* (Milan, 1942).

BONINI, SEVERO, *Discorsi e regole sopra la musica*, ed. L. Galleni Luisi (Instituta et monumenta, ser. 2, vol. 5; Cremona, 1975).

—— *Discorsi e regole*, ed. and trans. MaryAnn Bonino (Provo, Utah, 1979).

BONTEMPELLI, MASSIMO (ed.), *Il Poliziano, Il Magnifico, lirici del Quattrocento* (Florence, 1925).

BORREN, C. VAN DEN, 'Inventaire des manuscrits de musique polyphonique qui se trouvent en Belgique', *AcM* 6 (1934), 65–70 [A. Striggio, the Elder, 68].

—— 'Le madrigalisme avant le madrigal', *Studien zur Musikgeschichte: Festschrift für Guido Adler* (Vienna, 1930), 78–83.

BORSELLINO, NINO (ed.), *Commedie del Cinquecento*, 2 vols. (Milan, 1962–7).

BOTSTIBER, H., *Geschichte der Ouverture* (Leipzig, 1913; repr. 1969).

BOWLES, EDMUND A., *Musical Ensembles in Festival Books, 1500–1800: An Iconographical and Documentary Survey* (Ann Arbor, Mich., 1989).

BRAGAGLIA, LEONARDO, *Storia del libretto*, 3 vols. (Rome, 1970–1).

BRANCA, DANIELLA DELCORNO. See Delcorno.

BRANCA, VITTORE, *Poliziano e l'umanesimo della parola* (Turin, 1983).

—— 'Tra Ficino "Orfeo ispirato" e Poliziano "Ercole ironico" ', in *Filologia e forme letterarie: Studi offerti a Francesco della Corte* (Università degli Studi di Urbino, 1988?), 445–59.

BREIG, W., BRINKMANN, R., and BUDDE, E. (eds.), *Analysen: Beiträge zu einer Problemgeschichte des Komponierens. Festschrift für H. H. Eggebrecht* (Beihefte zum *AMw*, 23; Wiesbaden, 1984).

BRIDGMAN, NANIE, *La vie musicale au quattrocento et jusqu'à la naissance du madrigal (1400–1530)* (Paris, 1964).

BROWN, HOWARD M., 'A Cook's Tour of Ferrara in 1529', *RIM* 10 (1975), 216–41.

—— 'Emulation, Competition and Homage: Imitation and Theories of Imitation in the Renaissance', *JAMS* 35 (1982), 1–48.

—— 'How Opera Began: An Introduction to Jacopo Peri's *Euridice* (1600)', in Eric Cochrane (ed.), *The Late Italian Renaissance* (London, 1970), 401–43.

—— 'Psyche's Lament: Some Music for the Medici Wedding in 1565', in Laurence Berman (ed.), *Words and Music: The Scholar's View. A Medley of Problems and Solutions Compiled in Honor of A. Tillman Merritt* (Cambridge, Mass., 1972), 1–27.

—— *Sixteenth-Century Instrumentation: The Music for the Florentine Intermedii* (MSD 30; Rome, 1973).

—— 'Towards a Definition of Antonio Barré's *Madrigali ariosi*', *RIM* 25 (1990), 18–60.

—— 'A Typology of Francesco Corteccia's Madrigals: Notes towards a History of Theatrical Music in Sixteenth-Century Italy', in Caldwell *et al.* (eds.), *Well Enchanting Skill*, 3–28.

—— (ed.), *A Florentine Chansonnier from the Time of Lorenzo the Magnificent*, 2 vols. (Monuments of Renaissance Music, 7; Chicago and London, 1983).

BROWN, PETER M., *Lionardo Salviati* (Oxford Modern Languages and Literature Monographs; London, 1974) [*Il granchio*, 1567, 108–123].

BRYCE, JUDITH, *Cosimo Bartoli (1503–1572): The Career of a Florentine Polymath* (THR 191; Geneva, 1983).

BUCK, AUGUST, 'Camerata', *MGG* ii (1952), 719–22.

——— *Der Orpheus-Mythos in der italienischen Renaissance* (Schriften des Petrarca-Instituts Köln, 15; Krefeld, 1961).

BUJIĆ, BOJAN, ' "Figura poetica molto vaga": Structure and Meaning in Rinuccini's *Euridice*', *EMH* 10 (1991), 29–64.

BUKOFZER, MANFRED F., *Music in the Baroque Era* (New York, 1947; repr. London, 1948).

BUONAROTTI, MICHELANGELO, *Complete Poems and Selected Letters of Michelangelo*, tr. C. Gilbert (Modern Library; New York, 1965).

——— *Rime*, ed. Enzo Noè Girardi (Scrittori d'Italia, 217; Bari, 1960).

BURKERT, WALTER, *Ancient Mystery Cults* (Cambridge, Mass., 1987).

BURNEY, CHARLES, *A General History of Music*, 4 vols. (London, 1776–89; repr. in 2 vols., ed. F. Mercer, 1935; repr. 1957).

BUSH, DOUGLAS, *Mythology and the Renaissance Tradition* (Minneapolis, 1932).

BUSSI, FRANCESCO, 'Storia, tradizione e arte del *Requiem* di Cavalli', *NRMI* 10 (1976), 49–77.

BUTLER, GREGORY C., 'Music and Rhetoric in Early Seventeenth-Century English Sources', *MQ* 66 (1980), 53–64.

CABROL, F., and LECLERCQ, H. (eds.), *Dictionnaire d'archéologie chrétienne et de liturgie*, 15 vols. (Paris, 1903–53), xii, pt. 2, s.v. Orphée.

CACCINI, FRANCESCA, *La liberazione di Ruggiero*, ed. Doris Silbert (SCMA 7; Northampton, Mass., 1945).

CACCINI, GIULIO, *Le nuove musiche*, ed. H. W. Hitchcock (RRMBE 9; Madison, Wis., 1970; 2nd corr. printing, 1982).

——— *Nuove musiche e nuova maniera di scriverle (1614)*, ed. H. W. Hitchcock (RRMBE 28; Madison, Wis., 1978).

CALCATERRA, CARLO, *I lirici del Seicento e dell'Arcadia* (Milan, 1936).

——— *Poesia e canto* (Bologna, 1951).

CALDWELL, JOHN, 'The *De Institutione Arithmetica* and the *De Institutione Musica* [of Boethius]', in Gibson (ed.), *Boethius*, 135–54.

——— OLLESON, E., and WOLLENBERG, S. (eds.), *The Well Enchanting Skill: Music, Poetry, and Drama in the Culture of the Renaissance: Essays in Honour of F. W. Sternfeld* (Oxford, 1990).

CAMETTI, ALBERTO, *Il Teatro Tordinona, poi di Apollo* (Tivoli, 1938).

CAMPBELL, JOSEPH, *The Hero with a Thousand Faces* (Princeton, NJ, 1949; repr. London and Glasgow, 1988); index s.v. 'Orpheus', 'Orphic', 'Threshold'.

CANAL, PIETRO, *Della musica in Mantova* (Venice, 1881; repr. 1977).

CANDY, HUGH C. H., *Some Newly Discovered Stanzas written by John Milton on Engraved Scenes Illustrating Ovid's Metamorphoses* (London, 1924).

CANNABICH, CHRISTIAN, *Recueil des airs du ballet 'Orphée'* [. . . *arranged by Mozart]*, ed. Robert Münster (Zurich, [1973]).

CAPPELLI, ADRIANO, *Cronologia, cronografia e calendario perpetuo* (3rd edn., Milan, 1969 [1st publ. 1905]).

CARDUCCI, GIOSUÈ, *Su l'Aminta di Torquato Tasso* (Florence, 1896; repr. in *Opere*, xv; Bologna, 1905).

CARISSIMI, GIACOMO, *Jephte*, ed. J. Beat (London, 1974).

CAROSO, FABRITIO, *Nobiltà di dame [1600]*, ed. and tr. J. Sutton and M. F. Walker (Oxford, 1986).

CARTER, TIM, 'A Florentine Wedding of 1608', *AcM* 55 (1983), 89–107.

—— 'Jacopo Peri', *ML* 61 (1980), 121–35.

—— 'Jacopo Peri (1561–1633), his Life and Works', Ph.D. diss. (University of Birmingham, 1980); publ. in 2 vols., Outstanding Dissertations in Music from British Universities; New York, 1989.

—— *Mozart: Nozze di Figaro* (Cambridge Opera Handbooks; Cambridge, 1987).

CATTIN, GIULIO, 'Le rime del Poliziano nelle fonti musicali', in *Miscellanea di studi in onore di Vittore Branca*, 5 vols. (Biblioteca dell'Archivum Romanicum, 78–82; Florence, 1983), iii. 379–95.

CAULA, G. A. (ed.), *Balet Comique de la Royne* (facs. edn., Turin, 1965).

CAVALLI, FRANCESCO, *'Lament of Cassandra' from La Didone*, ed. Raymond Leppard (London, 1966).

—— *L'Egisto*, ed. Raymond Leppard (London, 1977).

—— *L'Ormindo*, ed. Raymond Leppard (London, 1969).

CAVICCHI, ADRIANO, 'La scenografia dell'*Aminta* nella tradizione scenografica pastorale ferrarese', in Muraro (ed.), *Studi sul teatro veneto*, 53–72.

—— 'Teatro monteverdiano e tradizione teatrale ferrarese', in Monterosso (ed.), *Claudio Monteverdi e il suo tempo*, 139–56.

CERRETA, F., 'The Sienese MS of Bargagli's *Pellegrina*', *BHR* 30 (1968), 601–16.

CESARI, G., and LUZIO, A. (eds.), *I copialettere di Giuseppe Verdi* (Milan, 1913; repr. 1973).

CHARTERIS, RICHARD (ed.), *Altro Polo: Essays on Italian Music in the Cinquecento* (Sydney, 1990).

CHIABRERA, GABRIELLO, *Canzonette, rime varie, dialoghi*, ed. Luigi Negri (Turin, 1964 [1st publ. 1952]).

CHIAPELLI, FREDI, 'Considerazioni di linguaggio e di stile . . . della *Mandragola*', *GSLI* 146 (1969), 252–59.

CHIARELLI, ALESSANDRA, ' "L'incoronazione di Poppea" o "Il Nerone", problemi di filologia testuale', *RIM* 9 (1974), 117–51.

CHIESA, RENATO, 'Machiavelli e la musica', *RIM* 4 (1969), 3–31.

CIONI, ALFREDO, *Bibliografia delle sacre rappresentazioni* (Biblioteca bibliografica italiana, 22; Florence, 1961).

CLARK, RAYMOND J., *Catabasis, Vergil and the Wisdom-Tradition* (Amsterdam, 1979).

CLUBB, LOUISE GEORGE, *Giambattista Della Porta* (Princeton, NJ, 1965).

—— *Italian Plays (1500–1700) in the Folger Library* (Florence, 1968).

—— 'The Making of the Pastoral Play: Some Italian Experiments between 1573 and 1590', in J. A. Molinaro (ed.), *Italian Criticism and Theatre* (Toronto, 1973), 45–72.

COLBY, ELBRIDGE, 'The Echo Device in Literature', *Bulletin of the New York Public Library*, 23 (1919), 683–713, 783–804.

COOPER, HELEN, *Pastoral: Medieval into Renaissance* (Cambridge, 1977).

COPELAND, ROBERT M., 'The Christian Message of Igor Stravinsky', *MQ* 68 (1982), 563–79.

Corago, Il. *See* Fabbri and Pompilio (eds.).

CORRIGAN, BEATRICE, 'All Happy Endings: Libretti of the Late Seicento', *Forum Italicum*, 7 (1973), 250–67.

CORTE, ANDREA DELLA. *See* Della Corte.

CORTECCIA, FRANCESCO, *Collected Secular Works*, ed. Frank A. D'Accone (Music of the Florentine Renaissance, viii–x; CMM 32; Neuhausen-Stuttgart, 1981).

CORTELAZZO, ANGELA T., 'Il melodramma di Marco da Gagliano', in Monterosso (ed.), *Claudio Monteverdi e il suo tempo*, 583–98.

COSTA, GUSTAVO, *La leggenda dei secoli d'oro* (Cultura moderna, no. 731; Bari, 1972).

COTTON-HILL, J. M. S., *Death and Politian* (repr. from *Durham University Journal* with corrections, appendices, and illustrations, 1954).

—— 'Ex Libris Politian', *Modern Language Review*, 29 (1934), 326–30; 32 (1937), 394–99.

—— 'Materia medica del Poliziano', in *Il Poliziano e il suo tempo: Atti del IV convegno internazionale di studi sul Rinascimento . . . Firenze, 1954* (Florence, 1957), 237–45.

—— *Name-List from a Medical Register of the Italian Renaissance 1350–1550* (Oxford, 1976).

CRAWFORD, DAVID, 'A Review of Costanzo Festa's Biography', *JAMS* 28 (1975), 102–11.

CROLL, MORRIS WILLIAM, *Style, Rhetoric and Rhythm* (Princeton, NJ, 1966).

CROSS, F. L., and LIVINGSTONE, E. A. (eds.), *The Oxford Dictionary of the Christian Church* (2nd edn., Oxford, 1983).

CULLEY, M. T., and FURNIVALL, F. J. (eds.), *Caxton's Eneydos 1490* (Early English Text Society, extra series, 77; London, 1890).

CULLEY, THOMAS D., *Jesuits and Music, i: A Study of the Musicians Connected with the German College in Rome* (Sources and Studies for the History of the Jesuits, 3; Rome, 1970).

CURTIS, ALAN, '*La Poppea Impasticciata*, or Who Wrote the Music to *L'Incoronazione* (1643)?' *JAMS* 42 (1989), 23–54.

—— *Sweelinck's Keyboard Music* (2nd edn., Leiden and Oxford, 1972 [1st. publ. 1969]).

CURTIUS, ERNST R., *European Literature and the Latin Middle Ages*, trans. W. R. Trask (London, 1953).

D'ACCONE, FRANK A., 'Heinrich Isaac in Florence', *MQ* 49 (1963), 464–83.

DANCKWARDT, MARIANNE, 'Das Lamento d'Olimpia "Voglio voglio morir"—eine Komposition Claudio Monteverdis?', *AMw* 41 (1984), 149–75.

D'ANCONA, ALESSANDRO, 'Del secentismo nella poesia cortigiana del secolo XV', in *Pagine sparse* (Florence, 1914), 61–181.

—— *Le origini del teatro italiano*, 2 vols. (2nd edn., Turin, 1891).

—— *La rappresentazione di Santa Uliva* (Pisa, 1863).

—— *Sacre rappresentazioni dei secoli XIV–XVI*, 3 vols. (Florence, 1872).

—— 'Il teatro mantovano nel sec. XVI', *GSLI* 6 (1885), 1–51, 313–51; 7 (1886), 48–93.

DANIELLO, BERNARDINO, *La Poetica* (Venice, 1536; facs. repr., Munich, 1968).

DANTE, *Opere*, ed. Fredi Chiapelli (Milan, 1978) [Bibliography of allegory in *Commedia*, pp. l–li].

D'ARIENZO, N., 'Origini dell'opera comica', *RMI* 2 (1895), 597–628; 4 (1897), 421–59; 6 (1899), 473–95; 7 (1900), 1–33.

DASSMANN, E., 'Sündenvergebung durch Taufe, Buße und Martürerfürbitte in den Zeugnissen frühchristlicher Frömmigkeit und Kunst', *Münsterische Beiträge zur Theologie*, 36 (1973), 9–25.

DAVARI, STEFANO, 'La musica in Mantova', *Rivista storica mantovana*, 1 (1885), nos. 1–2; repr. Mantua, 1975, ed. G. Ghirardini.

—— *Notizie biografiche del distinto maestro di musica Claudio Monteverdi* (Mantua, 1884–5).

DE BATINES, COLOMB. *See* Batines.

DE BOER, CORNELIUS. *See* Boer.

DEGRADA, FRANCESCO (ed.), *Andrea Gabrieli e il suo tempo: Atti del convegno internazionale (Venezia 16–18 Settembre 1985)* (Studi di musica veneta, 11; Florence, 1987).

DELCORNO BRANCA, DANIELA, 'Da Poliziano a Serafino', in *Miscellanea di studi in onore di Vittore Branca*, 5 vols. (Biblioteca dell'Archivum Romanicum, 78–82; Florence, 1983), iii. 423–50.

—— 'Il ms. Riccardiano 2723 e la formazione delle antiche sillogi di "Rime" del Poliziano', *Rinascimento*, 16 (1976), 35–110.

—— 'Note sulle tradizione delle "Rime" del Poliziano', *Rinascimento*, 15 (1975), 61–88.

—— 'Per un catalogo delle "Rime" del Poliziano', *Lettere italiane*, 23 (1971), 225–52.

—— *Sulla tradizione delle rime del Poliziano* (Florence, 1979).

DEL GIUDICE, LUISA, 'Armida: *Virgo Fingens* (Broken Mirror)', in *Western Jerusalem* (New York, 1984).

DELLA CORTE, ANDREA (ed.), *Drammi per musica*, 2 vols. (Turin, 1958).

DELLA SETA, FABRIZIO, and PIPERNO, FRANCO (eds.), *In Cantu et in Sermone: For Nino Pirrotta on his 80th Birthday* (Florence [and Perth], 1989).

DEL LUNGO, ISIDORO, *Florentia* (Florence, 1897).

DENT, EDWARD J., *Mozart's Operas* (2nd edn., London, 1947).

—— 'Music and Drama [1540–1630]', *New Oxford History of Music*, iv (1968), 748–820.

DESPORT, MARIE, *L'Incantation virgilienne: Virgile et Orphée* (Bordeaux, 1952).

—— 'Orphée dans le *Culex*', *Orphea Voce*, 1 (1980), 129–43.

DODDS, ERIC R., *The Greeks and the Irrational* (Berkeley, Calif., 1951).

DOGLIO, MARIA L., 'Mito, metamorfosi, emblema dalla "Favola d'Orfeo" di Poliziano alla "Festa de lauro" ', *Lettere italiane*, 29 (1977), 148–86.

DONATI, LAMBERTO, 'Edizioni quattrocentesche non pervenuteci delle "Metamorfosi" ', in *Atti del convegno internazionale Ovidiano*, i (1959), 111–24.

DONI, GIOVANNI BATTISTA, *Lyra Barberina*, ed. A. F. Gori, 2 vols. (Florence, 1763; facs. edn., Bologna, 1975).

DONINGTON, ROBERT, *Opera and its Symbols: The Unity of Words, Music and Staging* (New Haven, Conn., 1990).

—— *The Rise of Opera* (London, 1981).

DRONKE, PETER, *Medieval Latin and the Rise of the European Love Lyric* (rev. edn., 2 vols., Oxford, 1968).

—— 'The Return of Eurydice', *Classica et Mediaevalia*, 23 (1962), 198–215.

DRUMMOND, JOHN D., *Opera in Perspective* (London, 1980).

DUNNING, ALBERT, *Die Staatsmotette* (Utrecht, 1970).

DU ROCHER, RICHARD J., *Milton and Ovid* (Ithaca, NY, and London, 1985).

EGGEBRECHT, HANS HEINRICH, 'Figuren', *Riemann Musiklexikon* (12th edn.), iii (Sachteil) (Mainz, 1967), 286–8.

—— *Schütz und Gottesdienst* (Stuttgart, 1969).

—— 'Zum Figur-Begriff der Musica poetica', *AMw* 16 (1959), 57–69.

—— (ed.), *Handwörterbuch der musikalischen Terminologie* (Wiesbaden, 1972–).

EINSTEIN, ALFRED, 'Firenze prima della monodia', *La rassegna musicale*, 7 (1934), 253–74.

—— *The Italian Madrigal*, 3 vols. (Princeton, NJ, 1949; repr. 1971).

—— 'Orlando Furioso and La Gerusalemme Liberata as Set to Music', *Notes*, 8 (1950–1), 623–30.

—— (ed.), *Canzoni, sonetti, strambotti et frottole. Libro tertio (Andrea Antico, 1517)* (SCMA 4; Northampton, Mass., 1941).

EISLER, ROBERT, *Orphisch-dionysische Mysteriengedanken in der christlichen Antike* (Vorträge der Bibliothek Warburg, 2; Leipzig, 1925).

EITNER, ROBERT (ed.), *Die Oper* (Publikationen älterer praktischer und theoretischer Musikwerke, 10; Leipzig, 1881) [contains, among others, Caccini's *Euridice* and Gagliano's *Dafne*].

ELIADE, MIRCEA, *The Myth of the Eternal Return*, trans. W. R. Trask (London, 1955 [1st publ. Paris, 1949]).

—— *Rites and Symbols: The Mysteries of Birth and Rebirth*, trans. W. R. Trask (New York, 1965 [1st publ. Paris, 1959]).

—— *Shamanism: Archaic Techniques of Ecstasy* (rev. edn., trans. W. R. Trask, London, 1964 [1st publ. Paris, 1951]).

ELWERT, W. THEODOR, *Italienische Metrik* (Munich, 1968).

—— *La poesia lirica italiana del Seicento* (Florence, 1967).

—— *Traité de versification française des origines à nos jours* (Paris, 1965) [p. 150: Rime en écho].

—— *Versificazione italiana* (Florence, 1973; 2nd edn., 1976).

EMPSON, WILLIAM, *Some Versions of Pastoral* (London, 1935; repr. 1950).

Enciclopedia dell'arte antica, 9 vols. (Rome [1958–73]) ['Allegoria', 'Orfeo'].

ENGEL, HANS, *Luca Marenzio* (Florence, 1956).

—— 'Nochmals die Intermedien von Florenz 1589', in Walter Vetter (ed.), *Festschrift Max Schneider zum 80. Geburtstag* (Leipzig, 1955), 71–86.

ENGELS, J. (ed.), *Petrus Berchorius, Reductorium morale, Lib. XV*, 3 vols. (Utrecht, 1960–6): (1) cap. I: De Formis Figurisque Deorum [1509 print]; (2) cap. II–XV: Ovidius Moralizatus; (3) De Formis Figurisque Deorum [critical edn. based on Brussels MS].

EPSTEIN, PETER, 'Dichtung und Musik in Monteverdis "Lamento d'Arianna" ', *Zeitschrift für Musikwissenschaft* 10 (1927/8), 216–22.

ESSLING, Prince d'. *See* Masséna, André Prosper.

FABBRI, MARIO, 'La vita e l'ignota opera-prima di Francesco Corteccia musicista italiano del rinascimento', *Chigiana*, 22 (NS 2) (1965), 185–217.

—— ZORZI, E. G., and TOFANI, E. M. P. (eds.), *Il luogo teatrale a Firenze* (Milan, 1975).

FABBRI, PAOLO, *Monteverdi* (Turin, 1985).

—— *Il secolo cantante: per una storia del libretto d'opera nel Seicento* (Bologna, 1990).

—— and POMPILIO, A. (eds.), *Il Corago o vero alcune osservazioni per metter bene in scena le composizioni drammatiche* (Studi e testi per la storia della musica, 4; Florence, 1983) [an edn. of an anonymous treatise on opera, c.1630, in a Modena MS, possibly by the son of Ottavio Rinuccini].

FACCIOLI, EMILIO (ed.), *Representatione di Phebo et di Phetone, strenna per l'anno 1959*, a cura del Bolletino storico mantovano, Mantua, Biblioteca Communale, MS A. IV, 30 (Mantua, 1959).

—— DAVICO BONINO, G., and ARIANI, M. (eds.), *Il teatro italiano*, 7 vols. (Gli struzzi; Turin, 1975–8): (1) Vols. 1–2 (Struzzi, 75*, 75**), Faccioli, *Dalle origini al Quattrocento*; (2) Vols. 3–5 (Struzzi, 113–115), Davico Bonino, *La commedia del Cinquecento*; (3) Vols. 6–7 (Struzzi, 145*, 145**), Ariani, *La tragedia del Cinquecento*.

FANTUZZI, GIOVANNI, *Notizie degli scrittori bolognesi*, 9 vols. (Bologna, 1781–9; repr. Bologna, 1965).

FASSO, LUIGI, *Teatro del Seicento* (Milan, 1956).

FELLERER, KARL GUSTAV, 'Monodie und Generalbass', *Mf* 37 (1984), 99–110.

FELLOWES, E. H., GREER, D., and STERNFELD, F. W. (eds.), *English Madrigal Verse* (3rd rev. edn., Oxford, 1967 [1st publ. 1920]).

FENLON, IAIN, 'Music and Spectacle at the Gonzaga Court', *PRMA* 103 (1976/7), 90–105.

FERRARI, SAVERINO (ed.), [Pamfilo Sasso: Strambotti] in *Biblioteca di letteratura popolare italiana*, 1 (Florence, 1882), esp. pp. 284–90.

FERRONI, GIULIO, *'Mutazione' e 'riscontro' nel teatro di Machiavelli* (Biblioteca teatrale, Studi, 9; Rome, 1972).

FERRUA, A., 'Una nuova regione della catacomba dei Ss. Marcellino e Pietro', *Rivista di archeologia cristiana*, 44 (1968), 29–78.

FESTA, COSTANZO, *Opera omnia*, vii, ed. Albert Seay (CMM 25; Stuttgart, 1977).

FINNEY, PAUL CORBY, 'Orpheus-David: A Connection in Iconography between Greco-Roman Judaism and Early Christianity', *Journal of Jewish Art*, 5 (1978), 6–15.

FINSCHER, LUDWIG, *'Che farò senza Euridice?'*: Ein Beitrag zur Gluck-Interpretation', in *Festschrift Hans Engel* (Kassel, 1964); repr. in Hortschansky (ed.), *Gluck*, 135–53.

—— (ed.), *Monteverdi: Festschrift Reinhold Hammerstein* (Laaber, 1986).

Firenze e la Toscana. See Garfagnani (ed.).

FISCHER, P., *Music in Paintings of the Low Countries in the 16th and 17th Centuries* (Amsterdam, 1972).

FLANDERS, PETER, *A Thematic Index to the Works of Benedetto Pallavicino* (Music Indexes and Bibliographies, no. 11; Hackensack, NJ, 1974).

FLECHSIG, EDUARD, *Die Dekoration der modernen Bühne in Italien von den Anfängen bis zum Schluß des XVI. Jahrhunderts*, Teil I (Dresden, 1894).

FLETCHER, ANGUS JOHN S., *Allegory: The Theory of a Symbolic Mode* (Ithaca, NY, 1964 [paperback: 1970]).

—— *The Prophetic Moment: An Essay on Spenser* (Chicago, 1971).

—— *The Transcendental Masque: An Essay on Milton's 'Comus'* (Ithaca, NY, 1971).

FORSYTH, KAREN, *Adriadne auf Naxos by Hugo von Hofmannsthal and Richard Strauss: Its Genesis and Meaning* (Oxford Modern Languages and Literature Monographs; Oxford, 1982).

FORTUNE, NIGEL (ed.), *Music and Theatre: Essays in Honour of Winton Dean* (Cambridge, 1987).

FRAENKEL, GOTTFRIED S. (ed.), *Decorative Music Title Pages* (New York, 1968).

FRATI, L., 'Tasso in musica', *RMI* 30 (1923), 389–400.

FRAZER, JAMES GEORGE, *The Golden Bough*, 12 vols. (3rd rev. edn., London, 1911–15 [1st publ. 1890]).

FREEMAN, EDWARD (ed.), *Orphée: Jean Cocteau: The Play and the Film* (Blackwell's French Texts; Oxford, 1976).

FRIEDMAN, JOHN BLOCK, *Orpheus in the Middle Ages* (Cambridge, Mass., 1970).

FRYE, NORTHROP, *Secular Scripture: A Study of the Structure of Romance* (Cambridge, Mass., 1976), esp. pp. 106–10, 117, 152–7.

FULD, JAMES J., *The Book of World-Famous Libretti: The Musical Theatre from 1598 to Today* (New York, 1984).

FURTWÄNGLER, WILHELM, *Concerning Music*, trans. L. J. Lawrence (London, 1953 [1st publ. Zurich, 1948]).

FUX, JOHANN JOSEPH, *Orfeo*, facs., ed. H. M. Brown (Italian Opera, 1640–1770, 19; New York, 1978).

GAFFURIUS, FRANCHINUS, *De harmonia musicorum instrumentorum*, trans. Clement A. Miller (MSD 33; [Rome], 1977).

GAGLIANO, MARCO DA, *Dafne*, ed. and tr. J. Erber (London: Cathedral Music, 1978).

GALLENI LUISI, LEILA, 'Il "Lamento d'Arianna" di Severo Bonini (1613)', in Monterosso (ed.), *Claudio Monteverdi e il suo tempo*, 573–82.

GALLICO, CLAUDIO, 'I due pianti di Arianna di C. Monteverdi', *Chigiana*, 24 (1967), 29–42.

—— *Un libro di poesie per musica dell'epoca di Isabella d'Este* (Mantua, 1961).

GALLO, ALBERTO, *La prima rappresentazione al Teatro Olimpico: Con i progetti e le relazioni dei contemporanei* (Archivio del teatro italiano, 6; Milan, 1973).

GARDNER, HELEN, *The Business of Criticism* (Oxford, 1959).

GARFAGNANI, G. (ed.), *Firenze e la Toscana dei Medici nell'Europa del '500. Atti del convegno internazionale di studio, Firenze 9–14 giugno 1980*, 3 vols. (Biblioteca di Toscana moderna e contemporanea, Studi e documenti, 26; Florence, 1983).

GASPARI, G., *Catalogo della Biblioteca del Liceo musicale di Bologna*, v: *Libretti*, ed. U. Sesini (Bologna, 1943; repr. 1970).

GHISI, F. (ed.), *Feste musicali della Firenze medicea* (Florence, 1939; repr. Bologna, 1969).

GIACCOBBI, GIROLAMO, *Aurora (1608)*, ed. G. Vecchi (Bologna, 1954).

GIANTURCO, CAROLYN, 'Nuove considerazioni su il tedio del recitativo delle prime opere romane', *RIM* 18 (1982), 212–39.

GIBSON, MARGARET (ed.), *Boethius: His Life, Thought and Influence* (Oxford, 1981).

GIRAUD, Y. F. A., *La fable de Daphne* (Geneva, 1968) [reviewed by F. Lesure, *Revue de musicologie*, 1969, 233–4]).

GIUDICE, LUISA DEL. *See* Del Giudice.

GLOVER, JANE A., *Cavalli* (London, 1978).

—— 'The Teatro Sant'Apollinare and the Development of Seventeenth-Century Venetian Opera', D.Phil. thesis (University of Oxford, 1975).

GOLDSCHMIDT, H., 'Cavalli als dramatischer Komponist', *Monatshefte für Musikgeschichte*, 25 (1893), 45–8, 53–8, 61–111.

—— *Studien zur Geschichte der italienischen Oper im 17. Jahrhundert*, 2 vols. (Leipzig, 1901–4; repr. 1967).

GOOS, JERZY, 'Italian Baroque Opera in 17th Century Poland', *Polish Review*, 8 (1963), 67–75.

GRABES, HERBERT, *The Mutable Glass: Mirror-Imagery in Titles and Texts of the Middle Ages and English Renaissance*, trans. Gordon Collier (Cambridge, 1983).

GRAFTON, ANTHONY, *Joseph Scaliger: A Study in the History of Classical Scholarship*, i: *Textual Criticism and Exegesis* (Oxford, 1983).

GRANT, MARY (trans. and ed.), *The Myths of Hyginus* (Lawrence, Kans., 1960).

GRAYSON, CECIL, 'Dante's Theory and Practice of Poetry' in C. Grayson (ed.), *World of Dante* (Oxford, 1980), 146–65.

GREG, WALTER WILSON, *Pastoral Poetry and Pastoral Drama* (London, 1906; repr. New York, 1959).

GRIFFITH, J. G., *The Origins of Osiris and his Cult* (Studies in Histories of Religions, suppl. to *Numen*, 40; Leiden, 1980). [For 'death and resurrection' see 'Life after Death', pp. 64–8.]

GROUT, DONALD JAY, *A Short History of Opera*, 2 vols. (2nd edn., New York, 1965; 3rd edn., with H. W. Williams, New York, 1988).

GUARINI, G. B., *Opere*, ed. Luigi Fassò (Turin, 1955; 2nd edn., *Opere*, ed. Marzino Guglielminetti, Turin, 1971).

—— *Il pastor fido*, ed. Ettore Bonora (Grande Universale Mursia, 28; Milan, 1977).

GUTHMÜLLER, BODO, 'Lateinische und volkssprachliche Kommentare zu Ovids "Metamorphosen" ', in August Buck and Otto Herding (eds.), *Der Kommentar in der Renaissance* (Deutsche Forschungsgemeinschaft, Kommission für Humanismusforschung, Mitteilung I; 1975), 119–39.

—— 'Die literarische Übersetzung im Bezugsfeld Original–Leser (Am Beispiel italienischer Übersetzung der Metamorphosen Ovids im 16. Jhdt.)', *BHR* 36 (1974), 233–51.

—— 'Ovidübersetzung und mythologische Malerei. Bemerkungen zur Sala dei Giganti Giulio Romanos', *Mitteilungen des kunsthistorischen Institutes in Florenz*, 21 (1977), 35–68.

—— (ed.) *Ovidio metamorphoseos vulgare* (Veröffentlichungen zur Humanismusforschung, 3; Boppard am Rhein, 1981).

GUTHRIE, WILLIAM KEITH C., *Orpheus and Greek Religion* (London, 1934; repr. New York, 1966).

HAAR, JAMES, *Essays on Italian Poetry and Music in the Renaissance, 1350–1600* (Berkeley, Calif., 1986).

—— 'The *Madrigale Arioso*: A Mid-Century Development in the Cinquecento Madrigal', *SM* 12 (1983), 203–19.

—— 'Madrigals from Three Generations: The MS Brussels Bibl. du Conservatoire Royal, 27.731', *RIM* 10 (1975), 242–64.

HAAS, ROBERT M., *Mozart* (Potsdam, 1933).

—— *Die Musik des Barocks* (Potsdam, 1929; repr. 1949).

HAMMOND, N. G. L., and SCULLARD, H. H. (eds.), *The Oxford Classical Dictionary* (2nd edn., Oxford, 1970).

HANFMANN, GEORGE M. A., 'The Continuity of Classical Art: Culture, Myth and Faith', in K. Weitzmann (ed.), *Age of Spirituality: A Symposium* (New York, 1980), 75–100.

HANNING, BARBARA RUSSANO, 'Apologia pro Ottavio Rinuccini', *JAMS* 26 (1973), 240–62.

—— 'Glorious Apollo: Poetic and Political Themes in the First Opera', *Renaissance Quarterly*, 32 (1979), 485–513.

—— *Of Poetry and Music's Power: Humanism and the Creation of Opera* (Studies in Musicology, 13; Ann Arbor, 1980).

—— review of R. Donington, *The Rise of Opera* (New York, 1981), *JAMS* 36 (1983), 316–22.

HARRÁN, DON, 'Eloquence as a Concept in Sixteenth-Century Music Criticism', *Renaissance Quarterly*, 41 (1988), 413–38, esp. 435.

—— '*Maniera*' e il madrigale: Una raccolta di poesie musicali del Cinquecento (Biblioteca dell'Archivum Romanicum, ser. 1, 163; Florence, 1980).

—— 'Orpheus as Poet, Musician and Educator', in Charteris (ed.), *Altro Polo*, 265–76.

HARRIS, SIMON, 'The Significance of Ovid's *Metamorphoses* in Early Seventeenth-Century Opera', *MR* 48 (1988), 12–20.

HARVEY, DAVID I. H., *The Later Music of Elliott Carter* (Dissertations in Music from British Universities; New York, 1989).

HASTINGS, JAMES (ed.), *Encyclopedia of Religion and Ethics*, 13 vols. (Edinburgh, 1908–26).

HAYDN, JOSEPH, *L'anima del filosofo ossia Orfeo ed Euridice*, ed. Helmut Wirth (Haydn, *Werke*, ser. XXV, vol. 13; Munich, 1974).

HELL, HELMUT, 'Zu Rhythmus und Notierung des "Vi ricorda" in Claudio Monteverdis *Orfeo*', *AnMc* 15 (1975), 87–157.

HENKEl, M. D., 'Illustrierte Ausgaben von Ovids Metamorphosen im XV., XVI. und XVII. Jahrhundert', *Vorträge der Bibliothek Warburg*, 6 (1926–7), 58–144 (84 illustr.).

HILL, JOHN W., ' "O che nuovo miracolo!": A New Hypothesis about the "Aria di Fiorenza" ', in Della Seta and Piperno (eds.), *In Cantu*, 283–322 [supplementary information in reviews by Sternfeld, *ML*, 1990; Bujić, *Modern Language Review*, 1991].

—— 'Oratory Music in Florence', *AcM* 51 (1979), 108–36 and 246–67.

HINKS, ROGER, *Myth and Allegory in Ancient Art* (Studies of the Warburg Institute, 6; London, 1939).

HITCHCOCK, H. WILEY, 'Caccini's "Other" *Nuove musiche*', *JAMS* 27 (1974), 438–60.

—— 'Depriving Caccini of a Musical Pastime', *JAMS* 25 (1972), 58–78.

—— 'M.-A. Charpentier and the Comédie Française', *JAMS* 24 (1971), 255–81.

—— 'Scipione delle Palle', *New Grove*, v. 348–9.

HOLMES, WILLIAM C., 'G. A. Cicognini's and A. Cesti's Orontea (1649)', in William Austin (ed.), *New Looks at Italian Opera: Essays in Honor of Donald J. Grout* (Ithaca, NY, 1968), 108–32.

HORTSCHANSKY, KLAUS (ed.), *Gluck und die Opernreform* (Wege der Forschung, 163; Darmstadt, 1989).

HUFF, STEVEN R., 'The Early German Libretto: Some Considerations Based on Harsdörffer's "Seelewig" ', *ML* 69 (1988), 345–55.

HUIZINGA, JOHAN, *The Waning of the Middle Ages* (London, 1924; repr. Harmondsworth, 1955).

HULTKRANTZ, ÅKE, *The North American Indian Orpheus Tradition* (Stockholm, 1957).

HUNGER, HERBERT, *Die hochsprachliche Literatur der Byzantiner*, 2 vols. (Handbuch der klassischen Altertumswissenschaft, XII. 5. 1–2; Munich, 1978) [see index s.v. Anthologia Palatina, Anthologia Planudea, Echoverse, Leiterverse].

—— *Lexikon der griechischen und römischen Mythologie* (6th edn., Vienna, 1969).

HUNKEMÖLLER, JÜRGEN, 'Strawinsky rezipiert Monteverdi', in Finscher (ed.), *Monteverdi*, 237–47.

HUSKINSON, J., 'Some Pagan Mythological Figures and their Significance in Early Christian Art', *Papers of the British School at Rome*, 42 (1974), 68–97.

HUTTON, JAMES, *The Greek Anthology in Italy to the Year 1800* (Cornell Studies in English, 23; Ithaca, NY, 1935).

HYGINUS, *Astronomica*, ed. Émile Chatelain and Paul Legendre (Bibliothèque de l'école des hautes études, 84; Paris, 1909).

—— *L'Astronomie*, ed. and trans. André Le Bœuffle (Collection des Universités de France; Paris, 1983).

—— *Fabulae*, ed. Herbert Jennings Rose (2nd edn., Leiden, 1963).

HYNES-BERRY, MARY, 'Cohesion in *King Horn* and *Sir Orfeo*', *Speculum*, 50 (1975), 652–70.

IMBRIANI, VITTORIO, 'L'Eco responsiva nelle pastorali italiane', *Giornale napolitano di filosofia*, 2 (1872), 279–314 (on 'Cinquecento'); NS, 9 (1884), 843–65 (on 'Seicento').

INGEGNERI, ANGELO, *Discorso della poesia rappresentativa* (Ferrara, 1598); repr. in G. B. Guarini, *Opere*, 4 vols. (Verona, 1737–8), iii; also repr. Faccioli *et al.*, *Teatro italiano*, vii.

ISAAC, HEINRICH, *Messen*, ed. H. Birtner and M. Staehelin, 2 vols. (Musikalische Denkmäler, 7–8; Mainz, 1970–3).

—— *Weltliche Werke*, ed. J. Wolf (Denkmäler der Tonkunst in Österreich, 14/i; Vienna, 1907).

ISTEL, EDGAR, *Das Libretto* (Berlin, 1914).

IVANOVICH, CRISTOFORO, *Minerva al tavolino* (Venice, 1681; 2nd edn., 1688).

JACQUOT, JEAN, 'L'Opéra *The Rake's Progress*: naissance et formation', in Vaccaro (ed.), *Rake's Progress*, 57–82.

—— (ed.), *Dramaturgie et société: Rapports entre l'œuvre théâtrale, son interprétation et son public aux XVIe et XVIIe siècles*, 2 vols. (Paris, 1968).

—— (ed.), *La Fête théâtrale et les sources de l'opéra: Actes de la 4e session des Journées Internationales d'Étude du Baroque*, in *Baroque*, 5 (Montauban, 1972).

—— (ed.), *Le Lieu théâtral à la Renaissance* (Paris, 1963).

—— (ed.), *Musique et poésie au XVIe siècle* (Paris, 1954).

—— (ed.), *Les Tragédies de Sénèque et le théâtre de la Renaissance* (Paris, 1964).

—— and Konigson, E. (eds.), *Les Fêtes de la Renaissance*, 3 vols. [vol. ii, 1960, subtitled *Fêtes et cérémonies* . . .] (Paris, 1956–75).

JANDER, OWEN, 'Beethoven's "Orpheus in Hades": The *Andante con moto* of the Fourth Piano Concerto', *19th Century Music*, 8 (1985), 195–212.

—— 'Concerto grosso Instrumentation in Rome in the 1660s and 1670s', *JAMS* 21 (1968), 168–80.

—— 'Prologues and Intermezzos of A. Stradella', *AnMc* 7 (1969), 87–111.

JANNACO, C., *Il Seicento* (Storia letteraria d'Italia; 2nd edn., Milan, 1966).

JAVICH, DANIEL, 'Rescuing Ovid from the Allegorizers: The Liberation of Angelica, *Furioso X*', in A. Scaglione (ed.), *Ariosto 1974 in America* (Ravenna, 1976), 85–98.

JEPPESEN, KNUD, *La frottola*, 3 vols. (Copenhagen, 1968–70).

JOHNSON, M. F., 'Agazzari's "Eumelio" ', *MQ* 57 (1971), 491–505.

JOLY-SEGALEN, A., and SCHAEFFNER, A. (eds.), *Segalen et Debussy* (Monaco, 1961) [*Orphée-Roi*: pp. 217–341].

JOOSEN, J. C., and WASZINK, J. H., 'Allegorese', in Th. Klauser (ed.), *Reallexikon für Antike und Christentum*, i (Stuttgart, 1950), 283–9.

JOUKOVSKY, FRANÇOISE, *Orphée et ses disciples dans la poésie française et néo-latine du XVIe siècle* (Publications romanes et françaises, 109; Geneva, 1970).

JUNG, HERMANN, *Die Pastorale: Studien zur Geschichte eines musikalischen Topos* (Neue Heidelberger Studien zur Musikwissenschaft, 9; Berne, 1980).

JUNG, MARC-RENÉ, *Hercule dans la littérature française du XVIe siècle* (THR 79; Geneva, 1966).

JUST, MARTIN, and WIESEND, R. (eds.), *Liedstudien: W. Osthoff zum 60. Geburtstag* (Tutzing, 1989).

KAST, PAUL, 'Biographische Notizen zu römischen Musikern des 17. Jahrhunderts', *AnMc* 1 (1963), 38–69.

KELLER, PETER, *Die Oper 'Seelewig' von S. T. Staden* (Publikationen der Schweizerischen Musikforschenden Gesellschaft, ser. 2, vol. 28; Berne, 1977) [pp. 39–44: Echo: comparison with *Eumelio*].

KELLY, JOHN NORMAN D., *Early Christian Creeds* (3rd edn., London, 1972).

KENNEDY, GEORGE ALEXANDER, *The Art of Persuasion in Greece* (London, 1963).

KENNEDY, GEORGE ARTHUR, *The Art of Rhetoric in the Roman World, 300 B.C.–A.D. 300* (Princeton, NJ, 1972).

KERÉNYI, KARL, *Hermes der Seelenführer* (Zurich, 1944).

—— *Pythagoras und Orpheus* (3rd edn., Zurich, 1950).

KERN, O. (ed.), *Orphicorum fragmenta* (Berlin, 1922; repr. 1972).

KIDD, B. J., *The Thirty-Nine Articles, their History and Explanation*, 2 vols. (2nd edn., London, 1901).

KINKELDEY, O., *Orgel und Klavier in der Musik des 16. Jahrhunderts* (Leipzig, 1910; repr. Hildesheim, 1968).

KIRKENDALE, URSULA, 'The Source for Bach's *Musical Offering*: The *Institutio Oratoria* of Quintilian', *JAMS* 33 (1980), 88–141.

KIRKENDALE, WARREN, *L'Aria di Fiorenza* (Florence, 1972).

—— 'Cavalieri, a Roman Gentleman at the Florentine Court', *Quadrivium*, 12/2 (1971), 9–21.

—— 'Ciceronians vs. Aristotelians on the Ricercar as Exordium, from Bembo to Bach', *JAMS* 32 (1979), 1–44.

—— 'Emilio de' Cavalieri', *Dizionario biografico degli italiani*, 22 (1979), 659–64.

KIRKPATRICK, RALPH, *Domenico Scarlatti* (7th edn., Princeton, NJ, 1982; new rev. edn., 1983 [1st publ. 1953]).

KIRSCHBAUM, E., BANDMANN, J., and BRAUNFELS, W. (eds.), *Lexikon der christlichen Ikonographie*, 8 vols. (Freiburg, 1968–76).

KITZINGER, ERNST, 'Christian Imagery: Growth and Impact', in Kurt Weitzmann (ed.), *Age of Spirituality: A Symposium* (New York, 1980), 141–64.

KLAKOWICH, ROBERt, '*Scocca pur*: Genesis of an English Ground', *JRMA* 116 (1991), 63–77 [cf. also 324–5].

KNOCH, HANS, *Orpheus und Eurydike: Der antike Sagenstoff in den Opern von Darius Milhaud und Ernst Krenek* (Kölner Beiträge zur Musikforschung, 91; Regensburg, 1977).

KOSCH, WILHELM, *Deutsches Literatur-Lexikon* (3rd edn., ed. B. Berger *et al.*, Berne, 1968–).

KRISTELLER, J. P., *Early Florentine Woodcuts: With an Annotated List of Florentine Illustrated Books* (London, 1897).

KRÖHLING, WALTER, *Die Priamel (Beispielsammlung) als Stilmittel in der griechisch-römischen Dichtung* (Greifswald, 1935).

KROYER, THEODOR, *Die Anfänge der Chromatik im italienischen Madrigal des XVI. Jahrhunderts* (Publikationen der Internationalen Musikgesellschaft, Beihefte, 4; Leipzig, 1902; repr. 1968).

—— 'Dialog und Echo in der alten Chormusik', *Jahrbuch der Musikbibliothek Peters*, 16 (1909), 13–32.

KRUMBACHER, KARL, *Geschichte der byzantinischen Literatur* (Handbuch der klassischen Altertumswissenschaft, ix/2; 2nd edn., Munich, 1897) [see index s.v. Anthologia Palatina, Anthologien, Leiterverse, Spielereien]. See also Hunger's revision of this volume, 1978.

KÜFFEL, IRMGARD, 'Die Libretti Giulio Rospigliosis', diss. (Vienna, 1968).

KÜMMEL, W. F., 'Ein deutscher Bericht über die florentinischen Intermedien des Jahres 1589', *AnMc* 9 (1970), 1–19.

KUNZLE, DAVID, *The Early Comic Strip: Narrative Strips and Picture Stories in the European Broadsheet from c. 1450 to 1825* (History of the Comic Strip, 1; Berkeley, Calif., 1973).

LA FACE BIANCONI, GIUSEPPINA, and ROSSI, ANTONIO, '*Soffrir non son disposto ogni tormento*': Serafino Aquilano: figura letteraria, fantasma musicologico', in *Atti del XIV Congresso della Società Internazionale di Musicologia: Trasmissione e recezione delle forme di cultura musicale*, 3 vols. (Turin, 1990), ii. 240–54.

LAFFONT, ROBERT, *Laffont-Bompiani Dictionnaire de culture universelle*, 6 vols. (Paris, 1964).

LANCASTER, HENRY C., *A History of French Dramatic Literature in the Seventeenth Century*, 9 vols. (Baltimore, 1929–42; repr. New York, 1966) [Pt. II (Period of Corneille), i. 173, on the operatic qualities of Chapoton's *Descente d'Orphée*, 1640].

[LANDAU, HORACE DE], *Catalogue des livres manuscrits et imprimés composant la bibliothèque de M. Horace de Landau*, ed. F. Roediger, 2 vols. (Florence, 1885–90).

LANGLOIS, E. (ed.), *Recueil d'arts de seconde rhétorique* (Paris, 1902).

LANGMUIR, ERIKA, 'Nicolò dell'Abate's "Aristeus and Eurydice" ', *Burlington Magazine*, 112 (1970), 107–8.

LAUSBERG, HEINRICH, *Handbuch der literarischen Rhetorik*, 2 vols. (Munich, 1960) [see index s.v. anadiplosis, analepsis, anaphora, derivatio, geminatio, gradatio, klimakotos, palillogia, paronomasia; no entry s.v. 'echo', but see par. 622 concerning 'Klage-Echo'].

LAVIN, I., 'Cephalus and Procris: Transformations of an Ovidian Myth', *JWCI* 17 (1954), 260–87.

LAZZARI, A., *La musica alla corte dei duchi di Ferrara* (Ferrara, 1928).

LAZZERI, ELISABETTA (ed.), *Poliziano: Commento inedito all'epistola ovidiana di Saffo a Faone* (Istituto Nazionale di Studi sul Rinascimento, Studi e Testi, 11; Florence, 1971).

LEA, KATHLEEN MARGUERITE, *Italian Popular Comedy: A Study in the Commedia dell'Arte*, 2 vols. (Oxford, 1934; repr. New York, 1962).

—— 'The Poetic Powers of Repetition' (Warton Lecture in English Poetry), *Proceedings of the British Academy*, 55 (1969), 51–76.

LE MAÎTRE, H., *Essai sur le mythe de Psyché dans la littérature française* (Paris, 1939).

LEOPOLD, SILKE, 'Echotechniken bei H. Schütz und seinen italienischen Zeitgenossen', in *Kongreß-Bericht Stuttgart 1985* [Gesellschaft für Musikforschung, *Alte Musik als ästhetische Gegenwart: Bach, Händel, Schütz*], 2 vols. (Kassel, 1987), i. 86–94 [+ 5 music exx.].

—— 'Haydn und die Tradition der Orpheus-Opern', *Musica*, 36 (1982), 131–5.

—— 'Iacopo Sannazaro et le madrigal italien', in Vaccaro (ed.), *Chanson à la Renaissance*, 255–74.

—— 'Lyra Orphei', in Finscher (ed.), *Monteverdi*, 337–45.

—— 'Madrigali sulle egloghe sdrucciole di Jacopo Sannazaro: Struttura poetica e forma musicale', *RIM* 14 (1979), 75–127.

—— *Monteverdi: Music in Transition*, Engl. trans. Anne Smith (Oxford, 1991) [1st publ. as *Monteverdi und seine Zeit* (Laaber, 1982)].

—— ' "Quelle bazzicature poetiche . . . ": Dichtungsformen in der . . . italienischen Oper (1600–1640)', *HJMw* 3 (1978), 101–41.

—— *S. Landi: Beiträge zur Biographie: Untersuchungen zur weltlichen und geistlichen Vokalmusik*, 2 vols. (Hamburger Beiträge zur Musikwissenschaft, 17; Hamburg, 1976).

LINCOLN, HARRY B., *The Italian Madrigal and Related Repertories: Indexes to Printed Collections, 1500–1600* (New Haven, Conn., 1988).

LINFORTH, I. M., *The Arts of Orpheus* (Berkeley, Calif., 1941).

LIPPMANN, FRIEDRICh, 'Der italienische Vers und der musikalische Rhythmus', *AnMc* 12 (1973), 253–369; 14 (1974), 323–410; 15 (1975), 298–333.

LOCKWOOD, LEWIS, 'Music at Ferrara in the Period of Ercole I d'Este', *SM* I (1972), 101–31.

—— *Music in Renaissance Ferrara, 1400–1505* (Oxford, 1984).

LOEWENBERG, A., *Annals of Opera* (2nd edn., 2 vols., Geneva, 1955; 3rd edn., London, 1978 [1st publ. 1943]).

LOEWENSTEIN, JOSEPH, *Responsive Readings: Versions of Echo in Pastoral, Epic, and the Jonsonian Masque* (Yale Studies in English, 192; New Haven, Conn., and London, 1984).

LOMMATZSCH, ERHARD, *Beiträge zur älteren italienischen Volksdichtung: Untersuchungen und Texte*, 5 vols. (Deutsche Akademie der Wissenschaften zu Berlin. Veröffentlichungen des Instituts für Romanische Sprachwissenschaft, 2–4, 14, 17; Berlin, 1950–63).

LUISI, FRANCESCO, *Del cantar a libro – a sulla viola: La musica vocale nel Rinascimento* (Turin, 1977).

LUNGO, ISIDORO DEL. *See* Del Lungo.

Luogo teatrale a Firenze. See Fabbri *et al.*

MAASS, ERNST, *Orpheus* (Munich, 1895).

MACCHIA, GIOVANNI, *Vita, avventure e morte di Don Giovanni* (Bari, 1966).

MACCLINTOCK, CAROL, *Giaches de Wert* (MSD 17; Rome, 1966).

—— 'Giustiniani's *Discorso sopra la musica*', *Musica disciplina*, 15 (1961), 209–25.

—— 'Molinet, Music, and Mediaeval Rhetoric', *Musica disciplina*, 13 (1959), 109–21.

—— and MACCLINTOCK, LANDER (eds.), *Balet comique de la Royne* [*1581*] (MSD 25; Rome, 1971).

MACHIAVELLI, NICCOLÒ, *Opere*, ed. M. Martelli (Florence, 1971).

MAGAGNATO, LICISCO, *Teatri italiani del Cinquecento* (Venice, 1954).

MAIER, IDA, *Ange Politien* (THR 81; Geneva, 1966).

—— *Les Manuscrits d'Ange Politien* (Geneva, 1965).

MANIATES, M. R., 'Musical Mannerism', *MQ* 57 (1971), 270–93.

—— *Musical Mannerism in Italian Music and Culture 1530–1660* (Manchester, 1979).

MARTIN, JOSEF, *Antike Rhetorik* (Handbuch der klassischen Altertumswissenschaft, ii/3; Munich, 1974).

MARTINDALE, CHARLES (ed.), *Ovid Renewed: Ovidian Influences on Literature and Art from the Middle Ages to the Twentieth Century* (Cambridge, 1988).

MASSÉNA, ANDRÉ PROSPER, Prince d'Essling, *Les Livres à figures vénitiens de la fin du XVe siècle et du commencement du XVIe*, 3 vols. in 6 (Paris and Florence, 1907–14).

MASSENKEIL, GÜNTHER, 'Wiederholungsfiguren in den Oratorien Giacomo Carissimis', *AMw* 13 (1956), 42–60.

MATTINGLY, HAROLD, 'Virgil's Fourth Eclogue', *JWCI* 10 (1947), 14–19.

MEDICI, LORENZO DE', *Canzone a ballo composte dal magnifico Lorenzo de Medici et da M. Agnolo Politiano & altri autori* (Milan, 1812 [facs. of the Florence, 1568 edn.]).

MEER, J. H. VAN DER, *J. J. Fux als Opernkomponist*, 2 vols. (Bilthoven, 1961).

MICHELS, ULRICH, 'Das "Lamento d'Arianna" von C. Monteverdi', in Breig *et al.* (eds.), *Analysen*, 91–109.

MINOR, ANDREW C., and MITCHELL, BONNER (eds.), *A Renaissance Entertainment: Festivities for the Marriage of Cosimo I, Duke of Florence, in 1539* (Columbia, Mo., 1968).

MITCHELL, BONNER, *Italian Civic Pageantry in the High Renaissance: A Descriptive Bibliography of Triumphal Entries and other Festivals for State Occasions (1494–1550)* (Biblioteca di bibliografia italiana, 89; Florence, 1979).

MONTEROSSO, RAFFAELLO (ed.), *Claudio Monteverdi e il suo tempo* (Verona, 1969).

MONTEVERDI, CLAUDIO, *12 composizioni vocali profane e sacre (inedite)*, ed. Wolfgang Osthoff (Milan, 1958).

—— *L'Incoronazione di Poppea*, ed. Alan Curtis (London, 1989).

—— *Lettere, dediche, prefazioni*, ed. Domenico de' Paoli (Rome, 1973).

—— *Letters of Claudio Monteverdi*, tr. and intro. Denis Stevens (London, 1980).

—— *Tutte le opere*, ed. Gian Francesco Malipiero, 16 vols. (Asolo, 1926–42 [vol. xi, *Orfeo, Arianna*, 1930; vol. xii, *Ulisse*, 1930; vol. xiii, *Poppea*, 1931]).

MORELL, MARTIN, 'New Evidence for the Biographies of Andrea and Giovanni Gabrieli', *EMH* 3 (1983), 101–22.

MORELLI, G., and WALKER, T., 'Tre controversie intorno al San Cassiano', in Muraro (ed.), *Venezia e il melodramma nel Seicento*, 97–120.

MÜLLER, REINHARD, *Der stile recitativo in Claudio Monteverdis Orfeo* (Münchner Veröffentlichungen zur Musikgeschichte, 38; Tutzing, 1984).

MURARO, MARIA TERESA (ed.), *Studi sul teatro veneto fra Rinascimento ed età barocca* (Civiltà veneziana, 24; Florence, 1971).

—— (ed.), *Venezia e il melodramma nel Seicento* (Studi di musica veneta, 5; Florence, 1976).

—— (ed.), *Venezia e il melodramma nel Settecento*, 2 vols. (Studi di musica veneta, 6–7; Florence, 1978).

MURATA, MARGARET, 'Il carnevale a Roma sotto Clemente IX Rospigliosi', *RIM* 12 (1977), 83–99.

—— 'Classical Tragedy in the History of Early Opera in Rome', *EMH* 4 (1984), 101–34.

—— *Operas for the Papal Court 1631–1668* (Ann Arbor, Mich., 1981).

—— 'Operas for the Papal Court with Texts by Giulio Rospigliosi', Ph.D. diss. (University of Chicago, 1975).

—— 'The Recitative Soliloquy', *JAMS* 32 (1979), 45–52.

MURATORI, LUDOVICO ANTONIO, *Rerum italicarum scriptores*, 28 vols. (Milan, 1723–51).

MURPHY, JAMES J., *Rhetoric in the Middle Ages* (Berkeley, Calif., 1974).

—— (ed.), *Renaissance Eloquence: Studies in the Theory and Practice of Renaissance Rhetoric* (Berkeley, Calif., and London, 1983).

—— (ed.), *Renaissance Rhetoric: Key Texts, A.D. 1479–1602: A Microfiche Collection of Important Texts from the Bodleian Library, Oxford* (Elmsford, NY: Microforms International, 1986?).

MUSCH, H., *Costanzo Festa als Madrigalkomponist* (Collection d'études musicologiques, 61; Baden-Baden, 1977).

MYERS, ROLLO, 'The Opera that Never Was: Debussy's Collaboration with Victor Segalen in the Preparation of *Orphée*', *MQ* 64 (1978), 495–506.

NABOKOV, NICOLAS, *Old Friends and New Music* (London, 1951).

NAGLER, ALOIS M., *Theatre Festivals of the Medici, 1539–1637* (New Haven, Conn., 1964).

NERI, ACHILLE, 'Gli intermezzi del Pastor fido', *GSLI* 11 (1888), 405–15.

NERI, FERDINANDO, *Il Chiabrera e la pleiade francese* (Turin, 1920).

NICCOLÒ DA CORREGGIO, *Opere*, ed. Antonia Tissoni Benvenuti (Scrittori d'Italia, 244; Bari, 1969).

NICHOLSON, R. H., '*Sir Orfeo*: A "Kynges Noote" ', *Review of English Studies*, 36 (1985), 161–79.

NORDEN, E., 'Orpheus und Euridice', in B. Kytzler (ed.), *Kleine Schriften zum klassischen Altertum* (Berlin, 1966), 468–532.

—— *P. Vergilius Maro: Aeneis Buch VI* (4th edn., Stuttgart, 1957).

OBERTELLO, A., *Madrigali italiani in Inghilterra* (Milan, 1949).

OPITZ, MARTIN, *Weltliche Poemata, 1644, Erster Teil*, ed. E. Trunz (Deutsche Neudrucke, Reihe: Barock, 2; Tübingen, 1967).

OSTHOFF, WOLFGANG, 'Antonio Cestis "Alessandro Vincitor di se stesso" ', *SMw* 24 (1960), 13–43.

—— 'Contro le legge de' fati: Poliziano und Monteverdis *Orfeo* als Sinnbild künstlerischen Wettkampfs mit der Natur', *AnMc* 22 (1984), 11–68.

—— 'Dante beim späten Verdi', *Studi Verdiani*, 5 (1988–9), 35–64.

—— 'Maschera e musica', *NRMI* 1 (1967), 16–44.

—— *Monteverdistudien I. Das Dramatische Spätwerk Claudio Monteverdis* (Münchner Veröffentlichungen zur Musikgeschichte, 3; Tutzing, 1960).

—— 'Musica e versificazione', in Bianconi (ed.), *Drammaturgia musicale*, 125–41.

—— 'Die Opera buffa', in W. Arlt *et al.* (eds.), *Gattungen der Musik in Einzeldarstellungen: Gedenkschrift Leo Schrade* (Berne, 1973), 678–743.

—— 'Symphonien beim Ende des Zweiten Weltkriegs', *AcM* 60 (1988), 62–104.

—— *Theatergesang und darstellende Musik in der italienischen Renaissance*, 2 vols. (Münchener Veröffentlichungen zur Musikgeschichte, 14; Tutzing, 1969).

—— 'Zu den Quellen von Monteverdis *Ritorno d'Ulisse in patria*', *SMw* 23 (1956), 67–78.

—— 'Zur Bologneser Aufführung von Monteverdis "Ritorno di Ulisse" im Jahre 1640', *Österreichische Akademie der Wissenschaften, phil.-hist. Klasse, Anzeiger*, 95 (1958), 155–60.

—— 'Zur musikalischen Tradition der tragischen Gattung im italienischen Theater', in Hans Heinrich Eggebrecht and Max Lütolf (eds.), *Studien zur Tradition in der Musik: Kurt von Fischer zum 60. Geburtstag* (Munich, 1973), 121–43.

PALISCA, CLAUDE V., *Baroque Music* (2nd edn., Englewood Cliffs, NJ, 1981 [1st publ. 1968]).

—— 'The Camerata Fiorentina': A Reappraisal', *SM* 1 (1972), 203–36.

—— 'The First Performance of "Euridice" ', in Albert Mell (ed.), *Queens College Twenty-Fifth Anniversary Festschrift* (New York, 1964), 1–23.

—— *Humanism in Italian Renaissance Musical Thought* (New Haven, Conn., and London, 1985).

—— 'Rezitativ', in H. H. Eggebrecht (ed.), *Handwörterbuch der musikalischen Terminologie* (Wiesbaden, 1983).

—— 'Stile rappresentativo', *New Grove*, xviii. 145.

—— '*Ut Oratoria musica*: The Rhetorical Basis of Musical Mannerism', in Franklin W. Robinson and Stephen G. Nichols, Jr. (eds.), *The Meaning of Mannerism* (Hanover, NH, 1972), 37–65.

—— 'Vincenzo Galilei and Some Links between "Pseudo-Monody" and Monody', *MQ* 46 (1960), 344–60.

—— (ed.), *The Florentine Camerata: Documentary Studies and Translations* (New Haven, Conn., 1989).

—— (ed.), *Girolamo Mei: Letters on Ancient and Modern Music to V. Galilei and G. Bardi: A Study with Annotated Texts* (MSD 3; 2nd corr. edn., Rome, 1977).

PANOFSKY, E., *Hercules am Scheideweg und andere antike Bildstoffe in der neueren Kunst* (Leipzig, 1930).

—— *Dürer* (3rd edn., 2 vols., Princeton, NJ, 1948) [same page numbers apply to 4th edn., 1955].

PAOLI, UGO ENRICO, 'La trenodia del Poliziano "In Laurentium Medicum" ', *Studi italiani di filologia classica*, 16 (1939), 165–76.

PARKER, A. A., *The Allegorical Dramas of Calderón* (Oxford, 1943).

PASTOR, LUDWIG, *Geschichte der Päpste*, 16 vols. (1886–1933); trans. F. I. Antrobus, *History of the Popes*, 40 vols. (1891–1954).

PAULY-WISSOWA. *See* Wissowa.

PERI, JACOPO, *Euridice*, ed. Howard Mayer Brown (RRMBE 36–7; Madison, Wis., 1981).

—— *Le varie musiche*, ed. Tim Carter (RRMBE 50; Madison, Wis., 1985).

PERNICONE, VINCENZO (ed.), *Il Quattrocento* (Antologia della letteratura italiana, M. Vitale, gen. ed., 2, part i; Milan, 1966) [Poliziano, *Orfeo*: pp. 777–91].

PEROSA, ALESSANDRO, and SPARROW, JOHN (eds.), *Renaissance Latin Verse* (London, 1979).

PERRUCCI, ANDREA, *Dell'arte rappresentativa, premeditata ed all'improviso* (Naples, 1699).

PICCOLOMINI, ALESSANDRO, *Alessandro*, ed. F. Cerreta (Siena, 1966).

PIRROTTA, NINO, 'Il caval zoppo', *CHM* 4 (1966), 215–26 = *Music and Culture*, 325–34.

—— 'I cori per l'"Edipo Tiranno" ', in Degrada (ed.), *Andrea Gabrieli*, 273–92.

—— *Li due Orfei: da Poliziano a Monteverdi, con un saggio critico sulla scenografia di E. Povoledo* (Turin, 1969; 2nd rev. edn., 1975). For rev. Eng. trans., see *Music and Theatre*.

—— 'Falsirena e la più antica delle cavatine [D. Mazzocchi]', *CHM* 2 (1957), 355–66 = *Music and Culture*, 335–42.

—— *Music and Culture in Italy from the Middle Ages to the Baroque* (Studies in the History of Music, 1; Cambridge, Mass., 1984).

—— *Music and Theatre from Poliziano to Monteverdi*, trans. Karen Eales (Cambridge, 1982).

—— 'Note su Marenzio e il Tasso', in Riccardo Ricciardi (ed.), *Scritti in onore di Luigi Ronga* (Milan, 1973), 557–71 = *Music and Culture*, 198–209.

—— 'Scelte poetiche di Monteverdi', *NRMI* 2 (1968), 10–42, 226–54 = *Music and Culture*, 271–316.

—— *Storia dell'opera, anno academico 1972–73* (Rome, n.d. [?1973]).

—— 'Theater, Sets, and Music in Monteverdi's Operas', in *Music and Culture*, 254–70, 422–8 [1st publ. in Italian in Monterosso (ed.), *Monteverdi*].

POLIZIANO, ANGELO, *Miscellaneorum centuria secunda*, ed. Vittore Branca and M. Pastore Stocchi (Florence, 1978).

—— *Opera omnia*, ed. Ida Maier, 3 vols. (Turin, 1970–1).

—— *L'Orfeo*, ed. Ireneo Affò (Venice, 1776); trans. Louis E. Lord (London, 1931).

—— *Poesie italiane*, ed. Saverio Orlando (Milan, 1976).

—— *Prose volgare inedite*, ed. Isidoro Del Lungo (Florence, 1867).

POLIZIANO, ANGELO, *Rime*, ed. Daniela Delcorno Branca (Venice, 1990).
—— *Rime*, ed. Natalino Sapegno (2nd edn., Rome, 1967) [*Orfeo*: pp. 105–30].
—— *Le Stanze, L'Orfeo e le Rime*, ed. G. Carducci (2nd edn., Bologna, 1912 [1st edn., Florence, 1863]).
PORTER, W. V., 'Peri's and Corsi's *Dafne*', *JAMS* 18 (1965), 170–96.
POTTER, LOUIS, 'Realism vs. Nightmare: Problems of Staging *The Duchess of Malfi*', in J. Price (ed.), *The Triple Bond* (Tribute to A. C. Sprague), (University Park, Pa., 1975), 170–89 (on echo and mirroring).
POWERS, HAROLD S., 'L'Erismena travestita', in Powers (ed.), *Studies in Music History*, 259–324.
—— (ed.), *Studies in Music History: Essays for Oliver Strunk* (Princeton, NJ, 1968).
PRICE, CURTIS A., 'Italian Opera and Arson in Late 18th-Century London', *JAMS* 42 (1989), 55–107.
—— 'Orpheus in Britannia', in Anne Dhu Shapiro (ed.), *Music and Context: Essays for John Ward* (Cambridge, Mass., 1985), 264–77.
PRINCE, FRANK TEMPLETON, *The Italian Elements in Milton's Verse* (Oxford, 1954).
PRUNIÈRES, HENRY, *L'Opéra italien en France avant Lully* (Paris, 1913).
PYLE, CYNTHIA MUNRO, 'Politian's *Orfeo* and other *Favole mitologiche* in the Context of Late Quattrocento Italy', Ph.D. diss. (Columbia University, 1976).
—— 'Il tema di Orfeo, la musica, e le favole mitologiche del tardo Quattrocento', in Giovannangiola Tarugi (ed.), *Ecumenismo della cultura* (Acts of the Congress of the 'Centro di studi umanistici' Montepulciano . . . 1976), 2 vols. (Florence, 1981), ii. 121–39.
—— 'Towards Vernacular Comedy: Gaspare Visconti's "Pasithea" ', in *Il teatro italiano del Ri nascimento* (Acts of the Congress 'Renaissance Theater in Northern Italy: The Court and the City (1400–1600), New York, November 1978'; Florence, 1980), 349–60.
QUADRIO, FRANCESCO SAVERIO, *Della storia e della ragione d'ogni poesia*, 5 vols. in 7 (Bologna and Milan, 1739–52).
QUAGLIATI, PAOLO, *La Sfera armoniosa [1623], Il Carro di fedeltà [1611]*, ed. V. Gotwals and P. Keppler (SCMA 13; Northampton, Mass., 1957).
QUINONES, RICARDO JOSEPH, *The Renaissance Discovery of Time* (Harvard Studies in Comparative Literature, 31; Cambridge, Mass., 1972).
RASCHL, ERICH, 'Die musikalisch-rhetorischen Figuren in den weltlichen Vokalwerken des Giovanni Felice Sances', *SMw* 28 (1977), 29–103.
REANEY, GILBERT, 'Music in the Late Mediaeval Entremets', *Annales musicologiques*, 7 (1964–77), 51–65.
REINER, STUART, 'Preparations in Parma—1618, 1627/28', *MR* 25 (1964), 273–301.
—— ' "La vag'Angioletta" (and Others)', Part I, *AnMc* 14 (1974), 26–88 [part II not published].
—— 'Vi sono molt'altre mezz'arie' in Powers (ed.), *Studies in Music History*, 241–58.
RESTANI, DONATELLA, *L'itinerario di G. Mei: Dalla 'Poetica' alla 'Musica'* (Studi e testi per la storia della musica, 7; Florence, 1990).
RIDOLFI, ROBERTO, 'Ultime postille machiavelliane', *Bibliofilia*, 77 (1975), 65–76.
RINUCCINI, OTTAVIO, *Il Narciso . . . da un MS originale Barberiano*, ed. Luigi Maria Rezzi (Rome, 1829).

RITTER, A. G., 'Die musikalischen Chöre des Chr. T. Walliser zur Tragödie "Andromeda" ', *Monatshefte für Musikgeschichte*, 1 (1869), 134–41.

ROBSON, C. A., 'Dante's Reading of Latin Poets and the *Divina Commedia*', in C. Grayson (ed.), *World of Dante* (Oxford, 1980), 81–121.

—— 'Dante's Use in the *Divina Commedia* of the Mediaeval Allegories of Ovid', in *Centenary Essays on Dante* (Oxford, 1965), 1–38.

ROEDIGER, F. (ed.). *See* [Landau, Horace de].

ROLANDI, ULDERICO, *Il libretto per musica* (Rome, 1951).

ROLLAND, ROMAIN, 'The Beginnings of Opera', in *Some Musicians of Former Days* (New York, 1915), 25–69 [1st publ. in French, Paris, 1908].

—— *Histoire de l'opéra en Europe avant Lully et Scarlatti* (2nd rev. edn., Paris, 1931 [1st publ. Paris, 1895]).

RONSARD, PIERRE, *Œuvres complètes*, ed. Gustave Cohen, 2 vols. (Bibliothèque de la Pleiade; Paris, 1958).

RORE, CIPRIANO DE, *Opera omnia*, ed. Bernhard Meier, 8 vols. (CMM 14; Rome and Stuttgart, 1959–77).

ROSAND, ELLEN, 'The Descending Tetrachord: An Emblem of Lament', *MQ* 65 (1979), 346–59.

—— 'Lamento', *New Grove*, x. 412–14.

—— 'Monteverdi's Mimetic Art: *L'incoronazione di Poppea*', *Cambridge Opera Journal*, 1 (1989), 113–37.

—— *Opera in Seventeenth-Century Venice: The Creation of a Genre* (Berkeley, Calif., 1991).

—— 'The Opera Scenario, 1638–1655: A Preliminary Survey', in Della Seta and Piperno (eds.), *In Cantu*, 335–46.

—— ' "Ormindo travestito" in *Erismena*', *JAMS* 28 (1975), 268–91.

—— 'Seneca and the Interpretation of *L'Incoronazione di Poppea*', *JAMS* 38 (1985), 34–71.

ROSSI, VITTORIO, *B. Guarini e il Pastor fido* (Turin, 1886).

—— *Il Quattrocento* (Storia letteraria d'Italia; 6th rev. edn., repr. Milan, 1956).

ROTUNDA, DOMINIC P., *Motif-Index of the Italian Novella* (Indiana University Publications, Folklore series, no. 2; Bloomington, Ind., 1942).

RUBBI, A. (ed.), *Parnaso Italiano*, 56 vols. (Venice, 1784–91; repr. in 12 vols., Venice, 1832–51).

RUBSAMEN, WALTER, *Literary Sources of Secular Music in Italy, ca. 1500* (University of California Publications in Music, 1; Berkeley, Calif., 1943; repr. New York, 1972).

RUHNKE, MARTIN, *Joachim Burmeister: Ein Beitrag zur Musiklehre um 1600* (Kassel, 1955).

RUSSELL, D. A., and WINTERBOTTOM, M. (eds.), *Ancient Literary Criticism: The Principal Texts in New Translation* (Oxford, 1972).

RUTSCHMANN, E. R., 'Minato and the Venetian Opera Libretto', *Current Musicology*, 27 (1979), 84–91.

SABBATINI, NICCOLÒ, *Pratica di fabricar scene* (Ravenna, 1638; repr. Rome, 1955; French translation, Neuchâtel, 1942).

SADIE, STANLEY (ed.), *History of Opera* (New Grove Handbooks in Music; London, 1989) [Part I: Baroque Opera: pp. 15–68, bibliography, pp. 420–9].

SADLER, GRAHAM, 'Patrons and Pasquinades: Rameau in the 1730s', *JRMA* 113 (1988), 314–37.

SANDER, MAX, *Le Livre à figures italien depuis 1467 jusqu'à 1530*, 7 vols. (Milan, 1942–69).

SANNAZARO, JACOPO, *Arcadia and Piscatorial Eclogues*, trans. Ralph Nash (Detroit, 1966).

—— *Opere volgari*, ed. Alfredo Mauro (Scrittori d'Italia, 220; Bari, 1961).

SAPEGNO, NATALINO, *Il Trecento* (Storia letteraria d'Italia; 3rd edn., Milan, 1966).

SARTORI, CLAUDIO, *I libretti italiani a stampa dalle origini al 1800: Catalogo analitico con 16 indici* (Cuneo, 1990– [1st publ. as photocopy of typescript, 11 vols., Milan, 1980–2]).

SARTORIO, ANTONIO, *L'Orfeo*, facs., ed. Ellen Rosand (Drammaturgia musicale veneta, 6; Milan, 1983).

SASLOW, JAMES M., *Ganymede in the Renaissance: Homosexuality in Art and Society* (New Haven, Conn., and London, 1986).

SCHERING, ARNOLD, 'Die Lehre von den musikalischen Figuren', *Kirchenmusikalisches Jahrbuch*, 21 (1908), 106–14.

SCHLOSSER, JULIUS VON, 'Giusto's Fresken in Padua', *Jahrbuch der kunsthistorischen Sammlungen*, 17 (1896), 13 ff.

—— 'Heidnische Elemente in der christlichen Kunst des Altertums' [1894], in J. Schlosser, *Präludien, Vorträge und Aufsätze* (Berlin, 1927), 9–43.

SCHMITZ, ARNOLD, 'Die Figurenlehre in den theoretischen Werken Johann Gottfried Walters', *AMw* 9 (1952), 79–100.

SCHNEIDER, MAX, *Die Anfänge des Basso continuo* (Leipzig, 1918; repr. Farnborough, 1971).

SCHONDORFF, J. (ed.), *Orpheus und Euridice: Poliziano, Calderón, Gluck, Offenbach, Kokoschka, Cocteau, Anouilh* (Munich, 1963).

SCHRADE, LEO, *Monteverdi: Creator of Modern Music* (New York, 1950; repr. 1964).

—— *Tragedy in the Art of Music* (Cambridge, Mass., 1964).

—— (ed.), *La Représentation d'Edipo Tiranno au Teatro Olimpico (Vicence 1585)* (Le chœur des muses; Paris, 1960).

SCHULZ-BUSCHHAUS, ULRICH, *Das Madrigal: Zur Stilgeschichte der italienischen Lyrik zwischen Renaissance und Barock* (Ars poetica: Texte und Studien; Studien, 7; Bad Homburg and Berlin, 1969).

SCHWARTZ, RUDOLF, 'H. L. Hassler unter dem Einfluß der italienischen Madrigalisten', *Vierteljahrsschrift für Musikwissenschaft*, 9 (1893), 1–61.

SCOGLIO, E., *Il teatro alla corte estense* (Lodi, 1965).

SEAY, ALBERT, 'Arcadelt and Michelangelo', *Renaissance News*, 18 (1965), 299–301.

SEBILLET, THOMAS, *Art poétique Françoys*, ed. F. Gaiffe (Paris, 1910; repr. 1932).

SETTIS, SALVATORE, '*Citarea* "su una impresa di bronconi" ', *JWCI* 34 (1971), 135–77.

SEZNEC, JEAN, *The Survival of the Pagan Gods*, trans. B. Sessions (Harper Torchbooks, New York, 1961 [1st publ. in French, 1940]).

SHEARMAN, JOHN, 'The Florentine *Entrata* of Leo X, 1515', *JWCI* 38 (1975), 136–54.

—— *Mannerism* (Pelican Books; Harmondsworth, 1967; repr. 1973).

SIDNEY, PHILIP, *Poems*, ed. William A. Ringler (Oxford, 1962) [on Echo: p. 402].

SILBIGER, ALEXANDER, 'An Unknown Partbook of Early Sixteenth-Century Polyphony', *SM* 6 (1977), 43–67.

SILK, M. S., and STERN, J. P., *Nietzsche on Tragedy* (Cambridge, 1981).

SKERIS, ROBERT A., *Chroma Theou: On the Origins and Theological Interpretation of the Musical Imagery Used by the Ecclesiastical Writers of the First Three Centuries, with Special Reference to the Image of Orpheus* (Publications of the Catholic Church Music Association, 1; Altötting, 1976).

SLIM, H. COLIN, 'Un coro della "Tullia" di Lodovico Martelli messo in musica e attribuito a Philippe Verdelot', in Garfagnani (ed.), *Firenze e la Toscana dei Medici*, ii. 487–511.

——*A Gift of Madrigals and Motets*, 2 vols. (Chicago and London, 1972).

——'A Motet for Machiavelli's Mistress', in S. Bertelli and G. Ramakus (eds.), *Essays Presented to Myron P. Gilmore*, 2 vols. (Florence, 1978), ii. 457–72.

——'A Royal Treasure at Sutton Coldfield', *Early Music*, 6 (1978), 57–74.

SMITH, MORTON, 'Ascent to the Heavens and the Beginning of Christianity' *Eranos-Jahrbuch*, l (Zurich, 1981), 403–29 [subtitle: Aufstieg und Abstieg].

SMITH, PATRICK J., *The Tenth Muse: A Historical Study of the Opera Libretto* (New York, 1970; London, 1971).

SMITHER, HOWARD, *A History of the Oratorio*, 3 vols. (Chapel Hill, NC, 1977; Oxford, 1987).

SNUGGS, HENRY L., *Shakespeare and Five Acts* (New York, 1960).

SOLERTI, ANGELO, *Gli albori del melodramma*, 3 vols. (Milan, 1904–5; repr. 1969 and 1976).

——*Musica, ballo e drammatica alla corte medicea* (Florence, 1905; repr. Bologna, 1969).

——*Le origini del melodramma* (Turin, 1903; repr. 1969).

——'La rappresentazione della *Calandria* a Lione nel 1548', in *Raccolta di studii critici dedicata ad Alessandro D'Ancona* (Florence, 1901), 693–9.

——'Le rappresentazioni musicali di Venezia dal 1571 al 1605', *RMI* 9 (1902), 503–58.

——(ed.), *Ferrara e la corte Estense* (Città di Castello, 1891).

SOLMI, A. (ed.), [Rizzoli-Ricordi] *Enciclopedia della Musica*, 6 vols. (Milan, 1972).

SONNECK, OSCAR GEORGE, 'A Description of A. Striggio's and F. Corteccia's Intermedi "Psyche and Amor", 1565', in *Miscellaneous Studies in the History of Music* (New York, 1921; repr. 1968 [1st publ. 1911]).

——(ed.), *Library of Congress. Catalogue of Opera Librettos Printed Before 1800*, 2 vols. (New York, 1914; repr. 1967).

SONNINO, LEE ANN, *Handbook to 16th Century Rhetoric* (London, 1968).

SPARROW, JOHN, 'Latin Verse of the High Renaissance', in E. F. Jacob (ed.), *Italian Renaissance Studies* (London, 1960; repr. 1966), 354–409.

STADEN, SIGMUND, *Seelewig*, ed. Robert Eitner in *Monatshefte für Musikgeschichte*, 13 (1881), 53–147.

STAEHELIN, MARTIN, *Die Messen Heinrich Isaacs*, 3 vols. (Publikationen der Schweizerischen Musikforschenden Gesellschaft, 2nd ser., 28; Berne, 1977).

STÄUBLE, ANTONIO, 'Rassegna di testi e studi sul teatro del Rinascimento', 'Nuove pubblicazioni sul teatro del Rinascimento', 'Rassegna di studi teatrali', *BHR* 29 (1967), 227–45; 32 (1970), 649–75; 36 (1974), 361–96.

STECHOW, W., *Apollo und Daphne* (Studien der Bibliothek Warburg, 23; Leipzig, 1932).

STEINITZ, K. T., 'The Voyage of Isabella d'Aragon from Naples to Milan, January 1489', *BHR* 23 (1961), 17–33.

STERN, H., 'Orphée dans l'art paléochrétien', *Cahiers archéologiques*, 23 (1974), 1–16.

—— 'The Orpheus in the Synagogue of Dura-Europos', *JWCI* 21 (1958), 1–6.

STERNFELD, F. W., 'Aspects of Echo Music in the Renaissance', *SM* 9 (1980), 45–57.

—— 'The Birth of Opera: Ovid, Poliziano and the *lieto fine*', *AnMc* 19 (1979), 30–51.

—— 'Des intermèdes à l'opéra: la technique du finale', in Jean Jacquot and Elie Konigson (eds.), *Les Fêtes de la Renaissance*, iii (Paris, 1975), 267–80.

—— 'Écho et répétition dans la poésie et la musique' in Vaccaro (ed.), *Chanson à la Renaissance*, 242–53.

—— 'Expression and Revision in Gluck's *Orfeo* and *Alceste*', in Jack Westrup (ed.), *Essays Presented to Egon Wellesz* (Oxford, 1966); repr. Hortschansky (ed.), *Gluck*, 172–99.

—— 'The First Printed Opera Libretto', *ML* 59 (1978), 121–38.

—— 'Gluck's Operas and Italian Tradition', *Chigiana*, 29–30 (1972–3), 275–81.

—— 'Les Intermèdes de Florence et la genèse de l'opéra', *Baroque*, 5 (Montauban, 1972), 25–9.

—— 'The Lament in Poliziano's "Orfeo" and Some Musical Settings of the Early 16th Century', in J.-M. Vaccaro (ed.), *Arts du spectacle et histoire des idées: Recueil offert en hommage à Jean Jacquot* (Tours, 1984), 201–4.

—— *Music in Shakespearean Tragedy* (London and New York, 1963; 2nd edn., 1967).

—— 'A Note on *Stile recitativo*', *PRMA* 110 (1983/4), 41–4.

—— 'The "Occasional" Element in the Choral Finale from Poliziano to Rinuccini', in Marc Honegger, Christian Meyer, and Paul Prevost (eds.), *La Musique et le rite sacré et profane: Actes du XIIIᵉ Congrès de la Société Internationale de Musicologie, Strasbourg, 29 août–3 septembre 1982*, 2 vols. (Strasburg, 1986), i. 371–6.

—— 'The Orpheus Myth and the Libretto of "Orfeo" ', in Whenham (ed.), *Monteverdi: Orfeo*, 20–33.

—— 'Orpheus, Ovid and Opera', *JRMA* 113 (1988), 172–202.

—— 'Poliziano, Isaac, Festa: Rhetorical Repetition', in Garfagnani (ed.), *Firenze e la Toscana dei Medici*, ii. 549–64.

—— 'Repetition and Echo in Renaissance Poetry and Music', in John Carey (ed.), *English Renaissance Studies Presented to Dame Helen Gardner in Honour of her Seventieth Birthday* (Oxford, 1980), 33–43.

STIEGER, FRANZ, *Opern-Lexikon*, 10 vols. (Tutzing, 1975–82).

STRAUSS, WALTER A., *Descent and Return: The Orphic Theme in Modern Literature* (Cambridge, Mass., 1971).

STRAVINSKY, IGOR, and CRAFT, ROBERT, *Dialogues and a Diary* (2nd edn., London, 1968).

STROHM, REINHARD, *Die italienische Oper im 18. Jahrhundert* (Taschenbücher zur Musikwissenschaft, 25; Wilhelmshaven, 1979).

—— 'Die Tragedia per Musica als Repertoirestück: Zwei Hamburger Opern von G. M. Orlandini', *HJMw* 5 (1981), 37–54.

—— ' "Tragédie" into "Dramma per musica" ', *Informazioni e studi vivaldiani*, 9 (1988), 14–25; 10 (1989), 57–102; 11 (1990), 11–26; 12 (1991), 47–75.

—— 'Vivaldi's and Handel's Settings of *Giustino*', in Fortune (ed.), *Music and Theatre*, 131–58.

STRONG, ROY, *Art and Power* (London, 1984).

—— *Splendour at Court: Renaissance Spectacle and Illusion* (London, 1973).

STRUNK, OLIVER, *Source Readings in Music History* (New York, 1950).

STUBBS, H. W., 'Underworld Themes in Modern Fiction', in H. R. E. Davidson (ed.), *The Journey to the Other World* (London, 1975), 130–47.

SZWEYKOWSKA, ANNA, *Dramma per musica w teatrze Wazów 1635–1648* (Cracow, 1976).

TARR, E. H., and WALKER, T., '*Bellici carmi, festivo fragor:* Die Verwendung der Trompete in der italienischen Oper des 17. Jahrhunderts', *HJMw* 3 (1978), 143–203.

TASSO, TORQUATO, *Aminta*, ed. Luigi Fassò (5th edn., Florence, 1967).

—— *Poesie*, ed. Francesco Flora (Milan, 1934).

TERMINI, OLGA, 'From a God to a Servant: The Bass Voice in the 17th Century Venetian Opera', *Current Musicology*, 44 (1990), 38–60.

TERPENNING, RONNIE H., *Charon and the Crossing: Ancient, Medieval, and Renaissance Transformations of a Myth* (Lewisburg, W. Va., London, and Toronto, 1985).

TESTI, FLAVIO, *La musica italiana nel medioevo e nel Rinascimento*, 2 vols. (Milan, 1969).

THIEL, EBERHARD, and ROHR, GISELA (eds.), *Libretti: Verzeichnis der bis 1800 erschienen Textbücher* (Kataloge der Herzog August Bibliothek Wolfenbüttel, NS 14; Frankfurt am Main, 1970).

THOMPSON, STITH (ed.), *Motif-Index of Folk-Literature, Folktales, Ballads, Myths, Fables, Medieval Romances* (rev. and enl. edn., 6 vols., Copenhagen, 1955–8).

TISSONI BENVENUTI, ANTONIA, *L'Orfeo del Poliziano: con il testo critico dell'originale e delle successive forme teatrali* (Padua, 1986).

—— 'Il teatro volgare della Milano sforzesca', in *Milano nell'età di Ludovico il Moro* (Milan, 1983), 333–51.

—— 'Il viaggio d'Isabella d'Este a Mantova nel giugno 1480 e la datazione dell' "Orfeo" del Poliziano', *GSLI* 158 (1981), 368–83.

—— (ed.), *Teatro del Quattrocento: Le corti padane* (Turin, 1983).

TOFFANIN, GIUSEPPE, *Il Cinquecento* (Storia letteraria d'Italia; 6th rev. edn., Milan, 1960).

TOMLINSON, GARY A., 'Ancora su Ottavio Rinuccini', *JAMS* 28 (1975), 351–6.

—— 'Madrigal, Motet and Monteverdi's "Via naturale alla imitazione"', *JAMS* 34 (1981), 60–108.

—— *Monteverdi and the End of the Renaissance* (Oxford, 1987).

—— 'Music and the Claims of Text: Monteverdi, Rinuccini and Marino', *Critical Inquiry*, 8 (1982), 565–89.

—— 'Ottavio Rinuccini and the *Favola affettuosa*', *Comitatus*, 6 (1975), 1–27.

—— 'Rinuccini, Peri, Monteverdi and the Humanist Heritage of Opera', Ph.D. diss. (University of California, Berkeley, 1979).

—— 'Twice Bitten, Thrice Shy: Monteverdi's "finta" *Finta pazza*', *JAMS* 36 (1983), 303–11.

TORCHI, L. (ed.), *L'Arte musicale in Italia*, 7 vols. (Milan, 1897–1907).

TOSCANELLA, ORATIO, *Precetti necessarie . . . Grammatica, Poetica, Retorica* (Venice, 1562).

TRAVI, ERNESTO, 'L'esperienza mantovana del Poliziani: L'"Orfeo" ', in *Studi in onore di Alberto Chiari*, 2 vols. (Brescia, 1973), 1297–1314.

TRISSINO, GIOVANNI GIORGIO, *La 5. e la 6. Divisione della Poetica* (Venice, 1562).

TROWELL, BRIAN, 'Acis, Galatea and Polyphemus', in Fortune (ed.), *Music and Theatre*, 31–93.

TURCHI, MARCELLO (ed.), *Opere di G. Chiabrera e lirici non marinisti del Seicento* (Classici italiani; Turin, 1973).

UGOLINI, FRANCESCO A., *I cantari d'argomento classico con un'appendice di testi inediti* (Biblioteca dell'Archivum Romanicum, ser. 1, 19; Geneva and Florence, 1933).

UNGER, HANS-HEINRICH, *Beziehungen zwischen Musik und Rhetorik* (Würzburg, 1941; repr. Hildesheim, 1985).

VACCARO, JEAN-MICHEL (ed.), *La Chanson à la Renaissance, Actes du XXe Colloque d'Études humanistes du Centre d'Études Supérieures de la Renaissance de l'Université de Tours, juillet 1977* (Tours, 1981).

—— *The Rake's Progress . . . Études de J. Jacquot, J.-M. Vaccaro, et M. Chimènes* (Paris, 1990).

VAN GENNEP, ARNOLD, *The Rites of Passage*, trans. M. B. Vizedom and G. L. Caffee (London, 1960 [1st publ. in French, 1909]).

VASOLI, CESARE, *La dialettica e la retorica dell'umanesimo: 'invenzione' e 'metodo' nella cultura del xv e xvi secolo* (Milan, 1968).

VASSALLI, ANTONIO, 'Il Tasso in musica e la trasmissione dei testi', in M. A. Balsano and T. Walker (eds.), *Tasso: La musica, i musicisti* (Florence, 1988), 59–90.

VERDE, ARMANDO FELICE, *Lo Studio fiorentino, 1473–1503: Ricerche e documenti*, 4 vols. (i–ii, Florence, 1973; iii, Pistoia, 1977; iv, Florence, 1985). For additional recent information cf. *Renaissance Quarterly*, 44 (1991), 429–75.

VINGE, LOUISE, 'Chapman's *Ovid's Banquet of Sence*', *JWCI* 38 (1975), 234–257.

—— *The Five Senses: Studies in a Literary Tradition* (Lund, 1975).

—— *The Narcissus Theme* (Lund, 1967).

VITALE, MAURIZIO (gen. ed.), *Antologia della letteratura italiana*, 5 vols. (Milan, 1965–8).

VITALINI, MIRELLA, 'A proposito della datazione dell'*Orfeo* del Poliziano', *GSLI* 146 (1969), 245–51.

VOGEL, EMIL, 'Claudio Monteverdi', *Vierteljahrsschrift für Musikwissenschaft*, 3 (1887), 315–450 [transcription of *Lamento d'Arianna* from Florence MS, pp. 443–50].

VOLKMANN, RICHARD, *Die Rhetorik der Griechen und Römer* (3rd edn.; Handbuch der Altertumswissenschaft, 2/3; Munich, 1901 [1st publ. 1874, 2nd edn., 1885]) [see also Martin, Josef].

WAGENSEIL, GEORG CHRISTOPH, *Euridice*, facs., ed. Erik Weimer (Italian Opera, 1640–1770, 75; New York, 1983).

WALKER, DANIEL PICKERING, *The Ancient Theology* (London, 1972).

—— 'Musical Humanism in the 16th and Early 17th Centuries', *MR* 2–3 (1941–2) in 5 instalments; German transl., *Der musikalische Humanismus* (Kassel, 1949); also repr. in *Music, Spirit and Language* (London, 1985).

—— *Music, Spirit and Language in the Renaissance*, ed. P. Gouk (Variorum Collected Studies Series, CS 212; London, 1985) [a collection of the author's publications from 1941 to 1984].

—— 'Orpheus the Theologian and Renaissance Platonists', *JWCI* 16 (1953), 100–20 = *Ancient Theology*, 22 ff.

—— 'The *Prisca Theologia* in France', *JWCI* 17 (1954), 204–59 = *Ancient Theology*, 63 ff.

—— *Spiritual and Demonic Magic from Ficino to Campanella* (Studies of the Warburg Institute, 22; London, 1958).

—— (ed.), *Musique des intermèdes de 'La Pellegrina'* (Les Fêtes du mariage de Ferdinand de Médicis et de Christine de Lorraine, i; Paris, 1963; repr. 1986).

WALKER, JOSEPH COOPER, *Memoirs of Alessandro Tassoni; Also an Appendix Containing Biographical Sketches of O. Rinuccini, G. Galilei, G. Chiabrera and B. Guarini* (London, 1815).

WALKER, THOMAS, 'Gli errori di *Minerva al tavolino*: osservazioni sulla cronologia delle prime opere veneziane', in Muraro (ed.), *Venezia e il melodramma nel Seicento*, 7–16.

WALLS, PETER, 'The Origins of English Recitative', *PRMA* 110 (1983–4), 25–40.

WARBURG, ABY, 'I costumi teatrali per gli intermezzi del 1589', in *Commemorazione della riforma melodrammatica* (Florence, 1895; repr. in *Gesammelte Schriften*, 1932, i. 259–300).

—— *Gesammelte Schriften*, 2 vols. (Leipzig, 1932) [on Bercheur see ii. 462, 627–8].

WARD, JOHN, 'The Morris Tune', *JAMS* 39 (1986), 294–331.

—— *Music for Elizabethan Lutes*, 2 vols. (Oxford, 1992).

WARDEN, JOHN (ed.), *Orpheus: The Metamorphoses of a Myth* (Toronto, 1982).

WEAVER, ROBERT L., 'The Orchestra in Early Italian Opera', *JAMS* 17 (1964), 83–9.

—— and WEAVER, NORMA W., *A Chronicle of Music in the Florentine Theatre, 1590–1750: Operas, Prologues, Finales, Intermezzos and Plays with Incidental Music* (Detroit Studies in Music Bibliography, 38; Detroit, 1978).

WEBSTER, JOHN, *Complete Works*, ed. Frank Laurence Lucas, 4 vols. (London, 1927; repr. Staten Island, NY, 1966) [on echo: ii. 195].

WECKERLIN, JEAN-BAPTISTE, *Balet Comique de la Royne [1581]* (Chefs-d'œuvre de l'opéra français; Paris, *c.*1881).

WEINBERG, BERNARD, *A History of Literary Criticism in the Italian Renaissance*, 2 vols. (Chicago, 1961).

—— (ed.), *Trattati di poetica e retorica del Cinquecento*, 4 vols. (Scrittori d'Italia, nos. 247, 248, 253, 258; Bari, 1970–4).

WEITZMANN, KURT (ed.), *Age of Spirituality: A Symposium* (New York, 1980).

WEST, MARTIN LITCHFIELD, *The Orphic Poems* (Oxford, 1983).

—— 'Tragica, vi', *Bulletin of the Institute of Classical Studies*, 30 (1983), 64–82 [on the treatment of the Orpheus plot in Aeschylus' *Lycurgeia*].

WESTRUP, JACK A., 'Monteverdi's *Lamento d'Arianna*', *MR* 1 (1940), 144–54.

—— *Purcell* (8th rev. edn., London, 1980 [1st publ. 1937]).

WHENHAM, JOHN, *Duet and Dialogue in the Age of Monteverdi*, 2 vols. (Studies in British Musicology, 7; Ann Arbor, Mich., 1982).

—— (ed.), *Claudio Monteverdi: Orfeo* (Cambridge Opera Handbooks; Cambridge, 1986).

WHITMAN, JON, *Allegory: The Dynamics of an Ancient and Medieval Technique* (Cambridge, Mass. and London, 1986).

WIESE, BERTHOLD VON, 'Eine Sammlung alter italienischer Drucke auf der Ratsschulbibliothek in Zwickau', *Zeitschrift für Romanische Philologie*, 31 (1907), 310–51.

WILKINS, ERNEST H., 'Descriptions of Pagan Divinities from Petrarch to Chaucer', *Speculum*, 32 (1957), 511–22.

—— *History of Italian Literature* (Cambridge, Mass., 1954).

WILLE, G., *Musica romana* (Amsterdam, 1967).

WILLIAMS, PETER F., 'Encounters with the Chromatic Fourth . . . or, More on Figurenlehre', *Musical Times*, 126 (1985), 276–8, 339–43.

—— 'Figurenlehre from Monteverdi to Wagner', *Musical Times*, 120 (1979), 476–9, 571–3, 648–50, 816–8.

WILPERT, J., *Die Malereien der Katakomben Roms* (Freiburg, 1903).

WISSOWA, GEORG (ed.), *Pauly's Real-Encyclopädie der classischen Altertumswissenschaft* (Stuttgart and Munich, 1893–).

WITTSCHIER, HEINZ WILLI, *Giannozzo Manetti: Das Corpus der Orationes* (Studi italiani, 10; Cologne, 1968).

WITZENMANN, WOLFGANG, 'Autographe Marco Marazzolis in der Biblioteca Vaticana', *AnMc* 7 (1968), 36–86; 9 (1970), 203–94.

—— 'D. Mazzocchi', *AnMc* 8 (1970).

—— 'Die römische Barockoper *La vita humana*', *AnMc* 15 (1975), 158–201.

WOLFF, H. C.,'Italian Opera from the later Monteverdi to Scarlatti', *New Oxford History of Music*, v (1975), 1–72.

—— 'Ovid's Metamorphosen und die frühe Oper', *Quadrivium*, 12/2 (1971), 89–107.

—— *Die Venezianischer Oper in der 2. Hälfte des 17. Jahrhunderts* (Berlin, 1937; repr. 1975).

WOODHOUSE, WILLIAM JOHN, *The Composition of Homer's Odyssey* (Oxford, 1930).

WORSTHORNE, S. T., *Venetian Opera in the 17th Century* (Oxford, 1954; 2nd edn., with suppl. bibl., 1968).

WOTQUENNE, A. (ed.), *Libretti d'opéras et d'oratorios italiens du XVIIe siècle* (Catalogue de la Bibliothèque du Conservatoire de Musique de Bruxelles, Annex 1; Brussels, 1901).

YATES, FRANCES A., *Astraea* (London, 1975), esp. pp. 29–30, 33, 67 *et passim*.

—— *The Valois Tapestries* (Studies of the Warburg Institute, 23; London, 1959).

ZAMBOTTI, BERNARDINO, *Diario ferrarese 1476–1504*, ed. Giuseppe Pardi (Rerum italicarum scriptores, rev. edn., xxiv, part 7; Bologna, 1934–7).

ZELM, KLAUS, *Die Opern Reinhard Keisers* (Munich and Salzburg, 1975).

ZIEGLER, KONRAT, 'Orpheus in Renaissance und Neuzeit', in *Form und Inhalt: Festschrift Otto Schmitt* (Stuttgart, 1951), 239–56.

—— (ed.), *Der Kleine Pauly*, 5 vols. (Munich, 1965–75; repr. 1978).

Index of Subjects

academy, academies 8, 16–23, 49, 54, 82, 110, 113, 120
acts and act-division 28, 33, 45–6, 58, 84–6, 96–7, 99–117 *passim*, 123, 125–6, 132
  see also finale; plot, shaping of; scenes and scene-division; time-division
Aeolian mode 173
allegory 7–16, 20, 88, 113, 116, 137–8, 142
  see also rebirth
anadiplosis 197–8, 205, 207–8, 211–12
anaphora 89, 141, 181–2, 197–8, 205, 207–8, 211, 216, 219, 223
apotheosis, *see* rebirth
aria 31, 131, 140–1, 160, 194, 196
  aria 34, 46, 91, 122
  arietta 43, 45
  arioso 41 n. 12, 141
  definition 42–3

ballet 28, 33, 58, 66, 100, 108–11, 116, 120–2, 124, 136
  in intermedi 46–7, 64, 67, 71, 81, 86–97
  see also choreography; moresca
bass 42–3, 160–6, 176, 183–4, 194
  motion of 35, 43, 160, 163, 166, 186
  ostinato 41 n. 12, 91, 168–73, 177–8, 184, 187, 189, 218
  see also basso continuo; tetrachord
basso continuo 40, 116

cantari 22–3
cast 96, 111, 124, 133
Catholic drama, *see* sacred or spiritual drama
choral finale 21, 24–9, 43, 55–9, 61, 64, 70–2, 81–96, 98, 102–3, 108–14, 116–23, 130–1, 140, 143, 195
choreography 74, 91–2, 108, 110, 116, 120–1
  see also ballet
chorus, music for 25, 43, 47, 58, 67, 79, 82, 96–7, 130, 132, 178, 208
  see also choral finale
chroma 182–3
chromaticism 136, 142, 173, 180–3
  see also tetrachord, chromatic
comedies 32–3, 45–6, 53–5, 59–76 *passim*, 83–4, 187
commedia dell'arte 101, 125
concertato:
  choral, *see* choral finale
  instrumental 135–6, 167
contrafactum, *see* parody

couples 24, 51, 58, 100, 104, 111, 119, 123–34, 139, 194
  duets 59, 110, 122–3, 130–1, 139, 175
  see also homoeroticism

dancing, *see* ballet
descent 9, 11, 16, 28, 49, 88, 118, 120, 148, 184, 186
  see also *katabasis*
deus ex machina 26, 48–9, 58, 111, 117–22, 129, 132–3, 139
dismemberment, *see* rebirth and dismemberment
dramatic structure, *see* plot, shaping of; time-dimension
duets, *see* couples

echo effects 6–7, 18, 43, 46, 54, 67, 76, 116, Ch. 7 *passim*
echo laments 1, 4, 6, 26, 141–3, 153–60, 164–5, 194, 198
echo settings (in chronological order):
  Euripides 1, 6, 197–8
  Aristophanes 6, 197–8
  Callimachus 197
  Virgil 18
  Ovid 4, 18, 58, 124, 211
  Greek Anthology 198–9
  Poliziano 199–200, 212
  Poliziano–Isaac 205
  ?Serafino 203, 205
  'Quae celebrat' 213
  Santa Uliva 67, 217, 225
  Erasmus 212
  Sermisy 222
  Joannes Secundus 212
  Striggio 219–20, 225
  Du Bellay 221
  Palestrina 224 n. 46
  Le Jeune 213
  Marenzio 220, 224–5
  Guarini 197
  Peri 7, 153, 159–60, 165, 205, 220, 225
  Shakespeare 7, 159, 179
  Pastor fido 197, 225
  Monte 197 n. 1, 225
  1599 intermedio 4, 225
  Cavalieri 43, 46, 116, 225
  Agazzari 197, 225
  Monteverdi 126, 164–5, 225
  Gagliano 220, 225
  Narciso 221, 225
  Walliser 224–5

echo settings (*cont.*):
  Webster 197
  Landi 225
  Cifra 218–19
  Campion 197, 212
  Mazzocchi 225
  Schütz 224–5
  M. Rossi 225
  Vittori 225
  Marazzoli 225
  Ferrari 225
  Cavalli 225
  Carissimi 224–5
  Mazzocchi 225
  L. Rossi 225
  Staden 42, 224–5
  Cavalli 225
  Marazzoli 225
  Legrenzi 225
  Gasparini 225
  Vivaldi 7, 159, 225
  Handel 159, 225
  Gluck 1, 58, 119, 194, 225
  Hugo 221
  Verdi 1, 194, 225
  Strauss 224–5
  Hardy 197
  Eliot 197
  see also Index of Names s.v. Echo; *Echo et Narcisse*; *Narciso*
ethos 8, 11, 19, 30, 88, 171
euoe 59 n. 15, 72

fabula satyrica 53–5, 60, 79, 85
figura 9, 16, 27, 142, 185
Figurenlehre, *see* rhetoric
finale 24–5, Chs. 3–4, 140, 143, 176, 194–5
  operatic 99–139
  problem of 48–64
  in sixteenth century 65–98
  see also choral finale; *fine tragico*; *lieto fine*; *Orfeo* (Monteverdi); *Orfeo* (Poliziano)
fine tragico 49–51, 121, 133
folia 168 n. 24, 169
frottola 216

Golden Age 66, 68, 71, 74–5, 90

harp 28, 135–8, 149, 152, 167
homoeroticism 18–21, 27, 147
  see also misogyny
homophony 80, 85, 91–2, 186, 209–10
  see also melismatic vs. syllabic setting

instruments, instrumental music 71–2, 80–9
  passim, 92, 97–8, 103, 108, 111, 113, 116, 120, 132, 135–6, 140, 147, 153, 164–75
  passim, 183–4, 187, 192–4
  concealed 55, 85

intermedi 2–4, 35, 58, 65–6, 96–7
  definition 32–3
  Faenza, 1526: 68–70, 86
  Ferrara, 1529: 80
  Florence, *c.*1525 (*Santa Uliva*) 66–7, 217–18
  Florence, 1539: 66, 70–4, 80, 86
  Florence, 1565: 33, 81, 219, 225
  Florence, 1589: 7, 43–7, 66, 83, 86–95, 103, 153, 205, 220, 225
  Florence, 1616: 2, 33
  Lyons, 1548: 65–6, 74–5
  Mantua, 1598: 97, 197, 225
  Milan, 1599: 4
  Naples, 1558: 74–5

katabasis 9, 11, 15, 29
  see also descent

lament 5–7, 18–22, 25–6, 48, 54, 58–9, Ch. 6 *passim*, 207–9, 217–18
  function and vocabulary 140–4
  in Monteverdi 140–3, 164–83
  as 'number' 193–6
  in Peri 152–64
  in Poliziano's *Orfeo* 143–52
  see also echo laments; *Lamento d'Arianna*; *Lamento della ninfa*; 'Pianto della Madonna'
libretto, librettist 14, 21, 26, 28, 31–7, 141–2
  see also acts and act-division; finale; *fine tragico*; *lieto fine*; lines, number of; plot, shaping of; scenes and scene-division; time-dimension
licenza 27–8, 48–9, 86, 102, 120, 131
lieto fine vii–viii, 17–28 *passim*, 48–67 *passim*, 77, 79, 84, 86, 89, 98, 104, 110, 113, 118–24, 131–43 *passim*, 163, 176, 178, 187, 194–6
lines, number of 10, 20–8 *passim*, 46, 55–8, 82, 85, 110, 145, 178–81
  see also plot, shaping of; time-dimension

masquerades 32
melismatic vs. syllabic writing 89, 103, 120, 123, 160, 166, 170
  see also homophony
misogyny 17–30 *passim*, 133, 147, 165
  see also homoeroticism
modes, *see* Aeolian; Phrygian
monody, monodic style 31–47, 145, 178, 181, 186, 205
  definition 34–5
  see also *recitar cantando*; *stile monodico*; *stile rappresentativo*; *stile recitativo*
moresca 64, 72, 77 n. 22, 80, 98, 111–13

Neoplatonism 13–16, 20, 27, 113, 119, 133
Night 68, 71, 74–5
numbers, arias or laments as 14, 21, 43, 60, 71, 75, 80, 82, 123–5, 130, 145–6, 193–6, 216
obbligato 135, 165, 167–8, 171

occasional music 24, 49, 50, 119–21, 128–31, 139
  see also intermedi
ombra 128, 187
oratorio 32
overture 87

palillogia 141, 197, 203, 213, 220, 223
parody 179, 210
paronomasia 197–8, 200, 222
parlar cantando, see words and music
passamezzo antico 169–71, 175
pastoral, pastoral settings 4, 17, 32–3, 42, 53, 55,
    59–65 *passim*, 75–82, 84, 88–90, 95–8,
    111, 135, 197, 205, 223, 226
Phrygian mode 172–3
plot, shaping of 48–55, 124–33, 136
  in Poliziano 58–9
  see also lines, number of; time-dimension
polyphony:
    two parts 82, 112
    three parts 82, 88, 92–3, 103, 108, 112, 149,
      172
    four parts 70, 72, 116, 186, 211
    five parts 27, 70, 72, 82, 88, 92–3, 108, 111–12,
      116, 179, 186
    six parts 70, 82–3, 85, 88
    seven parts 140
    eight parts 70, 81, 116–17, 120
    more than eight parts 70, 87–90, 92, 213
preghiera 37, 145–6, 165
prologue 48, 54, 168, 172–3

rebirth and dismemberment 15, 20, 27–9, 49,
    55, 64, 117–19, 128–9, 132–9, 152
recitar cantando 35–9
  see also monody
recitative, vs. aria 31, 42, 57, 102, 110, 113, 123,
    136, 140–1, 187, 189
  see also *stile recitativo*
refrain 21, 55, 61, 71, 97, 108–9, 112, 120, 171–4,
    194
  see also ritornello
repetition 18, 71, 74, 104, 120, 143–4, 146, 149, 153,
    161, 163, 171, 174–89 *passim*, Ch. 7 *passim*
  in poetry 197–226
  see also anadiplosis; anaphora; echo;
    palillogia; paronomasia
rhetoric 63, 89, 161, 193, 197, 207, 226
rhetorical terms, *see* anadiplosis; anaphora;
    palillogia; paronomasia
Rhétoriqueurs 222
rhyme 60
rifacimento 20–3, 56, 79, 147
ritornello 24, 42, 74, 95, 103, 108, 110–11, 116–17,
    121
  see also refrain
romanesca 169, 175
ruggiero 168 n. 24, 218

sacra rappresentazione 66, 217
  see also *Santa Uliva*
sacred or spiritual drama 3, 9, 32, 224
  see also *Andromeda* (Walliser); *Eumelio*;
      Sant'Alessio; *Rappresentazione di anima e di corpo*
satyrs 54, 59, 64, 66, 71, 79, 80
scenes and scene-division 100, 102, 108
  see also acts and act-division
shepherds 53, 63, 68, 76–7, 79, 89–91, 96–7,
    111, 114, 120, 201
singers 89, 152, 160, 178
  primary and secondary roles 124–5, 129,
    132
  secondary roles 128–31
solo, soloist 25, 27, 33–4, 42, 44, 46, 55, 68, 71–
    2, 80, 82–3, 87–9, 102–3, 108, 110, 116,
    120–1, 123, 130, 132, 135–6, 140, 159–61,
    172, 176–9, 194–6
sonority 21, 24, 44, 48, 55–6, 82, 87, 71–2, 84–
    6, 92, 102–3, 108, 110, 116, 120, 123, 132,
    135, 137, 140, 172, 194, 222
stagecraft 117
stanza 42, 153, 163, 195
  in Cavalieri 92, 108, 116
  in Cavalli 187, 189, 194
  in Gagliano 24, 102–4
  in Monteverdi 25–7, 111–14, 164
  in Peri 24, 104–5, 109–10, 161
  poetic 200–1, 216, 218
  in Poliziano 21–3, 55–6, 61, 146–7
  see also *Lamento della ninfa*; 'Possente spirto'
stile monodico 38, 41
  see also monody
stile rappresentativo 3, 26, 38–43, 77, 172–3
  see also monody
stile recitativo 35, 38–46, 160, 167, 178, 186, 193, 224
  see also monody
strings 19, 30, 135–7
strophic forms, *see* stanza
syllabic, *see* melismatic vs. syllabic writing

tambourines 55, 92
tetrachord 171 n. 27, 175–6, 183–93
  ascending diatonic 152
  descending diatonic 147–9, 152, 171, 175–7
  ascending chromatic 176, 183, 185, 187, 192, 193
  descending chromatic 148, 167, 176, 183–93
    passim
theatre 32, 46, 48, 52, 66–7, 69, 80, 82, 102,
    116, 118, 125, 147, 224
time signatures 24, 74, 93–4, 103, 108, 110, 113,
    187
time-dimension 10–11, 16–17, 33, 44, 64, 69–71,
    75, 83, 84 n. 31, 86–7, 96, 102, 111–12,
    152, 171, 174, 179, 181, 193, 195, 197
  and Poliziano 55–8
  see also lines, number of; plot, shaping of
tragédie lyrique 125–6, 132

tragedy 24, 34, 49–54, 58–60, 64–7, 76, 79, 80, 83–6, 89, 118, 121, 133, 143, 153, 184, 194, 196, 208
tragicomedy 53–5, 59–60, 79, 83

verse-types 60
  blank 60
  endecasillabi 23, 60, 63, 72, 93, 97, 113, 117, 120 n. 23, 123, 141 n. 3, 200
  in Poliziano 59–64
  other types 60–1
  ottava rima 21–3, 42, 63, 71, 146–7, 186, 200, 205, 218–19
  ottonario 21, 24, 46, 60–3, 72, 90, 92, 97, 102–3, 109–17 *passim*, 120 n. 23, 123–4; examples of melodies for 73
  quaternario 60, 102
  quinario 46, 97, 200–1

senario 123
settenario 46, 60, 72, 92–3, 97, 109, 117, 123–4, 171
sdrucciolo 45–6, 60–4, 72, 92, 165, 201
terza rima 166, 168
tronchi 61
versi toscani 60–1, 69, 71–2, 80, 93, 102–3, 109, 113–17, 153, 161
variations 170–1
  over a bass 168

words and music 31–46, 49, 54–7, 68, 76–7, 80–3, 84 n. 31, 89, 91, 96–7, 104, 134, 146, 153, 160, 171, 173, 179, 182–3, 207, 216, 219
  Greek drama 31
  parlar cantando 35–8
  see also *recitar cantando*

Index of Names, Titles, and First Lines

'A Dio Roma' (Monteverdi, *Poppea*) 141–3
'A Dio terra' (Monteverdi, *Orfeo*) 142
Adone (Manelli) 7, 127
Adonis 8, 10, 185
Agazzari, Agostino:
  on recitative 40
  see also *Eumelio*
Agnelli, Scipione, see *Nozze di Tetide*
Agostini, Lodovico 213
'Ah, ah, questo, questo' (Cavalli, *Ormindo*) 176–7
Aida (Verdi) 143, 166
Alberti, Leon Battista 52–3
'Al canto, al ballo, all'ombre, al prato adorno'
  (Peri, *Euridice*) 109
Alceste (Gluck) 121, 131–2, 196
Alceste (Lully) 120–1, 131–2
'Alcun non sia che disperato in preda'
  (Monteverdi, *Orfeo*) 112
Alessandro (Piccolomini) 75
Algarotti, Francesco 25, 133
'Almo dio ch'il carro ardente' (Gagliano, *Dafne*)
  103
Ambra, Francesco d', see *Cofanaria*; *Furto*
Ameto (Boccaccio) 77
Aminta (Tasso) 33, 77–8, 81–2, 96
Amori d'Apollo e di Dafne (Cavalli) 123, 125, 127
Amphion 8, 9
Andromeda 6, 7, 65, 198, 226
Andromeda (Manelli) 127
Andromeda (Walliser) 224–5
Anerio, Felice 213
Anima del filosofo ossia Orfeo ed Euridice, L' (Haydn)
  128–36 *passim*
Anima e corpo, see *Rappresentazione di anima e di corpo*
Anne of Brittany 209
Antonio dal Cornetto 79
Apollo 3, 6, 8, 9, 19–30 *passim*, 49, 65, 71, 74–5,
  89, 101, 104, 108, 110, 113, 117–21, 125,
  133, 137, 139, 143, 220, 223
Apollo e Dafne (Cavalli), see *Amori d'Apollo e di
  Dafne*
Apollon musagète (Stravinsky) 71, 137
Arcadia (Sannazaro) 77–8, 185
Aretusa, L' (Lollio) 80
Argenti, A., see *Sfortunato*
Aria del Granduca 91
Aria di Firenze 91–2
'Aria di Ruggiero' (Cifra) 218
Ariadne 5–7, 10, 34, 37, 49, 54, 59, 65, 124,
  176–83
Ariadne auf Naxos (Strauss) 183, 224–5

Arianna (Monteverdi) 24, 26, 34, 36, 40, 44, 54,
  57, 85, 99–100, 102, 110, 117, 127, 177, 183
  finale 28, 114
  see also *Lamento d'Arianna*
Arianna (Rinuccini) 24, 34, 49, 86, 99–100, 102,
  127, 140, 177–8, 180–3
Arion 1, 7–9, 153, 159, 226
Ariosto, Lodovico, see *Orlando furioso*
Aristaeus 129–31, 133, 145
Aristophanes 6
Aristotle 51–2, 84, 101, 117 n. 21, 125, 198
Armenia (Visconti) 4, 225
Ars poetica (Horace) 52, 101, 110, 125
Arteaga, Esteban de 25, 133–4, 177
Artemisia (Cavalli) 225
Ashbery, John 128, 137
Atlas, Allan 210
Auerbach, Erich 9
Aureli, Aurelio 2, 128–9, 132
Auric, see *Orphée*
Aurora ingannata (Giacobbi) 39

Bacchus 15, 49, 55, 61, 66, 71–2, 79, 85, 89, 113,
  128
Baccio, see Ugolini
'Bacco, bacco' (Corteccia) 72, 73 (ex.), 74, 80
'Ballo dell'ingrate' (Monteverdi) 172
Bach, Johann Sebastian, see B minor Mass
Banchieri, Adriano 91
Banister, John (d. 1679) 224
Bardi, Giovanni 40, 88
Bardi, Pietro 40, 43
Bargagli, Girolamo, see *Pellegrina*
Bati, Luca 99
Beccari, Agostino, see *Sacrificio*
Beethoven, *see* Fourth Piano Concerto; Ninth
  Symphony; Pastoral Symphony
'Bella ninfa fuggitiva' (Gagliano, *Dafne*) 103–4
Belli, Domenico, see *Orfeo*
Bembo, Pietro 208, 216
'Ben venga maggio' (Poliziano) 201
Berg, Alban 59
Berlioz, Hector 135–6, 196
  see also *Mort d'Orphée*; *Troyens*
Bibbiena, Cardinal (Bernardo Dovizi) 65, 75
'Biondo arcier che d'alto monte' (Peri, *Euridice*) 109
Birtwistle, Harrison, see *Mask of Orpheus*
Blackburn, Bonnie ix
Blow, John 192
  see also *Venus and Adonis*

B minor Mass (Bach) 184
Boccaccio 21, 66, 77–8
Boethius 8, 13
Bonini, Severino 39–40
  see also *Lamento d'Arianna*
Boyé, – 196
Boyleau, Simon 216
Braunschweig 2
Bressand, Friedrich Christian 2
Brognonico, Orazio 96
Brown, Howard Mayer 24, 29, 100
Brunelli, Antonio, see *Lamento della ninfa*
Brunswick 2
Buchner, August 2
Burney, Charles 185
Busenello, Gian Francesco 100, 125, 127, 141
Buti, Francesco 2

Caccini, Giulio 29, 35, 38–44, 46, 75, 87, 89,
  102, 153, 160, 164
  see also *Cefalo; Euridice; Nuove musiche*
Cadmus 120
'Calami sonum ferentes' (Rore) 185
Calandria (Bibbiena) 65, 75, 80
Caldara, Antonio 126
Calderón de la Barca, Pedro 2, 3
Callimachus 197–8
Calzabigi, Raniero de' 3, 25, 58, 121, 128, 131–2,
  223
Cambio, Perissone 213
Campion, Thomas 4, 192, 212
'Canti ogn'un ch'io canterò' (Poliziano) 201–3
'Care selve beate' (Guarini; Agazzari) 197, 225
Carissimi, Giacomo, see *Jephte*
Carnaval des animaux (Saint-Saëns) 136
Caroso, Fabrizio 72, 91
Carter, Elliott, see *Syringa*
Carter, Tim ix, 29
Casentini, Marsilio 96
Cassandra 189–92
Castiglione, Baldassare, see *Tirsi*
Catalani, Ottavio, see *David musicus*
Catena d'Adone (D. Mazzocchi) 39, 127, 225
Cavalieri, Emilio 38–47, 96, 108, 226
  see also Aria di Firenze; 'O che nuovo
    miracolo'; *Rappresentazione di anima e di corpo*
Cavalli, Francesco 4, 33, 43, 49, 122, 148, 153,
  164, 185–7
  see also *Amori d'Apollo e di Dafne; Artemisia;
    Didone; Egisto; Ercole amante; Giulio Cesare;
    Nozze di Teti; Ormindo; Rosinda*
'Cease, sorrows, now' (Weelkes) 192
Cefalo (Caccini) 62, 99, 113 n. 15, 127, 166
Cefalo (Chiabrera) 99 n. 1, 113–14, 117, 127
Cefalo (Niccolò da Correggio) 58, 78–9, 86, 119
Cervantes Saavedra, Miguel de 77, 78
Chapoton, Sieur de 2
Charpentier, Marc-Antoine 2

'Che fai tu, Ecco' (Poliziano) 199, 213 n. 27
'Che farò senza Euridice' (Gluck, *Orfeo*) 195
Chiabrera, Gabriello 2, 21, 33, 61–2, 166
  see also *Cefalo; Galatea; Orfeo dolente*
'Chi ne consola ahi lassi' (Monteverdi, *Orfeo*) 112
'Chi non fa prova' (Verdelot) 69
'Chi se' tu che rispondi?' (Monte) 225
Chi soffre speri (Marazzoli and V. Mazzocchi) 225
Cifra, Antonio 218
Cini, G. B. 219
Cinthio (G. B. Giraldi), 81
  see also *Egle; Orbecche*
Clark, Raymond 15
Climene 189
Clizia, La (Machiavelli) 68–70
Cocteau, Jean 1
  see also *Orphée*
Cofanaria, La (Ambra) 74, 219
Colloquia (Erasmus) 211
'Combattimento di Tancredi e Clorinda'
  (Monteverdi) 172
Commodo, Il (Landi) 70
'Construe my meaning' (Farnaby) 192
Contarino, Pietro 199
Corsi, Jacopo 103–5
Corteccia, Francesco 70–5 *passim*, 80–3
  see also Index of Subjects under intermedi,
    Florence, 1539
Così fan tutte (Mozart) 137
'Crucifixus' (Monteverdi) 186
Curtis, Alan 122
Curtius, Ernst 11
Cyclops (Euripides) 54

Dafne (Gagliano) 24, 28, 99, 102–4, 106–7 (ex.),
  108, 220, 223, 225
Dafne (Peri) 29, 33, 57, 65, 79, 99, 101–2, 113,
  116, 127, 225
  Corsi's numbers for 103–4, 105 (ex.)
Dafne (Rinuccini) 3, 24, 57–8, 99, 100–5, 114,
  127, 220–5
Dafne (Schütz) 127, 224–5
Dalla Viola, Alfonso 80, 83
'Dal vago e bel sereno' (Cavalieri) 88
D'Ancona, Alessandro 67
Daniello, Bernardino, see *Poetica*
Dante 13
  on allegory 11
  see also *Divina Commedia*
Daphne 6, 10, 104, 123–5
David musicus (Catalani) 127
Dazzi, Andrea 209
Debussy, Claude, see *Pelléas et Mélisande*
De Cupis, – 2, 99, 127
Delia (Manelli) 127
Della Palla, Scipione 75
Dent, Edward J. 14–15, 27
Diana (Montemayor) 77–8

Dido 193
Dido and Aeneas (Purcell) 5, 183-4, 189-90 (ex.), 192
'Dido, chi giace' (Palestrina) 224 n. 46
Didone (Cavalli) 5-6, 127, 189-91 (ex.), 192
'Dieu gard ma Maistresse et Regente': (Claudin) 222; (Marot) 222
D'India, Sigismondo 39
Dittersdorf, Carl Ditters von, see *Orpheus der Zweite*
Divina Commedia (Dante) 9, 166
Donato, Baldassare 213
Don Giovanni (Mozart) vii, 50, 52, 59, 148, 173, 184, 195
Doni, G. B. 29, 35-6, 40-7, 123, 177, 226
    criticism of Cavalieri's music 43-7
Dorat, Jean 13
Dowland, John 192
Draghi, Antonio 2, 132
Dresden 2
Du Bellay, Joachim 221-3
Duboullay, Michel 2
Duchess of Malfi (Webster) 197
Dunning, Albert 210
'Dunque fra torbide onde' (Peri) 153-60 (ex.), 165, 168 n. 24, 221 n. 40, 225
'Dunque piangiamo, o sconsolata lira' (Poliziano) 146
D'Urfé, Honoré 77-8

'Ebra di sangue': (Gagliano) 220, 223, 225; (Marenzio) 221, 225; (Peri) 220, 225
Echo 1, 6, 10, 165, Ch. 7 *passim*
Echo et Narcisse (Gluck) 58, 119, 225
Eclogues (Virgil) 76-7, 80
Edipo tiranno (A. Gabrieli) 58, 82-6, 88, 89
Egisto (Cavalli) 130 n. 33, 189-90 (ex.)
Egle (Cinthio) 77-9
'E la virtute un raggio' (Monteverdi, *Orfeo*) 112
Elegiae (Campion) 212
Eliade, Mircea 15
Eliot, T. S. 197
Engel, Hans 212
Entführung aus dem Serail, Die (Mozart) 64
Erasmus 211
Ercole amante (Cavalli) 123
Erminia (M. Rossi) 127, 225
Este, Alfonso II d' 185
Eumelio (Agazzari) 2, 3, 27-9, 32, 39-40, 44, 99, 101, 115-17, 120, 127, 197, 225
Euridice (Caccini) 2, 3, 99, 168
Euridice (Peri) viii, 2-4, 16, 19, 23-44 *passim*, 49, 54, 57-8, 62, 65, 79, 93-4, 102-3, 108-11, 116-33 *passim*, 143, 160-4, 168, 172-3, 194, 223
    finale 29, 94 (ex.), 112-17 *passim*, 130, 134, 136
    ritornello 74
Euridice (Rinuccini) 8, 24-5, 54, 57-8, 99-104, 111, 113-14, 124, 127, 131-4, 140, 144, 223
Euridice (Wagenseil) 14, 128-32

Euripides 6, 8, 34, 54, 59, 64, 119, 132, 149, 185, 197-8, 208, 224
Eurydice 3, 5, 8, 13-26 *passim*, 54, 96, 100, 125, 128-45 *passim*, 149, 161, 164-5, 167, 185, 196
'Evohè, padre Lieo' (Monteverdi, *Orfeo*) 112

Fabula di Orpheo (Poliziano), see *Orfeo*
Falstaff (Verdi) 9, 59, 195
Fasolo, Il 175
Faustini, Giovanni 123, 176
Ferrara 4, 58, 65, 77-80, 82, 98, 185
Ferrari, Benedetto 122 n. 25, 175 n. 31
    see also *Maga fulminata*; *Pastor regio*
Festa, Costanzo 70, 86
    see also 'Qual sarà mai'
Finta pazza, La (Sacrati) 127
Fletcher, John 78
Fliegende Holländer, Der (Wagner) 50
Florence 2, 17, 31, 33, 40-1, 44-7, 54-5, 62, 65-70 *passim*, 74-5, 86, 91, 93, 98-9, 104, 123, 217
Follino, Federico 177-8
'Follow thy fair sun, unhappy shadow' (Campion) 192
'Forlorn Hope Fancy' (Dowland) 192
'Fortunato semideo' (Landi, *Morte d'Orfeo*) 114
Fourth Piano Concerto (Beethoven) 135
Frescobaldi, Girolamo 91
Frigimelica-Roberti, Girolamo 126
'Fuggi speme mia' (Striggio) 219-20 (ex.), 225
Furto, Il (Ambra) 74
Furtwängler, Wilhelm 51-2, 54
Fux, Johann Joseph, see *Orfeo ed Euridice*

Gabrieli, Andrea 213
    see also *Edipo tiranno*
Gagliano, Marco da 36-41 *passim*
    see also *Dafne*
Galatea (Chiabrera) 114
Galatea (Vittori) 225
Gasparini, F. 126
    see also *Tiberio*
Gastoldi, Gian Giacomo 96
Gauradas 199-200
Georgics (Virgil) 18, 76, 143
Gerusalemme liberata (Tasso) 186
Ghizzolo, Giovanni 96
Giacobbi, Girolamo, see *Aurora ingannata*
Giambullari, Pietro Francesco 71
Gibbons, Orlando 192
Giraldi, G. B., see Cinthio
Giulio Cesare (Cavalli?) 127
Giustino (Handel) 159, 225
Giustino (Legrenzi) 225
Giustino (Vivaldi) 7, 159, 225
Gluck, Christoph Willibald 6, 76, 120, 122
    see also *Alceste*; *Echo et Narcisse*; *Iphigénie en Aulide*; *Iphigénie en Tauride*; *Orfeo*

'Godi turba mortal' (Cavalieri) 88–9
Goethe 16
Goodson, Richard, see *Orpheus*
Götterdämmerung (Wagner) 51
Greek Anthology 198
Greene, Robert 17
'Gridan vostri occhi' 205–6 (ex.), 223
Groto, Luigi 216
Guarini, G. B. 63 n. 22
    see also *Pastor fido*
Guiniggi, Vincenzo 209

Hamlet (Shakespeare) 59
Handel, George Frideric 132
    see also *Giustino*
Hanning, Barbara Russano 29, 100
Hardy, Thomas 197
Hasse, Johann Adolf 194
Hassler, Hans Leo 213
Hastings, James 15
Haydn, Joseph, see *Anima del filosofo*
'Heaven and earth' (Wyatt) 143
Hecuba 189
Hercules Oetaeus (Seneca) 208
Heroides (Ovid) ix, 183, 211
    musical settings based on 6–7
Hidalgo, Juan 2
Hill, John W. 91
Hofmannsthal, Hugo von vii, 36, 49, 59, 183,
    196, 224
Homer 9, 66, 198
Horace, see *Ars poetica*
Hugo, Victor 221
Hyginus 1, 19–20, 134

Idylls (Theocritus) 76–7
Ingegneri, Angelo 85
Innocenza difesa (V. Mazzocchi) 225
'Io che d'altri sospiri' (Peri, *Euridice*) 41 n. 12
'Io non l'ho perchè non l'ho' (Chiabrera?) 61 n. 17
Iphigénie en Aulide (Gluck) 121
Iphigénie en Tauride (Gluck) 121
Isaac, Heinrich 199–200
    see also *Missa Salva nos*; 'Quis dabit capiti
    meo'; 'Quis dabit pacem'

Janequin, Clément 223
Jason 65
Jephte (Carissimi) 224–5
Jonson, Ben 38, 42
    see also *Sad Shepherd*
Josquin des Prez 211
Julius Caesar (Shakespeare) 64
Just, Martin 210

Kapsberger, Johann, see *Lamento della ninfa* ·
Keiser, Reinhard, see *Orpheus*
Kroyer, Theodor 185, 212

Lamento d'Arianna (Bonini) 39–40
Lamento d'Arianna (Monteverdi) 6, 27, 34, 37–42
    passim, 49, 140, 177–83 (ex.)
Lamento d'Arianna (Rinuccini) 40, 171, 174, 183 n. 44
Lamento della ninfa (Brunelli) 173
Lamento della ninfa (Kapsberger) 173, 174 n. 30
Lamento della ninfa (Monteverdi) 33, 86, 173–5,
    183, 186–7
Lamento della ninfa (Piazza) 173
'Lamento di Madama Lucia' (Il Fasolo or
    Manelli) 175
Landi, Antonio, see *Commodo*
Landi, Stefano 2, 3
    see also *Morte d'Orfeo*; *Sant'Alessio*
Landini, Francesco 1
'La pastorella se leva per tempo' 200–3 (ex.), 205
'Lasciatemi morire', see *Lamento d'Arianna*
    (Monteverdi)
'Là tra 'l sangu'e le morti' (Monteverdi) 185
'Laura suave' 72, 74 (ex.), 91
Layolle, Francesco 147–8
Legrenzi, Giovanni, see *Giustino*
Le Jeune, Claude, see 'Quae celebrat Thermas
    Echo'
Leopold, Silke 133
Liszt, Franz, see *Orpheus*
Locke, Matthew , see *Orpheus*
Loewe, Johann Jacob, see *Orpheus*
Lollio, A. 80
London 2, 4, 78, 87, 95, 128, 132
Love's Labour's Lost (Shakespeare) 16, 81–2
Lowinsky, Edward E. 185
Lucchesini de' Guidiccioni, Laura 91
Lully, Jean-Baptiste 2, 5, 33, 49, 122, 125–6
    see also *Alceste*
Lully, Louis, see *Orphée*

Lulu (Berg) 59
Luzzaschi, Luzzasco 96
Lyons 65–6, 74–5, 87

Machiavelli, Niccolò 67–9, 86
    see also *Clizia*; *Mandragola*
Madrid 2
Maga fulminata, La (Ferrari) 127
Malipiero, Gian Francesco 178–81
Mandragola, La (Machiavelli) 68–71
Manelli, Francesco, see *Adone*; *Delia*; 'Lamento di
    Madama Lucia'
Mantua 2, 4, 24–5, 31, 34, 41, 78, 80, 91, 97–9,
    111, 123, 178
Manucci, Piero 65
Marazzoli, Marco, see *Chi soffre speri*; *Vita humana*
Marenzio, Luca 221, 225
    see also 'Solo e pensoso'
Marot, Clément 222
Mask of Orpheus (Birtwistle) 128
Mask of Time (Tippett) 16, 128, 138

Mazzocchi, Domenico 31, 41
  see also *Catena d'Adone*
Mazzocchi, Virgilio, see *Chi soffre speri; Innocenza difesa*
Medea 6
Medici, Lorenzo de' 61, 63, 147, 205–9, 211
Mei, Girolamo 88
Menander 101 n. 6
Merchant of Venice (Shakespeare) 68
Metamorphoses (Ovid) 1–11 *passim*, 18, 65–6, 211–13, 217
Metastasio, Pietro 126, 132, 134, 195
Midsummer Night's Dream (Shakespeare) 17, 125
Milan 2, 4, 65, 209
Milton, John 51, 224 n. 48
Minato, Niccolò 2
Miscellanea (Poliziano) 199–200
Missa Salva nos (Isaac) 210
Molinet, Jean 222
Momigny, Jérome-Joseph de 193
Monte, Philippe de 225
Montemayor, Jorge de, see *Diana*
Monteverdi, Claudio 1–4, 16–60 *passim*, 64, 74, 80, 86, 88, 96, 100–45 *passim*, 153, 160, 164–87 *passim*, 198, 211 n. 21, 213, 225–6
  madrigals 39, 185
  see also *Arianna*; 'Ballo dell'ingrate';
    'Combattimento di Tancredi e Clorinda';
    'Crucifixus'; *Lamento d'Arianna*; *Lamento della Ninfa*; *Nozze d'Enea*; *Nozze di Tetide*;
    Orfeo; 'Pianto della Madonna'; *Poppea*;
    Ritorno d'Ulisse; *Selva morale*
Mort d'Orphée (Berlioz) 128, 135
Morte d'Orfeo (Landi) 27, 28, 33, 113–15 (ex.), 127–30, 134
Mozart, Wolfgang Amadeus 76, 79, 121, 136, 141, 160, 196, 226
  see also *Così fan tutte*; *Don Giovanni*; *Entführung aus dem Serail*; *Nozze di Figaro*; String Quartet in D minor; *Zauberflöte*

Naples 70, 74–5, 122
Narciso (Rinuccini) 28, 221, 225
Narcissus 6, 54, 58, 65, 67, 211, 213, 217–18, 221
'Nel pur ardor' (Peri, *Euridice*) 42
Niccolò da Correggio, see *Cefalo*
Nietzsche, Friedrich vii, 54 n. 10
Ninth Symphony (Beethoven) 184
'Non piango e non sospiro' (Peri, *Euridice*) 54, 160–4 (ex.), 172–3, 194
'Non si nasconde in selva' (Gagliano, *Dafne*) 103
Nozze d'Enea, Le (Monteverdi) 127
Nozze di Figaro, Le (Mozart) 140
Nozze di Teti, Le (Cavalli) 127
Nozze di Tetide, Le (Agnelli) 35
Nozze di Tetide, Le (Monteverdi) 35
'Nud'arcier chi l'arco tendi' (Gagliano, *Dafne*) 103

'Nulla impresa per huom si tenta in vano' (Monteverdi, *Orfeo*) 112
Nuove musiche (Caccini) 36, 39–40
'Nymphes des bois' (Josquin) 211

'O che nuovo miracolo' (Cavalieri) 72–3 (ex.), 87–93 (ex.), 94–5
'O dolce notte' (Verdelot) 68–9, 71, 74, 80
Offenbach, Jacques, see *Orphée*
'O fortunato giorno' (Cavalieri) 88
'Ohimè il bel viso' (Monteverdi) 198
'O qual resplende nube' (Cavalieri) 88
Orbecche (Cinthio) 80
'O regnator di tutte quelle genti' (Poliziano) 146
Orestes (Euripides) 198, 209
Orfeo (anonymous settings) 2
Orfeo (Belli) 2–3, 33
Orfeo (Gluck) vii, 1, 3, 14, 16, 19, 23, 25, 27, 49, 128, 131–2, 134–7, 194–6, 225
Orfeo (Monteverdi) vii, 2, 3, 8, 16–43 *passim*, 53–8 *passim*, 99–100, 110–18, 127, 130 n. 33, 142–3 (ex.), 164, 176, 184, 194, 221 n. 40
  Apollo finale 20, 25, 29, 49, 55, 57, 80, 111, 115 (ex.), 121, 124, 128, 133–4, 138, 152, 165
  Bacchic finale 25, 120, 124
Orfeo (Poliziano) 4, 9, 14–23 *passim*, 27, 57, 63–5, 78–9, 96, 125, 143–52, 163
  dating 56
  finale 24, 55–64 *passim*, 72, 80, 86, 102, 113
  libretto 58
Orfeo (L. Rossi) 2, 125, 128–9, 130 n. 33, 134
Orfeo (Sartorio) 2, 128
Orfeo dolente (Chiabrera) 114
Orfeo ed Euridice (Fux) 14, 128–32
Orlando furioso (Ariosto) 42, 168, 218
Ormindo (Cavalli) 123, 175–7, 186–9 (ex.)
Orphée (Auric and Cocteau) 3, 128, 137
Orphée (L. Lully) 2
Orphée (Offenbach) 3, 14, 128, 136
Orpheus 1–30
  act-division 100
  allegorical interpretation 8–16, 88, 142, 185
  compared with Sethos 15
  descent 9, 11, 13, 15
  intermedi 2, 33
  lament 143, 145–9, 161, 164–8, 194–5
  musical settings of legend, see *Anima del filosofo*;
    Eumelio; *Mort d'Orphée*; *Morte d'Orfeo*; *Orfeo*;
    Orfeo dolente; *Orfeo ed Euridice*; *Orphée*; *Orpheus*
  plot 37, 54, 64, 104, 110, 124–5, 128–39
  rebirth 9, 18–19, 49, 111, 117–18, 152
Orpheus, treatments of myth (in chronological order):
  Euripides 1, 8
  Phanocles 18–19
  Virgil 1–9, 18–21, 125, 132, 143
  Ovid 1–11, 17–21, *et passim*
  Hyginus 19–20, 134

Orpheus, treatments of myth (*cont.*)
  Boethius 8, 13
  Dante 9, 11, 13
  Ovide moralisé, 9, 11–13
  Poliziano 4–27, 54–64, *et passim*
  Ronsard 13
  Schiaffinati 2, 4
  Peri 2–29, 39, *et passim*
  Agazzari 2–3, 9, 27–9, 32, *et passim*
  Monteverdi *passim*
  Belli 2, 33
  Landi 2–3, 27–8, *et passim*
  Calderón 2, 3
  Schütz 2
  Chapoton 2
  L. Rossi 2, 125–34 *passim*
  Loewe 2
  Sartorio 2, 128
  Goodson 2
  Keiser 2, 128–9, 134
  Fux 14, 128, 130–1
  Wagenseil 14, 128
  Gluck 1, 3, 25, 27, 49, 128–32, 195–6, 225
  Haydn 128, 132
  Berlioz 128, 135
  Offenbach 3, 14, 128
  Cocteau 1–3, 128, 137
  Stravinsky 28, 49, 128, 137, 149, 152
  Carter 128, 135, 138
  Tippett 16, 128, 135, 138
  Birtwistle 1, 8, 128
Orpheus (Goodson and Weldon) 2
Orpheus (Keiser) 2, 128–9, 134
Orpheus (Liszt) 3
Orpheus (Locke) 2, 224
Orpheus (Loewe) 2
Orpheus (Schütz) 2
Orpheus (Stravinsky) 20, 28, 49–50, 118, 128, 135–9, 149, 152 (ex.)
Orpheus der Zweite (Dittersdorf) 14
Osthoff, Wolfgang ix, x, 4, 29, 56, 69, 71, 79, 80, 113, 122, 210
Otello (Rossini) 50
Otello (Verdi) 50, 194–5, 225
Othello (Shakespeare) 79, 194
Ovid 3–11, 17–21, 27, 33, 58, 80, 104, 118, 132, 134, 185
  musical settings based on 5
  see also *Heroides*; *Metamorphoses*
Ovide moralisé 9–13
Ovidius moralizatus 9, 13
Oxford 2

Palazzo incantato, Il (L. Rossi) 225
Palestrina, Giovanni Pierluigi da 224 n. 46
Panofsky, Erwin viii
Paris 2, 6, 27, 31, 33, 38, 121, 123, 125, 128, 133, 225

Parsifal (Wagner) 50
Pastoral Symphony (Beethoven) 77
Pastor fido, Il (Guarini) 53 n. 9, 71, 77–81, 91, 95–8, 125, 147, 197, 225
  chronology 97
  influence 95–6
Pastor regio, Il (Ferrari) 225
Pathétique Symphony (Tchaikovsky) 184
'Pavana Dolorosa' (Phillips) 192
Pelléas et Mélisande (Debussy) 118, 176
Pellegrina, La (Bargagli) 87
Pergolesi, Giovanni Battista, see *Serva padrona*
Peri, Jacopo 1, 35, 43, 89
  1589 intermedi 7, 87, 93, 153, 205
  see also *Dafne*; 'Dunque fra torbide onde'; *Euridice*
'Per quel vago boschetto' (Peri, *Euridice*) 41 n. 12
Pesaro 4, 65
Petrarch 143–4, 198, 216, 221
Petrouchka (Stravinsky) 117
Phanocles 18–20
Phillips, Peter 91, 192
'Piangete, O Ninfe, e con voi pianga Amore' (Gagliano, *Dafne*) 103
'Piangete valli abbandonate' (Caimo) 185
'Pianto della Madonna' (Monteverdi) 179, 181
Piazza, Giovanni Battista, see *Lamento della ninfa*
Piccolomini, Alessandro 75
Pirrotta, Nino x, 4, 56, 69–71
Pisano, Bernardo 216
Plato 17, 82, 88
Plautus 101
Plutarch 15
Poetica (Daniello) 84, 89
Poetica (Trissino) 63
Poetics (Aristotle) 52, 84, 117 n. 21, 125
'Poi che gl'eterni imperi' (Peri, *Euridice*) 109
Poliziano, Angelo:
  echo poems 199–212 *passim*, 221
  and Ovid 212
  poems in ottonari 62
  see also *Miscellanea*; *Orfeo*; 'Qual sarà mai'
Pollarolo, Carlo Francesco 126
Poppea (Monteverdi) 28, 122–3, 127, 131, 141–3 (ex.), 164, 166, 175–6, 192 n. 56
Pordenone, Marc'Antonio 216
'Possente spirto' (Monteverdi) 30, 37, 43, 145, 165–70 (ex.), 171, 175, 184
Prodromos 198
Purcell, Henry 224
  see also *Dido and Aeneas*

'Quae celebrat Thermas Echo' (Anon.) 213; (Le Jeune) 213–16 (ex.)
'Qual sarà mai si miserabil canto' (Festa) 147–8 (ex.), 149–51 (ex.), 152–3, 160, 172; (Layolle) 147–8 (ex.); (Poliziano) 146; (Verdelot) 147–8 (ex.)

'Questi i campi' (Monteverdi, *Orfeo*) 129, 164, 194, 225
'Quanto sia lieto' (Verdelot) 69, 80
'Quis dabit capiti meo' (Isaac) 146–7, 205, 207–8 (ex.), 209–11 (ex.)
'Quis dabit pacem populo timenti' (Isaac) 208

Rake's Progress (Stravinsky) 28, 59, 184–5, 194–5
Rampollini, Matteo 147
Rapimento di Cefalo, Il (Chiabrera), see *Cefalo*
Rappresentazione di anima e di corpo (Cavalieri) viii, 3, 29, 32, 36, 39, 43–4, 46, 66, 80, 83, 99, 101, 108, 110, 115–16, 120, 126–7, 225
Requiem 186 n. 52 (Cavalli), 194 n. 58 (Verdi)
Rilke, Rainer Maria, see *Sonette an Orpheus*
Rinuccini, Ottavio:
    intermedi of 1589 87, 224
    as librettist 2, 3, 21, 29, 110, 117–19, 124–5, 130, 139
    use of ottonari 24
    see also *Arianna; Dafne; Euridice; Lamento d'Arianna; Lamento della ninfa; Narciso*
Ritorno d'Ulisse, Il (Monteverdi) 6, 28, 122–7 *passim*, 176
Roggeri, Francesco 209
Rome 2–5, 7, 9, 31, 40–1, 44–5, 65, 80, 99, 128, 141, 164, 197
Ronsard, Pierre 13
Rore, Cipriano de 213
    see also 'Calami sonum ferentes'
Rosand, Ellen 186
Rosenkavalier, Der (Strauss) 59
Rosinda (Cavalli) 123
Rossi, Michelangelo, see *Erminia*
Rossi, Luigi, see *Orfeo; Palazzo incantato*
Rossini, Gioacchino, see *Otello; Semiramide*
Rousseau, Jean-Jacques 196
Ruffo, Vincenzo 216
Ruggiero (bass) 168 n. 24, 218

Sacrati, Francesco 122, 148, 175 n. 31
    see also *Finta pazza; Ulisse errante*
Sacrificio (Beccari) 77–81
Sad Shepherd (Jonson) 78
Salzburg 2
Samson Agonistes (Milton) 51
Sannazaro, Jacopo 221
    see also *Arcadia*
Sant'Alessio (Landi) 32, 66–7, 120, 127
Santa Uliva 66–7, 217–18
'Sa quest'altier ch'io l'amo' (Ariosto) 218, 224; (Cifra) 218–19 (ex.)
Saracini, Claudio 39
Sartorio, Antonio, see *Orfeo*
Sassi, Pamfilo 208
Scarlatti, Alessandro 126
Schiaffinati, Camillo 2, 4, 225

Schönberg, Arnold, see *Verklärte Nacht*
Schopenhauer, Arthur 51
Schürmann, Georg Caspar 132
Schütz, Heinrich 42, 193
    see also *Dafne; Orpheus*
Sebillet, Thomas 222
Secundus, Joannes 212
'Se de boschi i verdi onori' (Peri, *Euridice*) 109
Seelewig (Staden) 42 n. 15, 224–5
Selva morale (Monteverdi) 179
Semiramide (Rossini) 50
Seneca 208
Serafino Aquilano 63, 200–23 passim
Sermisy, Claudin de 222–3
Serva padrona, La (Pergolesi) 177
Settle, Elkanah 2
'Severed Head' (Tippett) 135
Sfortunato, Lo (Argenti) 80
Shakespeare 4, 100, 139, 166
    see also *Hamlet; Julius Caesar; Love's Labour's Lost; Merchant of Venice; Midsummer Night's Dream; Othello; Venus and Adonis*
Sidney, Philip 77
'Si dolce non sono' (Landini) 1
Silbiger, Alexander 213
'S'i' 'l dissi mai' (Petrarch) 216; (Tromboncino) 216–17 (ex.)
Silenus 65–6, 71
Silvae (Johannes Secundus) 212
'Si suave è l'inganno' (Verdelot) 69
'Soffrir i' son disposto' 203–4 (ex.)
Solerti, Angelo 99–101, 177–8
'Solo e pensoso' (Marenzio) 184
Sonette an Orpheus (Rilke) 16, 128, 135, 138
'Son io, son altri. Echo' (Sperindio) 212 n. 26
'Sospirate aure celesti' (Peri, *Euridice*) 109
Spenser, Edmund 77–8
Sperindio, Bertoldo 212
Staden, Sigmund Theophil, see *Seelewig*
Staehelin, Martin 210
Stilbes 198
Stoa, Joannes Franciscus Quintianus 209
Strauss, Richard vii, 36, 49, 50 n. 3
    see also *Ariadne auf Naxos; Rosenkavalier; Tod und Verklärung*
Strauss, Walter 15–16
Stravinsky, Igor 9, 193
    see also *Apollon musagète; Orpheus; Petrouchka; Rake's Progress*
Striggio, Alessandro (elder) 74
    see also 'Fuggi speme mia'
Striggio, Alessandro (younger) 36
    libretto for *Orfeo* 2, 24–9, 57, 59, 72, 99–102, 110–17, 127
String Quartet in D minor (K. 421) (Mozart) 184, 193
Strozzi, Pietro 99
Strungk, Nicolaus Adam 132

Sweelinck, Jan Pieterszoon 91, 193
Syringa (Carter) 128, 135, 137

Tasso, Torquato 98, 168, 211
  see also *Aminta*; *Gerusalemme*
Tchaikovsky, Peter Ilich 184
Terence 101, 143–4
Terrasson, Jean 9, 14–15, 23, 133
Theocritus, see *Idylls*
Thompson, Stith 14, 67
Tiberio (F. Gasparini) 225
Tippett, Michael, see *Mask of Time*; 'Severed Head'
Tirletti, – 2, 99, 127
Tirsi (Castiglione) 77 n. 22, 78, 80, 98
Tissoni Benvenuti, Antonia ix, 4, 20–3, 55–6, 144–6
Tod und Verklärung (Strauss) 51
Trissino, Giovan Giorgio, see *Poetica*
Tristan und Isolde (Wagner) 51, 118, 176, 184, 194
Tromboncino, Bartolomeo, *see* 'S'i' 'l dissi mai'
Troyens (Berlioz) 5
Tzetzes, John 52–3, 198

'Udite, selve, mie dolce parole' (Poliziano, *Orfeo*) 146
Ugolini, Baccio 145
Ulisse errante (Sacrati) 127

'Vanne, Orfeo, felice a pieno' (Monteverdi, *Orfeo*) 112, 114
Vecchi, Orazio 213
Venice 2, 4, 7, 14, 34, 68, 82, 121–2, 128, 176, 189, 208
Venturi, Stefano 99
Venus 5, 6, 8, 35, 92, 118, 120, 129, 185
Venus and Adonis (Blow) 7
Venus and Adonis (Shakespeare) 7, 159, 197
Verdelot, Philippe 67, 69, 83, 86, 213
  see also 'O dolce notte'; 'Qual sarà mai'; 'Quanto sia lieto'

Verdi, Giuseppe 194 n. 58
  see also *Aida*; *Falstaff*; *Otello*; 'Willow Song'
Verklärte Nacht (Schönberg) 51
Viadana, Lodovico 91
Viardot-Garcia, Pauline 23, 196
Vienna 2, 29, 31, 52, 96, 123, 128, 131, 134
Virgil 1, 4–9 *passim*, 19–21, 125, 132
  see also *Eclogues*; *Georgics*
'Virgo prudentissima' (Josquin) 211
'Vi ricorda o boschi ombrosi' (Monteverdï, *Orfeo*) 42
Visconti, Giovanni Battista, see *Armenia*
Vita humana (Marazzoli) 225
Vittori, Loreto, see *Galatea*
Vivaldi, Antonio, see *Giustino*
Vogel, Emil 177

Wagenseil, Georg Christoph, see *Euridice*
Wagner, Richard, see *Fliegender Holländer, Der*; *Götterdämmerung*; *Parsifal*; *Tristan und Isolde*
Walker, D. P. 1, 15, 88, 90–2, 95
Walliser, Christoph Thomas, see *Andromeda*
Webster, John 197
'Weep for Adonis' (Stravinsky, *Rake's Progress*) 185
Wert, Giaches de 213
Westrup, Jack 181
'When I am laid in earth' (Purcell, *Dido and Aeneas*) 189–90 (ex.)
Willaert, Adrian 213
'Willow Song' (Verdi, *Otello*) 194–5
Winckelmann, Johann Joachim 131
Winterfeld, Johannes 180
Wolff, H. C. 5
Wozzeck (Berg) 59
Wyatt, Thomas 143

Zauberflöte, Die (Mozart) 14–17, 23, 133
Zeno, Apostolo 126
Ziani, Pietro Andrea 132
Ziegler, Konrat 1, 8